# Beyond Document

# Beyond Document

## Essays on Nonfiction Film

edited by Charles Warren

Wesleyan University Press
Published by University Press of New England
Hanover and London

Wesleyan University Press

Published by University Press of New England, Hanover, NH 03755

© 1996 by Wesleyan University

All rights reserved

Printed in the United States of America   5 4 3 2 1

CIP data appear at the end of the book

"Memory's Movies" copyright © 1995 by Patricia Hampl. Used by permission of the Rhoda Weyr Agency, New York.

"The Camera People" copyright © 1992 by Eliot Weinberger. Reprinted by permission of the author.

# Contents

# Acknowledgments

**T**his book began with filmmaker Robert Gardner's idea that writers and poets should be asked to consider what faculties "beyond document" might lie in films of actuality. All the writers in the book are grateful to Gardner for starting the project, and to Vlada Petric, curator of the Harvard Film Archive, and Stanley Cavell, professor of philosophy at Harvard, for their role in planning and developing the project originally with Gardner. The book's writers are very grateful to Gardner and Petric in a more special way, for much help in seeing films and videotapes. A generous grant from the Billy Rose Foundation made possible the series of Harvard symposia where some of the essays were first presented, and made possible subsequent development of the book. Arthur Cantor of that organization showed himself, as in other instances, a true friend of the study of film.

The Museum of Modern Art in New York has been very helpful to a number of the writers here in making films available, and we would like to acknowledge our gratitude. I want to say a special word of thanks to Sally Berger of the Museum's Film and Video Department for some late help in circulating a videotape. Patricia Hampl was kindly aided in her research by the Jerome Foundation and by Saint Catherine's College, both in St. Paul, Minnesota, and by First Run Features, New York, who distrib-

ACKNOWLEDGMENTS

ute Ross McElwee's films. Maureen Howard would like to thank Walter Bernstein, Janet Mason, contributing editor at *Time,* and the University of Houston Film Department, which made it possible for her to see films while she was teaching at the University. Susan Howe and I made some inquiries of filmmaker Chris Marker in Paris, and we thank him for his very helpful responses. Others of our authors have made notes of personal thanks at the ends of their essays.

The illustrations in this book are images taken from films. We are grateful to the Harvard Film Archive for supplying most of the prints used. Dana Bonstrom at the Film Study Center at Harvard was instrumental in the process of transforming film frames for book publication purposes, and we are grateful for his expertise and devoted work on the project. The following directors kindly gave approval for using images from their films: Robert Gardner, Barbara Kopple, Richard Leacock, Ross McElwee, Dušan Makaveyev, and Chris Marker. We would also like to thank Anatole Dauman and Argos Films, who produced *Night and Fog*, for approval to use a frame from that film; Glorianna Davenport and the M.I.T. Media Laboratory for the loan of a print of *A Happy Mother's Day*; José Lopez and New Yorker Films for the loan of a print of *Sans Soleil* with permission to copy frames; Jonas Mekas and Anthology Film Archives for lending us *Film Portrait* with permission to copy frames; Jessica Rozner and Kino International Films for permission to use their print of *Mirror* when it came our way; the Boston Public Library for the loan of their print of *Night and Fog*; and First Run Features for the loan of *Time Indefinite*.

In my work as editor, I have benefited very much from consultation with Robert Gardner, and with Vlada Petric also. Stanley Cavell and I spent many pleasant hours discussing the book as it took shape, for which I thank him; and all of us involved in the book thank Cavell for his "Words of Welcome." I am grateful to Suzanna Tamminen of the Wesleyan University Press for ideas and much assistance, and to Terry Cochran, formerly of the Press, for early interest in the book and suggestions about it. All the writers here have been a pleasure to work with. I am particularly grateful to Patricia Hampl, Susan Howe (twice over), Helene Keyssar, and William Rothman, for consultation about the book as a whole and my own work. I also want to thank, for consultation and invaluable help of other kinds, James Maraniss at Amherst College, filmmaker Richard Rogers, Steffen Pierce at the Harvard Film Archive and the Film Study Center, Heidi Bliss at Harvard's Office of Light and Communication, William Kimball, and, above all others, Katherine Kimball.

—C.W.

STANLEY CAVELL

# Words of Welcome

**W**ho would doubt, in 1995—the hundredth anniversary of the invention of the moving picture—that this technological event, and then the event of film's emergence, no more than two decades later, as the newest of the great arts, imply leaps within the history of the arts, and in human consciousness generally, whose consequences we are still just beginning to measure? Nor do I doubt that film has barely begun, with certain revelatory exceptions, to inspire a degree and continuity of critical or philosophical response worthy of itself. It seems to me a cause of wonder that universities at large remain unpuzzled by this lag. Say that the art of film occurs in two main branches or states, call them fictional and factual film (setting aside animated film—allowing that not all moving pictures are animated). Since the branch of the factual or documentary film has captured no general audience for itself (it exists generally in connection, for example, with museum programs or as part of popular science education on public television), the community of those seriously interested in making and viewing documentaries tend to find one another in regions of the modern university. But the university is mostly silent about them; which is to say, it does not behave like a university with regard to them.

Such is the problem of film that even these few opening words will, and should, seem prejudicial. Some will continue to feel that film is receiving at least as much academic attention as a popular art deserves. This is perhaps no longer as common a sentiment as it was, but the falseness or philistinism of this sentiment always masked a more troubling concern that even among those who know the marvels of the heights and depths of film, not many have allowed themselves to bring film into their classrooms and writings, at least not as something more than a kind of exotic intruder. Is this out of institutional or intellectual intimidation? Or is it out of a still-unrecognized fact that film presents a standing challenge to the received distinction between popular and serious art and shows that we do not know what these words are good for? (I do not take our intellectual or academic position to have exactly improved by the introduction of courses on film that take it as a popular art, true as in some sense that is.) Some may object that the distinction between fictional and factual film is not a pure one, that fact and fiction spill into one another, that these concepts mark not separate genres of film but linked dimensions of all film. However correct this is, it leaves the contrast unarticulated, and leaves untouched the difference along these lines between dimensions of film and analogous dimensions of any representative art. Some will still feel that the real distinction is not between the fictional and the factual within the art of film but between film as art and film as document. But it is not easy to understand how one who has experienced even a small set of the great documentary films discussed in the essays that follow could go on with a clear mind insisting that the documentary film, whatever else it is, is not a medium of art.

It is against such a background of issues that I imagine Robert Gardner to have been led to the idea of sponsoring a lecture series out of Harvard's Carpenter Center for the Visual Arts, under the title *Beyond Document*. The idea was to invite a set of interesting writers, not necessarily or even preferably writers who had previously published thoughts about film, to deliver a lecture designed to help form the basis of an accompanying symposium, and to later take its place in a volume collecting the texts together. Vlada Petric, curator of the Harvard Film Archive, began putting the idea into practice, and I was enlisted to sound whatever connecting notes might prove useful in the course of introducing each of the invited lecturers. The charge to the speakers was to take up any issues of the documentary film and to concentrate on any film or set of films that genuinely engaged them. Five such lectures and symposia were held over the five semesters from the spring of 1989 to the spring of 1991. The result was a satisfyingly intense and varied sequence of texts, but at its conclusion those of us involved in turning the lectures into a volume found that some supplementation was in order—even considering the originally envisioned additions to the volume: a contribution by Robert Gardner meditating on his experience of his work as a maker of films; one by Vlada Petric epitomizing his scholarly knowledge of Dziga Vertov's significance in the history of the documentary; and two by Charles Warren, the editor of the volume, one on Dušan Makaveyev's WR: *Mysteries of the Organism*—surely among the richest films ever made on the very subject of the incorporation of fiction and fact by one another, in film and in history—and a second contribution sketching enough of a history of the documentary to allow readers new to the subject to place the names and titles invoked in the essays to follow.

Three people were approached to help further fill the frame we seemed to have in mind. Patricia Hampl and Susan Howe, superb writers who had not before written about film, were invited to think whether accepting an assignment to do so might not prompt a direction they wanted to explore. They thought, and the estimable results are here. Hampl elegantly takes on in her prose the signature moral problem of documentary film, that of exposing the lives of others, or rather causal imprints of fragments of those lives, to serve one's own story. Her discovery of her townsman Jerome Hill's remarkable work should find further friends for it. Howe's discovery of already acclaimed—and always underknown—masterpieces of Vertov and of Chris Marker incorporates the thrill of meeting artists who uncannily confirm strains of her ecstatic ways with writing, picking up the pieces in mourning. And Helene Keyssar was asked to look for a way of constructing an account of nonfiction filmmaking by women— the single instance here of an essay in which a massive case in the history of the documentary was meant to be covered. She proved able to turn an awkward, not to say impossible, task into a beautifully practical one by reflecting a sea of work through a pool of resounding examples.

The resulting book is thus meant to document a period of time, and a place, in which certain strangers and friends have undertaken to chart ways of addressing the documentary in film so as to prompt others to notice their own involvement in this hemisphere of the newest of the great arts, and therewith, with encouraged attention, in the world of film as such. To preserve the formative event of the original five public lectures, they are printed here in the order in which they were delivered, as essays 1, 3, 5, 7, and 9. The justifications for the dispersal of the seven further contributions went through a succession of phases in which thematic connections and contrasts, stylistic consonances or dissonances, large and small diameters of reference, were juxtaposed differently. In the end the decisions manifest the intuitive sense of balance and movement that was ascendant when time for further experiment was called.

It is further to preserve or recapture some sense of the five double occasions of lecture and symposium, which my introductory words of welcome for those occasions were meant to facilitate, that they are reprinted essentially as they were given, but collected in this one prefatory space, less most of the professional facts about each speaker that are now collected more handily at the end of the volume. I had contemplated composing new introductions to each of the additional texts, but the misguidedness of such an idea swiftly revealed itself: the public lectures variously honor a commitment to immediate discussion that was not part of the mission of the later texts. Indeed, a reason for inviting additional texts was to allow certain dimensions of the experience of film to come to the fore that the format of the accompanying symposia would in some cases have kept back. I note that since Robert Gardner's contribution differs from the others, as befits that of the only filmmaker whose words are presented here, I further extend the modes of discourse exemplified in this volume by including here my introductory appreciation of his film, *Forest of Bliss*, written for its premiere in 1985.

## Jay Cantor

The opposition between documentary and fictional film signifies two great branches of the art of film, each with its own history, its own audience, and on the whole its own directors in obedience to their own imperatives of art and politics and culture and morality and perhaps religion; and at the same time it signifies two dimensions or directions of all film, no more to be kept from touching or pervading one another than are fantasy and reality, or myth and ritual, or language and the world. The mutual attraction between the documentary and the fictional has become a great subject of each branch, as, say, in the narrative of Robert Gardner's filming, which inevitably intrudes upon, and bears consequences of, the narrative of the ritual that inspires it; the use of documentary procedures to compose what are for all the world, or for some of it, feature (autobiographical) films in the form of Ross McElwee's *Sherman's March* and *Time Indefinite;* or in the excavations faced and effected in Dušan Makaveyev's *WR: Mysteries of the Organism* and *Sweet Movie,* which may be articulated as a struggle against the invasion of fact by fiction conducted by an articulation of fiction by fact.

The films Jay Cantor asks us to think about—*Night and Fog; Shoah;* and *Hotel Terminus*—have taken upon themselves, in the topic of the extermination of the Jews of Europe, some ultimate site of the suffocation of fact and fantasy in one another. Such films create, by means of our surviving intelligence, and of the complicitous, violent, redemptive camera, a refusal of this process of the ridding of the human voice, and the coordination of human choice.

Cantor calls his most recent fiction *Krazy Kat,* "a novel in five panels." One way to describe its work is to say that it undertakes to depict the conditions—psychological, political, economic, cultural, historical, critical, philosophical—under which a cartoon is possible, for the moment *this* particular one, that with the simplicity of figures and the repetitiveness of situations of the Krazy Kat cartoon strip afforded pleasure and instruction for the crazy quilt of American immigrant society in the decades before World War II; the novel goes so far as to depict the failures of those conditions after the invention of nuclear destruction that closes that war.

An immediate extension or guise of this investigation, in the novel's third or center panel, is to depict the conditions under which the pleasure and instruction of film is possible—that is, of talking, moving pictures, or talking, moving panels. Allow me to read a passage from that region, since Cantor has left himself in his present essay no time for comedy. It is a scene in which the Producer is talking to Krazy about the idea of her making a comeback in the, for her, drastically new medium of film; to get her, as Cantor puts it, to work again. The panel takes Krazy and her companions over the novel's landscape of the concepts of character and star, of producer and audience, of seduction and writing and death; and through topics of dream and skepticism and of the relation of the popular and the serious in the arts. At a certain point it gives us what is—or becomes, in the Producer's mouth—an American explanation of the successful occupation of American literary studies (hence film studies) over the past two decades or so by the forces of European critical theory:

> "Look, Kat," the Producer said, "anyone tells you that they know what they're doing in this business, they're lying. Because I want to tell you something: Nobody knows nothing about this business!" He shook his head, muttering sadly, "Crazy business. Crazy business." He smiled at her. "OK, Kitty. Get up off your knees. You don't have to beg anymore. I'll tell you how I learned the secret of picking b.o. smashes. Come backstage with me, darling, and I'll show you the wires and gizmos. You'll like that! You'll be in on the secret, see—American audiences love to be in the know. They love to go backstage. They want to see the machinery that fools them, the back projections, the special effects. Right? Right! They don't realize that showing them the machinery is the show, and while they're hypnotized by the gears going round, the microchips blinking on/off, while you let them see the marketing surveys that reveal their kinky emotional ratchets and levers, you can really get your hands deep down into their pockets. They get hypnotized thinking they're learning how the rubes get hypnotized.

On the next page the panel takes a further leap:

> "Audiences are children, Krazy." He smiled sadly. He straightened
> up and put his hand to his forehead in salute: "They're geniuses,"
> he concluded. "You're a woman, right, Krazy? I mean it's hard to
> tell. My research people tell me that sometimes the others call you
> her, sometimes him. That's depraved. It's decadent. It's disgusting.
> Very Now, right? I like it."

A great question of the novel is whether we can wish for happiness
in a world in which we are faced so continuously with our apparently limitless taste for cynicism and destruction. It raises from an unexpected angle
Kant's frightening question whether we may act so as to deserve happiness.

Forced by Cantor's choice, in the essay he has prepared for this
occasion, to think back to three documentary interrogations of the extermination of European Jewry, I turned from his text, for the moment adrift
in a sense of my helplessness, to further writing that his writing may at any
moment call upon (as if to keep open the circles in which we may be
shocked at ourselves)—to, among others, a haunting remark in
Wittgenstein's notebooks during the last year of World War II: "The whole
planet can suffer no greater torment than a single soul." (Is this echoing
Kierkegaard somewhere, or a predecessor of his?) This makes it
imaginable, it seems, for another to help bear the greatest torment, contain
it. Then this is a promise that, one to one, link by link, we may bury the
helplessness of our past. Then art—for us, the art arising from the fact of
film—may be measured by its readiness for such a move. It is the measure
I grant to such writing as Jay Cantor offers us.

## William Rothman

At one point in William Rothman's intricate text, as he is unraveling certain of the overlapping conceptual strands in the relation between
film and literature, and between a classical fiction film and a screenplay for
that film, and between imagining or envisioning a film and interpreting or
transcribing a film, he turns aside and says: "I find myself feeling homesick
for the field of philosophy." Not everyone is in a position to feel and say

quite that, but I trust everyone who cares for film knows an analogous longing and perhaps a counterpart metaphysical surprise verging on fear at an
instant when the sheer *fact* of film seems remarkable—that it is at once the
most obvious and the most mysterious of the arts, and that its advent into
human culture raises afresh every question philosophy has ever raised
about the arts, from the endless question about what art is, and what its origin and history and its makers and its audiences are; to whether the arts are
a unity, and what the gains and losses are of their interactions; to the roles
of technology and representation in the various arts, and their various relations to reality and dream and illusion and nature and politics; to the distinction between the high and the low in human culture.

The statement announcing the *Beyond Document* lecture series
orients itself toward the denial—and with an understandable impatience
that the denial remains necessary—that the nonfictional camera is a simple
instrument of recording; and it enters a call for further consideration of
what that camera's instrumentality or agency is, what it is that the documentary inflection creates a medium for. William Rothman's extraordinary
first book on film—*Hitchcock: The Murderous Gaze* (1982)—may be taken
as a study of the camera's agency, its tracking and magnification of the
lucidities and obscurities, and the subtleties and banalities, of human
agency, hence of human passion. His essay here takes it as given that the
cameras of nonfictional and fictional film are each inextricable from human
activity and passivity. He takes it as a fact of our experience that the best of
the films called documentaries contain the intelligence (hence the power
of questioning intelligence), and the poetry and drama (hence the heart for
questioning poetry and drama), that one expects of the best of the films
called features. Starting from this commonality, Rothman in effect asks on
what grounds, if any, these different regions of film are interestingly different.

He finds ground between specific territories within these regions
of the world of film—between a territory of fictional film he calls the classical system and a territory of nonfictional film he (with reservations) per-
sists in calling cinema-verité—sufficiently common to allow an orderly consideration of differences. One of the ways Rothman marks a commonness

between these specified regions is to say that in both of them the photographic grounding assures that the world has made its impression. The invitation is unmistakable, since philosophy has been invoked, to think of this grounding in terms of the classical Empiricists' picture, as in Locke and Hume, of impressions as the basis of human understanding, scoring the tabula rasa of the mind. In Rothman's view impressions enter the mind's camera obscura, which is evidently the last place to take impressions for granted, since the mind will have its designs upon them. The common ground of the world's impression stands out against the yet different region of the world of film called animation, where instead of impressions of the world—say of its oscillation between the theatrical and the private—we are presented with drafts of the world's animism, perhaps of its circulation or metamorphosis out of and into the human organism, made explicit, within the precincts of the Carpenter Center, in the work of Suzan Pitt.

In Rothman's cover letter accompanying the distribution of his paper to participants in the symposia, he notes that his text turned out to be more abstract than he had expected. I am for my part happy about this surprise. He and I have long shared the sense that something about film makes the fact of its making, of the choices it represents, peculiarly invisible to its audience; and I have experienced over many years Rothman's combating of this invisibility in the particular way he takes his classes through the shot-by-shot events of a sequence of film—a practice whose range is reflected in his collection of essays entitled *The "I" of the Camera*. But just because of my admiration for his pedagogy, I greedily wanted him also to devote that kind of attention to theorizing his practice. And because I knew his talent for providing the pleasures of abstract thought, as well as for respecting those of concrete objects, I would recurrently try to encourage in him a homesickness for philosophy.

Perhaps I had been thinking about Novalis's remark that philosophy is essentially homesickness (sick of it, sick for it). I know I had been thinking about what film is.

## Eliot Weinberger

Eliot Weinberger reports that after attending the most recent Margaret Mead Film Festival, he found himself generally in agreement with "nearly all ethnographic filmmakers [who], in interviews, have remarked that the genre of ethnographic film is still in its infancy." Only generally in agreement, however, since he emphatically recognizes, as in his passages that read moments of Robert Gardner's *Deep Hearts* and *Forest of Bliss*, that "there are certain films [categorizable as ethnographic, or at any rate, ethnopoetic] which contradict this notion." It follows that it is not exactly ethnographic film as a genre that remains in an undeveloped state, but a general run of ethnographic filmmakers, as if their relation to the camera remains what it is generally for tourists—amateurish, obvious, repetitive, imitative.

Allowing that this is true, what could account for it? We might ask: If the ethnographic film remains generally in its infancy, in what state does the writing about ethnographic film find itself? What is the state of the genre's critical community?

It is my impression that Eliot Weinberger writes—as in certain ways others in this book write—out of a sense of an absence of such a critical community or communities. Some such sense is indeed one of the motivations in establishing this whole series of contributions, to create a momentum of discussion of nonfictional film that gets beyond undeveloped, repetitive quarrels over what the concept of the documentary implies—quarrels over whether it obviously asserts an epistemological claim to have found the royal road to cultural reality, or whether any such claim instantly betrays its ignorance in the face of the mechanism of the camera, with its innocence or decadence in the face of the unrolling of politics.

But again—supposing this sense of absence of a critical community is accurate—what would account for the implied ignorance and inno- cence, and for the reactive arrogance that must claim to reveal it? Weinberger explores an answer in a quarrel between science and art, epitomized among other places in what he calls a "scary comment" that he quotes from Timothy Asch: "The camera can be to the anthropologist what the telescope is to the astronomer or what the microscope is to the biologist." Weinberger notes the apparently false assumption here that "the matter on the other side of the ethnographic lens is as imperturbable as galaxies or amoeba." But couldn't one go on to develop some theory about the perturbations the camera causes? It takes considerable theory, after all, to understand what the telescope or microscope tell us. Is it Weinberger's point that Asch is not aware, or denies, that this place of theory is required also in anthropological understanding? Another apparent assumption that may be taken in Asch's comment—not a necessary one, but easily recruitable in advancing the claims of science over those of art—is that the training and experience that goes into making a film is closely analogous to the training for making and reading microscopic slides or telescopic photographs. That all are practices related to theory, and that their results may all be beautiful and useful, seems obvious enough. But it should be no less obvious that variations in the quality of the evidence that microscopes or telescopes provide and discrepancies in the interpretation of this evidence are communally resolvable (except in a stage of scientific crisis), whereas the quality and interpretation of a film—as with any artifact showing the work art does—is inherently, permanently contestable (which is perhaps to say that the arts are always in a state of crisis). From which it does not follow (a point Weinberger emphasizes) that the evidence provided by film regarded ethnographically is less rich or necessarily less objective than that provided by more elaborate scientific instrumentation. What follows is that there is no standing set of procedures—no unargumentative paradigm—to help articulate the camera's ethnographic significance. Which in turn is to say: a practice of criticism is required.

Weinberger begins by telling of a peculiar tribe of people he calls Ethnographic Filmmakers. Among many other fascinating characteristics Weinberger has discovered, they worship a deity known as Reality, whose chief enemy is Art. It is irresistible to summarize what I have said in giving an initial response to Weinberger's text by adding to Weinberger's myth: these filmmakers have an unhealthy relation with a tribe called Critics, with whom they speak solely in a language of conflict, called Philosophy, which no one knows very well but no one knows so much less well than everyone else that arguments cannot begin. They merely cannot end. And these filmmakers tend to spend most of their days in corners of places called Universities, which do not really seem to want them, any more than they really want philosophy past a certain point. So that instead of trying to turn their intimate but unfruitful exchanges to better use, filmmakers and philosophers may each exert themselves to prove that they belong precisely in the University, and the direct route to such conviction is to appear as part of or as adjunct to Science.

### Maureen Howard

When Robert Gardner and Vlada Petric first asked me to introduce the progress of lecturers in the envisioned *Beyond Document* series, I recognized a pair of guiding ideas in their initial description of the series: there was, first, the plain wish to call attention to the massive fact, and comparatively neglected dimension, culturally and theoretically, of the documentary in the world of film; and a wish, second, to invite writers from outside the dominance of academic film studies, whose ways of addressing issues of film as document—epistemological and political and artistic issues—could not be confined to the conventions and discourses of the professional study of film. Every academic field has, and needs, such conventions—it is what establishes the field as (in the European, not quite American sense) "scientific," fit for orderly presentation in a university. But every healthy field also has, and needs, a sense of itself as intelligibly related to some social good not defined by its professional necessities.

Maureen Howard has picked for her subject the treacherous and popular form—treacherous emotionally as well as intellectually—called the docudrama, in which fact is more or less knowingly fictionalized and fiction more or less unknowingly treated as ponderous fact. Among writers and readers there is common agreement that—in the words of one of our celebrated short-story writers—"Maureen Howard belongs in any list of the best American novelists practicing today." The statements on the cover of her fifth novel, entitled *Expensive Habits*, stress its intelligence, elegance, and complexity. Having just finished reading that work I can testify to the clear presence throughout it of those admirable qualities; but they do not capture the particular sense, reading it, of something harrowing the moments we are shown—not alone because the events depicted are, openly and hiddenly, hard to bear, in their violence and their pathos, but because the text's responsiveness to the events it depicts is as relentless as the events themselves are, so that you sometimes feel, remembering it, as you do with writing at its best, frightened by your ignorance of the significance of your everyday hours, that their richness and their deadliness are passing unnoticed before and behind you. This is something the documentary is meant to document.

Science and art can both be said to check experience, habitually to overthrow it. Science accomplishes this by beginning from, and maintaining, its perspectives of lucidity, seeing where to discount irrelevance; art accomplishes it, taking itself unawares, continuously, beginning with its opacities, not placed to discount irrelevance, searching for perspective.

In *Expensive Habits,* Howard further anticipates our subject of the documentary in obvious and unobvious matters of its content. Its principal character is a novelist who also writes for movies, and it contains a couple of scenes with an old lover of hers, a movie producer, and his new young wife, a heavy-metal singer, making bravura fun of the pair's preparations for filming an authentic docudrama about Nazis. How Howard's novel takes up the cost of its own fun is essential to its business—relating in plot and prose the antics of this pair who are contending for the fables and images of our public lives, to the psychic dangers of clapping individual lives into the space of a serious book, such as the one happening before us.

Howard's complex awareness is always at work in the tactfully straightforward manner of the essay she has prepared for us. In *Expensive Habits*, its central woman implicitly relates her writing, hence herself, to the profession of her first husband, a surgeon, as well as to astronomy, the intellectual passion of her adolescent son: writing as opening the heart and as scanning the heavens. In her essay on docudrama, Howard identifies herself with two further characters from that novel: in her superstitious invoking of Christ she invokes the superstitions with which she endows the writer's Central American housekeeper, fatefully connected with the docudrama under construction in that book—mockudrama she calls it; again, in naming herself, in her essay, "a back number," she identifies herself for the moment with the writer's present husband in *Expensive Habits*, to whom that writer assigns the epithet "former," meaning particularly an aristocratically derived former radical of the 1960s, an emissary to the present, sent from no one.

In her essay she invokes the grief, along with the rage, out of which her novel is written, almost always within earshot of a sociable tone (as if not to make the all-but-unbearable world more irrelevantly unbearable); she even repeats the novel's occasional trick of casting a strategic sentence, in whole or in part, in iambic pentameter. A full sentence about her father reads: "We fell apart, no setting that aside." The idea is not to write poetry. It serves, rather, to demonstrate the truth of Nietzsche's remark that writing good prose is a constant battle against writing poetry— call this a battle against the (always dangerous, sometimes essential) unwillingness to make yourself sociable, here and now, to friends and strangers.

To deal with the modern interpenetration of fact and fiction, of document and drama—or, as Nietzsche more or less puts it in *The Use and Abuse of History*, the twisting of one's culture with the history of one's culture—is not the work of a moment or of a known theory (since part of the struggle is precisely against the expensive habit of substituting theory for experience); it is rather the long task of modern life, in which grief and rage, or love and hate, are to distinguish themselves as best they can from one another, and both from the intolerance of irony that rests itself in cynicism.

### Phillip Lopate

Philosophy has announced for two and a half millennia that the mind, or a language, or any image, does not merely, or not at all, mirror what we may call reality, or may call the world, or nature; yet in each generation there are individuals, even crowds, who discover some idea of language's prejudices with a sense that they alone realize the idea's validity or its power, as if each is discovering philosophy itself. I think there is good reason why this banal discovery—or discovery of banality—should take this enthusiastic form: philosophy exists only in discovering for oneself the power of such a thought.

Phillip Lopate is a helpful voice to have join our explorations beyond the document. One of his recent books, *Against Joie de Vivre* (1989), is a collection of what Lopate calls personal essays. In one of these essays, with the title "What Happened to the Personal Essay?" he characterizes "informal, personal essays [as tending] to seize on the parade and minutiae of daily life: vanities, fashions, oddballs, seasonal rituals, love and disappointment, the pleasure of solitude, reading, going to plays, walking in the street"—the banalities of life, as most of life is, one may think. And yet Lopate, invoking Montaigne, declares that "in an essay, the track of a person's thoughts struggling to achieve some understanding of a problem is the plot." The strength to come to an understanding of one's banal plots and repetitive tricks (call them one's melodrama) is not banal; but neither need it be as rare as it seems to be. To put this strength into our hands is a precious gift of the essayist, as that figure is described in Lopate's essay; it is the gift not to fear the finality of the banal, a perspective philosophy endlessly fails, for all its perspectives, to possess for itself, something it endlessly seeks and almost always disparages.

Phillip Lopate invokes another, perhaps companion, fear dogging these still early years of academic film study: the fear, and fact, of ignorance—the fact not only that no one knows everything required to know what film is and has been, but that no one knows the dimensions of our ignorance. Suppose we may assume a certain working knowledge, if sketchy, of the chronologies of film in two or three cultures. Which is more important for our purposes in the neighborhood of film studies: the philosophy or the history of art, or of theater, or of art criticism; the sociology of institutions or the economics of entrepreneurship; or the history or philosophy of technology or of perception and cognition? Lopate, as a writer and a teacher of writing, and with the contrariness he values in the essayist, in the long, disturbing essay that ends *Against Joie de Vivre*, "Suicide of a Teacher," asks: "What else was being a teacher but trying to respond as humanly as possible to problems that would not wait for an expert?"

He also (despite, or as a way of qualifying, his professional writing about film and his official participation in such institutions as the New York Film Festival) identifies himself as a film buff, in the complex and evocative essay, "Anticipation of *La Notte*: The 'Heroic' Age of Moviegoing." A certain sense of paradox arises in putting this direct claim of a buff's enthusiasm together with the book's title that questions our grounds for joyfulness. But this sense of paradox conveys a spiritual or human crisis that runs through the book: its title essay epitomizes the crisis by invoking a great passage from a text of Simone Weil's that ends: "So much for joie de vivre. . . . I don't really know what I'm waiting for. But I think it hypocritical to pretend satisfaction while I am still hungry." This testing of the claim of pleasure, or enthusiasm, is painfully pertinent at this moment of film studies, or generally in what mostly administrators still call the humanities—when the ancient question, cyclically repressed, of the nature of the pleasure of works of art, or of enthusiasm in works of the mind, is newly under investigation or suspicion. Surely it calls for a renewed investigation of the equally ancient question of the nature—of the dangers, and of the necessities, you may say of the politics—of pleasure as such.

In his essay here Phillip Lopate specifies his hunger in the special case of film—despite, as it were, the joys he evidently also encounters there. He calls for more or better or clearer work in a genre of film his essay strives to define, and that several times he suggests may not quite even—or yet—exist. I predict that many of you will search your memories for instances of film that ought to satisfy his hunger; and I expect he means you to—if you first recognize the hunger in yourself.

## Robert Gardner

*Forest of Bliss* is the latest in Robert Gardner's body of films— joining among others *Dead Birds* and *Rivers of Sand*—which is increasingly recognized as among the most significant accomplishments in the world community of nonfiction filmmaking, call it anthropological or documentary filmmaking. But these titles, or any others that seek to limit in advance the achievement of work such as Gardner's, will be overcome by the very power, the poetry of that achievement. As creative work may in any genre or form of art, *Forest of Bliss* acts to burst its form, as if its maker is challenging its origins, taking his work into its own exploration of the conditions of art and of life that make it possible, as if becoming answerable for, and to, the medium of film itself. It is to Gardner's engagement of this answerability—the questioning of the limits of his art—that I call your attention.

  You do not need words of mine to help you recognize that you are confronted by images of extreme beauty in *Forest of Bliss*; that in it some ritual of the dead, hence of the living, is being approached (never as a whole, as if one might be finished with it); that the approach is at every turn forwarded and threatened by the commercial traffic in ritual, where flies tramp across warm coins; and that the absence of Western words among the film's eloquent tracks of sound is one sign of the film's respect for difference, for otherness, respect both for the other's mystery and for its own power to communicate what it wishes known. It is a version of that respect for his or her subject or material that every true artist manifests. Genuine filmmakers, documentary or nondocumentary, will, for example, take it as part of their artistic mission to locate and account for their presence at lives and deaths, at tears and cries and laughter not their own. The absence of voiced narration in *Forest of Bliss* accepts this issue as a standing one—the issue of intrusion or of false domination—an issue accepted as well by the explicit virtual absence of awareness on the part of the living subjects of the film that they are under surveillance by a camera.

  How, then, does *Forest of Bliss* achieve its account of itself, its declaration of its subjects' independence of its camera's capture, its answerability to the condition of film by its questioning of its own existence? The answer I ask you to consider as you view this film is that it allows its making, its presence to its world, not just here and there to be noticed by that world, not just there and here to comment on our uncanny sense of familiarity with and of difference from that world, but to let that world as a whole interrogate every moment of the film's presence, of its life, hence of our own viewing of it—as if the cremation ritual in the holy city of Benares asks us to account for the rituals of our lives that so essentially absorb, among other things, cameras—that is, our lives that feed on our views of the lives of others, as if the reality of our own lives is no longer authorizable by themselves. The rhetorical texture of the film that moment to moment reflects our viewing as our being viewed—our being discovered by what we discover—is woven by the sequence of identifications to which Gardner's camera declares or exposes itself.

You will see, for example, breathtaking shots of wild dogs; of enchanted sails; of a river in which things and steps and days begin and end; of children's tiny red kites drawing in a red sky; of structures that are and are not ladders; of marching hand-prints and histories of marigolds; of clumps of logs balanced for honest sale and then balanced on a human back for trotting to their part in the endless transmission of fire. And in each case an allegory is proposed of this camera's (perhaps not just this one's) life—of what it hungers for and would be eaten by, of its roving and floating and flowing and standing, and its aspiration to ascend to heaven while it is bound to the hands of a human child, of its readiness to adorn the world that lends itself to its traffic, of its labors of measuring and carrying that at every moment threaten to overtake the quest of transcendence. Perhaps above all one will consider the camera's self-exposure in subjecting itself to the fact and the idea of a ritual of cremation, of a ritual figured as transfiguration itself: film is the medium of transfiguration—as painting is the medium of representation, or its denial; as theater is the medium of impersonation, or its denial; as music is the medium of transformation, or its denial—blessed or cursed with the fate, in the same gestures, to destroy and recreate everything it touches. So that I see *Forest of Bliss* as staking itself on its strength to participate in the fact and the idea of life and death as cycles of metamorphosis, hence in the human effort to redeem the violence of death and the violence by which life sustains itself—that they may not be stupid and inconsequential separations, but fruitful, faithful, and memorable, as in the perpetuations of ritual, and as in the transfiguring provocations of such a film as this one.

# Beyond Document

CHARLES WARREN

# Introduction, with a Brief History of Nonfiction Film

**T**his book explores nonfiction film as an artful, moving, humanly rich medium of expression. One might say medium of expression, or medium of discovery and understanding, or medium for the world itself to show a face.

The filmmaker may be an arguer or a poet, and the nonfiction film the expression of the filmmaker's perceptions and way of coming to terms with the world. We may relish a film for the filmmaker's insight or sensibility. Or we may be grateful to the filmmaker as a sympathetic, perhaps unassuming, helper for our own desire to see, and to mold the world with feeling. Or it may seem the world is more than anyone's seeing and hearing, or filming, or ordering of parts, and that the world, in our time, has found filmmakers and film and the film audience as a way of making itself known—a way of being. Film is a way for the world to be.

The history of nonfiction film is an abundant one, with many kinds of things being done. The standard accounts—and they are good, and readable, such as Erik Barnouw's or Lewis Jacobs's—emphasize overmuch the aspect of social analysis, scientific inquiry, educational mission.[1] And recent work in academic film studies still worries the issue of truth and

1. Erik Barnouw, *Documentary: A History of the Non-Fiction Film*, rev. ed. (Oxford University Press, 1983). Lewis Jacobs, *The Documentary Tradition*, rev. ed. (Norton, 1987).

directness in presenting facts and information, finding that many nonfiction films are not the true representations of life they pretend to be.[2] A film is either an educational success or, simply, an educational failure.

The writers in this book have sought to open themselves to the real variety, power, and imagination of nonfiction films over the years. There is a dimension of art and imagination to these films, and viewers find themselves caught up in this and find that it can lead to truth and understanding—though a truth and understanding that could not have been conceived of in advance of the films.

Each notable nonfiction film is an experiment with reality and asks —radically, if we will accept the challenge—what is going on in this film? What is a fact? What are *these* facts? What is it to reflect on them, or memorialize them, in this way? Acts of criticism are called for.

The writers here take up films that have moved them to think about how the art of film works and where it is taking us, to say why the films matter, and to think through broad issues of art and its treatment of reality. Guided by and responding to films, the writers consider major human experience in the twentieth century and how we regard it: the Holocaust, the catastrophe of war, the West's discovery of Africa and of the East, the life of women as it seems different from men's, the individual's struggle to find coherence in personal life, people's very craving to understand reality and to have the means to see the facts of the world clearly.

Readers will hear very different voices in this book, as one writer after another presses forward with something important to talk about. In a number of instances, the writer identifies with a filmmaker or with a certain way of making a film by virtue of the writer's own work in poetry or fiction or nonfiction. This artistic identification illuminates how nonfiction films work and what they aim for. Writers speak in the first person here, making plain their interests. And the writers create their own ways to talk about film and its issues; form and style and the way of approaching a film differ in each essay. The result, over the course of the book, is an abundant presentation of films, viewers' responsiveness, and thought.

2. See Bill Nichols, *Ideology and the Image* (Indiana University Press, 1981) and *Representing Reality* (Indiana University Press, 1991); Alan Rosenthal, ed., *New Challenges for Documentary* (University of California Press, 1988); and Michael Renov, ed., *Theorizing Documentary* (Routledge, 1993). Rosenthal takes more of the older line of aspiration toward truth-telling about society, but many of his writers do not.

Since the writers here delve deeply into selected films and issues, it seems helpful to provide a sketch of the past and present of nonfiction film. This account has no thought of being complete; interesting work in nonfiction film worldwide is all but overwhelming (readers are referred to our Bibliography). What follows is meant as an orientation for appreciating the essays in the book, filling in some of the history and marking where the writers take things up. It seems good, moreover, to recall in one place what a wonderful series of films there has been over time, where both observation of actuality and imagination come into play, where there is a fruitful meeting of these spheres of existence.

Short documentaries—films of brief events, or brief looks at places—were a major part of cinema exhibition in its first days. Beginning with the Lumières' *Arrival of a Train*, in 1895, the Lumières and their agents and then others shot many, many short actuality films. Such films were made and shown all over the world, by traveling agents and by local people trained in the new equipment. Familiar things seem to have looked wonderful up on the screen; and the unfamiliar was seen, too—the East saw the West, and vice versa.

The appetite for films of actuality lies at the origin of the making of film and film's finding of a public. This kind of film largely gave way, however, by 1905 or so to fiction film; and between 1910 and 1920, the one-to-two-hour fiction film became the standard for exhibition. This change away from actuality is sometimes spoken of as a seduction of the public into fantasy and romance. But so many of the films here are so deeply interesting—Griffith, Chaplin . . . —as not to permit such a crude view of what was happening.

Actuality is a powerful element in fiction film. The mixing of the filmed real with the imagined constitutes the very interest of fiction film. In the first two decades of the century the appeal of films of actuality was worked into fiction films of various kinds, finding new ways to thrive. Think of city streets in early comedies, or of the outdoors in Griffith, and, above all, of people—in roles in stories, yes, but still endlessly interesting actual people.

In the 1920s, suddenly, remarkable extended experiments were made in filming the world without a fictional story and characters and in putting together substantial, sophisticated films from this material. The experiments were diverse, each asking its own response. There was no agreed-upon way of making documentaries, as indeed there never would be for more than a short time and in only one or two places.

Robert Flaherty, beginning with *Nanook of the North* in 1922, showed that compelling films can emerge from going to unfamiliar places, facing the life there, living there for a time, learning, working a film up slowly. *Nanook* was followed by *Moana* (1926), in the South Seas, *Man of Aran* (1934), and other films, concluding with *Louisiana Story* (1948). Flaherty has been accused of imposing himself on those before his camera, getting people to do things they did not ordinarily do, making up stories, evoking, romantically, old ways of life. He does bring himself as a person with distinctive feelings to his documentary work; he does bring poetry to the medium, in the sense of *making* something of his material and his feelings. Flaherty's films have held the world's attention since they first appeared, and the point seems to be, after all, that this *is* Nanook on film, to a remarkable extent; this *is* the North; this is the sea about Aran; these are ways of life that have been lived—this filmmaker has lived them to a degree and has cared about them. His care is there in the films, and is interesting in itself.[3]

Poetry can work for good or for ill with the facts of the world. Eliot Weinberger's essay in this book deals with the issue in the area of ethnographic film, Flaherty's and that of later filmmakers—Jean Rouch, Robert Gardner, Trinh Minh-ha, and others. Objectivity and transparency are impossible ideals here, and the methods of science seem not to ensure enlightenment. A filmmaker, as it were acknowledging great barriers, may negotiate a kind of poetry as a way toward facts and unfamiliar people, or a way to allow facts and people to answer back to the filming and film-maker. Weinberger speaks about this negotiation in a number of different films.

3. For a positive view of Flaherty's "intensely active attitude" toward his material, see Nagisa Oshima, *Cinema, Censorship, and the State: The Writings of Nagisa Oshima, 1956–1975*, ed. Annette Michelson, trans. Dawn Lawson (MIT Press, 1992), 45.

Nothing could be more different from Flaherty than the work of his contemporary Dziga Vertov in the Soviet Union. Editing newsreels, filming modern Russia, writing manifestos about documentary, putting together the complex masterpieces *The Man with the Movie Camera* (1929), *Enthusiasm* (1931), and *Three Songs about Lenin* (1934), Vertov was a lover of modernity and the future, of machines, of fast editing in film, and altered motion and superimpositions. He was a strong advocate for actuality film over fiction, but with actuality shot and edited to stimulate audiences toward a future consciousness: admiration for labor, disavowal of the barriers of geographic space and racial identity, disavowal of the time between present and future. Vertov was famous for a decade or so in the world of Russian film, but his career was stopped in the 1930s and his films suppressed as formalist and useless. He remained an obscure figure for a long time. In the 1960s a revival took place, spirited by Jean-Luc Godard and others, and Vertov's films and writings became much looked at and talked about again, inspiring filmmakers and students of film everywhere.[4]

Vlada Petric concentrates here on *Three Songs about Lenin*, explaining Vertov's theory and practice for presenting "Life-As-It-Is" and at the same time creating the "Film-Thing," something new in the world, which yet takes us back to reality with better insight and an expanded sensibility. Shots must have documentary authenticity, though they are carefully chosen and framed, with an eye toward movement and light and other factors; then the shots are edited together and combined with sounds and written titles to create a new world of sensation, emotion, and meaning. Petric shows how Vertov beautifully met the challenge of transforming reality on film, but came to tragic failure in trying to do the work he wanted to do in the face of a Stalinist regime hostile to experimental art and to radical political idealism such as his.

Susan Howe in her essay on Chris Marker and post–World War II film takes up Vertov as a background figure whose enthusiasm, brilliance, and belief in the world seem hardly possible in a later era. The work of mourning of *Three Songs about Lenin* is forward-pressing and open-

4. Very valuable for study are *Kino-Eye: The Writings of Dziga Vertov*, ed. Annette Michelson, trans. Kevin O'Brien (University of California Press, 1984); and Vlada Petric, *Constructivism in Film—"The Man with the Movie Camera"* (Cambridge University Press, 1987).

ended, unlike the mourning of more deeply blighted later films. In all Vertov's films there are touching positive images, so many, one after another, of people, of work being done, of buildings, of old Russia with its earthiness and defects even as it becomes a new Russia of spirit and technology. How can there *be* such images? Howe asks. What are the pressures of feeling that bring Vertov to encounter facts, or half make them, rendering them on film this way? What is the source of such?—poetry, Howe calls it.

Vertov worked very closely not only with his brother, Mikhail Kaufman, as cameraman, but with his wife, Elizeveta Svilova, as editor—both Kaufman and Svilova are shown very prominently in *The Man with the Movie Camera* doing their work and appearing to shape the film as it unfolds before us. Women have played a crucial role in many instances editing nonfiction films, as they have editing fiction films in Hollywood, Europe, and elsewhere. Vertov and Svilova's contemporary Esther Shub made an art of finding old documentary footage and putting it together to create powerful films, *The Fall of the Romanov Dynasty* (1927) and others. Helen Van Dongen worked closely with documentary director Joris Ivens, and with Flaherty on *The Land* (1942) and *Louisiana Story*, collaborating on the planning and structuring of the latter prior to shooting, as well as editing the footage.[5]

The 1920s saw further important experiments. Merian Cooper and Ernest Shoedsack shot *Grass* (1925) in dangerous mountain terrain in Turkey and Persia, keeping a certain amazed distance on the events of an arduous tribal migration with cattle herds. Walter Ruttmann made his influential *Berlin: Symphony of a City* (1927), where the city seems to take on a life of its own, dawn to dark, and the filmmaker enjoys his bravura in putting together images. The film of the life of a place met with a deep, imaginative artistic temperament in the case of Jean Vigo's *A Propos de Nice* (1930). Here everything looks strange, though it is plain footage from the streets. The unfolding of the images is surprising, but organic—one's

5. For an account of this see Richard Meran Barsam, *The Vision of Robert Flaherty: The Artist as Myth and Film-maker* (Indiana University Press, 1988). This is a good modern study of Flaherty, drawing on earlier treatments.

attention is held in a way it is not with Ruttmann's film. Is this the naturalness of the world, never before revealed as it is here? Or is it the strength of an artist's personality?

A similar phenomenon to the Vigo is Luis Buñuel's *Land Without Bread (Las Hurdes)* (1932), with images of the debased life of a remote Spanish small town, overlaid by a dry, seemingly not fully aware commentary and the romantic, deeply ordered orchestral music of Brahms. The place itself is there, somehow more realized, not dissipated, by virtue of Buñuel's temperament and discomforting sense of humor. With Vigo and Buñuel we meet the commandingly interesting filmmaker who will work in both nonfiction and fiction—one should perhaps mention Leni Riefensthal right off in this regard, and later figures include Alain Resnais, Agnès Varda, Lindsay Anderson, Marta Meszaros, Werner Herzog, Nagisa Oshima.

In the 1930s there was consolidated in Britain and the United States the idea of documentary film as a sort of social truth-telling, an educational project (in a much soberer and more widely accepted and practiced style than Vertov's). The thirties gave us the documentary as it is commonly thought of, and many viewers have never shaken off the idea, despite the radical, deviant—in these terms—artistic work in nonfiction that has gone on through the decades.

A key figure of the thirties and forties is John Grierson, who directed *Drifters* (1929), about herring fishermen, and went on to produce many films for commercial and governmental agencies in Britain, and later in Canada, coordinating the talents of many, writing and lecturing all the while, in every way promoting his goals. He sought to educate the public about common work, social processes, the good citizen's obligations, and, sometimes, foreign places.[6] Much of the British Documentary Movement, as it came to be known, will look slow and empty (or not full enough, not vital and intelligent enough) to viewers now. But sometimes exceptional talents came to the fore, as in Basil Wright's poetic *Song of Ceylon* (1935), or perhaps in Wright and Harry Watt's *Night Mail* (1936), a high-spirited film about work on an overnight mail train, with rhythmic commentary written by W. H. Auden and music by Benjamin Britten. Certainly

6. See John Grierson, *Grierson on Documentary*, ed. Forsyth Hardy (Harcourt Brace, 1947).

Humphrey Jennings was an exceptional talent, emerging during World War II after Grierson had left for Canada. His *Listen to Britain* (1942) is a compelling assemblage of images of work, the performing arts, and daily life in wartime, with natural sounds (sometimes music in performance, or an actor's recited words) and no commentary. *Fires Were Started* (1943) is a basically nonfiction film, with some staging (as has been the case, actually, in many nonfiction films), about firemen who cope with the aerial bombing of London during the war. *A Diary for Timothy* (1945), about the end of the war in Britain and future prospects, is full of pain and fear, but with a positive spirit that is forced only as such spirit can be in real situations of distress.

Films made in the United States in the 1930s also helped set the idea of documentary as an educational tool: coming out of left-oriented journalistic and photographic circles, Pare Lorentz and others made *The Plow That Broke the Plains* (1936), about the Dust Bowl; and *The River* (1937), about the Mississippi Valley, the destructiveness of floods, and the work of the TVA. These films were widely seen and admired. The didactic commentary and the music seem overbearing now. But the images of depredation in the Dust Bowl accumulate powerfully as *The Plow That Broke the Plains* comes to an end on a downbeat, open note—reminiscent of the ending of *Nanook*. And the sequence of flood images in *The River* amazes the viewer, that such beautiful photographing could go on in the midst of, and could seem to capture, such chaos. The Dutch filmmaker Joris Ivens, who had begun with studiedly artistic work such as *Rain* (1929; Amsterdam in the rain), collaborated with Ernest Hemingway on *The Spanish Earth* (1937), a project started and funded by concerned American writers and artists to tell what was going on in the Spanish Civil War. The film was premiered for the Roosevelts at the White House, and became quite famous. It is a film actually shot in war conditions, showing the defense of Madrid and the work in a supportive agricultural community not far away. One sees and sees, and learns gradually about the overall situation as more and more of Hemingway's spare commentary is spoken. The film, as put together, really works as one of step by step discovery.

In Germany in the 1930s Leni Riefensthal made *Triumph of the Will* (1935) and *Olympiad* (1938), films that disturb, or horrify, viewers, but that are impossible to get over. Riefensthal had earlier done very interesting work acting in and directing fiction films of a romantic, mystical sort, and her documentaries seem especially inventive ones. They raise in, as it were, nightmare fashion the issue of artistic imagination meeting reality. *Triumph of the Will*, about a Nazi Party rally in Nuremberg, with youth camps, torch-light parades, gatherings in a huge stadium, does not so much film Nazism as invent or construct it, or sing about it, the reality coming through only as the grubby leaders face the camera and make their speeches. But then hope, strange as it sounds, an excited, visionary hope, was a real element of early Nazism—Riefensthal has managed to record this. *Olympiad* is about the 1936 Berlin Olympic Games. The film's presentation of divers, runners, horse-riding, with images of Hitler and his associates intermixed, has been called fascist because of the abstraction and idealism—though an idealism that could focus on an American Negro, Jesse Owens.[7] Abstraction and ide-alism are qualities that make possible much of music and dance. Riefensthal works in this mode, bringing it to nonfiction film, and she seems not so much to participate in a fascist artistic sensibility as herself alone to *be* that sensibility, if that is what it is. There is no work like hers, after all. Her films seem finally personal, even inner, and not political, though she blamably aided the Nazi regime with this work.

Propaganda was the route for documentary during World War II—explaining, advocating, urging on. In the United States there was a notable transfer of talent from Hollywood to the war effort—Frank Capra, John Ford, William Wyler, John Huston. Capra's clear, forceful *Why We Fight* series did its job best for the government, educating soldiers and clearing their thoughts for their work. John Huston's beautifully intimate *Let There Be Light* (1945), about shellshock invalids in a soldiers' hospital, was too realistic for the times and was suppressed.

Jean-Luc Godard has said that cinema was invented to film the concentration camps. And surely in this film footage, some of it taken by

7. The most forceful attack on Riefensthal has been Susan Sontag's "Fascinating Fascism," in *Under the Sign of Saturn* (Farrar, Straus and Giroux, 1980).

those who ran the camps, some by the liberating armies, the great rebarbative fact is there to be faced as perhaps it could not be otherwise. Alain Resnais's *Night and Fog* (1955) brings the forces of art to bear on this material, this history—selecting, juxtaposing, taking new color footage to go with the old black-and-white film, supplying music and the fine, plain writing of Jean Cayrol for the spoken commentary. This half-hour film, intense but giving some precious breathing spaces, is everywhere admitted to have worked, to have served the purpose—a supreme case of art and feeling meeting its subject.

To look into the camps and the catastrophe of World War II generally has been a preoccupation of film ever since the war, directly and indirectly. Jay Cantor, Maureen Howard, and Susan Howe argue here that film in many areas simply cannot get over the war. Korea, Algeria, Vietnam seem to have compounded the original pressure. Marcel Ophuls's *The Sorrow and the Pity* (1970) was one of the most widely seen and talked about nonfiction films ever. Many viewers returned to this four-and-a-half hour film a second and third time out of sheer fascination. The reconstruction of collaboration and resistance and everyday life in a city in occupied France is intelligent, flexible, compulsively observing. It is a large, complex work, where we face and listen to people in the present, and sometimes look at old footage, and the past comes entirely to life. Ophuls's *Hotel Terminus* (1987) concerns Klaus Barbie's brutal regime in Lyons and the C.I.A.'s use of and protection of Barbie after the war. This film puts Ophuls forward more as a discomfort-causing investigator than in *The Sorrow and the Pity*. The facts are harder to extract here—they are more consistently horrible. In Claude Lanzmann's *Shoah* (1985), the simple shooting and construction of the film, the repetitious interviews over some nine hours, miraculously manage to build the events of the camps up into reality again, from the earth up.

Jay Cantor talks about *Night and Fog*, *Hotel Terminus*, and *Shoah* here, and the way one kind after another of art, method, filmmaking style—often working like psychoanalytic therapy—is brought to bear to elicit the facts and affect the viewer. How, Cantor asks, and finds answers, can film confront death—non-being—and not distance or avoid it? How can film honor the dead, positively and without false sentiment?

World War II's indirect effect on film might be charted in a number of ways—the change of mood in the postwar films of John Ford, Alfred Hitchcock, and Japanese directors; the emergence of a figure such as Ingmar Bergman, determined not to get over confronting an unfathomable evil, taking various forms. The pressure may be seen behind Georges Franju's choice of subject in his nonfiction studies, *Blood of Beasts* (1949), about a slaughterhouse, and *Hôtel des Invalides* (1952), about the grand old museum for the military in Paris, hollow-seeming here. Robert Gardner's *Dead Birds* (1964), about warring tribes in New Guinea, works like Simone Weil's essay on the *Iliad*, to project acceptance of war as a way of life.

One of the most intriguing and intelligent figures working in nonfiction film since World War II is Chris Marker, who has made films all over the world—*Sundays in Peking* (1955), *Letter from Siberia* (1957), *Cuba Si!* (1961). He finds a predilection eventually for Japan—*The Kuomiko Mystery* (1965), *Sans Soleil* (1982)—as very much a post-Hiroshima and life-over-the-abyss world, and at the same time a world of beauty and of an intensely imagined way of life, even in Japan's great progressiveness in technology. Marker is a political activist and an intellectual, and film is his way of working. There is a wonderful convergence in his films, of images with the rational and verbal. He is an eager and curious filmmaker, an explorer; but there is a somberness about the socialist hope of his 1950s films and *Le Joli Mai* (1963), his famous large-scale study of life in Paris at the end of the Algerian war. *Sans Soleil* is melancholy and inward-turning, for all its imagery from all over the world, as if from an inveterate extrovert.

Susan Howe insists on the way all Marker's work is scarred by the Second World War, the broad catastrophe of the 1940s. She concentrates on *Sans Soleil* and on Marker's one fiction film—how different is it? Howe asks—*La Jetée* (1962), the intense half-hour work made almost wholly of still images, as if more real thereby, a romance set in a war of the future. These films are mourning what is almost inconceivable loss, Howe says. This is the pressure behind their documentary and imaginative moves. Marker leads Howe into Andrei Tarkovsky's work, where the fictional *Ivan's Childhood* (1962) seems to reconstruct real war memories rawly, and where in *Mirror* (1974) found nonfictional war footage breaks in and takes over the film, showing its deep source and motive.

In the 1940s and 1950s there were changes in the look and the subject matter of much fiction film, as it became more like documentary in immediate, obvious ways. André Bazin argues that the war and the postwar years impressed on people how bound they were to a particular time and place, giving rise to the new developments in film.[8] Italian Neorealism— Roberto Rossellini's *Open City* (1945) and *Paisan* (1946), Vittorio De Sica's *Bicycle Thieves* (1947) and *Umberto D* (1952), and other films—used the real settings of city streets and people's dwellings and workplaces (not in good shape at this point in history), used nonprofessional actors in many instances, and told stories of everyday people and everyday crises at the end of the war. These films were seen all over the world and have been much discussed. They inspired new movements in filmmaking, even non-fiction filmmaking, in Europe, Latin America, India, and elsewhere.

Beginning as early as Neorealism, so-called docudrama became an important mode in the United States. These films tell true current sto-ries, usually involving spying or crime, sometimes quite mundane crime, and use real, nonstudio settings, and nonprofessional actors to a degree, sometimes people who were involved in the original events—Henry Hath-away's *The House on 92nd Street* (1945) and *Call Northside 777* (1948); Elia Kazan's *Boomerang* (1947), *Panic in the Streets* (1950) (the right style, though not a true story), and *On the Waterfront* (1954); Hitchcock's *The Wrong Man* (1957). Maureen Howard discusses these films here and their links to newsreels and other documentary forms of the time. She sees all this fictional and nonfictional work as part of a history of shock at the war and anxiety to understand the mechanisms and methods of documentation of facts of all kinds, to make out what might be threatening one's commu-nity or one's private world. Maureen Howard and Susan Howe talk most about history in this book—how films and filmmakers and the appeal of films to audiences are pressured by a consciousness of current history.

As if in response to fiction film's greater realism, in style at least, a new experiment was undertaken on a large scale in nonfiction film in the late 1950s and on into the next decades, the movement known loosely as cinema-verité. There is something of a foretaste in the British Free Cinema

8. See the essays on this era in André Bazin, *What Is Cinema?*, vol. 2, ed. and trans. Hugh Gray (University of California Press, 1971).

movement of the 1950s, with films such as Lindsay Anderson's *Every Day Except Christmas* (1957), observing night and early morning work at Covent Garden Market, using new lighter camera and sound equipment for more intimate and flexible observation, the subject seeming really to lead the filmmakers, who have no Griersonian instruction or case to present. The term cinema-verité was first used by Jean Rouch in his influential 1961 film, *Chronicle of a Summer*, about ordinary Parisians and their assessments of their lives; and this film and Rouch's extraordinary African ethnographic films—*Les Maîtres Fous* (1955) and many more—make a decisive contribution to the new experiment. (In some films—*Moi, un Noir* [1957], *Jaguar* [1967], and others—Rouch merges nonfiction and fiction in a daring way.)[9] Then the new approach to filming blossomed in America with the work, often sponsored by television, of Richard Leacock, D. A. Pennebaker, Albert and David Maysles, and others—films such as *Primary* (1960) and *Crisis* (1963), watching political campaigning and government in everyday action; Leacock and Joyce Chopra's *A Happy Mother's Day* (1963), about a South Dakota family with quintuplets; Leacock and Pennebaker's *Don't Look Back* (1967), about Bob Dylan; and the Maysles' *Salesman* (1969), about door-to-door Bible selling, and their later, notorious *Grey Gardens* (1976), about well-born women living in squalor in their rundown Long Island mansion.

These films have principles. They eschew commentary from outside the world of the film, using the natural words and sounds that go with the images, often seeming to welcome accidental or confusing sounds (though some of them do have some voiceover commentary). The films try for long-lasting shots, the camera usually handheld, staying with the subject, moving to follow events or to reveal nuances of the scene. Cutting is held to a minimum, as if the juxtapositions of a filmmaker's editing would make too much of a statement, imposing something on the material, forcing it. These films seem to bring viewers closer than ever to everyday, even sordid, reality (the Americans liked to call it "direct cinema"), yet they can also convey a certain delirious impression of reality floating by, or of being unmoored and afloat in winding space and drawn-out, almost stopped

9. A good introduction to Rouch is *Anthropology-Reality-Cinema*, ed. Mick Eaton (British Film Institute, 1979). This book gives brief accounts of all Rouch's films (to 1979) and reprints an excellent article on him by Jean-André Fieschi, dealing with the reality/fiction issue.

time. One's means of distancing and comprehending material can seem taken away, or made to alter. This is a particular experiment with reality, not simply the throwing over of filmic conventions—there has never been one set of conventions for nonfiction film.

William Rothman discusses the cinema-verité movement here, its principles and some of its notable films, inquiring into the element of imagination at work. Cinema-verité is romantic, Rothman says, in ways it inherits from classical Hollywood film; and the latter is real, if we will attend to it, in its ways of discovering people and behavior. Rothman focuses on the fascinating issue of a *conceivable* screenplay for cinema-verité films. What does it mean, deep down and after all, that some films are scripted and some are not?

The effect and the kinship of cinema-verité can be seen in a great deal of film in the 1960s and later. The burgeoning of ethnographic film, discussed by Eliot Weinberger, was made possible by the new lighter equipment and easier methods for sound recording, which had inspired cinema-verité in the United States and Paris; and many ethnographic films follow the principles of cinema-verité in treating reality. Weinberger discusses a number of films and the debates about procedure in this area of filmmaking. One of his subjects is Robert Gardner, and Weinberger's essay is followed by Gardner's. This is the one occasion in the book where we are able to have a filmmaker, in this case one who is also a writer, come forward and speak about what making nonfiction films means to him. Gardner comments on films that have influenced him—work by Maya Deren, Basil Wright, and others—and looks back at his own filmmaking in New Guinea, India, and elsewhere. He speaks of the meeting of filmmaker's feeling and outer reality in film, the camera's active and eliciting, yet not overbearing, role, the trance-like state of attunement needed in the filmmaker.

Features of cinema-verité—its spontaneous-seeming camera, its following of the naturally unfolding event, its disdain of the pictorial—are there in Marcel Ophuls's interview films, in *Shoah*, in Shirley Clarke's *Portrait of Jason* (1967), about an elegant middle-aged black male hustler, who gradually comes to show profound distress as he talks on and on to the camera. And the style of cinema-verité can be felt in some fiction films of the French New Wave (handheld camera, natural light, accidental sounds, staying a long time with a mundane subject), or in films of Robert Altman or John Cassevetes.

Frederick Wiseman's distinguished series of films about American institutions—*Titicut Follies* (1967), *High School* (1968), *Basic Training* (1971), *Welfare* (1975), and many more—share with cinema-verité a presentation without commentary, and a sense of letting the subject lead; but Wiseman's is decidedly a cinema of editing (with some late exceptions), of relatively brief shots, many cuts. Wiseman's films raise the question about editing: must it make a point, as Wiseman plainly does sometimes, or can editing work more like the constantly running camera, as a means to follow events and material? In Robert Gardner's *Forest of Bliss* (1986), shot in Benares, India, with no spoken commentary, every cut seems a major event, but one very hard to paraphrase or specify—while Wiseman's cuts, for all his purpose as a social critic, often do *not* seem strong events, but rather flow by. Relatively speaking, we forget the editing, feeling we are just absorbed in the subject—or is Wiseman seducing us into his point of view?[10]

Jean Rouch put himself forward in his films as provocateur, or at least let it be clear how the situation of filming is itself provocative or reality altering for people being filmed. Ed Pincus, who made cinema-verité films about conditions in Mississippi in the 1960s (*Panola*, *Black Natchez*), made *Diaries* over a period a years in the 1970s, filming himself and his family and friends, his marriage in progress and in crisis, all very much in the real countercultural Boston and Vermont of the time. It is always clear, as Rothman points out here, that Pincus's life is not just there to be filmed, but that filming affects the life. *Diaries* is the film of a life to some extent formed by the filming.

The personal development continues in much work of the 1970s, 1980s, and 1990s: to name a few films, Joyce Chopra and Claudia Weill's *Joyce at 34* (1972), about Chopra at a certain stage of her life, just having a child; Amalie Rothschild's *Nana, Mom, and Me* (1973), about the film-

---

10. Three good studies of Wiseman are Thomas Benson and Carolyn Anderson, *Reality Fictions: The Films of Frederick Wiseman* (Southern Illinois University Press, 1989); Barry Keith Grant, *Voyages of Discovery: The Cinema of Frederick Wiseman* (University of Illinois Press, 1992); and Alan Robert Cholodenko, *The Films of Frederick Wiseman* (Harvard Ph.D. thesis, 1987, available through University Microfilms International).

maker and her mother and grandmother; Rob Moss's *The Tourist* (1992), about the filmmaker's travels abroad on film-shooting assignments, and his and his wife's efforts at home to overcome infertility. Ross McElwee's *Backyard* (1982, shot earlier) and *Charleen* (1978) introduce the filmmaker and other people who will appear in subsequent films of his, as the film about the filmmaker's life becomes a series and looks to become a life's work. *Sherman's March* (1986) was a considerable commercial success, presenting McElwee, with his dry, but lively, temperament of a Southern young man who now lives in the North, traveling through the South again on a filmmaking grant, confronting Civil War history and modern fears of nuclear devastation (shades of Susan Howe's theme), meeting family and old friends and old girlfriends, and cultivating new ones—giving, above all, a series of remarkable portraits of women. *Time Indefinite* (1993) continues McElwee's story, with his marriage and the death of his father and the birth of a son. The mode of this film is denser, more suggestive of an essay, reflecting on death and birth, with images and episodes more made to collide and to cast meaning on one another, less a linear flow of marvels than is *Sherman's March*.

The personal kind of nonfiction film raises the issue of the relation of nonfiction to avant-garde film, film as extreme—is it?—formal experimentation. The question might well have come up before, with Vigo or Buñuel, or indeed Vertov. The restless-seeming camera of cinema-verité has some kinship to Stan Brakhage films of the 1950s and later, and Brakhage writes about the camera eye and what it can see and do, with a fervor that recalls Vertov's manifestos.[11] Is Brakhage's film about his wife's giving birth, *WINDOW WATER BABY MOVING* (1959), to be considered nonfiction, documentary, for all its unusual assertive editing? Is a certain amount of Warhol to be thought of as documentary? Filmmakers in the avant-garde, from Maya Deren in the 1940s onward, frequently portray themselves, their intimates, and their familiar places, sometimes we might want to say in creative storytelling or the making of fantasy, but often (even in these same cases) to reveal what they themselves and others and places and things actually are.

11. See Stan Brakhage's writings in *Film Culture Reader*, ed. P. Adams Sitney (Praeger, 1970).

Patricia Hampl discusses the autobiographical film here, where a filmmaker's voice is heard and images of the life are seen, or summoned up in the viewer's mind. Hampl's principal figure, Jerome Hill, comes from the world of the avant-garde, where he was a highly respected artist and friend to artists from the 1930s on. With the great Whitmanesque *Film Portrait* (1971), Hill presents his own life, with some found material in photographs and film, and with strongly experimental film techniques to represent his angles, as Hampl puts it, upon himself and the world he is reflecting on—techniques to represent, to be, really, his voice in full, himself as we have him. Another of Hampl's figures is McElwee, with his looser style of filming and talking about life as it occurs. What is *this* voice? What is the presence in life of filmmaker and filming, which people in McElwee films so often shy from or rebuke (as well as play up to)? A third figure for Hampl is Su Friedrich, whose *The Ties That Bind* (1984), about her mother, and *Sink or Swim* (1990), about herself and her father, hark back to Hill and Deren and other avant-garde figures with a desire to order images precisely, to let the personal voice emerge indirectly in the very ordering of things, presenting the film as very much made rather than as freely and, perhaps, submissively observing (of course, the latter impression in McElwee or Pincus is only a first impression . . .).

Helene Keyssar's essay on several women filmmakers takes up instances of the avant-garde, films by Deren from the 1940s and Yvonne Rainer several decades later, as well as political/sociological films such as Barbara Kopple's *Harlan County, U.S.A.* (1977) and *American Dream* (1990), and films that seem to lie between these two kinds, Chopra and Weill's *Joyce at 34*, Roberta Cantow's *Clotheslines* (1983), presenting a series of suggestive images of hanging out the wash, and Jennie Livingston's *Paris Is Burning* (1991), about transvestite competitions in Harlem. Keyssar concentrates on the positive, valuable irritation a viewer is made to feel with all this work. It is work that realizes active thinking—film as thinking—and provokes thinking in the viewer. Deren's "lyrical" films tutor us about women's lives and the way the collective mind works. The "personal" film *Joyce at 34* becomes a philosophical dialogue between two filmmakers about the nature of being filmed.

*Paris Is Burning* and Rainer's *Film about a Woman Who . . .* (1974) in their different ways challenge emphatically a viewer's sense of identity. The very popular *Paris Is Burning* is a cinema-verité look at showy public drag competitions and behind-the-scenes talk about the downbeat lives of the participants. This woman filmmaker's film, as it goes on, grows in sympathy, or acknowledgment of oneness, with its subject, drawing the viewer along. Where does this leave viewers who are not gay black males? Yvonne Rainer, beginning with *Lives of Performers* (1969), has made a series of films that seem to find ways to film pure thought or feeling or human motive—but whose? *Film about a Woman Who . . .* (like other Rainer films) moves forward fully unpredictably—like music by Arnold Schönberg—asking the viewer to rethink what the medium of film is: what is it showing us? what is *there* in these images and protracted scenes of plausible and implausible activities? If the viewer grasps in the end a basic thought or motive for the whole thing—say, a woman's feeling about a man—is this the filmmaker's feeling or the struggling, thinking viewer's? Where is the line between filmmaker and viewer, person and person?

Later in the book Phillip Lopate returns to the question of thought in film (as do Petric and Howe, whose essays follow his, on Vertov and Marker). Lopate discusses the personal film where it becomes in his view an essay, reflective, pursuing a general subject and coming to a conclusion, interesting in the writing itself of the spoken commentary. Lopate is a lover of film as well as of the written word, and he is not look-ing for a good lecture well illustrated: the point is a melding of words and images, or the setting up of a valid interchange between the two. *Night and Fog*, with Cayrol's writing, is an important instance. Chris Marker is a crucial figure with a number of films, right up to his recent *The Last Bolshevik* (1993), about the career of filmmaker Alexander Medvedkin in the Soviet Union. And Godard is formidable here with his political essays *Letter to Jane* (1972), on Vietnam, codirected with Jean-Pierre Gorin, and *Ici et Ailleurs* (1977), on Palestine; and Orson Welles is very satisfying with his thoughtful late videotape *Filming "Othello"* (1978). Lopate takes the discussion into quite personal films with Ralph Arlyck's *An Acquired Taste* (1981) and Vanalyne Green's *A Spy in the House That Ruth Built* (1984).

The present situation in nonfiction film is not dominated by the personal. That is a rich vein, and varied in itself, but recent work shows diversity and experimentation more than ever. We have seen a large commercial success for left-oriented films on public issues—Barbara Kopple's films; Michael Moore's *Roger and Me* (1989), about harsh labor policies of General Motors, with Moore portraying himself as the bumbling investigator. Errol Morris's *The Thin Blue Line* (1988), about a Texas murder case, was widely seen and caused the case to be reopened, with the result that a man falsely convicted under police pressure was exonerated. The film includes stagings of the roadside crime, depicting various conceivable ways it could have been committed, the stagings done in eerie color light at night, with music by Philip Glass—speculation about the crime thus falls in the realm of the fantastic as well as that of logic. What most gives the film its powerful effect is extensive interviews with the accused man, Randall Adams. This material is natural and direct, though Adams becomes in the course of it a charming film presence, a creature of film. This film had its public effect by virtue of revelation of (probable) reality; should the stress fall on the art of revelation or on the reality?

*Pictures from a Revolution* (1992), by Susan Meiselas, Richard Rogers, and Alfred Guzzetti, about the Nicaraguan Revolution and life there in the ten years following, had a very successful screening at the New York Film Festival, and has been memorable for those who have seen it, and much talked about. The film did not go into wide distribution. It is available on videotape, but not easy to find, and this is eminently a film to be seen screened from a good print, on a large screen. The problem is a typical one with good nonfiction films. Meiselas published a famous book of photographs she took in Nicaragua during the revolution, and she returns with filmmakers Rogers and Guzzetti to see what life is like after years of economic isolation and war with the Contras, and to find out what has become of the people she photographed. The depressed vitality of the Nicaraguan people and the devastation of war are conveyed in rich, beautiful color images and very immediate sound, and by means of some highly artistic interworkings of the older still photographs with present action. The film is a remarkable meeting of the artistic with the real, with an important stretch of the history of our times.

A great deal is shot on videotape these days, for practical and for aesthetic reasons. (Trinh Minh-ha describes video as sometimes being a very interesting sketch-like or watercolor-like material—one doesn't always want the ripeness of film, like oil painting in this comparison.) Video made possible a project such as *Silverlake Life: The View from Here* (1993), where two men with AIDS film their life in its last year. The practiced filmmaker of the two, Tom Joslin, is dying faster, and indeed seems gone from the start. But he wanted to do this film, and with limited funds and the limited technical expertise of his partner, Mark Massi, video was the way to do it. The material was edited and transferred to film after the death of both men by a friend and sympathetic filmmaker, Peter Friedman. It is a work of collaboration, made, it almost seems, by the very situation that is its subject. It is always moving; heartbreaking at the moment Joslin's newly dead corpse is seen, and his partner sings over him; sometimes bright, as with the remembered high spirits of Joslin, seen in old films, and the daily good humor of Massi. This work seems all the truer for the look of video, the mode of home movies at present, which perhaps more than film now, reminds us that things are gone.

New people are doing new kinds of work in nonfiction film now. Most of the filmmakers who have emerged since World War II are still at work, trying new things—Chris Marker, working in videotape; Agnès Varda, honoring her deceased husband, Jacques Demy, with the biographical-fantastic *Jaquot de Nantes* (1992); D. A. Pennebaker, making *The War Room* (1993) with Chris Hegedus, about James Carville and the managing of Bill Clinton's presidential campaign. Sometimes an odd being, rooted in the fictional imagination, wanders into the world of non-fiction film and creates enduring work, part of an individual journey. Such was the case with Michelangelo Antonioni, many years after his early documentary shorts, when he made his film about China, *Chung Kuo Cina* (1973); and with Werner Herzog and his spooky *Fata Morgana* (1971), about a barren African landscape with industrial trash, gradually peopled, with spoken words from creation myths and a diverse mix of music, or his *Land of Silence and Darkness* (1972), a very moving, down to earth yet intensely transcendent film about the blind-and-deaf and their schooling and their families.

Dušan Makaveyev became known for his fiction films in Yugoslavia in the 1960s, part of an Eastern European renaissance in film at the time. The extraordinary *WR: Mysteries of the Organism* (1971) and *Sweet Movie* (1974) were made in more than one country and are part nonfiction, part fiction. Then, settling in the West, Makaveyev went his way with further fiction films. *WR: Mysteries of the Organism* is a documentary about sexual-social theorist Wilhelm Reich and his ideas, their ramifications in America and in an imagined—but certainly real, in many ways—Eastern Europe. The film presents archival and newly shot footage, nonfiction and fiction, and becomes an instruction in what fiction and nonfiction are, what reality and perception are, perception and imagination, acceptance of the world, and desire. It is a wild and disturbing film, heated about politics and sex, and heated in its sudden moves from one kind of material to another. This film is constantly on the verge of becoming discourse—not moralizing discourse, but one that opens up questions—and my own essay here offers to take the film the one step farther it seems to want to go, into writing, writing that throws us back into film.

The essay on *WR* is the one instance in this book of dealing entirely with one film, staying with it from beginning to end. Many films invite and deserve such treatment, but it is only one way among others of talking about film. Many ways are needed, with their various perspectives; many ways give valuable insight, as this book proves. To read through the essays here is to come closer to a wonderful body of films, the powerful effects they can have, the thoughts they provoke, as writers analyze passages of film, or talk philosophically about reality and imagination, or testify to the experience of watching film and having to reflect, not being able to get over the experience of film.

JAY CANTOR

# Death and the Image

*for Stanley Cavell*

In *The World Viewed*, the philosopher Stanley Cavell places Film in the volume marked Memory; for films, like memories, give us a world that is ours, yet that we are barred from entering. Memories, of course, may, on certain remarkable occasions, be vividly reborn as part of one's current telling; they enter us reincarnated, rich with anxiety and the demand that we change our lives, that we continue our narratives, in light of their questions, to a new momentary stopping point. But only some films are such inspired memories; others are that failed sort of memory called nostalgia. Nostalgia: because we think of the time we remember as a time we have survived; and because we dream we have survived it—its challenges, its interrogations—we think we watch a history that is simply past, incapable of troubling us in the present. We are fond spectators of a calm time, lulling, purged of that constant moment-to-moment anxiety for one's survival that edges each present moment with pain. It's as if the nostalgic film (both fiction and documentary) longs to attain the status of the snapshot, the perfect form, Kodak and Polaroid reassure me, for nostalgia, the past not as question, but as possession.

I think that the continual consumption of such images-become-snapshots in the T.V. news, newspaper photos, magazine photo-essays, films, and videos makes us feel immortal; not alive as humans once were;

and, like gods, not quite capable of imagining our death. One figure for this in my thinking is Patty Hearst's demonic kidnappers, who, when their not-so-safe-house was surrounded, stayed inside, watching themselves on T.V. as the police burned them up. I imagine they felt they couldn't really be dying because they were watching themselves on television, and so were outside the flames that consumed them. Besides, they could always change the station.

Death is the absent guest in most of the images we use to divert ourselves—not death as subject or as spectacle but felt death, our transience, our violence, and our will to end our lives. Did the artist's shaping violence form the image or do we feel that at most he shot a camera and the mechanism did the rest? We know better; every great cinematic artist teaches that each frame must be formed by the artist and by the viewer's imagination. Yet it is easy also to deceive, to make us feel that the camera, that machine, doesn't have full implication in what it records. Our entertainments are often bloody minded, but the violence is usually localized in one kill-crazy hero, rather than experienced as the force that forms the world we see on (and perhaps off) the screen. And viewers need not quite acknowledge that they, too, imagine the world in the image, and so participate in what it represents; rather, one pretends that one *sees* it. The image overwhelms the imaginative faculty, that sense, redolent with instinctual involvement, that we collaborate in making the world through our shaping violence and our love. (Imagination, that is, as opposed to fixation, when one is fixed on, impaled upon, a world simply seen.)

But we cheat ourselves, I think, when we deaden our uneasiness before death, that fiercely beseeching anxiety that is the "gift" of the death instinct. That invaluable anxiety might make us acknowledge our desire to die, and our violence, and so (if we bear it, if we do not simply repress or deaden it) it might cause us to call on the god Eros. It might opportune our political imaginations to create a new dispensation for ourselves, one equal to the magnified means of annihilation that we have put at the service of the death instinct.

To speak of the images of the destruction of European Jewry, in the films I will write of here—*Night and Fog* (1955), *Shoah* (1985), *Hotel Terminus* (1987)—as if such pictures might be deadening, soothing, distracting or nostalgic, seems absurd. Yet often in considering these events, one slips into melancholy, or dark mourning, or a too insistent piety, when, if death were truly in what we imagine, one would feel, as the narrator of Alain Resnais' documentary *Night and Fog*, reminds us, "endless, uninterrupted fear." What I think the filmmakers I will speak about demand of us seems almost inhuman; that the death instinct, and our anxiety, might be felt by us and in us, in each of its manifestations, that the viewer might play every role in the film: executioner, spectator, victim, and the artist whose violence forms the image of this kingdom of death. Resourceful animals, we need all exits closed or we will avoid this confrontation. The viewer must feel the death instinct operates not only in the characters, but in the theme, not only in the theme but in the way the film's world was made, and in the way his or her mind operates in its understanding and enjoyment.

I do not mean, please understand me, that we are all responsible for the Holocaust. But I do think that if we cannot enter imaginatively into history—even this history—then our world will be a delusion, and our history a spectacle, and eventually, as the drugs wear off, an intolerable weight. In describing the cure of the neurosis, D. W. Winnicot speaks of the neurotic's first step towards cure coming when she reincludes her history, even its traumas, in the domain of infantile omnipotence. For the neurotic either represses the offending event, making the world and her personality unreal; or the trauma is experienced as an utterly external event that has crushed her. She, like us, must regain that sense the healthy infant has that her cry helps make the breast, that her desire collaborates in the creation of the world. Without this sense, half-illusory though it may be, our imagination is stunned by the inert mechanical mass of the world, incapable of creating the new dispensation we require, and we ourselves become machine-like in our pleasures or our destruction.

Each of these films begins by acknowledging the near impossibility of even representing the Holocaust. In part this is a piety; to admit that the Holocaust might be represented seems almost to deny the enormity of its horror, and its singularity. The Holocaust is, in a phrase borrowed from Rilke, "the bottle filled full of death . . . out of which people were forced to drink a bitterness of undiluted death." Impossible to represent this, for, as Freud writes, the death instinct is never simply, singly, manifested; death is always fused with eros. Or, perhaps, as the world was about to learn, not always; and then how can it be represented? We have no forms for such an unknown thing. "The problem of my film," the director of *Shoah*, Claude Lanzmann said, "was to show death." But can it be shown? For what one wishes to show does not adhere precisely in any of the documents the executioners left, any of the traces the victims made; even the survivors' voices. Those are papers; artifacts; sounds; and being adheres in each, when what the film wants to give is, precisely, non-being.

But if it could show us that blackness, we would become "frantically terrified"; death as catastrophe, death as drive—each is the signal for an anxiety beyond bearing. "If you could lick my heart," one survivor tells Lanzmann, "it would poison you." The Holocaust survivor's problem is the film's problem: death cannot be shown; it must be shown, must be felt, or all reality is drained from this world. It must, frame by frame, be remembered; it must be forgotten or life cannot continue.

"We should need the very mattress," the narrator of *Night and Fog* says as the camera pans over the dormitory at Auschwitz, "at once meat safe and strongbox . . . the blanket that was fought over, the denunciations and oaths. Only the hush and shade remain of this brick dormitory." [The camera pans outside.] "Here is the setting . . . an autumn sky indifferent to everything . . . evokes a night shrill with cries . . . " Can we hear those cries? Resnais and Cayrol—the camp survivor who wrote the extraordinary narrative—here present the fundamental difficulty of the Holocaust documentary as if it were a difficulty of evidence, of having the right documentation, the actual mattresses the victims slept on. As if one could believe the past only if it were no longer past, or as if documents and artifacts could return it to us (when, equally, documents, mattresses, in their very quiddity, hide non-being from us)! This is the mark of the greatest piety, and the greatest mischief. The piety: such an event should not be spoken of, cannot be spoken of; one cannot enter into the register of the historical order, of memory, what ended, or should have ended, history. And it marks the greatest evil: those who say that such a thing could not have happened.

Resnais shows us one face of the greatest evil, a still photo of a camp commandant "who pretends to know nothing . . . How discover what remains of the reality of the camps, when it was despised by those who made them and eluded those who suffered there . . ." [The camera pans past beds.] "Where sleep itself was a danger . . . no description, no shot can restore their true dimension, endless interrupted fear." What new forms, what new apprehensions, might restore our anxiety, and help us to bear it as well, not despising the events, repressing them, piously or evilly denying them—even if we must, then, also despise ourselves?

Resnais begins by reversing the expected terms of some problems. He makes the horrible ordinary, so we might believe it; and then he makes the ordinary horrible, so that we might fear it. "An ordinary road," his film begins, "an ordinary village . . . names like any other on maps and in guide books . . ." The camps are built, and the Jews, interned, "go on living their ordinary lives six hundred miles from home." The SS, with its registrars, Kapos, commandants, prostitutes, "managed to reconstitute the semblance of a real city." The ordinary becomes horrible—the tracks from our city of the living lead to the camp. The horrible becomes ordinary. The camp becomes a city. Not our city? Perhaps, but not, anymore, *not* our city, either.

Yet this is hardly enough to bring death into the image and into our consciousness. For that, the artist must understand the making of this city not simply as ordinary but in its deepest congruence with his own manner of making his film. For Resnais, the most lyric of the directors I will discuss, and the finest craftsman, it is art that builds the walls of the city; our city; the camps; his film. Death is most felt not in the voices of survivors, not in the silence of nature, but in all these things only when the artist has found a way to make himself and us participate in the *building* of these images of the destruction of the Jews, and so, in that limited, symbolic, so necessary way, in what the images show. We can participate, then, *symbolically* in the destruction of the Jews, and in our own destruction; for to imagine properly is also, symbolically, to perform and to suffer. The filmmaker must apprehend that the bringing of death can come from the way his sensibility operates. His sensibility, too, is what made the camps, made death, and if this were not the case, he would not, I think, be an artist, for in this manner, too, death is crucial in giving a world. One might say that each artist finds his sensibility, is given it as his, by apprehending—and bearing the knowledge—that his sensibility imaginatively makes death also.

So for Resnais, the most formally elegant, the most artful and elegiac of the filmmakers I'm going to discuss, the camp is made by art and by craft: "A concentration camp is built like a grand hotel—you need contractors, estimates—

"The camps come in many styles: [shots of guard towers accompany the list] Swiss, Garage, Japanese, No style." Whereas for Claude Lanzmann, the director of *Shoah,* the Final Solution is a matter of methodical, step by step, engineering, for Resnais it's a matter of art; as we come to the entrance to Auschwitz, the narrator says, "The leisurely architects plan the gates no one will enter more than once."

Within those crafted gates, some prisoners are classified as "Night and Fog," a piece of Hitler's poetry; the Jews were to disappear into the night and fog, their fate forever unknown. Poetry—art and craft—made the camp; poetry—art and craft—makes Resnais' response to the camp, its representation. Poetry is complicit with death—with the real death of the camp, and with what makes the representation of the camp. If Resnais' art did not openly display this complicity it would distance him and us from the camp, turn us into spectators, and the camp into spectacle.

In the Talmud, it is asked, how, now that the Temple is destroyed, are we to make sacrifices? And why, now that the Temple is destroyed, do we study in such detail how sacrifices were made there? The sages answer that our way of making a sacrifice at the Temple is, of course, *to study* how the sacrifice has been made, to sacrifice one's life briefly through study, in remembering the sacrifice, remembering it meticulously, step by step. In this way we symbolically enact sacrifice; our own detailed delineation, which calls upon all our powers of imagination and interpretation, both describes and is symbol for the sacrifice. The manner, that is to say, of a true representation is where the activity of representation itself is a symbolic equivalent for the act to be represented. Such symbolic sacrifices are not bloodless, not without scars; and it is a dangerous philistinism not to appreciate that the death instinct truly operates in the symbolic sacrifice as well as in the more cowardly literal one.

So "arts and crafts" here make the way death is represented and the way literal death is carried out: "Each camp has its surprises: a symphony; a zoo [we see a bear]; hothouses; Goethe's oak . . . " Resnais then shows, using still photos—using film to animate the still—the role call of naked prisoners; the piles of the dead; the lashings and gallows. And then adds: "The mind works on. They [the prisoners] make spoons, boxes, marionettes . . . while they hide notes, dreams." Art also entwines life with death, making the unbearable momentarily tolerable. (Is there anywhere art is not present, not formative?) The film then takes us to the hospital, a place for prisoners to be mocked with paper bandages—props, one might say—or murdered medically. We see footage in color, from present time, of empty rooms. The camera then pans across black-and-white stills of patients—or so one thinks, until an eye blinks. One thinks (forced to a telling misapprehension): so it wasn't a photo (though of course it is). If motion-pictures-become-snapshots describe nostalgic images, then here nostalgia is defeated by momentarily making the moving picture seem like a still—and then the slight motion of the patient's eye makes a mournful scene horrifying. Death enters because we had felt protected, because we had thought we were looking at a still, at history that had already happened. Outside history's narrative, we did not have to participate in its forward motion. But because the man will die, because he has returned for a moment to life, we try to grasp him at the edge of the precipice; and feel our failure, and await death, again, with him.

The hospital, the narrator says, "is set-up and scenes." What is behind them? "Useless operations, amputations." Set-up and scenes, as in a film. And a crematorium, too, can be a set—a work of art that is a lie. "An incinerator can be made to look like a picture postcard. Later—today—tourists have themselves photographed in them." Beware, then, of settings and sets. Beware of picture postcards, backdrops, photo opportunities, snapshots. Beware, this artist says, of art; it might make you nostalgic; it might make you a spectator; it might help you forget; and it might help you commit murder. Beware of arts and crafts. "Nothing is lost . . . women's hair" [a lovely shot of masses of hair, almost abstract in composition, until we might forget for its beauty what we are looking at] "is made into cloth, 15 pfennigs a kilo." Bones, "for manure." "Bodies . . . there's nothing left to say." [Shot of chopped off heads.] "Bodies . . . were meant for soap. As for skin . . ." [—the film shows images painted on skin. That is to say: *we watch images of images painted on skin.*]

Then: "Nothing distinguished the gas chamber from an ordinary block. What looked like a shower room welcomed the arrivals. The doors were closed. A watch was kept. The only sign—but you have to know—is this ceiling scored by finger nails." Why, I wondered, after all the horror we have seen, does the narrator add, "but you have to know"? Clearly, this moment has engrossed Resnais' imagination, for hands scraping stone is an image that will recur in his *Hiroshima, Mon Amour*, where the lover repeatedly scars her own hand by dragging her fingers against a cellar wall. The image must have spoken precisely *to him*, to his sense of himself and his project. I felt almost as if Resnais was defining himself by responding to an image in Rilke's essay, "In Regard to Art." Art, Rilke says, is "the sensuous possibility of new worlds and time . . . the artist is a dancer whose movements are broken by the constraints of his cell. That which finds no expression in his steps and limited swing of his arms, comes in exhaustion from his lips, or else he has to scratch the unlived lines of his body into the walls with his wounded fingers." Art, for Rilke, is Eros, sensuousness not yet able to be born, blocked by the recalcitrant unreadiness of history. But art, too, built these camps as well their sensuous representation. Is there art then in marks the victims' fingers made in *these* walls? Is this the end of art, or its grim mockery, or what defeats it—its hidden residue? Those who love art must stop, here, in stunned wonder. Are these markings ugly? beautiful? sublime? Here are the dancers; the unlived lines; the wounded fingers. " . . . but you have to know."

Resnais' film concludes that the Nazis' arts and crafts, "[t]he skill of the Nazis[,] is child's play today . . . There are those who take hope again as the image fades, as though there were a cure for the scourge of these camps . . . Those who pretend all this happened only once at a certain time and at a certain place. Those who refuse to look around them. . . Deaf to the endless cry." Art made the camps, and their representation, and art, too, can be used to uncover that endless cry which is perhaps now also the truth of the world art sometimes makes—a cry revealed by art that may destroy art. Is this art's point of reversal, where art creates for itself a world where art can no longer exist—where "the sensuous possibility of a new world and time" becomes the sensuous embodiment of no world, and no time? Will it destroy the telling if we hear the cry, know of the marks?

**Alain Resnais, *Night and Fog* (1955)**
**"The only sign — but you have to know — is this ceiling scored**
**by fingernails."**

Perhaps. Art must be, from now on, poised on a knife's edge, aware of its blandishments, its dangerous penchant for deception, its implication in catastrophe. *Night and Fog* provides, I think, both the sense of danger, and the program for Resnais' later fictional meditations. Film must now take on the task of warning us about art, must become a self-examining instrument, philosophical towards itself; uncovering through its representations and its manner of representing its own implications in the horror it reveals, and in the forgetting of that horror, uncovering again that final null point of art that may destroy art—the cry itself, the marks scratched in the wall.

In contrast to Resnais' elegiac and piercing tones in *Night and Fog*, Claude Lanzmann's *Shoah* seems more the work of an engineer than an artist—or the artist as engineer. Lanzmann is stupefyingly literal mind-ed. Everything said must be shown. If Filip Müller, survivor of Birkenau and Auschwitz, an engaging man of almost preternatural self-possession, describes marching to work at the crematoria, Lanzmann shows the path with hand-held camera, as if walking it. Literal-minded here often means both boring and bloody-minded, the combination forming, very intentionally, I think, Lanzmann's equivalent for "the banality of evil." Lanzmann means, I think, to be banal in his artistic means, inhibited in his visual vocabulary; zoom shots and pans with little variety in camera angle (usually overhead shots) make up most of his repertory. He is maddeningly compulsive in his repetition of sequences: the pan (over the former site of the camp, over the surrounding forests, over the Ruhr valley); the shot of the train crossing in front of the camera; the train arriving at Auschwitz; all are numbingly reshown.

From moment to moment there is little new to look at in *Shoah*. We hear the location of the gas chamber at Treblinka, and we see bricks and snow. A survivor describes the construction of the crematoria and we see bricks and snow. A former SS officer speaks of the "undressing room" with its deceptive signs about cleanliness and work. But we see bricks and snow. Until, from a desire for variety, our imagination becomes complicit in the process and we make the camp arise from the stones. We project upon the screen's projections, and now bricks and snow fill one with horror. (Over and over the same scene in the consulting room: the therapist's impassive face; his poorly chosen tie. We repeat the same story over and over, as we lie, like a corpse, on the couch, until our imagination—perhaps in part from boredom, from a desire for variety—projects a past on this meager screen.)

Literal-minded, bloody-minded, Lanzmann asks his informants, Was the path the gas vans went down paved? Or: how did the train get from here to there? Were the trains pushed the last kilometers into the camp? (Literal minded, bloody minded, he must walk that part of the way.) Was the train track inside the camp, or outside? He goes over the track with a train engineer. And from here to the camps was how far? "Here," he says, "was the Polish part, and here death." In this concentration on detail, on process, Lanzmann seems very much the obsessive; as if, if the right careful rituals were followed, death might be isolated in one part. But his obsession is too profound, too complete, too tireless, and soon death spills over, here and everywhere, for if the tracks go *there*, then they can also go *here*.

How were the gas chambers built? we hear Lanzmann's voice asking the SS man Suchomel. Who built them? What was their capacity?

(Jewish survivors, Suchomel thinks, tend to exaggerate it.) Lanzmann's voice asks for more details on the precise location of the undressing area, the gas, the crematoria. As we listen to these voices we see a van drive up outside Suchomel's house with a large antenna on top. We enter the van and see a technician focusing Suchomel's image on a television screen. On the T.V. screen, we hear and see Lanzmann lie to Suchomel, telling the SS officer that his face won't be shown, his name won't be used. Reassured, Suchomel, using a long pointer and a wall chart, describes the layout of the camp. "I don't see," Lanzmann said later, to an interviewer, "why I should keep my word to these people. Did they keep their word? I refuse to enter the psychology of the Nazis. I decided to have only technical conversations." But throughout the film this choice pushes Lanzmann farther beyond ordinary probity than such transparently poor self-justification; in fact what he achieves is a kind of *necessary* near-identification with the Nazis. He, *like them*, will lie. He, like them, will, *in his way*, kill. "How could I stand this, not to jump at [Suchomel] and kill him?" he says to an interviewer. "This was not my purpose. My purpose was to kill him with a camera." He, like them, is only interested in technical conversations; he, like them, wishes to make the Final Solution an engineering problem.

"I refuse," Lanzmann says, "to enter the psychology of the Nazis. I decided to have only technical conversations." Instead of why—and what answer would we accept here?—we have how. But in an age when psychology is what makes souls, to substitute (as Lanzmann does) how for why —is to seem oneself the soulless, the repetitive, the machine. How far from ramp to camp? "Four kilometers." "Was the road paved?"

The victims, too, wonder *how* such a thing might be done. "We were like stones, we couldn't mention what had happened to the wife," Abraham Bomba says. "Nobody is anymore alive. How could they gas so many people at once? But they had their way how to do it . . . It was impossible to believe that just a minute . . . before you were part of a family, you were part of a wife, a husband. Now all of a sudden, everything is dead." When the mind is stunned by what the mind can do, one asks not why but how, by what techniques, can we do such things. So this machine makes us into machines:

I looked around me [Filip Müller says]. There were hundreds of bodies, all dressed. Piled with the corpses were suitcases, bundles, and scattered everywhere, strange bluish, purple crystals. I couldn't understand any of it. It was like a blow on the head, as if I'd been stunned . . . Above all, I couldn't understand how they managed to kill so many people at once . . . Suddenly an SS man rushed up and told me . . . "Go stir the bodies!" What did he mean, "Stir the bodies?" . . . At that point I was in shock, as if I'd been hypnotized, ready to do whatever I was told. I was so mindless, so horrified, that I did everything . . . So the ovens were fed . . .

Lanzmann, stunned, refuses to enter the Nazis' psychology, to grant them inwardness. But this is, of course, the terrifying double bind that Hitlerism, perhaps all racism, confronts us with. He will not be like the Nazis; they must be utterly alien to him; they cannot even be imagined, granted insides; they are not human. But the Nazis knew better than us that technique of making their opponents *not human!* And so the machine has made him into a machine; he has become like them, for not to grant others inwardness means not to have it oneself. His outrage, his obsessive defense ("I decided to have only technical conversations"), meant to ensure that he remain uncontaminated, instead brings about the very thing he *seemingly* wants to avoid.

Lanzmann's *impersonation* is so complete that we begin to make equivalence after equivalence: the gas vans used at Chelmno are, one survivor has told us, like green vans one sees delivering cigarettes in Israel, are like, one supposes, the van we saw drive up to Suchomel's apartment. The SS lured the Jews with lies (and, one must add, unlike Lanzmann, forced them with unparalleled brutality). Lanzmann deceives Suchomel, and traps him in the van. No, not him—one must remind oneself—*his image.* Near the beginning of the film a survivor is shown a forest in Israel—why, one wonders, would Lanzmann bother with this, instead of simply showing him an image of the original forest? It is, the survivor agrees, something like the forest in Ponari where the Jews were burned. We then pan, at high angle, a forest at Sobibor. "That's the charm of our forests: silence and beauty," a Pole, Jan Piwonski, says. "But . . . there was a time when it was full of screams . . . and that period . . . is engraved on the mind of those who lived here then." This forest is like that forest . . . these vans are like those vans that deliver cigarettes. Our half-fare railroad tickets for children are like the pricing policies used by the Nazis for deportations. This train station is like that train station. Here are suitcases, like the suitcases that the dead left after they were "processed." The dead were called puppets; shit; bricks; rags. This is like that: metaphor, the trope which gives value, that makes a world, here destroys it by yoking our present with the kingdom of death. Through metaphor our world is unmade; replaced by another.

There is little new to look at in this film because it is not the new that interests Lanzmann but the eruption of the past. Lanzmann's method is the creation of transference—new editions, as Freud called it, of old conflicts; the sudden, almost epiphanic emergence of the spectral past to obliterate or reshape the present in its own image; in this case, to turn the apparent life of the present into the death that was the past; to kill the present, until this forest in Israel is for a moment that forest in Poland. Transference teaches a new lexicon: A river = a sewer for ground bones; stones = corpses; trees = deceptive propaganda to hide a killing ground; shoes = corpses; suitcases = corpses; clothing = corpses; rags = corpses; a field = a sorting place for dead people's clothing; shit = corpses; puppets = corpses; bricks = corpses; workers = cogs in a killing machine; to process = to kill people. And, of course, I must add film to this lexicon: when the Nazis rounded up the Jews of Corfu a survivor says that many gentiles came to watch. The subtitle says, "for the show," but the survivor has actually said "pour le cinéma." Lanzmann makes us mad with analogies that annihilate the present: we are silent in the theater, politely not interrupting, as if we were good Germans; afraid to scream, as if we were prisoners, stunned like Muller into stirring the bodies; we look towards the flickering light, as if we were prisoners in the gas vans. And we will emerge at the end, like the survivor of the Warsaw ghetto, the last Jew on earth, stunned now by life as the others had been by death, shocked to find that "In Aryan Warsaw life went on as naturally and normally as before. The cafes operated normally, the restaurants, buses and streetcars . . . were open."

When Lanzmann's necessary, difficult, arduous, techniques bear their bitter, invaluable fruit, all these equivalencies, and all the boredom and repetition, become ways of making the moments of transference bloom into a continuous transference neurosis. To accomplish this, Lanzmann, like a good analyst, is unfailingly dogged; and he is not (on rare occasions) beyond a little artifice. For Abraham Bomba, a Jewish survivor who had worked at Treblinka cutting hair, Lanzmann finds a barbershop, though he doesn't mention in the film that Bomba is now long retired. (Resnais, whose quarry is art itself, would have reminded us that this is a set, a setting.) We see Bomba working on a man's hair—but not actually; the scissors cut air; or the man, by the end of the scene, would have no hair. The Nazis used actual barbers at Treblinka to deceive the women about to be gassed, so the victims "could sit and not get the idea that this is their last day or the last time they are going to live or breathe or know what's going on." The barbers were a piece of art on the Nazis part: to make the Jews think that they were still part of a human community, not animals being shorn of their hair to make clothing and pillows for the Wehrmacht. Bomba, speaking somewhat impassively, says that the barbers tried "to do the best we could—to be the most human we could." Lanzmann, seemingly still the obsessive engineer, doesn't, at first, ask him how he felt about this, or what he thought, but how the gas chamber looked, and where, in relation to the gas chambers, he was standing when he performed the haircuts. Bomba begins to answer and then insists, "We know already that there is no way of going out from this room, because this room was the last place they went in alive and they will never go out alive again." Lanzmann then asks again, as if that fact were not at issue, or not of interest, what the room looked like. "Can you describe it precisely?" And "You cut with what—scissors?" And "There were no mirrors?" And "Can you imitate how you did it?" And: "Where did you wait [for the next group to arrive]?" And: "You cut the hair of how many women in one batch?" *Then* Lanzmann asks Bomba, "What was your impression the first time you saw these naked women arriving with children? What did you feel?"

Bomba's reply is in every way extraordinary. First, he reminds us that "it was very hard to feel anything, because working there day and night between dead people, between bodies, your feeling disappeared, you were dead." But then he says, "As a matter of fact, I want to tell you something that happened." *As a matter of fact*—and what he has been telling us previously have not quite been facts, for something has been screened out of them—he tells us that he knew many of the women whose hair he cut, yet he could not tell them anything of what awaited them. He begins to speak, as patients often will (or those in severe psychological trouble, or artists) not of himself, but of a double, a barber who recognizes among his "clients" his wife and sister. Then: "I can't. It's too horrible. Please." Bomba weeps.

The dialogue that follows between Lanzmann (off-screen) and Bomba (in a barber's smock, with a mirror behind him, standing over a man in a barber chair) is reminiscent of Beckett's tramps, or a director and an actor, or of any patient and therapist:

> "We have to do it. You know it."
> "I won't be able to do it."
> "You have to do it. I know it's very hard. I know and I apologize."
> "Don't make me go on please."
> "Please. We must go on."

Bomba, crying, finishes his story. "They could not tell them this was the last time they stay alive, because behind them was the German Nazis, SS men and they knew that if they said a word, not only the wife and the women, who were dead already, but also they would share the same thing with them. In a way they tried to do the best for them with a second longer, a minute longer, just to hug them and kiss them, because they knew they would never see them again."

Bomba is right, of course. In a machine world, stunned, half-hypnotized, it is very hard to have a feeling. Lanzmann has asked us, impelled us, through his incessant repetition of scenes, the film's long silences, the pauses for translations, the obsessive attention to details, to enter boredom, that fake death, like the psychoanalytic patient, that fake corpse on the couch. The boring details have given us the sense that we have the freedom to look away, when really we are hypnotized by the repetition of

DEATH AND THE IMAGE

actions, the familiarity, only to find that the repetition has lulled us, the affectlessness has allowed for an eruption of feeling, and we, along with Bomba, are—to use the Nazis' word—*transported,* transported back to the camp. Bomba then incarnates the past. He reads the memory traces inscribed on his body; he enacts the kinetic memories, relives the event. (Poetry, here, is the marks the prison made on the dancer's body.)

One of the SS men interviewed, assistant Nazi head of the Warsaw ghetto, says to Lanzmann, "We're reaching no new conclusions."

Lanzmann says, "I don't think we can."

But Lanzmann doesn't want new conclusions, he wants the old ones revived. And perhaps some resonance of the Holocaust has unknowingly scarred us as well, for sometimes, through identification, or because of something we find in ourselves, we, too, accompany Lanzmann's subjects. To bring about transference, Lanzmann has played the part of fellow victim and Nazi. Like the therapist, he has impersonated both the ego's ally, and the monstrous figure from the past, so he might guide Bomba and the others to go back, to enter death again. "To accompany the dead," Lanzmann called it in an interview. "To resurrect them. And to make them die a second time, but to die with them."

Or almost. Filip Müller tells this story:

> The violence climaxed when they tried to force the people to undress. A few obeyed, only a handful. Most of them refused to follow the order. Suddenly, like a chorus, they all began to sing. The whole "undressing room" rang with the Czech national anthem, and the Hatikvah. That moved me, terribly . . . That was happening to my countrymen, and I realized that my life had become meaningless. Why go on living? For what? So I went into the gas chamber with them, resolved to die. With them. Suddenly, some who recognized me came up to me . . . A small group of women approached. They looked at me and said, right there in the gas chamber . . . "So you want to die. But that's senseless. Your death won't give us back our lives. That's no way. You must get out of here alive, you must bear witness to our suffering, and to the injustice done to us."

This reprieve—we're just reprieved corpses, one of the Jewish camp workers had told a Kapo—is not, precisely, a cause for rejoicing. If Müller is willing to die with them—as the movie asks us to die with them—he is granted life again. But only if he accepts the task they, the dead, offer him, and that task is to remember more than he knows he can remember, to show more than he can say, to enact for others, over and over, their entry into the gas chamber, his desire to die, their death, his reprieve; he is spared if he is willing to make his life an abreaction, an incarnation of their dying, if he allows death to be endlessly reborn in him. Müller's story warns me, too, of one of the costs of the tradition represented by the Talmud's injunction to repeat in the ritual of study the activities of the dead. Such an incarnation may require the help of others, but it may also annihilate the present that one shares with them. Perhaps that's why Lanzmann found the work of making *Shoah* so isolating, why, in addition to the carnage that surrounded them, several of the survivors speak of having this same thought: that if they survived, they would be the last Jew left alive.

Lanzmann's technique is the inducement of transference: at whatever cost—even if it obliterates the present—the past must live in us. Marcel Ophuls's film *Hotel Terminus*, produced by his company, Memory Pictures, might be compared to that aspect of analysis that aims for knowledge. Patient and analyst methodically analyse repressions, not to bring about a reconnection between the ego and its stores of buried feeling, but so that one might accurately know the past again, and confront a present that, though bitter, is purged of distortions.

Ophuls's film, his analysis, traces the hidden—repressed, one might say—career of Klaus Barbie, the Nazi torturer of Lyon, murderer of Jews and resistance leaders, who was used and protected by the American government after the war. The neurotic—or historical actors—have, from Ophuls's point of view, disorders of memory. The neurotic tells the story of his life with the parts in the wrong order; or with gaps; or he contradicts himself; and he denies or distorts the reality of anything he sees in the present that might challenge his fantastical past. Eventually he becomes incoherent. The neurotic cannot remember, for example, that, after the war, he recruited the Nazi torturer Klaus Barbie to work for U.S. intelligence. He cannot remember if he knew that Barbie was a torturer, or how he avoided knowing. Or he cannot remember if he collaborated with the Nazis, or made false papers for the resistance. The neurotic cannot remember if, when he worked as a bellboy at the Hotel Terminus, he saw the SS officers bring suspects through the lobby in handcuffs. He cannot remember if, at the police station where he worked, he heard people scream. He cannot remember if he saw Jewish children being deported. "Did I say that?" the U.S. agent Kolb says in this film. "Then I was wrong in my memory." Ophuls reads to the U.S. agent Taylor his own memo calling Barbie a Nazi idealist, and asks what "idealist" means, as we look at a picture of Barbie's eyes. "I don't know. I wish I could rewrite that today." ("Perhaps," Ophuls says, with mild, characteristic cruelty, "especially today.") Madame Hammerle, a collaborator, says she saw the death camps in "propaganda films." Such exaggerated, impossible to believe events! Ophuls asks, "Propaganda films? Was that *Night and Fog*?" But Hammerle can't recall that, either. Wolfgang Gustmann, a former SS officer, thought Barbie was a "fantastic guy"; as for talk of Nazi crimes, it's "time to be done with it." The massacre at Oradour? "I'm still not sure what happened . . . If such a thing really happened." The deportation of the Jews, the Final Solution? "Maybe we'd like a pact of silence about some things."

Because of what one knows but doesn't want to know, there are soon many related matters one must distort or avoid without knowing, of course, one is avoiding them. Kolb didn't know the resistance leader Jean Moulin had died under Barbie's torture, or even that he had died. Or that he was really a resistance leader. "I knew Moulin was a resistance fighter or something like that," Kolb says.

Ophuls, an amiable but tenacious interrogator, presses him, "Why do you say 'something like that'"?

"Well, I'm a political scientist, so I like to know what the fellow's orientation is." He means, of course, as neurotics often do, the reverse of what he says: he doesn't want to know what a person's political orientation is, or even that the person existed. The neurotic devises strategies of disingenuous denial. Kolb says, "[Barbie] didn't strike me as the sort of person who would need to torture." Or as Gustmann, the former officer, says, using a vicious kind of magical thinking, Barbie couldn't have been that sort of person, because dogs liked him. Forced to admit his crimes, Barbie's allies must make torture not matter, because those Barbie murdered were communists, and thus not resistance fighters but "something like that," and, really, enemies. Besides, the accounts were undoubtedly exaggerated.

Ryan, the State Department lawyer who was forced to confront the charge that the United States might have employed Barbie, says, "controlled ignorance is still ignorance." Actually, it's not; it's repression. Such repression requires scrupulous avoidance of knowledge. Kolb denies he knew about the trial of Hardy, the man accused of betraying Moulin, for if he had, he would have learned that Barbie, his prize agent, had tortured resistance members. Kolb and his superiors say they only read the army paper, *The Stars and Stripes*. Like Omercamerim, the Vatican official who collaborated with the United States in smuggling Barbie out of Europe, they followed "the Catholic principal, no questions asked." (Besides, Omercamerim says, there are Jews with immense riches "who are vengeful and fabricate crimes to accuse Barbie of.")

Those collaborating with Barbie, using him and being used by him, must either have known with whom they collaborated, or must have particularly not wanted to know, which is, psychoanalytically, the same—for how do you know what you want to repress unless you know it? So for those engaged in repression, self-deception, and deception of others, the great luxury—reserved for psychotics and those at the pinnacles of power—is to be "out of the loop," to have what one wishes happen, without knowing about it. "Do what you have to do," the head of the U.S. Army intelligence service says, "but keep me out of trouble."

"I've forgotten," Barbie says. "If they haven't, it's their problem." But Barbie, who is not simply a liar, but more disastrously, a cause of lies told by others, is the corrosive principal itself. In this he is reliable: everything he says, as in this last remark, is backwards. Their problem, our problem, is that we have forgotten. What those with power do not want to remember is, of course, what Barbie did at the Hotel Terminus. In Lanzmann's movie we see trains arriving at the death camps, over and over; in Ophuls's film, we see elevator doors closing in front of an opulently decorated floor of a prosperous hotel. What went on behind those doors—obscene? It's impossible to see, but not impossible to know—in fact, one can easily know, if one wishes. Behind those doors Barbie walked through his domain, looking at a floor littered with those torture victims too weak to stand anymore. He picked up their faces with the tip of his boot, and if the face looked Jewish to him, he crushed it. (We learn this just after Kolb has told us Barbie was not anti-Semitic.) Women had their backs broken, their hands and arms put into manacles with spikes pointing into the flesh. Victims were given "ice baths," the water poured from an old tin container. They were beaten. (As one victim says, "I passed out a respectable number of times.") Torture, death, and deportation of Jews is what is not seen, and, again, though we can know it, we can—like the victim's bed whose absence is lamented in *Night and Fog*—no longer precisely see it. But Barbie's effects can be seen, not simply the marks he left on the victim's bodies, but the effects wrought by denying how much of our world is still connected to that once luxurious hotel. For after so much evasion, the neurotic begins to make mistakes in the present, and soon forgets what to call things anymore. As Barbie's daughter says, "I can't exactly say what a National Socialist is." And Barbie, deported from Bolivia under guard, feels he can safely challenge an interrogator: "Can you explain what 'Nazi' means?"

Fear of communism and, in most of the collaborators, hatred of the Jews, made them ally themselves with Barbie, and Ophuls pays due attention to their motives. But it is the effects that concern Ophuls—how a once shared world has been corroded till the meaning of words, of symbols, of feelings, is confused, distorted, lost. The multiform, exfoliating denials soon seem part of a deeper, wider, darker forgetting of the Holocaust itself, as if our everyday actions, our comfort, our ease (who is putting us at our ease?), even our prosperity—based in part on a war machine that did perhaps, as the defeated Nazis wished, "continue east"—might perhaps be a way of forgetting. The documentary's job is to put elements back in their proper place, but not so much to rebuild a present—something outside the strength of even the best analyst—as to show that this world we take for real, of amiable billiard games, cards, of beer and ease, camaraderie, fellowship, cognac and brandy snifters, Lenten masks, Christmas ornaments, and what we think they stand for, doesn't, in fact, anymore quite exist. Like a good analyst, Ophuls uses forcefully put questions or well-chosen quotations from our past, or rapid editing that brusquely points out contiguous matters strangely overlooked or denied. Ophuls's constantly inquiring camera darts over the subject's shoulder to his shelves, or into the filmmaker's archives, bringing related or seemingly disparate elements into the frame. His editing montages the truth, as when Kolb's mild assessment of Barbie is put over Christmas tree ornaments, and then beside the accounts of those he tortured. It is easy, of course, to surrender one's faith in nation-states or in the U.S. intelligence community, and perhaps even in religion, but the corrosions linked to Barbie seemed to me both deeper and more widespread than that, and I soon felt as if, if I continued to believe in the blandishments of patriotism or radicalism, if I continued to accept the comforting illusion that the world of neighborliness, of home, of friendship and loyalty existed when that is so rarely the case, then I would destroy even that world's possibility.

At one point, Kolb, a virtuoso of denial, tries to save our American amour propre by denying that Barbie was a torturer. In the process Kolb helps destroy morality. He reassures himself that Barbie was so skillful an interrogator that he wouldn't need to torture. With impressive worldliness, Kolb adds that this does not mean that Barbie was a decent man. "There's a world of difference between intelligence," Kolb instructs us, "and high moral standards, and the ability to manipulate people—which is what intelligence work is about." It is a chilling moment in the film, not because what it reveals about the world is so awful, or for what it says about Kolb, whom one has long ago begun to despise. One's discomfort goes deeper. You see, Kolb is saying, I, too, am a professional of interrogation—it's not that I have some moral objection to torture, the world is now far too cynical, too sophisticated for moral objections. And you, Mr. Ophuls, as a man of the world, wouldn't accept such moral objections anyway—you, Mr. Ophuls are an artist, too, an artist of interrogation, so you understand that one might be against torture aesthetically (for no other standards exist). Torture is unprofessional; it lacks an economy of means; excessive force is ugly. (If others, one might say, think too much of the shared world still exists, Kolb thinks that wisdom is to deny that any of it exists. Or as he puts it, with contented despair, "The whole world is shot through with moral ambiguities.") So Barbie, Kolb says, wouldn't have used torture. He would, like you, Mr. Ophuls, have been a better manipulator of people and images, of the image of himself, and of the world, and taken you out for a few beers and bratwurst, as I would have done, as I in fact did with Barbie, when I interrogated him on whether he was guilty of torture, and as we often see you do with your victims in this film. And so Barbie would put his subject at his ease, as you do with your subjects—and your film (Kolb might have said) is filled with images of ease, of after-dinner liqueurs, of subjects at their favorite billiard tables or by their swimming pools. (Who is putting us at our ease?)

Kolb is telling us of Barbie's genius as an interrogator, but he indicts Ophuls, too. I recognize myself in the style of Kolb's far from fool-ish cynicism, so, though I despise him, I cannot simply ignore his indict-ment. And, as I have identified with Ophuls, thinking that Ophuls's posi-tion was a protected and innocent one, Kolb speaks of me as well. Resnais is an artist who finds art in the making of the death camps; Lanzmann is an obsessive engineer, who methodically rebuilds the camps; and Ophuls—how could I have ignored this?—is, like Barbie, an interrogator, a man after information.

But, again, the specific cure for the death brought into reality by Barbie's methods, is Ophuls's methods, their modelling of a therapeutic use of the death instinct to find, again, correct information, and to make this representation. Of course, Ophuls is no torturer, yet even he, quite pointedly, causes psychological pain to some of those he interviews. We watch Ophuls, for example, talking to a colleague about a man he will film, as the man, Barbie's South American assistant, waits in another room, being filmed as he fidgets and waits. Ophuls remarks that the man must be squirming by now, and we cut to him squirming. Polk, a German who worked for U.S. intelligence, says, worriedly, "this film won't be shown in Germany, will it?" Polk desperately fears "repercussions." Ophuls reminds Polk, a seemingly weak and insecure man, that he has already signed a release; Polk blanches, shudders, shrinks within himself. It is not simply that Ophuls, unlike Lanzmann, will not play the Nazi liar. Rather, he has a different role to play. Ophuls, like Barbie, is good at manipulating people; his subjects say more than they mean to, and their discomfort is one of his tools. In this film we often look at still photos of resistance leaders and politicians and Nazis, but when we move into close-ups of these photos, it is only the torturers whose eyes are shown. Torturers have eyes, and viewers, like ourselves, have eyes (for we, too, are after information), and so the question is not, can we be innocent, or can we avoid our own violence, for death, here, too, will form the world of information; the question is what sort of tormentors will we be? Like Barbie or like Ophuls?

But what kind of interrogator is this Ophuls? There is a scene in the first half of the movie that spoke to me of Ophuls's character in this film, and that persona is, I think, one of the films' most striking creations. Ophuls is speaking with Monsieur Zuchner, who, as police chief of Lyon, sometimes interceded with the SS on behalf of French citizens, and sometimes, perhaps, collaborated. In any case, like many of those Ophuls interviews, he is uneasy, and has surrounded himself with books and papers that he hopes will document his good works. Ophuls, if not positively gleeful, smiles broadly, far from indifferent to Zuchner's unease. Zuchner speaks of those he helped, including the son of the man who owns the Bel Cheese Company. We see for a moment the familiar emblem of the company, La Vache qui Rit, the Laughing Cow. The innocent emblem curdles as I watch it, another small reminder now of the Occupation, of the manifold forms that collaboration takes, and I think, Well, the Laughing Cow hasn't heard the bad news yet. Zuchner is proud not only that he interceded for a French citizen, but, more particularly, for a powerful man's son. Ophuls laughs, and says, "Perhaps there are times, not just in wartime, when it's better to be rich and famous than not rich and famous," and I thought, that's a remark worthy of Lear's fool. Zuchner smiles at Ophuls and agrees, not quite realizing what he's agreeing to. In a small way, as in *King Lear*, such remarks restore a knowable world for us, with continuities that, though painful, are almost bearable. The fool won't allow us to live in a world of lies. He laughs at us as we try to squirm away from the past and its errors, contort ourselves to protect our wounded dignity, attempt to cover ourselves with hypocrisy or, as in Kolb's case or Edmund's, with cynicism. When the king is stripped of his protections, lost in the emptiness of the bitter present, the fool may give him a piece of the world, a refurbished truism become a timeless truth. But can we bear that either?

Barbie, deported from Bolivia, on his way to the airport, says, "Only the winner can speak." We know, then, that this truism must be the reverse of the truth, so only the loser is given speech. For the winner is power, propaganda, the unreal world of ideology. Those, like Verges, Barbie's lawyer, a petty demon who has the audacity to say he sees himself as defending the individual against state power, are, in their self-deception (or their lies) particularly dangerous, for they, too, are really cogs in some power machine's ideology. (Ophuls briefly interviews Claude Lanzmann about Verges. Lanzmann says, devastatingly—for we know how much horror *Shoah* has acknowledged—"I don't understand lawyers.") We can be, it would seem, a part of the awful grinding machinery of history, or victims of that machinery, or, taking our modern image-anodynes, we can, though both parts of the machinery *and* its victims, dream that we are only spectators. The novel, my own blessed form, has many times specialized in making a triumph of such defeats. Accepting that there is no alternative to the machinery of the state, many novels teach that we might at best be willing victims, those who love their fate, prodigies of suffering, heroes and heroines of sensibility. But Ophuls has, I think, remembered another path: We can be, like him, fools. The fool does not deny death, either his own catastrophe, or his violence. He tells the truth to power, tells Lear that he lives in an imaginary world, provoking Lear's rage, not only for his truths, but because the fool is often, and intentionally, mean; capable of sorrow over Lear's naked state, but also amused by it. He won't allow evasions, and insists on getting everything right. (Everything about the past, that is. At one point in the film, Ophuls cannot remember the current date.) The trick of the fool's survival is, in part, that he lacks pomp; apparently unthreatening to all, and so tolerated by those he will mockingly undo. Ophuls, a shaggy, amiable man, has great integrity, but little dignity. Denied an interview with the Nazi Bartlemus, he walks through a garden looking for Bartlemus under cabbage leaves, until a housewife, evoking the sanctity of private property, shoos him away. (A good analyst would also, one assumes, be similarly lacking in dignity, for pomp is based on a denial that the way up is the way down, on denying, for example, that the accumulation of money satisfies the infant's desire to accumulate his powerful shit.) The fool and the analyst are the curative forms of the torturer, the way that the death instinct might be used to overcome the death instinct that is embodied in repression. And, like a good analyst, the fool reminds us of some truths, some almost unbearable continuities between our lives and our parents' lives.

The fool, and the analyst, know that only if the false world is properly and thoroughly destroyed, not nihilistically but slowly, meticulously, piece by piece; and only if one acknowledges its destruction, and so the destruction of one's false self, can the world given by the past be even in part returned to you. I am reminded here of one of the analyst D. W. Winnicot's patients, who had developed a "false self" to please her mother, her lovers, her friends. When her false sense of herself and the world was undone by analysis, she was able to remember, with great sorrow, and a pleasure beyond words, the feel of her mother's coat against her cheek as a child. Around this fragment she will have to construct a less prosperous, less hyperbolic self. The ending of *Hotel Terminus* is, I am inclined to say, like the ending of Winnicot's case history, sentimental, but I am inclined to say that, and preserve my dignity, only because I often do not hold to the wisdom of foolishness, but to the Kolb-like worldliness of corrosive sophistication, soured idealism become irony. The foolish truth of my response was that I found the film's conclusion almost unbearably moving. At the end of Ophuls's film we meet the woman who cared for the Jewish children of Izieux—a spot on the continent, she calls it—children who were deported by Barbie to be murdered in the camps. The children, she says, knew that their parents had already been deported, and we see a photo of the wan face of Meyer Bulkha, a little boy depressed by the world he must inhabit, as Ophuls here almost dares us to feel sentimental towards the past, dares us (in J. D. Salinger's brilliant definition of sentimentality) "to love the world more than God does." We see the countryside of Izieux, the snow melting, water dripping from the eaves, and hear a letter of one of the children, a young woman. She speaks of the beauty of the snow. She thanks her parents for sending clogs. "Now my feet will be warm . . . The snow is melting." We see the countryside from a window.

"Soon Spring will be here. I will never forget what the south is like." She thanks her parents for a blue checkered shirt . . . Only the victims can speak, and perhaps only the dead can, if we have been sufficiently harrowed, if we have acknowledged the bitter emptiness of our unreal present, return a few bits of the world to us (clogs, snow, a checkered shirt).

It is hard (because so foolish) to speak of my mingled feelings of pain and relief, when those few objects were handed to me. I have spoken previously of the cost of remembering, as it is embodied in *Shoah,* and perhaps in Jewish ritual, how the constant remembering of the dead can obliterate the present. But there are, apparently, gifts given by the dead as well, the utterly powerless, infinitely greedy, not always innocent dead. (And how foolish they are as well, so silly as to have died!) Perhaps they can, from time to time, grant us, for our service to them, our costly, pious continuity with their tradition, some small fragments of the world (the ritual candle? a cup of wine?).

In the final moments of the film, Mme. Kaddoush, a survivor of Auschwitz, speaks to Ophuls outside the house in Lyon where she and her family had once lived. She remembers that her neighbors had shut their doors as her family was led away. I am almost a proper fool by this time, and know (though I cannot bear) what "home" means: not nothing, and not very much. Ophuls and Mme. Kaddoush climb the stairs she had descended with the Nazis, and she speaks of Mme. Bontout who, as the Nazis led her family away, tried to pull the little girl into her apartment. "I feel a fondness for her, not for the others." One of the Germans saw Mme. Bontout try to snatch the child from death. He grabbed the girl back, and slapped Mme. Bontout so hard she fell backwards. The movie, the voice of Jeanne Moreau says, is dedicated to her, a good neighbor.—Supposing you are so foolish as to think such people might exist!

What D. W. Winnicot, that humane man, wishes for his patients—that they might take their trauma back into the realm of infantile omnipotence—is, I realize now, the impossible, not quite secular, psychoanalytic equivalent of saying Kaddish. Kaddish, the Jewish prayer for the dead, praises God, his justice and his power. One hopes for the survival of the Jewish people, but there is little in the prayer that pleads with God to restore loss. One praises God, and death comes from God, even the death of one's beloved, as all things do, even what we call evil. Kaddish is the cure for piousness and sentimentality; through the right worship of God we come to prize the world properly, not to love it more than God does. Can we say Kaddish for the dead of the Holocaust? Can we refuse?

I think sometimes, as many others have before me in remembering these horrors, of the end of the book of Job, where God Himself says Kaddish for Job's family, singing a hymn of praise to His own power, to the pattern, beyond Job's understanding, that makes Job and destroys Job, and could not create him and sustain him if it did not also destroy him. When I spoke of these films helping us take events back into our infantile omnipotence—reconnecting them with our instinct for survival, but most especially also for destruction and for our own death—I mean that these artists are fitfully trying to reinvent a way to say Kaddish. These events must be inhabited by eros and death, those forces whose struggle makes us. To join oneself to that which wills one's own death, to occupy every position, would be a way of accepting that death is a part of the pattern that gives us; to be, in imagination, victim and executioner is to accept, and even to praise, God. But this talk is speculative; perhaps Kaddish cannot be said in this attenuated, secular, immanent way, and I am nauseated when I even imply that there is such a pattern that includes Auschwitz; Bergen-Belsen; Chelmno; Treblinka; Sobibor; Burkinau; Belzec; Buchenwald; Theresienstadt; Dachau.—Yet surely the forces that formed us formed the world, surely history is not simply outside us, something that happens; surely we might, with proper instruction, join the world in mutual reformation. And surely Kaddish, that prayer I cannot yet say, the prayer for the dead, must precede imagining the new dispensation I longed for at the beginning of this essay, a new political (or is it religious?) vision, which does not deny, but will re-vision our use of the death instinct, so that life might continue.—But this essay can only mark my intention to say that prayer; my desire; my as yet repeated failure.

PATRICIA HAMPL

# Memory's Movies

"**D**o you write from your life, or from," she paused, like someone hesitating on the edge of a diving board, and then plunged in, "or from imagination?"

The two of us were sitting on a slate terrace cantilevered off a hotel in Spello, one of the hill towns of "mystical Umbria," as the guidebooks say. The light was draining from the day, and the lovely view was disappearing. We had spent the hot afternoon hiking through this rolling landscape. Now, bathed and rested, we were waiting for drinks and dinner.

We weren't friends. It just happened that we had signed up for the same hiking trip, advertised in a British travel magazine. After three days of hiking, Edna, who asked the question, and I, who had been discovered earlier in the day to be a writer, still did not know each other very well. I had betrayed myself with an offhand remark about a piece I had finished before coming on the trip. "You write?" Edna had asked. She sounded appalled, but really she was thrilled: "I've never met an actual writer before," she said shyly.

Edna was a large woman with a small, tentative voice. Her slim husband Cecil had let it be known that he was forty-eight, seven years younger than Edna. One evening I heard him urging her to pass up the tiramisu at dinner ("You're thickening, old girl"). When the waiter came by, she murmured no, she thought she'd skip dessert. Usually she was silent, leaving the stage to Cecil. Now, perhaps emboldened by his absence, she sounded a little breathless. *Do you write from your life, or from imagination?*

I didn't answer. I didn't know what to say. Edna didn't seem to mind. She launched into a story of her own, a recent memory of an incident at Heathrow when she and Cecil had failed to help an African woman who was lost. She brooded over the episode: "She couldn't find Gate 36. Why didn't we help her? We should have seen her to Gate 36." She described the woman's tall body sheathed in a bright cotton gown, her elegant head wrapped in the same print fabric, her luggage two black plastic garbage bags, crammed full.

The image would not leave her alone; she woke in the night, haunted by the woman dragging her garbage bags, as far as Edna knew, in eternal friendless search of Gate 36.

I sensed dimly that the story had something to do, however obliquely, with the question she had posed and I had not answered. She had instinctively latched onto a conflicted moment, a frame of unfinished action that refused either to disappear or to be satisfactorily completed. She ran it through her mind in a kind of stuttered projection, over and over, looking for its correct finale. She knew she was overreacting: "Isn't it ridiculous, I've lost sleep over this." She was racking her imagination to make her life come out right.

And then Cecil appeared on the terrace, rubbing his hands along his damp hair, telling her there was no Cinzano *bianco*, he'd gotten her the *rosso* — "Is that all right, old girl?" And it was clear we were not to pursue the question further.

There is something suspect about my tongue-tied silence in response to Edna's question. Like most writers, I find it tantalizing to speculate on how "experience" (or, more accurately, how memory) is rendered into narrative. If fiction writers refuse to discuss the matter, they usually claim a kind of high superstition: if I knew, I wouldn't be able to do it. For writers of nonfiction the question is dicier; nonfiction demands of its audience the naïve, or at least indulgent, assumption that nonfiction is experience.

That, in fact, is the fundamental fiction underpinning nonfiction narration.

But my silence had a baser motive. Edna had caught me red-handed: I had taken the hiking trip because I was writing a book in which I was going to "use" a hiking trip. As it eventually turned out, I was going to use her and her husband, too, and even, briefly, her story about the lost African at Heathrow. The book is written now, and she's in it, sitting on the terrace in the Spello twilight, telling her trouble to the dark. The book, *Virgin Time*, is a memoir, and is classified as nonfiction, as autobiographical works are. Presumably, it is "from my life."

What Edna presented from her life that night was not so much a story, in the usual narrative sense, as it was a series of images she ran through fitfully, looking frame by frame for a solution, for a proper shape. She had not helped the woman dragging her garbage sacks through Heathrow, but revisiting those indelible images might provide a different kind of help, if one wholly of the imagination. It might *settle* things. Not fix what was broken or undone, but *settle* in the sense of placing things, housing them. She jumped around with her memories as she attempted to show me the scene. It was all jumbled up. Sometimes she panned across the entire airport, then she came in for a tight close-up of the African woman's high-boned face. She jumped back to cue her first encounter with Cecil (at a concert at the Wigmore Hall; he was with someone else and hadn't noticed her). Then back to the beautiful African. Then fast-forward to her troubled dreams about the African woman.

Her question about the relation between life and imagination was genuine, even urgent. Maybe that's why it has stayed with me. It wasn't a polite cocktail-party inquiry: she needed to know. There was something distinctly covert about her question: she hoped I would tell her the secret.

The mind presents two innate models of the imagination, and both are movie models—dream and memory. Naturally enough, film has been drawn to these two rich sources of narrative. Feature filmmakers as frankly autobiographical as Bergman and Fellini have attempted to convey both the dreamlike life of their lost past and the drama of night dreams. Even other people's memoirs can compel filmmakers: Jane Campion turned Janet Frame's autobiography, *An Angel at My Table*, into a feature film.

Perhaps it is inevitable that film, so wedded to surfaces, to the look and texture of the material world, finds it difficult to sustain dreams. Ironically, the fantastical quality of dreams, absorbed in fluid action, that makes them appear so movie-like to the sleeper, renders them tedious when they are forced to the surface of the material world where their illogic becomes insupportable. Dreams brought to film can seem arch, literary—strangely lacking in the intimacy and authority they have as they play across the sleeper's dream screen. Dreams live in the unconscious, which, although it has mythic properties, is profoundly interior, idiosyncratic, elusive.

Memory, on the other hand, positively begs to have its past made real again. Our memories may be our most personal possessions, but they are housed not only in ourselves but in the historical, and therefore social, past. Memory invites the camera as dreams do not because its landscape is a shared one, a kind of communal dream. Get out the period cars and costumes—memory loves a movie.

So it would seem that autobiography, always intimate with the shared historical past, would be a natural, even popular, form for film. Prose memoirs can win a wide readership, after all. Yet, the truth is that most film autobiographies live the limited, very un-Hollywood lives of most contemporary lyric poetry, and must be searched out in the garrets of special collections and libraries. They tend to be the products of fellowships and grants rather than of investment, here, too, relying upon the charity that sustains lyric poetry. Unlike either feature films or documentaries based on history that are perennial nonfiction favorites (think of the popularity of Ken Burns's *Civil War* series), the frankly autobiographical film is an acquired taste, a minor genre even in nonfiction film—and this, oddly, in a culture that alternately boasts of and bemoans its preoccupation with the individual.

Part of the reason for the marginal status of autobiographical film is, obviously, the matter of economics. Books—memoirs as well as novels—are written by a person alone in a room with words. The "production" of the book is an activity entirely separate from its creation. Movies, on the other hand, including autobiographical movies, are the product of dozens, even hundreds, of people. While it is possible to assemble the money and the production staff to film the biography of a single figure (especially someone widely acknowledged as a worthwhile subject), what filmmaker can find for an *autobiography* either the investment or the grants to cover the lush and complete renderings of a fully realized feature film?

But maybe the money would be there if the interest were there first. In spite of the fascination American culture has for the confessional, even the invasive, there remains a repulsion, even a mistrust, towards self-display. How, after all, can anyone pretend to present personal truth except under the veil of fiction? Books based on personal disclosure manage to be commercial staples of publishing (any question about whether Princess Di's autobiography would make the best-seller list?), but the big block-busters in this category are usually dependent on the celebrity of the subject/author.

Whatever the reason, autobiographical film, like lyric poetry, remains largely a cottage industry. Its methods tend to be humble, even homely. This is filmmaking sometimes as unadorned as the home movie — as Ross McElwee's investigations of his Southern family and background in *Backyard* (1982) and *Sherman's March* (1986) and *Time Indefinite* (1993) display. McElwee apologizes now and again in the voiceover when he runs out of film or when the camera unaccountably breaks down.

Constrained as it is, memoir film achieves a certain autonomy born of its poverty. Autobiography, the one-person show, breaks free of the usual haggle and compromise of an art fraught with collaboration. Jerome Hill, whose autobiographical movie, *Film Portrait* (1971), places him in the first rank of filmmakers in the genre, established his name first as a maker of biographical films (of Albert Schweitzer, Grandma Moses, and C. G. Jung). His style as biographer and autobiographer remains quite similar, urbane and detached. Hill claimed that he was drawn to biographical film precisely because it freed him to make movies "without having to struggle with actors, producers, unions and studios." The autobiographical film was, for him, a natural next step, not a radical shift.

But the memoir film's fundamental freedom is not simply an escape from other people engaged in the creative process who might gum up individual vision. The liberation is more radical, more subversive, than that. Oddly enough, the simplicity of its habits seems to free memoir film from the sovereignty of the image. The pictorial nature of film—seemingly its very essence—requires the form to be dramatic, to *show* things, to be active, not reflective. And obviously, pictures remain central and compelling in any movie. This is the art of moving *pictures,* after all. But in the memoir film, voice becomes unusually powerful, definitive even. When, occasionally, McElwee's camera breaks down, he leaves these glitches in the finished film: they are not simply part of the story—they are reminders to the audience of the art form itself, apparently unassuming, shorn of artifice, burdened with the accidents and limitations of the lowest of budgets. And though the image stutters and gets lost when the camera breaks, McElwee keeps talking. We may lose some footage, but never his voice.

McElwee even makes the breakdown of the image essential to the story: it is, he tells us, somehow meaningful that he always has these technical troubles when he is filming his father, who, he says in exasperation, seems to give off "a sort of Freudian force field." McElwee assumes that he is *telling* a story, not showing it; the failure of the camera can be used effectively as part of this story—but only if the voice says so. Without the reflecting, musing voice to guide it, the broken camera is only a technical snafu. With the voice, it becomes useful, even symbolic.

With the powerfully foregrounded voice of autobiography, the camera is freed to go about its pictorial business of showing, while the reflective mind is liberated to tell. But to tell what? A story? Not necessarily. More than most written memoirs (though even here an exception comes to mind: *Speak, Memory* by Nabokov, that most deliciously visual of writers), autobiographical film is preoccupied not with telling a life story but with conveying perception itself, with searching for the peculiar character of the perceiving consciousness. There can be something strikingly impersonal in these autobiographical works, in spite of the private impulse compelling them. They can be more detached than confessional.

Voice in these films—I'm thinking of works as varied as those by McElwee, Jerome Hill, and Su Friedrich—serves neither as dialogue nor as caption. It is, technically, voiceover, but this memoir voice reigns over the narrative more boldly, and is more invasive, than movies usually allow. (In feature films, the heavy use of narrative voiceover is a standard occasion for criticism. Most recently, the screenplay of *The Joy Luck Club* has been reproached in numerous reviews for relying too heavily on this device. The assumption, of course, is that showing, not telling, is the proper business of movies.)

The memoir film's voice does not transmit a story, although it is often used to provide basic background information. More fundamentally, though, as it does in contemporary lyric poetry, voice in the autobiographical film conveys individual consciousness. Typically, it is a thinking voice, an interior voice, not a telling or reporting voice, although it must convey a certain amount of information. It speaks in order to muse, to wonder, not to convey what it already knows. It is a voice assembling its pictures.

It is the voice, not simply the pictures themselves, that is *moving* in these films. More exactly, the voice lords over the picture so completely that it sets the rhythm, the pace, and therefore establishes the character of the images. For the still stranger fact that emerges from these personal films is that, in spite of their forays into the past, their subject is not, after all, the story of a personal self—though that would seem to be the point of autobiography. These filmmakers have discovered the extraordinary pliancy of the first person: not simply that it *has* a story, but that it can *tell* one. The self is not a source or a subject; it is an instrument.

In *The Ties that Bind* (1984), Su Friedrich, the daughter of a German woman who married an American GI after the Second World War, is not "seeking a self" as the cliché sell-line of contemporary memoirs so often promises. She is not even seeking her mother's life as she intercuts interview segments with period footage and film from her own contemporary visit to Ulm, her mother's hometown. Friedrich is after a shard of the historical puzzle, a small but essential fragment she feels capable of placing in the abiding mystery and misery of that war. The story may be "personal," but it is autobiography more in the service of history than psychology.

Even Ross McElwee, a considerably more self-reflective (even self-absorbed) memoirist, is unable to consider his own life or his family's without betraying his preoccupation with the South, its meaning, its history. His travels from his chosen, adult-life New England to his childhood North Carolina inevitably reprise the marches of the Civil War and draw attention to the breach between two essentially separate cultures. (In an early film, *Backyard*, the reverse relationship plays out the same way.

McElwee announces that his intention has been to make "a film about the South—which for me meant a film about my family." The apparent oppositions of family and nation, personal and public, prove to be inseparable twins.)

But even involvement with a social or national past does not leave the memoir voice of these films comfortably settled in history. In the spiral that their narrative voices follow, these memoirists start out with an autobiographical story and move into historical preoccupations, emerging with films that return the whole enterprise to a visual field. For the real fascination—the real subject—of these films is the fact of perception. Beyond the autobiographical narrative, beyond the larger story of history, there is the mystery of individual perception, the question of how consciousness frames its subject, how it *sees*—which makes all that voiceover in autobiographical films very movie-like, after all.

"The me that am . . . but never will be again. Hold on to a single moment, even for a second, and it already belongs to the past." With this prosaic observation, spoken in an attractively laconic voice, Jerome Hill begins his narration of his autobiographical film, *Film Portrait*. The voiceover accompanies a sequence of Hill shaving, and revolves around a triad of images: his face as he shaves, a sink full of water where he periodically rinses the razor, and his face again, this time reflected in the mirror as he shaves.

At the time, Hill was in his mid-sixties, and *Film Portrait* was his last film, although apparently he did not yet know about the cancer that would end his life late in 1971. *Film Portrait* won a 1972 London Film Festival award for documentary film. In 1957 Hill had won an Academy Award for Best Documentary for his portrait of Albert Schweitzer, but in general he steered clear of Hollywood. He spent most of his adult life in France and considered himself an independent filmmaker, drawn to documentary largely because of its autonomy. He was especially at home with the avant-garde and its preoccupation with underlying questions of form. He belonged to the first generation of moviegoers, and the prevailing theme of *Film Portrait* (and certainly the reason for its title) is that he and the art form were born at the same moment and, in his view, grew up together. For him, movies were always new, young, experimental. It was in their nature to be provisional and independent, a matter of one person with a magic box of film seeing the world afresh.

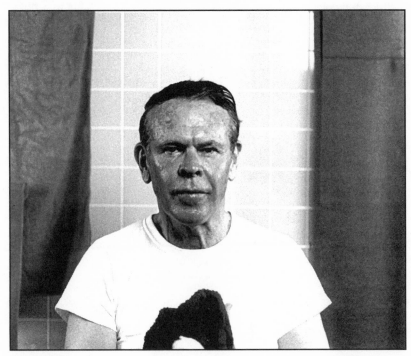

**Jerome Hill, *Film Portrait* (1971)**
**Hill presents "the me that am" before going into the past**
**and future.**

In spite of its position as Hill's final and only frankly autobiographical film, there is no elegiac feeling or sense of farewell in *Film Portrait*. The ordinariness of that opening sequence—the routine activity and the unremarkable, if philosophical, voiceover—perfectly represents his style: casual, benignly wry, cheerfully aristocratic, and modest. This is a man who can spend many frames on close-ups of his own face and convey not intimacy but an almost scientific, or at least objective, detachment.

Hill's own face is not even as compelling to his camera as the sink full of water is that he manipulates with strange, irradiated colors—the water at one point a gory red that seems molten, a malignant mass swirling like cells under a microscope when the razor disturbs the surface. The association with a primal, unformed existence is obvious: life begins in this undifferentiated, though fascinating, swirl. There is something anonymous and impersonal in this smallest smear of creation. In another sequence, the water turns a shocking aqua. Hill's face, in another frame, is stunned with light, his hair a blinding white. Angles of vision, points of view—that's all we have when we face ourselves in the mirror. Meanwhile, the easy, even lighthearted voice of the narrative carries on about the inability to capture the past or to frame the future.

And it is to the future that Hill goes as he ventures away from the mirror and the swirling water that looks like a slide of cellular material. To the future—and to fiction. "The me that will be," he announces, and runs through a series of staged and costumed possible future selves beginning with an elderly invalid surrounded by nurses and aides who treat him like an ancient rag-doll propped in his wheelchair. "It could be worse," he says, cutting to a homeless self, sleeping under newspapers on a park bench. "Or better," he concludes, and appears dressed in evening clothes, a cape, and top hat—for the opera, we assume. But when a woman, also dressed formally, appears, he helps her into a horse-drawn carriage—and hops up to take the reins as her driver. It is vintage Hill humor, the deft schoolboy gag, appealingly self-deprecating.

He rushes through a series of fantasy futures: quick clips of himself decked out in white as a surprisingly convincing Pope blessing the multitude from his window; then, signing documents at a great mahogany desk, a lean, faux-executive President in the Oval Office; finally, as family patriarch surrounded by an unreasonable number of children, all bearing his own adult deadpan face. "Impossible," he says.

The parade of possible/impossible selves goes on, from astronaut and symphony conductor to a pedestrian attacked in an alley and left for dead. He even invades his real adult past—a quick clip of his moment at the 1957 Academy Awards ceremony when Gina Lollobrigida hands him the Oscar; a skiing sequence that alludes not only to his love of the sport but to his first documentary film. "But enough of speculations on the future," he says abruptly after this dash through what amounts to a Cindy Sherman–like series of costumed tableaux. "Let's look at the me that was."

Jerome Hill is still referred to by those who knew him as a "Renaissance man." He had many gifts, "almost too many," his friend Otto Lang says in *The Man in the Portrait*, a film eulogy to Hill made shortly after his death. He took his degree in music composition at Yale and wrote music throughout his life (including the score for *Film Portrait*—impressionistic, French in style). He went on to become a serious filmmaker. He thought of himself perhaps primarily as an artist and devoted himself steadfastly to painting. He wrote poetry. And he gave away money.

He had a lot of it to give. He was born in Saint Paul, the grandson of the railroad baron, James J. Hill, "the Empire Builder." His childhood was positively Nabokovian in its splendor, with a background not simply of wealth, but of taste, art, thoughtful travel, and long dreamy days. There was an elegant house on Summit Avenue next door to the Empire Builder's gloomy gothic pile, trips to France, long train rides into Indian country, seasons riding horses at North Oaks, the immense family farm outside Saint Paul. It was a privileged, liberal American childhood with a late Russian Empire feeling to it. It seems to have been a life destined by birth and sensibility for art. "Good," the Empire Builder is reported to have said observing his two little grandsons, "one for business and one for the arts," as if the whole of life arranged itself solely into these two categories.

When Jerome Hill turns to "the me that was" in *Film Portrait*, he turns not to himself but, as if instinctively, to time itself. "1905," he says in his dry, faintly amused voice. "More curious than glorious, the year of my birth." The crammed interiors of the age appear festooned with aspidistras and antimacassars. In an invitation to shared judgment, he remarks, "Was there ever a period more ugly?" A nonchalant comment, but it establishes an authority for his voice, and therefore for his story: a man of unquestioned aesthetic judgment is running this life, this movie. "Thank God for Louis Tiffany," he says, and the camera surveys a series of Tiffany glass lampshades and windows glowing and manipulated by the painterly hand of Hill's editing.

We do not simply *see* the Tiffany objects; the camera closes in on the small, leaded shards of glass as if entering the jewel-colors of memory while Hill's music, tinkling like a dreamy wind chime, haunts the soundtrack. The point of this tour of Tiffany images seems to be not the display of individual decorative objects, but the occasion they afford to render Hill's first sensation of the gorgeous. There is an unmistakable pleasure, entirely sensuous, in this extreme close-up of bits of intense color. As if to frame this intensity, Hill cuts to the sad winter landscape of Saint Paul and the first flash of his family mansion.

He plays the high card of his family wealth and prominence early, and with characteristic ease. "My grandfather," he acknowledges as a portrait of the steely old man appears. And adds laconically, "He was in the railroad business." But this understatement is not a refusal to acknowledge facts. Hill is not coy, any more than he is confessional. He mentions the family's Scotch-Irish immigration to Canada, and then, in a single sentence, places his family in a world that explains his background: "They had, in one immense leap, become important people." Not rich, not successful—important.

I relished that line when, almost twenty years ago, I first saw *Film Portrait*, a movie so different from my notion of what a movie was—and showing pictures of my own hometown of Saint Paul—that I was captivated. *Film Portrait* conveyed a familiarity that had nothing to do with personal revelation, but relied on the unexpected intimacy of the narrator's voice. I hardly understood that this was "an experimental film." I had no curiosity about experiments with movies, for one thing.

This was simply the first time a movie had ever come to me like a personal letter, as direct and unmediated an utterance as poetry, one human being to another—or to himself, musing. I did not expect movies to speak directly to me, or to speak somehow to themselves as books did, as poems did. Movies were immense seductions, grand and imposing "pro-ductions"—the word was a movie word, and apt. Didn't everyone love the movies? But they were not the human voice, alone and free, telling its bit of life-news to a single listener in the way that a book did. There was some-thing large and communal about movies. It was right that they were on "the big screen"—they were writ too large for anything but a wall.

But here was a movie that belonged to a more modest, intimate world. It did not speak solely through pictures and "dialogue" as feature films (still, to me, "real movies") did. Nor was this man speaking in the godly style of documentary as "a narrator," nor in the anonymous informa-tion-giving voiceovers of certain old-fashioned feature films, usually adap-tations from classic novels.

Besides, I knew Jerome Hill spoke the truth: in Saint Paul, the Hills *were* important. Indeed, they were important beyond Saint Paul, but somehow it was a Saint Paul way of looking at things, of saying things. On the one hand eliding any crude reference to money, on the other inflating the condition of wealth with magnificent radiance. A very F. Scott Fitzgerald way of seeing things—which is itself a very Saint Paul way of seeing things. Hill's was a real voice, speaking from a life, not from a "narration." He cast a slight wash of irony on his remarks—but both the content and tone sug-gested that he and I understood, *we* knew that 1905 had been an unfortu-nate era for the refined eye, and that it both did and did not matter much to note this. For the first time, I was *listening* to a movie, the way you lis-ten for voice in a poem or a story, captivated by the subtle but decisive tonal presence that, in a book, carries personality and style—which is to say, spirit.

And I was listening to a memoir, a genre that inhabits a fascinat-ingly indeterminate narrative space between fiction and documentary. Here the presence of voice, of point of view, can be more crucial even than the story the voice is telling. The first-person voice, which sustains mem-oir, cleaves more to its angle of vision, its take on things, than to the clean arc of plot that rules the novel and feature film. As it refines its point of view, lavishing itself on the curious habits of personal consciousness, mem-oir achieves a rare detachment even as it enters more deeply into the rev-elation of individual consciousness. Its greatest intimacy (the display of perception) paradoxically reveals its essential impersonality. It wishes to see the world—not itself. At this core of the memoiristic enterprise, the narrator is more eye than I.

So, strangely enough, this first memoir film I saw captivated me with its voice, its way of telling, but I was also brought directly to the sources of the visual. Hill's real subject was individual perception—not simply what was *experienced,* but how it was *seen.*

I liked Jerome Hill. I trusted his voice precisely because I felt confident he was presenting the contours of his way of looking at things. It did not bother me that he was not telling me his secrets, that I was not getting the scoop. Some years later, when I learned that he was homosexual, I wondered whether he had felt constrained from allowing that fact to surface in the film, whether he had wanted to speak of it. But he seemed so intent on his life-long love affair with film that it felt like a rude presumption to push the question. In any case, I did not feel cheated that he had suppressed or avoided the subject. (Though the case for conscious suppression is right in the film: in his visual list of possible selves, he displays a photo of himself with Brigitte Bardot, very *intime* on the Cote d'Azur where he had his main residence. Without other information, the photo steers the viewer naturally to assume this is one possible scenario he would relish living more fully.)

Who can say—Hill made his movie in 1971, a time that is already very distant culturally; a 1991 *Film Portrait* might have been very different in its approach to sexual identity. In any case, Hill makes it clear that, autobiography or not, his film is not about *him*—it is about his twin, film itself, born as he was with the century.

Jerome Hill wanted to relive what it had been to grow up with the movies. That is his plot, such as it is. Beyond that, his film is an emblem for perception itself, a way he could display back to the world his interior take on all its swirling life—as that opening scene displays, with Hill shaving over the primal (but ordinary) ooze of a sinkful of water. Like all true memoirists, Hill is drawn more to shards than to stories. He notes his recollection of first sounds (chimes of a clock: "the fact that it told time only interested me much later"), early sensations of light. His first "moving picture," recreated in *Film Portrait*, is a series of drawings on the corners of pages of the dictionary that could be flipped to show the Titanic going down. An innate fascination with illusion, magic tricks, and mystery pervades all his games. "Where," he asks, "do children's games lead?"

It is a reprise of Jung's question, which sent the adult psychiatrist back to making again the sand castles of his boyhood. Hill had apparently been analyzed by Jung. He devoted himself to an unfinished documentary on Jung and attempted to incorporate some of Jung's ideas about the unconscious in his own avant-garde films. Jung encouraged him to work on films that would illustrate Jung's theories of the unconscious. Hill was a willing disciple. His best known attempt in this regard is *The Sandcastle*.

Hill's question about children's games draws him to an early memory of napping on a chaise longue in his mother's room. The memory is presented in a sequence of watercolors. (Hill is very painterly, using animation, working directly on negatives by hand, presenting cut-outs and drawings throughout, as if he can't keep his hands off the film.) In these drawings, a boy is put to bed near a window by a woman in a long Edwardian gown. The figures are manipulated slowly, like stately paper dolls: the child lies in bed and the woman tenderly (if rather stiffly, given the purposely crude animation) draws a coverlet up to his chin.

The paper-doll mother pulls down the window's dark outer shade and then an inner white shade. Outside, the sound of horses' hooves can be heard—the sounds of a dying era, premovie sounds. (Hill paints bright, jumping animated cars in front of the photograph of the mansion with its horse-drawn carriage.) The boy is drawn to a hole ("like an eye") in the shade. Pulling the inner shade closer, away from the darker outer shade, the child discovers the principle of the camera obscura, his Empire Builder grandfather's castle appearing suddenly tiny and complete, upside down on the "screen" of the shade. A profound intimacy radiates from this sequence. Children's games lead, it seems, directly to the adult imagination.

Cut to a close-up of a photograph of him as a child, next to his grandfather at some civic function. He is a beautiful child with a mass of golden curls and a markedly serious, direct gaze. "I am ten years old," the voice says. "Cinema has made its entrance into the family."

In a fortunate coincidence of wealth and hobby, Hill's father was a camera buff. Very early he became a movie buff, too. Films were brought to the house for private showings—to avoid the "microbes" of the public movie house. The reels of these early emulsion films could not be rented; they had to be bought. "What a privilege," Hill says, "to learn pieces of film by heart, as if they were music." The humble reverence of his voice is another reminder of how far in the cultural past 1971 is: the world before Blockbuster Video and the home VCR.

In addition to clips from some of the very early films of Georges Méliès and others, there are professional-quality home movies, shot by a Pathé cameraman who "came frequently to film us kids." And there they are, young people on horses at the North Oaks Farm, the Pathé cameraman displaying his revolutionary technique, the traveling shot. It was an advance in filmmaking that appeared in the Hill home movies before some people had seen it in feature films in the movie house.

This display of family moments has a homely charm, everyone mugging for the camera, tumbling around in a Buster Keatonish way. And then, disrupting the high jinks, the voice again: "These people to whom I belonged curiously did not belong to me," Hill says—as usual with an easy neutrality. "Of everything they did so well, I was incapable." It is not clear what they did "so well"—ride horses? Anyway, he goes on to make his point: "I was living a life apart." It is one of the film's two most personal moments.

I thought of this moment in the film when I learned of Hill's homosexuality. Exactly *here,* I thought, is where he veered from the directly personal pursuit of a self. It would be easy—and defensible—to claim that this is where Jerome Hill censored himself. It is possible to wish that he had spoken of his sexuality and whatever else separated him from his family. Yet I have always resisted that reading of his reticence (if that is what it is). Not only is such a critique insensitive to the cultural shifts over time and the only relatively recent openness about sexual orientation, but it presumes to decide what, exactly, was Hill's reading of his own life. Just because sexuality registers an intimate fact of one's identity does not mean it is one's subject.

Hill chooses not to investigate either specific family relationships or sexuality as the cause of this "life apart." Rather, he says, it was "the mysteries of the unconscious" that set him off from everyone else. Perhaps this sounds, in 1991, faintly arty. Talk of "the unconscious" is rather like talk of the soul—it takes some doing to make it feel authentic. This language can feel like a move away from an encounter with mystery and toward an intellectual relationship with the materials of personal experience. For an artist the unconscious must always be revealed in the curious, even bizarre details of personal experience. "Caress the details," Nabokov, that arch memoirist, advised, "the divine details." Caress them—don't analyze them. Present them as alive and radiant, not as workings of the faculty of mind called "the unconscious."

*Film Portrait* does move away from the radiance of its details and into a fascination with art and movie technique after Hill grows from childhood into adulthood. But before he departs for good into a more analytical self, he concludes this first movement of his life with the film's only extended narrative sequence, a trip he and his family took across his grandfather's rails into Indian country. In yet another link between his life experience and the history of film, Hill uses the regularly spaced vertical lines of telegraph poles, seen outside the moving railroad car, to suggest the frames of a film as the ride begins. We see each segment ever so briefly slowed and framed—again, Hill is pointing as much to the nature of perception and the formation of images as to the content of the event itself.

Hill has some magnificent period footage from the family archive of the trip, and he works deftly with Indian designs to create a kind of camera eye for these images, a brief travelogue within the film. The trip was a diplomatic mission of sorts to the Blackfoot Indians, to gain access across their lands. The voice remains detached, capable of remorseless statement: The railroad—his family—had "no scruples about moving in and disrupting the lives of these people," he says.

As for himself, a boy of twelve, he absorbed "the beauty of this aboriginal world." He learned the complicated Blackfoot sign language, and played games with the children. At the end of the summer he was accepted into the tribe by an ancient blind woman. "I had become a Blackfoot," he says. "At last I had a name I didn't share with anyone else. Here ends my childhood."

And here, in this second intensely revealing line, ends the self-as-camera part of the film, the deep immersion in the mysterious sources of perception that belong to childhood. Hill neatly skips from age thirteen to twenty-three (he uses two photographs of himself, bounding back and forth between them, the voice repeating, "Thirteen, twenty-three, thirteen, twenty-three . . . "). He leaps over those key developmental years without incident or remark, arriving at adulthood from childhood as if by parachute. From then on, the memoir belongs to the movie camera and follows more closely his observation and involvement in *its* technical coming-of-age. For by the time he is twenty-three, he—the conscious artist—holds the movie camera, not his hobbyist father, and not the hired Pathé cameramen.

The rest of *Film Portrait* is an archive of Hill's work displayed in relation to various technical advances. The voice of the teacher, the historian of film, takes over. The film does not cease to be of interest, and his teaching voice retains the winning freshness of the childhood half of the movie. But the urgency of unraveling a mystery gives way to a lesser impulse: a retrospective of his work. The emphasis is not on accomplishment or self-display, however. The film never becomes a self-advertisement. Hill uses his beloved villa at Cassis and the early experimental films from the thirties (if some of his sillier stuff deserves to be weighed down by the term "experimental"—a whole short film, for example, with everybody doing everything backwards) to return, again and again, to the idea of the birth of film as an art. As it happens (or maybe it is no coincidence, but a fact integral to his relation to Cassis), the very first strip of film ever shown in public was of a train arriving at the Cassis platform. Hill tucks the historic clip into *Film Portrait*, of course—more than once—and includes his own contemporary homage-shot of the same location at the end of his film.

It may be unfair to dismiss the adult part of *Film Portrait* as significantly less compelling (to students of film history it might seem the central point), but the palpable sense of mystery and discovery, the perfect register of self and subject, child and camera, is inevitably lost as Hill moves into his adult life. Actually, he seems to move away from his adult life, substituting film history (and his passionate involvement in it) as his subject. It's a fair choice—he lived the life. But it cannot claim the intensity of the earlier subject of perception itself when the boy and the art form entered together into the radiance of seeing the world for the first time.

Toward the end of *Film Portrait*, Hill stresses the idea of filmmaker as alchemist (and presents himself decked out, as at first it appears, as a medieval alchemist, who proves to be, after all, a man editing film). But an alchemist is a magician, one dealing in illusion, committed to hiding, not revealing, the truth. Nor are we given further tantalizing personal remarks about his "life apart." The life of film itself, having absorbed him so completely, is meant to hypnotize—and satisfy—us as well.

It cannot, quite. Yet *Film Portrait* continues to be a touching document as well as an instructive one. Why, I wondered, as I sat watching the movie again recently at a library archive in Saint Paul, is this man so moving—a man who does not display himself, who prefers the gracious surface to the frank revelation? Is it *because* of his essential shyness in the face of the personal genre he has chosen? Because he *can't* tell all or even much about himself?

Long ago I came to believe the impulse toward autobiography has naturally as much to do with reticence as it does with revelation. It is not only Hill who cannot get to the core of himself via memoir: the genre, ducking and feinting, laughs at that naïve impulse. For once entered, the house of memory claims power even over the alchemist, that identity Hill chose for himself as filmmaker. In the end, the magic man with all the tricks up his sleeve is no match for time's imperial transformations.


Ross McElwee cannot claim film as his twin, the historical partner of his life, as Hill does, but he too is determined to represent the camera as a self. "It seems I'm filming my life," he says uncomfortably in *Sherman's March*, "in order to have a life to film, like some primitive organism that somehow nourishes itself by devouring itself, growing as it diminishes."

Hill's claim to kinship with film stemmed from the magical luck of their arrival in the world at the same time, two fresh babies forever discovering vision. For McElwee, the camera is an eye far older than his own, taking in everything with a fierce neutrality. Whereas Hill's memoiristic voice sounds astonished by the radiance of its images, McElwee's voice seems weighted with all the footage he accumulates. He frets over his tendency to become entangled in a "morbid metaphysical feedback loop" of his life's images. If he is caught in radiance, it belongs not to his own perception, but to the past and someone else's camera, as with an old home movie of him and his mother (who died of breast cancer when he was 27) in *Time Indefinite*. "Everything seems to shimmer in the light," he says with wonder in the voiceover, "Everything is sort of quivering with a kind of life that would be very difficult to reenact. Everything's in movement—the shadows, the lights, the hand-held camera."

In *Time Indefinite*, his most ambitious film to date, McElwee returns to territory common to his earlier films—his Southern family, the South itself, and perhaps centrally, the attempt to become the next generation rather than to remain in a sort of fixated passivity relative to the previous ones, impotently observing their effects. In this film McElwee, a very Hamlet-like hesitator in his earlier films, marries, fathers a child, and loses his father to sudden death. In other words, there is plenty of story. The "action" of the film is decisive, but the spirit (the voice) is meditative, reflective.

Even with all the action, the voice dominates, trying to make sense of it all. The film opens at an annual family reunion by the ocean. McElwee is not the only person-as-camera in this family: several video cameras are running, including one held by his stepmother which captures McElwee. It is somehow startling to realize that every person who talks to him in the film is talking to a machine. His family seems long ago to have accepted gamely the inevitable substitution of the camera for eye contact. There may be a slight wariness as they speak, but not self-consciousness. Of course, we know that the camera is always there in every film, but we conveniently forget it. It is the filmic form of willing suspension of disbelief. But when McElwee is revealed by his stepmother's video camera as an anonymous hulk with a literal chip on his shoulder, there is a chilly awareness of the artist's essentially distant relationship from other human beings who are his subjects—and his relatives. "I'll be glad when that big eye is gone," his father says with barely controlled irritation in

*Backyard.* One hardly blames him. But when the big eye goes, presumably the beloved son goes with it; it's not at all clear, even to his father, where McElwee's camera stops and McElwee begins.

In fact, people frequently ask, and finally command, McElwee to turn off his camera. They tend to ask at moments of deep feeling or of private meaning, as a token of respect for the ineffable, as a recognition of some sacred patch of experience outside the scope of the big eye. In their requests and commands there is an implicit assumption that the visual record is uncaring, remorseless—fundamentally inhuman, and invasive. McElwee always obeys these direct requests: the camera shuts down but his voice continues, musing, speculating, wondering. "Cut that thing off," his poet friend Charlene (the subject of a film portrait as well as a tart, muse-like presence in *Time Indefinite*) says peremptorily as she gets deep into a consideration of her husband's suicide. When McElwee is following his bride Marilyn around minutes before their wedding ("When are you going to change, Ross?" someone off-camera asks), she finally indicates with a gently reprimanding look that he must shut off the camera. Not because anything too personal has been revealed but because, obviously, it is time to be *in* the action. As Charlene, in her best Southern country voice, practically hollers at him elsewhere, "This is not art, Ross, this is life." Off the camera goes.

But it seems McElwee must be guided on this matter. He cannot seem to stop the camera on his own, cannot recognize the sacred moments that others around him all acknowledge instinctively, moments that require not silence, but darkness—the closed eye casting its gaze within, acknowledging the abyss there.

No one, of course, tries to silence McElwee's narrative voice, the soundtrack of his thinking self, for no one has to contend with this voice as they do with the big eye. This voice, sorting its images, is the inner voice that cannot intrude because it speaks to and for itself. It is alone. It is after the fact. Its job is to *regard* the action. A visual word for a verbal action: the voice of the film regards the images of the film, through voice giving vision. We are allowed to eavesdrop. "My real life," he says at the end of *Sherman's March*, "has fallen into the crack between myself and my film."

**Ross McElwee, *Time Indefinite* (1993)**
**"When I was little my father would take me to this pier. Being underneath it was like being in an exotic temple or a cathedral."**

Not until his father dies suddenly in *Time Indefinite* does McElwee put down his camera of his own volition. Death alone liberates the father from the son's cold eye. "I didn't film anything for months," McElwee says. Even Charlotte, North Carolina's worst blizzard of the century, which blew in on his father's funeral day, does not compel him to record; the video clips of the storm in *Time Indefinite* are borrowed from a local television station.

McElwee is relentlessly self-aware and self-inquiring in his films, in a way foreign to the dispassionate manner of Hill. He is a child of a psychological culture as Hill, for all his fascination (even reverence) for Jung, never was. *Time Indefinite* has layers of memory that invite McElwee to revisit and revise his past again and again from before and after various turning points in the film's action: before and then after his (happy) marriage; before and after his father's death. (There is no foreshadowing of the death; even to the viewer, it comes as a shock. McElwee succeeds in presenting The Father as a protean force without ever stepping outside the simplicity of the man's modest life as a dedicated Charlotte physician. His bedrock family commitment makes it impossible that such a force should ever disappear from the family scene.)

In a telling moment during a visit home the spring after his father's death, McElwee opens the door to a Jehovah's Witness and his young daughter who have come calling. The earnest young father commiserates over the loss of McElwee's father. McElwee, of course, is regarding the man with "the big eye" hoisted on his shoulder, "pretending to be Monet with a movie camera," he says ironically of himself in the voiceover as he works for angles of light and composes the frame. Composing pictures, working with position and light, creating radiance. Meanwhile, he notes with sudden astonishment, "This man is trying to save my soul. The least I can do is pay attention." It's an odd remark: as if the presence of the camera, which would seem to be an unusually obvious kind of concentration, were in fact evidence of his not paying attention.

Shortly after this brief awakening, he finds a movie of his parents' wedding, a home movie he had never seen before. The business of life took over—medical school, internship, children, medical practice—"and there was never any time to look at the wedding footage." Now both the stars of this brief film within his film are dead, and McElwee runs it alone for himself. "I wish I could believe my parents had 'gone home,'" he says, "as Lucille says." This is a white Southern family. Lucille and her husband Melvin, black people who are his family's long-standing household workers, have outlived their employers. Later, aimless with his inability to find peace, despite attempts to interview himself, his doctor brother, and his sister about their father's life, McElwee gladly accepts Lucille and Melvin's request to film their fiftieth wedding anniversary. Finally he is using his big eye for a family who want him to keep the camera rolling.

The next time the screen goes dark, it is for joy: McElwee's son Adrian is born, and only Marilyn's crying voice and the baby crying are heard briefly. "I didn't film the birth," McElwee says in the voiceover, "because I wanted to help the midwife." He remains entranced by his new son, and says, as if offering proof positive of his devotion, that he hasn't been able to pick up a camera for six months. And indeed, when the film ends where it began—at the following year's family reunion at the beach—the footage is a home movie taken by his cousin Mary of all the babies in the extended family. McElwee is too busy holding his son to hold a camera.

Of course, this is a way of giving the camera, by its very absence, the final frame, the final power. Late in the film McElwee takes his wife and new baby to visit Charlene, his blowsy, poetry-crazed muse. It is she who seems to understand his endeavor best. When, in *Sherman's March*, she takes him to some of the ruins of that fateful destruction, she warns him about trying to connect things too neatly. In a sense she is warning McElwee about breaking faith with the essential fragmentation of memory, its natural state of decay. Charlene is encouraging a severe allegiance to the inevitable isolation of separate moments in a life and in history. In film terms, she is telling McElwee to frame (and thereby to honor) all the separate takes. "You never solve everything, Ross," she tells him, warning him against his desire to discover (or fabricate) more clarity or more sense than life can offer. "The only thing you've got," Charlene says, "is a chance at a few passionate hits. You see how foolish it all is. It's all a tragedy. It's just a matter of how you get through it. You see what the army comes to—the bunkers, the island, the burned-out house. Hell, it's all a tragedy. It's just a matter of how you get through it. And the most interesting way to get through it is to say, *I can't help it, I'm full of passion and I'm going to die this moment*. It's the only way to pretend you're alive."

The voice of memoir may be the voice of radiant perception as it is in Jerome Hill's recreated childhood, or it may be the anxious voice of Ross McElwee trying to make everything come out right. Or, if not "right," to come out as a unified tissue of meaning rather than the tangled (though "shimmering," to use McElwee's word) strands of separate moments forever lost to each other. But memoir is not, apparently, merely the impulse of reminiscence.

Remembering is not the point. Memory seeks coherence. And because it cannot give itself to plot as the novel or the feature film can, the memoir must find a different kind of glue. And in the absence of what Charlene calls "solving everything," the memoirist's voice comes forward with the only possible organizing principle: asking questions, noting confusions and absences, counting the family's emotional silver.

Jerome Hill is elusive, as fragmentary as the images he presents. Ross McElwee in his steadfast way talks the viewer through every twist and turn of his attempt to make sense of his life. There is a straightforward assumption of the first-person narrative voice in both of their films. The voice you hear is the voice of the filmmaker; its very timbre is an indication of the nuance of the narration.

But voice can be powerfully present without the literal voice of the filmmaker. Su Friedrich, in her beautiful bookend films of her mother (*The Ties That Bind*) and her father (*Sink or Swim*, 1990), is closer to Hill's elliptical method. Her "voice" in *The Ties That Bind* is often a black card cast on the screen with a question scrawled in white—the animated scrawl is carefully calibrated to suggest levels of emotion. The presentation is jerky, even frantic as the subject gets desperate. The technique is particularly effective when Friedrich is trying to elicit information about her German mother's awareness of the treatment of the Jews and the existence of the death camps during the war years. You can sense the whisper and the scream as the questions play across the screen as she tries to track down her mother's experience as a young girl in wartime Germany. In her poetic tracking of her father's flight from the family in *Sink or Swim*, she manages with great forbearance to tell a tale that is essentially a story of abandonment without once slipping into self-pity or outrage. She casts the memoir in the third person so that "the girl," "the father," and "the mother" are the characters. A child's voice, arrestingly pure, tells a series of Greek myths as various vignettes with titles (Zygot, Virginity, Seduction, Realism, Pedagogy, Nature, Memory . . .) pass across the screen.

The "story" is cut into fragments, as memory itself is. Friedrich does not approach with her own voice. Her "voice" is all over the images of the film. The place where image makes itself distinct from voice is less clear in her work—or perhaps the two are more harmoniously united. The "sound" of words cast on the screen is the sound the viewer's inner voice makes upon reading them rather than the literal sound of the filmmaker's voice. Here indeed is the entry to the unconscious Hill was hoping to convey. And as it happens, Hill did help Friedrich achieve her film: in the credits for *Sink or Swim* she acknowledges a grant from the Jerome Foundation, Hill's charitable trust for artists.

✦

Every person's life, we say, is a story. When it becomes story, a person knows he has a life, she has a life. The forming instinct sorts, orders, represses, highlights, and finesses its way to a certain contour—not to "reality," but to shapeliness. To represent the whole of reality is, of course, beyond the capacity of art, even outside its desire. In fact, the inability to limit the flow of reality is one definition of madness.

This forming instinct is true for all fiction, on the page or on the screen. And it is true for nonfiction, though out of a strange decorum about the "reality" of nonfiction, we are usually expected to wink—or frown—at this unavoidable habit of invention that it shares with all narratives. "Nonfiction" is a big, frayed umbrella, with a motley crew of genres sheltering under it. In film, just about anything short of a feature can nudge its way under the cover. A documentary about Salvadoran rebels, a historical panorama of the Civil War, a home movie shot at a wedding—they're all nonfiction. Perhaps the oddest figure of all under that umbrella is the memoir.

The materials of memoir may be nonfiction and from your life, as my hiking companion Edna put it as we sat together on the terrace in Spello. But the deeper instinct, which cries out to the prodigality of perception for some kind of shape—that is certainly the business of imagination.

But Edna's first question about the relation between memory and imagination collapsed under the pressure of her other worried self-inter-rogation: *Why didn't we help?* she cried when she reviewed her experience at Heathrow with the lost African woman she and her husband had failed to help. Still, the two questions were linked, indivisibly part of each other in her mind. When I did not respond to her first question, which belonged to the world of the imagination, she moved without hesitation to the moral ground of experience, to life itself. There her more vexed question stood incriminating her with its autobiographical fragment. It ran like a video loop in her waking and sleeping mind.

We say everybody has a story. That makes it sound as if everyone were an incipient writer with a finished novel in the drawer. But really everybody has snippets, a weight (a wealth) of footage we keep intending to edit into meaning. Edna hadn't helped the beautiful African looking for her way, and I hadn't helped Edna either, who seriously needed to know where stories come from, burdened as she was by the freight of unsorted images she carried. I could give her nothing at the time. I let her disappear down her own echoing interior hall as we sat together on the terrace at Spello while night fell and she cast her unedited footage, as if on a screen, before us in the dark, where I see it still.

WILLIAM ROTHMAN

# Eternal Verités

**T**he year 1960 was a watershed in the history of film in America. I think of the release of *Psycho* in 1960 as marking the definitive end of the classical era of American movies. 1960 was the year the French "New Wave" broke on American shores. Perhaps not entirely coincidentally, 1960 also marks the emergence of what has been called "cinema-verité." (This term is hopelessly inadequate, of course, yet I persist in using it. Alternatives such as "direct cinema" are no less inadequate and far more misleading. These days one is far less likely to fall into the error of supposing that "cinema-verité" films are guaranteed to be truthful than the error of taking them to be "direct," that is, unmediated.)

Cinema-verité, of course, is a form of documentary film, or a method of making documentary films, in which a small crew (often a cameraperson and sound recordist, sometimes only a solitary filmmaker) goes out into the "real world" with portable synch-sound equipment and films people going about their lives, not acting.

Jean Rouch, collaborating with the sociologist Edgar Morin, made *Chronicle of a Summer* (1961) in France simultaneously with the earliest cinema-verité films in America, such as the Drew Associates productions, of which *Primary* (1960) is perhaps the most famous. Nonetheless, for a number of reasons, I think of cinema-verité as an essentially American phenomenon, not a European one. It is in America that the grandest hopes for cinema-verité have been harbored. In the past thirty years, American filmmakers working within the cinema-verité tradition have created a remarkably impressive body of work. And cinema-verité has been perhaps the fullest inheritor of the concerns of America's "classical" cinema, the popular movies associated with the name "Hollywood."

Rouch's approach to cinema-verité was highly sophisticated. He anticipated, and quite shrewdly addressed, the problems and paradoxes— epistemological, aesthetic, and moral—that, as subsequent practitioners were to discover, inevitably attend this new, apparently more direct way of filming. Rouch understood that however "invisible" the man-with-the-movie-camera might make himself, and however unselfconscious the camera's subjects might appear, filming is a real act performed in the real world with real consequences. He understood as well that sometimes a filmmaker has to forsake the passivity of a place behind the camera to provoke reality into revealing its deepest truths. For Rouch, already a veteran of over a decade of ethnographic filmmaking among the Songhay and Dogon peoples in West Africa, the new lightweight synch-sound equipment became an indispensable instrument of a life-long cinematic enterprise poised between science and poetry, between anthropological research and a personal need to give poetic expression to his conviction that "primitive" societies possess knowledge that modern science must find ways to acknowledge.

For a maker of very American films such as Richard Leacock, who was Robert Flaherty's cameraman on *Louisiana Story*, cinema-verité was what film itself was to Griffith a half-century earlier: it promised a radically new way of revealing the truth about humanity. This truth was to be found not in Flaherty's romanticized vision of man's struggle against the elemental forces of nature, but in the everyday struggles of ordinary men and women to retain their humanity in a hypocritical America of sex, lies, and exploitation. The human truth was to be found in the coarseness and ugliness of that America, but also in the flashes of beauty, tenderness, and compassion revealed to Leacock's camera.

For Leacock, the beauty fleetingly glimpsed by cinema-verité offered the promise of redeeming America. Since it seems that this promise was fated not to be kept, cinema-verité also meant, for Leacock, a threat of disillusionment and despair. But he has remained faithful, in his filming, to the strict cinema-verité discipline, as have Robert Gardner, John Marshall and Frederick Wiseman, to name several of the great masters of cinema-verité whose work I deeply admire and who happen to be based in the Boston area, where I was able to become acquainted with them personally during the years I was teaching film at Harvard.

David Hume withdrew into his study, shutting out the world in order to contemplate whether it was possible that the world does not exist. The author of *Walden* withdrew from society and spent two years at Walden Pond in order to gain a new perspective on the world and learn how he might live in it. In order to film the world, the cinema-verité filmmaker, too, withdraws from the world. To effect this withdrawal, he needs only to assume a place behind the camera. His philosopher's study, his Walden, so to speak, is the camera itself. This is a Walden one can bear on one's shoulder.

Behind the camera, practitioners of the cinema-verité discipline forsake their ordinary lives to become observers who wait selflessly for the people they are filming to reveal themselves in their own good time and on their own terms.—But are cinema-verité filmmakers selfless? What are the fantasies that animate their hours of silent watching? Writing about Alfred Hitchcock's neglected early masterpiece *Murder!,* and hence in a rather dark mood, I argued that the role of cinema-verité filmmaker has an inhuman, murderous aspect:

> The cinema-verité filmmaker withholds himself from the world in order to film it. Stepping behind the camera may appear an act of perfect innocence and purity. But it expresses, it does not overcome, the fantasy of power and murderousness that *Murder!* declares to be an inalienable constituent of authoring a film. The cinema-verité filmmaker's fantasy of virginity and impotence has as its secret other face the fantasy of being author to the world, commanding it to unmask itself. Claiming exemption from responsibility for forging community within the world he is filming, he trains the camera's eye on that world, wreaking vengeance on it. These twin fantasies of impotence and omnipotence come together in cinema-verité's underlying vision of a world con-

demned to a lack of human community by virtue of the act of filming.[1]

Led by Edward Pincus and his students at the M.I.T. Film Section—for years, Pincus was codirector with Leacock of this unique cinema-verité training ground—a new generation of filmmakers attempted to break away from the inhuman aspect of the cinema-verité filmmaker's role while remaining faithful to the spirit of cinema-verité. Their aspiration was to reconcile the conflicting demands of filming and living by learning to film the world without withdrawing from it. Inevitably, the filmmaker's life and the demands of the filmmaker's role became the increasingly explicit subjects of films by Pincus, Steve Ascher, Ross McElwee, Jeff Kreines, Joel DeMott, Mark Rance, Ann Schaetzel, Robb Moss, and others. Their explorations culminated in two extraordinary epics, Pincus's *Diaries 1971–76* and McElwee's *Sherman's March* (1986).

In *Diaries,* a conflict emerges, seemingly inevitably, between the filmmaker's experiment of filming his life, a project only he can call his own, and the claims made upon him by his wife, children, parents, lovers, and friends who call upon him to acknowledge them as human beings separate from him and his film. The filming of *Diaries,* which has the aspect of a romantic quest, threatens to seal the filmmaker's isolation rather than liberate him to live freely within a human community, to turn him into a hero not of romance but of tragedy. This conflict between the romantic and the ordinary, between filming and living, emerges in *Diaries,* at least on the surface, as the primary obstacle to the filmmaker's goal of becoming fully human.

In the more ironic *Sherman's March*, the conflict between filming one's life and living it in a fully human way is equally central. In McElwee's film, too, the filmmaker takes his project to be a romantic quest. But *Sherman's March*, made a full decade after *Diaries,* presents its filmmaker as a comical character whom it treats ironically. Viewed from this perspective, the filmmaker's attempt to become more human by filming his life necessarily seems a foolish one doomed to failure. If *Diaries* tells its story with a gravity akin to that of tragedy, *Sherman's March* tells the same story as farce. They both, however, surely demonstrate that there is an irre-

---

1. William Rothman, *Hitchcock —The Murderous Gaze* (Harvard University Press, 1982), 105.

ducible aspect of withdrawal and isolation, and of violence, in the cinema-verité filmmaker's role, even if people directly address the filmmaker behind the camera; even if other people are allowed to turn the camera on the filmmaker, rendering him or her visible; and even if the filmmaker breaks his or her silence and enters into conversations with other characters in the film.

Reflecting on a history of cinema that is still far from perspicuous, it can seem quite remarkable that, despite film's long and illustrious documentary tradition, cinema-verité only emerged as late as 1960. There were isolated experiments such as Flaherty's celebrated *Nanook of the North* (1922). But most documentary filmmakers—even Dziga Vertov, so often claimed by cinema-verité filmmakers as a precursor—had little inclination to follow *Nanook*'s example. In part influenced by Marxist ideas about the necessity of transcending the individual protagonist, they veered in a different direction. In the films made in England by the talented filmmakers gathered around John Grierson, and in the work of Pare Lorentz, Willard Van Dyke, and others in America, a dominant form of documentary emerged in the thirties whose influence remains strong to this day. These documentaries composed their views of people lyrically or expressionistically, and used them rhetorically in advancing a social thesis, usually explicitly stated by a (typically male) narrator's authoritative voice.

In postwar Italy, the neorealist movement championed the use of nonprofessional actors and "real" locations in fiction film, and strove to discover dramatic subjects in the realm of the everyday. But the neorealists never took the decisive step of dispensing with scripts altogether and venturing into the world to film "reality itself." Nor did André Bazin, France's great theorist of cinematic realism, advocate this step. Above all, Bazin was a champion of film as a medium of authorship. How can a cinema-verité filmmaker claim to be an "author" in Bazin's sense, since in a cinema-verité film the world remains, as it were, a free agent?

In the thirties and forties and even the early fifties, the technology for portable synch-sound shooting was unavailable. Yet filmmakers could have made silent films that followed the lead of *Nanook of the North*, or they could have shot their films silent and postdubbed them in the studio as the neorealists did. For whatever reasons, however, filmmakers were not interested in filming this way.

Most American cinema-verité films could not but be in synch-sound, could not but have people who speak spontaneously and in their own voices. When and why and how people speak, the powers and limits of language in our human form of life, remain central concerns of American cinema-verité. This concern is manifest even in cinema-verité's refusal to use "authoritarian" voiceover narration. In cinema-verité, truth is to be revealed, not asserted by a narrator whose authority is beyond question. In cinema-verité, words are spoken in particular ways by particular people to particular people on particular occasions for particular reasons. No one's authority is beyond question. (Perhaps it is no accident that the emergence of cinema-verité in America was simultaneous with the impact of the "ordinary language" philosophy associated with the names of Wittgenstein and J. L. Austin.)

In the sixties, when the classical tradition had broken down and Hollywood's audience had become fragmented, cinema-verité promised a new way to make movies that might seem as vivid and "real" as Hollywood films of the thirties and forties had been, in their day, to their audience of all Americans (and to their audiences worldwide). By the sixties, the classical conventions seemed to have lost their vitality and relevance, and America had even lost the memory of the wonderful conversation its movies had once sustained with their culture. Thus it was possible for filmmakers and audiences to be convinced that cinema-verité owed nothing to classical movies, to think of Hollywood as the sworn enemy of all that cinema-verité stands for. Yet, in truth, cinema-verité owes far more to popular Hollywood movies than it does to most earlier documentary films. In the sixties, cinema-verité represented a new way of making films that inherited the concerns of popular genres such as the "comedy of remarriage" and the "melodrama of the unknown woman" (as Stanley Cavell has named them) that had crystallized in Hollywood in the thirties and forties. And cinema-verité derived from classical cinema its picture of human being-in-the-world as an expression of a dialectical opposition between the theatrical and the nontheatrical. In *The "I" of the Camera*, I characterized classical cinema's picture of, and way of picturing, the human form of life:

Film's opposition between the theatrical and the nontheatrical is grounded in, and grounds, its conventions for presenting human beings in the world. Typically, the camera alternately frames its human subjects within public and private spaces. The frame of an 'objective' shot is a stage on which human beings perform, subject to view by others in their world. Within the frame of a reaction shot, a subject views the spectacle of the world, reacts privately to it, and prepares the next venture into the public world. Point-of-view and reaction shots together combine to effect the camera's penetration of the privacy of its human subject, who alternates tensely and hesitantly between acting and viewing as he or she prepares an entrance onto the world's stage, performs, and withdraws again into a privacy to which only the camera has access.[2]

As we shall see, cinema-verité did not follow classical cinema in its use of point-of-view shots as a technique for distinguishing between the theatrical and the candid. Nonetheless, cinema-verité inherited classical cinema's great stake in the realm of privacy, and in the realm of the every-day. Cinema-verité inherited as well classical cinema's understanding that, within these realms, "the non-candid—the unspontaneous, the manipulated and the manipulative, the theatrical—is everywhere to be found."[3] And it inherited classical cinema's conviction that our happiness as individuals—and America's as a nation—turns on our ability to reconcile our private and public selves.

In thinking historically about the emergence of cinema-verité in America, it is important to keep in mind that early cinema-verité films such as *Primary* or *Crisis* (1963) were made not for movie theaters with their dwindling audience, but for network television, newly crowned as America's dominant medium. In the context of television programming, these films' identity was divided: like "real movies," or television dramas, or even soap operas, they appealed to human emotions. Yet, as documentaries, they were public-affairs shows, news.

2. William Rothman, *The "I" of the Camera* (Cambridge University Press, 1988), 69–70.

3. Ibid., 189.

Typically, news is presented on television by newscasters who address the camera directly. When news footage is shown, it is accompanied by a newscaster's voiceover that tells us how to understand what we are viewing. The newscaster is always "on." Television provides no system for distinguishing the person of the newscaster from the role she or he is performing—no system for acknowledging, for investigating, or even for exploiting, the dialectic between theatricality and nontheatricality that is at the heart of cinema-verité as well as classical movies.

Over the years, the format of television news has evolved to convey the impression that we do know the private person behind the newscaster mask. Walter Cronkite ended each of his broadcasts with a seemingly privileged moment, as he looked directly at the camera with an expression that told us he was taking us into his confidence. Person-to-person, he acknowledged that he was no impersonal newscaster; he was a human being who had in some particular way been moved, just as we had been, by the story chosen to close the show. He had taken the story to heart, like a *mensch*. Then, with an authority grounded in this display of emotion, he summed up his philosophy of life, always with the same words but every evening with a new inflection, one tailored to match the prevailing mood. "And that's the way it is." This nightly ritual put Uncle Walter's personal stamp on the role of newscaster, and thereby revised that role, paving the way for others who have gone much farther—indeed, much too far, as evidenced by the nauseating, shameless conviviality of local "news teams"—in incorporating displays of "personality" into a once rigidly impersonal role. The point is that the newscaster's role, however revised, however "personalized," nonetheless remains a role, a mask, no less so when the newscaster appears to be dropping his or her mask. The format of television news still provides no system for acknowledging even the possibility of such theatricality.

In classical cinema, we view "stars" continually putting on masks and taking them off. In most forms of television programming today, the mask is never dropped, unless another mask is already firmly in place beneath it. To be sure, when television was primarily live, masks often slipped, or cracked, or were inadvertently put on crooked. Already by 1960, though, the nature of television was changing from a primarily live medium to one in which no discernible sign distinguished what is "live" from what is, shall we say, canned. The result is not to make the canned seem live, but to make even the live seem canned. (This effect is, in a sense, a denial of the uncanny.)

Thus when it first appeared on television in America, cinema-verité represented, at one level, an assault from within against television's deadening denial of the distinction between theatricality and candor that has been the basis of American movies. By letting the audience view, say, John Kennedy when he was not performing in public (or at least by purporting to reveal the "private" man), *Primary* (and to a lesser degree *Crisis*) granted Americans a new perspective on Kennedy the public figure. (Of course, Kennedy's mask was hardly dropped completely. The camera was not granted access, for example, to his boudoir, to his private life as a stud.) All in all (and surely Kennedy himself anticipated this), these films served to reinforce Kennedy's public image, which was that of a man who "had it all together," who was enviably successful in his career and enviably lucky in his marriage, and whose public and private selves were, even more enviably, a harmonious match.

What I am suggesting is that cinema-verité was meant to undermine television's practice of packaging public figures as exploitable images. Ironically, cinema-verité itself quickly became a favorite tool of image-packagers who have learned to fabricate tolerable imitations of the look of spontaneity and candor. The famous Nixon-Kennedy debates helped Kennedy and hurt Nixon because both men, forced to be at least a little spontaneous, revealed something of their "true" characters to a camera that neither man was in a position to control, hence which took on something of the penetrating power of the camera in cinema-verité. When Nixon was in a position to control the camera (as, for example, with his staging of the infamous "Checkers" speech, which saved his political neck), he was free to perform his "sincere act" on television without the threat that its theatricality might be exposed.

Many of the earliest cinema-verité films in America revolved around celebrities, and portraits of celebrities—political figures, sports heroes, movie stars, singers and musicians—remain a staple of cinema-verité. No political convention or major sporting event is complete without minidocumentaries that make public figures private by presenting them, in ABC's immortal phrase, "up close and personal." Cinema-verité brings celebrities down to earth by filming them the same way it films ordinary people (which, of course, celebrities also are). The filmmaker's task in filming any human subject is to create a compelling figure on the screen, to make that figure as known to us, and as unknown, as James Stewart, Cary Grant, Katharine Hepburn, or any other star of classical cinema. Cinema-verité transforms an ordinary person into a star, or reveals, as it were, the "star within"—at least if that person happens to "have what it takes." But classical cinema has always made its stars out of ordinary people who happen to "have what it takes."

Classical cinema instituted a system of production in which, first, a screenplay is authored; then that screenplay is realized by a process of filming in which the director plays a central role; finally, the film is edited in a process that reconciles the screenplay with what might be called the "accidents of filming." In a cinema-verité film, there is, at least in theory, no directing of actors, and the camera's gestures, too, are improvised, not directed; and, of course, there is no screenplay.

D. W. Griffith did not write or work from screenplays as such, although his films were hardly "unscripted." Griffith was able to envision the film he wanted to make and to realize his vision in the act of filming without first putting into writing what he saw in his mind's eye. However, as the Hollywood system of production became rationalized, Griffith's method was superseded. Screenplays assumed a central function as blueprints for filming and editing, no doubt partly because studios wished to limit the risky (and potentially expensive) unpredictability inherent in the filming process.

In the voluminous writings about adaptations of literature to film, the screenplay has received virtually no attention. Perhaps the most surprising formal feature of the classical screenplay is that it employs no pictures or diagrams to help guide the reader in visualizing the film. The screenplay is made up of nothing but words.

In the classical system of production, the screenplay functions as an envisioning-in-advance, an imagining, of the film. One might think that yoking films to screenplays in this way subordinated cinema to writing. Yet the development of this mode of writing can also be thought of as an affirmation of cinema's authority over the written word. Screenplays demonstrate and declare film's powers, which are also writing's limits. For film has the power to make real, or to reveal to be real, what the words of a screenplay can never more than "envision." To read a good screenplay and then to see the film made from it—if it is well made—unfailingly restores one's wonder at the power of cinema.

By enforcing the discipline that films were to be "realized" only after first being envisioned in advance through the medium of the written word, the classical system also acknowledged the power of writing. This acknowledgment immeasurably strengthened the affirmation of film's authority. For film possesses precisely the power to reveal writing's limits, as I have suggested: Writing is not film. In turn, writing possesses precisely the power to challenge film to declare itself: Film is not writing. (In Griffith's hands, film comparably declared its authority over theater, hence revealing the limits of theater even as it affirmed theater's power: Theater is not film, and film is not theater.)

Nonetheless, within the classical system, no film is made without a screenplay. In this system, film may appear to lord it over writing, but it is dependent upon it. Cinema-verité constitutes an alternative system, one in which filming proceeds by improvisatory encounters with the world, by chance and whim (the filmmaker's whim, and the world's).

When cinema-verité dispensed with the screenplay, it was a declaration of film's independence from writing. Yet by issuing this declaration, cinema-verité was also following (or paralleling or leading) a literary trend, joining ranks with the self-conscious "nonfiction novel" (*In Cold Blood* is the most famous example) that is cinema-verité's exact contemporary. This suggests that cinema-verité was not breaking with the written word, but with the discipline of composing the film in advance, the yoking of filming to envisioning or imagining.

To say that a screenplay envisions or imagines a film in advance implies that filming is a process of realization, or interpretation, of the text of the screenplay, in the sense that a performance of a musical composition is an interpretation of the written score. In realizing a screenplay, the director directs the actors in interpreting their roles as written, as in theater (the casting of a particular actor in a role is already an act of interpretation). The director also directs the camera, interprets the camera's role as written. Part of the actor's role, to be interpreted by the actor under the director's direction, is to present himself or herself to the camera in particular ways, ways that may encompass an interpretation of the way the camera views that actor. In turn, the camera—also under the director's direction—addresses the actor—self-presentations (and interpretations of the camera) and all—as a subject in his or her own right.

No text has one and only one possible interpretation. If a classical film is an interpretation of its screenplay, this implies that other interpretations of the screenplay are also possible. Thus a screenplay can determine a film only up to a point, and can never fully determine a film in its concrete actuality. No moment of any film can be completely envisioned in advance. The actual filming transforms the screenplay in ways that are not perfectly predictable as well.

Film is photographic; there is an irreducible element of automatism in the way it reproduces the world. Nonetheless, screenplays bind classical film to the realm of interpretation, and to words. (Or do they reflect the fact that film is so bound by its nature?) Indeed, classical film is doubly bound to interpretation and to words because it is always possible, in the face of a realized classical film, to write in screenplay form what might be called a "transcription." Such a transcription is not an envisioning of the film in advance, nor is it an interpretation of the screenplay realized by the film. Rather, it is an interpretation of the film itself.

In transcribing moments of a classical film, one must find words that objectively characterize particular gestures, intonations, glances, facial expressions, or movements of the camera. But these are things one cannot objectively characterize apart from characterizing, interpreting, one's subjective experience of them. Screenplays, too, routinely characterize such things as gestures, intonations, glances, facial expressions and camera movements—things one cannot describe without interpreting one's own experience. In a screenplay, as in a transcription of a realized film, "objective" description and interpretation cannot, logically, be separated.

That directing a film from a screenplay is a discipline that can be mastered, that masters of this discipline are capable of creating compelling, expressive, endlessly exhilarating and moving films by interpreting screenplays that are made up of nothing but words, is an inherently unpredictable fact about words, and about film. Writing a transcription of a realized film is also a discipline that can be mastered. Every masterfully written transcription "is a study in the limits of what can be said. It is also a study in the limits of what goes without saying. What the possibility of such mastery reveals is that the limits of language and the limits of film coincide. That is, there is a boundary between them."[4]

The screenplay of which a classical film is an interpretation and the transcription that is an interpretation of that film cannot be expected to coincide word-for-word. In principle, such coincidence is not impossible; it only requires a miracle. Some films (and hence their transcriptions) fail to acknowledge or realize the screenplay's own perspective on the world it envisions. Other films go beyond their screenplays in the sense of acknowledging and revising the screenplay's own interpretations (I am thinking, for example, of the ending of *Now, Voyager*. The screenplay takes the woman still be in love with the man, still to be putty in his hands, while the realized film understands her to have attained a transcendental perspective.) When a film does revise and deepen its screenplay, this revision could always in principle have been anticipated and incorporated into the screenplay. After all, in writing a screenplay, the writer continually revises and (we hope) deepens his or her imagining and understanding of what is being imagined.

This suggests that while a classical screenplay is an imagining of the realized film that constitutes an interpretation of it (and which can, in turn, be interpreted by a transcription), the original screenplay, too, can be thought of as a transcription of a film that exists only in the screenwriter's imagination. (One might wish to speak, further, not only of a film that exists only in the screenwriter's imagination but also of a [different?] film that exists in the imagination of each reader of the screenplay [a different imaginary film for each reader?], and, crucially, in the imagination of one particular reader, the director [who may or may not also be the screenwriter] whose task it is to interpret the screenplay in the act of filming.)

4. Ibid., xiii.

Of course, it is not necessarily the case that a screenwriter first sees a film in the mind's eye and then subsequently transcribes it. The writing of the screenplay may also serve as an instrument of this imagining. Perhaps it is better to think of "the film envisioned by the screenplay" as having no prior existence apart from the specific words and literary form of the screenplay itself. (As I become more and more deeply mired in such distinctions, I find myself homesick for the field of philosophy.) In any case, what is imagined in this imagining? What is this "film that exists only in the screenwriter's imagination?" Is it a film at all? (If it isn't a film, what is it?)

It would be obviously misleading to speak of a novel as a transcription of a "novel that exists only in the novelist's imagination." This is because a novel, like a screenplay, is made up only of words, while presumably the novelist imagines not words but a world—a world that it is part of the discipline of the novelist to render in words.—But how do we imagine a world? What is the medium of our imagining?

The way we imagine a world is akin to the way we dream. It is often said that we dream in images, but it is more precise to say that we dream in views, or, rather, that we dream by imagining views. Views are always of the world. It is of the nature of views that they are from particular perspectives, that they correspond to positions *in* the world that nonetheless provide vantage points on the world.

We have no other way of imagining the world than by imagining viewing the world from vantage points that are at once inside and outside the world being viewed. This may seem an insignificant distinction, yet it is precisely where film's uniqueness lies. The material basis of film, Stanley Cavell argues in *The World Viewed*, is a succession of automatic world projections. Film is the medium in which the world leaves its impression in the form of a succession of views. To imagine the world is to imagine the world viewed, and to imagine the world viewed is, in effect, to imagine a film. This is what novelists do, for example, when they imagine the worlds of the novels they are writing.

But when a screenwriter envisions a film, isn't she or he imagining the world present in all its substantial reality, rather than imagining the shadowy projections of a world already past? Doesn't the screenwriter imagine not a film but a world as it presents itself to be filmed? Doesn't the screenwriter imagine what the field of film study calls "profilmic reality," not views of reality? But what is it to imagine reality (at least in its visual aspect) if not to conjure views of reality in one's imagination? The imagination itself is a faculty of projection. Nothing we can imagine is more real to us than views.

Views are the medium of imagining the world; imagining the world (in its visual aspect) is always imagining viewing the world; what one imagines are always views. Yet there is a difference between imagining and viewing. In viewing, the world makes its impression on me, although my imagination must meet the world halfway. By contrast, in imagining, I conjure views from within. Having conjured them, I have no need actually to view them, any more than I have a need, when I am dreaming, actually to view the views that constitute my dream; I need do nothing with the views in my dream other than dream them. And the screenwriter envisioning a film imagines the world viewed, imagines views of the world, but these views need only be imagined to be rendered in words, they do not need also to be viewed.

In imagining the film that is to be transcribed in the screenplay he or she is writing, the screenwriter does not imagine it as a film that has to be scripted and then realized by filming. To exist in the screenwriter's imagination, this film only has to be imagined. As it exists in the screenwriter's imagination, it is not a product of the classical system of production. (This is not to deny, of course, that the films a screenwriter is willing or able to imagine may be inspired, or constrained, by a lifetime of movie viewing.)

Paradoxically, then, a classical film is authored by first being envisioned as a film that has no author, as a film that comes into being through spontaneous encounters with unscripted, undirected "reality." Thus it is tolerably close to the truth to say that, in the imagination of the screenwriter (and in the imagination of the director whose task it is to interpret the screenplay), a classical film is a cinema-verité film.

A cinema-verité film is not envisioned in advance, and hence does not have a screenplay. However, insofar as it allows for transcription in screenplay form, it remains bound to the realms of interpretation and words. But is it possible to transcribe a cinema-verité film? This question is akin to asking whether jazz can be transcribed. In the case of cinema-verité there is no special problem in transcribing the gestures and expressions of the camera's human subjects. What poses special problems for transcription, or challenges, are the movements and vicissitudes of the camera itself.

Screenwriters are habitually advised to write as few "camera directions" as possible, the ostensible reason being that directors are said not to like it when writers encroach on their prerogative. Yet one cannot envision actions in the world in concrete detail without at the same time envisioning particular vantages on those actions, which correspond, in film, to positionings and movements of the camera. Shrewd screenwriters specify framings or camera movements only when they are surprising or especially significant, and most often leave the camera to the director's imagination. They know full well, however, that the conventions of classical cinema all but dictate that the director imagine a long shot here, a medium shot there, and so on.

In classical cinema there are conventional categories of shots and conventions for their use, although, to be sure, on occasion framings or camera movements may be called for that are so idiosyncratic that they require individualized descriptions. When an occasion does arise for specifying particular framings or camera movements, the screenwriter thus has at hand a repertory of conventional categories (close-up, two shot, point-of-view shot, and so on), screenwriters' terms that evolved hand in hand with the conventions of cinematography. Even in the forties, when the "long take" style flourished as an alternative to "analytical" editing, the "long takes" tended to take the form of stable framings—each virtually a separate shot, conventional in format—linked by reframings instead of cuts.

Typically, cinema-verité is shot as close to "real time" as possible, and by one hand-held camera. Thus the cinema-verité frame is rarely stable or fixed. Rather, there is continual reframing, and also zooming in and out (the zooms have the consequence that image size does not necessarily correspond to spatial distance). The camera is never completely still, but most of its movements have little or no particular significance apart from their status as indicators of two related conditions. First, the incessant movement of the camera indicates that the camera is hand-held, that it is an extension of the filmmaker's bodily presence. Second, in their characteristic hesitations, indecisions, incessant revisions of focus and framing, these movements are also indicators that this is not a scripted film, that the filmmaker is only a human being, not an omniscient author.

It is not just for technical reasons that cinema-verité films tend to approach as nearly as possible to the condition of complete continuity. This style also offers formal testimony to the method of filming—as if any cut would threaten the viewer's assurance of the filmmaker's dedication to the cinema-verité discipline. Every cut could be a splicing together of shots taken at different times or different places. In terms of cinema-verité discipline, every cut could be an instance of "cheating."

A corollary of this avoidance of cuts that break up continuity is that cinema-verité abandons the point-of-view technique that is a stable of classical cinema. Point-of-view technique requires cutting back and forth between viewer and viewed, instantaneous shifts of perspective not possible for a filmmaker shooting with one camera in "real time." In cinema-verité films, point-of-view shots can only be simulated. The motivation for dispensing with this technique, too, is not just technical, however: because the cinema-verité camera is perceived as an extension of the filmmaker's body, the camera's presence is identified first and foremost with the person of the filmmaker. This means that there is a limit to the camera's ability to establish an identification with its (other) human subjects. Point-of-view shots would risk transgressing that limit, hence they are to be relinquished. In avoiding point-of-view shots, and in the motivation for this avoidance, cinema-verité surprisingly reverts to Griffith, who never allowed the camera's gaze to stand in for the perspective of a character. Griffith's camera was always to be identified, first and foremost, with the perspective of the invisible author of the film.

The camera's "normal" state of incessant motion in cinema-verité contrasts strikingly with the classical camera's "normal" state of motionlessness. In classical films, the camera's stillness is punctuated only by specific, composed gestures of the camera. Not moving the camera may itself, at times, constitute a gesture of this kind, and such privileged moments of stillness might be specified in the screenplay. Ordinarily, though, the classical camera's fixity of position, like the incessant motion of the cinema-verité camera, has no particular significance apart from marking the camera's presence. The incessant motion of the cinema-verité camera binds it to the bodily presence of a human filmmaker whose hand and eye are continually and unavoidably revealed by this motion. By contrast, the camera in classical cinema breaks its stillness to declare itself in specific, self-possessed gestures that call for acknowledgment.

Interestingly, when the camera is referred to in a classical screenplay, it is treated as if it were a character, except that, by convention, references to characters are capitalized only when they are introduced, whereas references to the camera are capitalized throughout. It is as if every time we are called upon to take note of the camera, an introduction is performed, as though we had forgotten ever having encountered the camera before. The camera has been present all along, of course, but only on such occasions does it call for acknowledgment. Part of what is then to be acknowledged is that the camera has already, has always, been present. The significant point here is that the vantage of the camera is always open to being specified because, at every moment of every film, the camera frames the view, and it always does so from some particular vantage. This is an ontological condition of film.

A transcription of a cinema-verité film could not be expected to register every movement of a camera that is constantly in motion. Yet some movements of the camera would have to be noted and interpreted—perhaps because they are deliberate gestures, statements, on the part of the filmmaker, perhaps because they are spontaneous expressions in which the self of the filmmaker is especially tellingly revealed.

For example, in the climactic passage of Richard Leacock and Joyce Chopra's *A Happy Mother's Day* (1963), a South Dakota woman who has given birth to quintuplets is stoically enduring a luncheon in her honor. As an amateur soprano sings with a perkiness she takes for sophisticated sauciness, Leacock's camera dwells on the mother for whom this luncheon is supposed to be, as one town booster puts it, "her own fun time." The camera remains on her so long that we may well begin to wonder what, if anything, it can possibly hope to discover in her plain face. As if suddenly sensing that the camera has been attending to her, she steals a glance at it. Her suspicion confirmed, she furtively shifts her gaze away.

**Richard Leacock and Joyce Chopra, *A Happy Mother's Day* (1963)
Mrs. Fischer acknowledges the camera.**

But then, no longer willing or able to continue the pretense that she is uninterested in its interest in her, she deliberately meets the camera's gaze with her own. At this moment, we feel that anything can happen, and everything is at stake. What does happen next, miraculously, is that Mrs. Fischer breaks into a sly grin in recognition of the camera's capacity to acknowledge her.

Then, as if authorized by Mrs. Fischer, and in secret conspiracy with her, Leacock's camera pans from person to person in the hall, finding obliviousness in the eyes of all the people gathered to honor this woman they do not really know. Unless a transcription notes and characterizes these gestures of the camera, the power and meaning of this wondrous passage is lost.

Within limits, then, a cinema-verité film does allow for a transcription in screenplay form. In principle, such a transcription could have been written prior to the filming, and could have functioned as an envisioning of the film and as a blueprint for filming, the way a screenplay functions in classical cinema. A cinema-verité film can always be imagined to be a classical film. But can we imagine the reverse? Is it possible to imagine that a given classical film was really unscripted, was really made by the cinema-verité method?

There are special cases, of course, in which this can readily be imagined: films designed to simulate the appearance of cinema-verité, such as Mitchell Block's *No Lies* (1973), or specialized classical films like those of John Cassavetes in which the actors appear to be engaging so extensively in improvisation that it seems the camera, too, must improvise, giving rise to a cinematic style virtually indistinguishable, formally, from that of cinema-verité. But what of classical films that are not special cases? What would we say if someone claimed that *Casablanca* was really a cinema-verité film, or *The Philadelphia Story*, or *Gaslight*, or *Psycho*? Our first response would probably be that this is impossible, if only because, with the available technology, no cinema-verité filmmaker could have shot, say, *Psycho's* shower-murder sequence, with its instantaneous shifts of camera vantage. The same is true, if on a less dramatic scale, for any classical sequence that employs analytical editing.

Apart from this problem, which is in a sense only a technical one, the camera in a classical film always seems to know exactly where to be to frame every action, and often seems to know this in advance, before the action takes place. The filmmaker would have to possess godlike powers always to be in the right place at the right time, or else the filmmaker would have to be the beneficiary of an incredible succession of implausible coincidences. Such a run of luck is not impossible, nor is it unimaginable. After all, it cannot be unimaginable for any given classical film to be a cinema-verité film, because, as I have argued, every classical film is, in fact, first imagined this way, first envisioned as a creation of chance and whim, first envisioned as a cinema-verité film.

It would take a miracle for a classical film, so self-possessed and composed, really to be unscripted and undirected. Yet every masterful cinema-verité film, too, has a miraculous aspect. In every great cinema-verité moment, the filmmaker happens on a situation so sublimely poignant, or so sublimely absurd, that we can hardly believe the stroke of fortune that reveals the world's astonishing genius for improvisation.

Indeed, we never would believe it, were it not on film. That the cinema-verité method, too, is capable of creating compelling, expressive, endless-ly exhilarating and moving films is another inherently unpredictable fact about the world, and about film. In the fact of their unexpectedly felicitous marriage, how can we not believe in miracles?

HELENE KEYSSAR

# The Toil of Thought:
## On Several Nonfiction Films by Women

> *The toil*
> *Of thought evoked a peace eccentric to*
> *The eye and tinkling to the ear.*
> —Wallace Stevens

have always been irritated by nonfiction films. To begin with, I am bothered by the apparent ease with which films seem to divide into fiction and nonfiction, and the different reception a film receives dependent on whether it is labeled fiction or nonfiction. So I am troubled simply by the act of analyzing a film from a perspective that emphasizes its qualities as fiction or nonfiction. Notably, this is not an apparent problem when I am writing or thinking about most so-called fiction films. This is not to deny that we test fictional films against the "nonfictional" or historical world. It is sometimes the whole point of a mainstream movie: Michelangelo Antonioni's *Blow-Up* (1968) illustrates this in one way, Steven Spielberg's *Schindler's List* (1993) does so in another. But this is rare with fiction films.

My interest lies in my knowledge that the moment I am put in front of a nonfiction film I begin to wonder about its position *as* a nonfiction film. This is in part a matter of the ostensible status of a nonfiction film in relation to context: in academic and other intellectual or art arenas, nonfiction film has a higher status generally than fiction film; nonfiction film is assumed to be serious, noncommercial, educational, and, implicitly, not entertaining. It is assumed to be either art or information. Simultaneously, if I make a general comment about "film," the concrete instances I and others will recall are likely to be fiction films. If I ask if you have seen any good movies lately, I am not referring to nonfiction films. (I am not excluding them either; I am just not thinking about them). At least as an apparent element of modern life, fiction movies are paradoxically of low status precisely because they are well attended as "popular culture" whereas nonfiction movies, which are seen by and known to an elite audience and are anathema to most spectators, carry a high status. All this I find perturbing, confusing, and not simply foolish or mistaken.

As André Bazin famously argued, in contrast to other art forms film requires the physical world; it does so whether the sounds and images it projects are transformed from another state and thus thought of as invented by that phenomenon we call the imagination, or are found in the world and, seemingly mechanically, recorded. This is to say that a second irritation with nonfiction films is their resistance to our desire to take film as a medium for escape from ordinary life. Nonfiction films do not transport us away from ordinary life (although they may deny or ignore it), and it is that transportation that most of us wish from the movies.[1] In a nonfinite number of ways, nonfiction films insist on our self-conscious presence —both to film and the world—as spectators. Nonfiction film is the tool Emerson might have dreamed of, the shadow of presentiment in Emily Dickinson's eye.

Women filmmakers have known this, have had to know this, since early on in film history. Stanley Cavell may be right when he claims that a woman has often been the whole reason for the existence of a film, but that only reminds us that the sound and look of some women can transport spectators from the ordinary to the extraordinary world of desire that is at once shared and private. Cavell's comment does not reveal why many women have attempted to speak through the language of film and in that language to use and create a filmic vocabulary that resists the most stereotyped images of women and transcends what we have come to call the male gaze.

In recent years, women critics of film have illuminated the gendered traps and seductions, the structures and symbols, that have made film the twentieth-century locus of visual pleasure for men. We—I include

---

1. Sometime in the late seventies George Kateb told me that what he wanted from a movie was "to be transported." This notion is central to my essay on *Adam's Rib* and *Casablanca*, "As Time Goes By: Justice, Gender, Dramas and George" in *Democracy, Culture, and the Engagements of Politics: Essays in Honor of George Kateb*, ed. Austin Sarat and Dana Villa (forthcoming). The idea of film's ability to transport the spectator also appears in my *Robert Altman's America* (Oxford University Press, 1991).

myself—have not been as clever at clarifying why women appear to enjoy most movies, nor have we done much to analyze seriously the struggles of the women who control the images behind the camera. And, despite the fact that women in increasing numbers have directed nonfiction films over the past twenty-five years, to a great extent precisely because women as "auteurs" have generally been excluded from the mainstream worlds of commercial fiction films, critics, including myself, have paid far more attention to the "reverence and rape"[2] of women on the screen in conventional fiction films by men than to the hundreds of films made by women internationally that have been classified as nonfiction. This is not unreasonable. Perhaps I come to any nonfiction film and especially one by a woman in an uneasy state precisely because I know that I will have few people with whom to share the experience of my viewing, and fewer still for whom I might write about a nonfiction film by a woman. But if this state is comprehensible, it is also self-fulfilling.

Although my ambition here is less to rectify film history than to reflect on and with a handful of films, I puzzle at the absence of a detailed historical account of women making films. Despite the other richness of the histories of nonfiction film by Eric Barnouw, Richard M. Barsam, and Lewis Jacobs, nonfiction films created by women are hardly mentioned in these volumes. For many years, Julia Lesage, Christine Gledhill, and a handful of other women and men took responsibility for critical writing about nonfiction films made by women; more recently, as feminist film criticism has grown in both power and domain, articles about nonfiction films by women have appeared with some regularity, and perhaps a dozen books about women and film contain sections on nonfiction film.[3] But these mark only a beginning to a history and a critique.

The eleven films I address here, while drawn from fifty years of women's filmmaking, are not intended to represent a history of nonfiction film by women, but to remark some of its most telling moments. All of these films are, with varying degrees of effort, available at least on video-

2. My reference here is implicitly to Molly Haskell's *From Reverence to Rape: The Treatment of Women in the Movies* (Holt, Rinehart, Winston, 1973, 1989). This is one of the first books to focus on the roles of women in film.

3. Several useful books are *Multiple Voices in Feminist Film Criticism*, ed. Diane Carson, Linda Dittman, and Janice R. Welsch (University of Minnesota Press, 1994); *Films for Women*, ed. Charlotte Brunsdon (British Film Institute, 1986); Catherine Portuges's *Screen Memories*, about the work of Hungarian filmmaker Marta Meszaros (Indiana University Press, 1993); Barbara Quart's *Women Directors: The Emergence of a New Cinema* (Praeger, 1988); and Ally Acker's *Reel Women* (Continuum, 1991).

tape. They are, in the order in which I will talk about them: Maya Deren's *Meshes of the Afternoon* (1943), A *Study in Choreography for Camera* (1945), *Ritual in Transfigured Time* (1946), *Meditation on Violence* (1948), and *The Very Eye of Night* (1952–1959); Barbara Kopple's *Harlan County, U.S.A.* (1976) and *American Dream* (1990); Joyce Chopra and Claudia Weill's *Joyce at 34* (1972); Roberta Cantow's *Clotheslines* (1982); Yvonne Rainer's *Film about a Woman Who . . .* (1974) and Jennie Livingston's *Paris is Burning* (1991). They vary in length from four minutes to one hundred and five. In juxtaposition, the diversity of their settings is almost comic: there is no calculating, in conventional terms, the distances from Deren's filmically invented worlds to Austin, Minnesota, where we witness the plight of meat packers on strike, to the New York City palaces that present balls in which gay black men perform spectacular cross-dressed roles.

I am less interested in these differences than in the odd similarities I find in these films, similarities beyond their basic commonness as nonfiction films made by women directors. The constant presence throughout these films of unfixed ideas of women defies essentialist feminisms while invoking women's distinctive ways of seeing and being. These are films, as Cavell might say, the viewing of which is an education in itself. I should add here that my decision to focus on American films is one of both access and knowledge. I have seen magical and disturbing nonfiction films by Russian, Chinese, French, British, Hungarian, and Italian women, several of which have inspired serious critical attention, but, as one attribute of many nonfiction films is the foregrounding of context, I prefer to move within the sufficiently challenging territory of American films.

Several of these films approach the extreme points in a spectrum of nonfiction film by women (and perhaps by men, as well); most of them describe the larger field between those points. Uncomfortably, I think of this spectrum in literary terms: at one side of the field is nonfiction film that has many of the attributes of poetry; at the other side of the field are nonfiction films that are prosaic and, more precisely, similar in tone and strategy to the essay form in literature. However, all of the films I will discuss here resist reductive binary positioning. Those that are least like each other in categorical ways, those by Maya Deren on the one hand and by Barbara

Kopple on the other, are not so different as one might imagine from each other or from the other films of concern to this essay. I would be more comfortable if I could replace the spectrum image with the idea of genres, a term that works well in thinking about fiction films, especially American fiction films. The idea of genre, however, requires deliberate convergences of conventions and ideas that are inimical to nonfiction film. Genre also cannot be employed arbitrarily; a particular genre only exists as an understanding gained from several particular instances of the cultural form. From these instances, genre acquires a name, and that name implies a set of attributes that determine the inclusion and exclusion of particular texts, say of films, in the genre. Something close to notions of genre but not identical with it emerges in the accumulation of my commentaries, but, were we able to think clearly in terms of genre about nonfiction film, we would have had to resolve the problems raised earlier concerning the basic distinction between fiction and nonfiction film.

I turn first to a set of films by the "mother" of American underground film, Maya Deren. Born in 1917, Deren is the founder of the independent film movement in the United States; her only woman predecessor is Germaine Dulac, who began to make "film for art's sake" in Paris a generation before Deren. The position Deren marks is not just that of "first" historically but that of the "mother" of the school of film as poetry. In that role, she explicitly rejects key elements of film as prose: character and narrative are, at the least, to be sapped of conventional moves and meanings. Deren's first film, *Meshes of the Afternoon* (1943), is consistently talked about in terms of poetry and dreams: "We see there is the magical . . . built in the vertical dimensions of dream to become complicated metaphors," writes Parker Tyler about Deren's films in general and *Meshes* in particular.[4]

As dream, what I see in *Meshes* is hauntingly familiar. Over and again, the camera accompanies a woman from outside her house to her

4. Cited in Acker, *Reel Women*, 96.

front door, which she opens, after first dropping her key. We see a living room from the woman's point of view before we have seen any of the woman's body above her waist. Inconsistently, but emphatically, there is a rare sense of firstperson point of view here. We move through the house, sighting objects—bread, a phone, stairs, a knife, a chair vividly covered in a floral slipcover. The entire journey through the house is repeated, with the camera revealing the whole body and face of the woman; she is Deren herself. This time, she picks up the knife. In this iteration of the journey through the house, unconventional, awkward camera angles and an annoying humming sound disrupt the pattern. The basic sequence recurs once more with even more distorting, disturbing camera angles as the woman moves up the stairs. Now there is a man in the bedroom. He sees himself in a mirror and takes the mirror with him as he approaches the woman, who is lying on the bed, a knife near her head. The woman grabs the knife and makes a quick gesture towards the man; we see shattered pieces of mirror, then the shards reappear on a shore where they gradually vanish into the sea. In the last sequence the man approaches the house, turns the key in the door, opens it, and, the camera taking his point of view, stares at the floor, which is littered with shards and pieces of objects. The camera then cuts to the chair where the woman (Deren) appears at once to be part of the flowered upholstery, and, on closer view, limp, perhaps dead. A streak of dark liquid runs from her mouth.

Deren described *Meshes of the Afternoon* as an expression of a particular, unconscious self. As such, it calls forth expressionism in painting and drama. The most frequently remarked shot in the film, of Deren herself pressing her hands against what John Hanhardt aptly calls "a membrane of glass," explicitly separates the director and the world of her film from the real world. "As she stares through that reflecting surface, . . . she becomes a reflection of herself mediated by the projected film image."[5] My own strongest memory of *Meshes* is of a recurrent image of a figure, shrouded in black, moving stealthily through the house, and moving swiftly, in another segment, outdoors, around the house. Where her face should be, there is, instead, a pentagonal mirror. This figure appears both to

5. John Hanhardt, "Introduction," *Video Culture: A Critical Investigation*, ed. John G. Hanhardt (Visual Studies Workshop Press, 1986), 14.

accompany and reflect the woman at the center of the film. In black and white, with only erratic percussion and increasingly intense humming sounds, *Meshes* finds a woman imagining herself more and more detached from her physical world and from others. She is woman as fish, woman proliferating as her image is multiplied, woman slowly approached as time seems to slow almost to a stop, as, after interacting with a man, she becomes a woman dead, in a still, dead frame.

Meshes of the Afternoon has become a cult film among independent filmmakers. Why so, I ask myself, intrigued yet a bit angry. Despite its disorienting camera angles, its vocal silence, and its rhythmic repetitions, *Meshes* functions both narratively and symbolically more than I anticipate; no matter how many times I watch or what I read about Deren or her films, this film yields just enough obvious meaning to make me wish for something more—or less. I remember images, slightly varied, of an anxious woman, searching, finding a flower, finding her house, finding shadows and reflections and ideas of herself, finding herself as victim of a phallic symbol, and I remember movement, but movement that is almost self-indulgent because I so welcome it, given little else that differentiates this from a conventional melodrama. And I am reminded of how much *Meshes* is like my own dreams of haunting the house in which I tried to grow up. But is it about me?

In none of her subsequent films is Deren far from what she is doing—and not doing—in *Meshes,* but in *A Study in Choreography*, *Ritual in Transfigured Time*, *Meditation on Violence*, and *The Very Eye of Night*, I am less frustrated, and I find more rewards, even though I cannot easily remember, even with my notes, where one film begins and another ends. *A Study in Choreography for Camera* discovers a male dancer in a birch woods; he is so lean and graceful that he appears to be part of the forest. The man at once seems to be duplicated among the trees—as birches are of a kind and yet each in its separate place—and to be leaping away from us, away from the camera, through the woods, to and from no locatable place. In the next series of shots, the man continues leaping, but now he is moving through a broad, open, tiled space, marked by a double-faced stone bust of an ancient figure. At the end of this brief (four-minute) film, the man reappears in the woods and himself becomes a statue.

**Maya Deren, *A Study in Choreography for Camera* (1945)**

Several of the visual motifs of *Ritual in Transfigured Time* are so reminiscent of moments in *A Study in Choreography* and *Meshes* that I repeatedly mix these pieces in my mind. *Ritual* initially captures a woman posing in *her* ritual of winding a skein of yarn. Almost immediately, another woman (who may, indeed, be the same woman) appears daringly close to the camera and raises a hand as if to say, "Come with me, through the screen, into my world." A subsequent segment visually ritualizes a social scene of men and women gathering, by following the movement of conversations as if there were literally a flow to this party. Then yet other contexts that, momentarily, seem out of context tease, challenge our desire for stability: a man, reminiscent of the dancer in *Choreography*, leaps through arches which might be on the Rue de Rivoli in Paris, or in Rome. A woman appears and runs from him, distracting us from thinking about where we are, specifically. The woman is next in water, moving, as a body moves, more fluidly in water. The camera cuts away from faceless, moving beings to shots of tissues of fabric; these, too, move, gently, vertically, finally revealing a face veiled by tissue, then enclosed by more fabric. Again, as in so many of her visions, Deren's "rituals" are at once fleeting and recurrent.

*Meditation on Violence* begins with sound that suggests to my Western ear a Chinese flute. As always in Deren's films, images are in black and white. The camera finds a single man. Here he is moving his arms, his hands, in a way that seems practiced, part or all of a ritual. The camera finds shadows of the man on a white wall; together, these images are vaguely frightening; danger is here, and is increased when the man reappears, bare-chested, with his head bound in a black kerchief tied at the side of his face. This figure draws attention to the space around him, which he appears to shape, but mostly the still camera watches his arms, torso, and, occasionally, his legs move in a very small area, as drumbeats gradually replace and sometimes augment the sound of the flute. Just at the edge of my patience, the figure on the screen beckons again at the audience and adds a wide, flat sword to his space. He swirls the sword around his head, moves in circles, edging the frame of film, then suddenly grabs the sword and points straight down the middle of the frame, from a distance, towards the camera, freezing, as the camera freezes him, pointing the sword at it, at us, as he rises from a crouch to a standing position. And this is not the end. Sound becomes louder and more intense, and the film cuts from a vaguely outdoor space to an empty room. By these last frames of *Meditation on Violence*, it has become clear that this film relies on trying the patience of the viewer. Here, as indeed in all her films, just at the moment when I might walk out of the screening, Deren presents some small surprise, a new and intriguing sound or a camera angle that reconfigures previous images. The intervention will be commanding enough, but no more than enough, to sustain my attention.

*The Very Eye of Night*, subtitled "A Choreography for Camera," made between 1952 and 1959, is Deren's last film. It is initially less intimidating than her earlier films, in part because it immediately offers a few referents to the spectator: a diagram of Shakespeare's *A Midsummer Night's Dream*, which includes the names Ariel, Oberon, and Titania; an animated image of the yin/yang symbol in stark black and white; a starry sky that suggests a finely wrought paper doily (or the set of a 1930s MGM entertainment); and, with decreasing recourse to referents, paper-cut characters that float upwards, transforming screen to sky to screen again, new figures white on black like a photographic negative floating before us, the figure of a woman with long white hair especially vivid. This figure, in silhouette, a negative image replacing the positive, is joined by a similar figure of a man; together, they dance with the freedom of spirits, loosed from gravity's pull and classical ballet's conventions, yet notably embodied still and unwilling to resist the old gestures of flight and romance as she rises on point, as far as she can alone reach upwards, and he lifts her. Now, finally, the filmmaker becomes an explicit partner, tripling the image of the woman, projecting three where there was one, inserting marked variations in music from wind instruments to percussion to chimes and bells to initiate visual changes. The rhythms of shots and the superimpositions of editing make the figures before us dance in a space that is sometimes sky, sometimes water, until they float together and become one strange, fishy creature that, finally, yields to the fabricated starry sky of the beginning, and then to black.

In all of these films, but most successfully in *The Very Eye of Night*, Deren relies on, dwells with, dance. I was at first surprised, but then it seemed somehow obvious, predictable, that Deren and dozens of other women filmmakers have been serious dancers before they came to film. Deren's films are not, however, records of dance. They are collaborations between dance and film.[6] Like both these forms, Deren's films hint of flight within the frame and dwell in repetition. They propose the conjoining of the self-reflexivity of the modern in art with the redundancy of ritual so available to both dance and film. Deren's films do stunningly what she writes that film should do:

> If cinema is to take its place beside the others as a full-fledged art form, it must cease merely to record realities that owe nothing of their actual existence to the film instrument. Instead, it must create a total experience so much out of the very nature of the instrument as to be inseparable from its means. It must relinquish the narrative disciplines it has borrowed from literature and its timid imitation of the causal logic of narrative plots, a form which flow-

6. See William C. Wees, "The Legend of Maya Deren," in *Film Quarterly* 43:2 (Winter 89–90), 57. In this review of VèVè Clark et al., *The Legend of Maya Deren: A Documentary Biography and Collected Works*, vol 1, pt 2: *Chambers (1942–1947)* (Anthology Film Archives/Film Culture, 1988), Wees suggests that *Meshes of the Afternoon* was a collaboration between Deren and her second husband, Alexander Hammid. Hammid also assisted Deren on other films.

ered as a celebration of the earth-bound, step-by-step concept of time, space and relationship which was part of the primitive materialism of the nineteenth century. Instead, it must develop the vocabulary of filmic images and evolve the syntax of filmic techniques which relate those. It must determine the disciplines inherent in the medium, discover its own structural modes, explore the new realms and dimensions accessible to it, and so enrich our culture artistically as science has done in its own province.[7]

While these are claims from Deren's late writings, the notions of what film is and should be are confirmed in all her filmmaking. Read with no experience of Deren's films, this summary manifesto seems not much more than a powerful echo of one side of the earliest debates in film history over film's proper use as a record of the world or as a creator of new worlds. Read with Deren's films in mind, there is something else available to us that does more than note the ongoing relevance of this argument. One part of that something else is the recognition of the power of the film images we have seen that correspond to Deren's call. I think here of the consanguinity in ambiance as well as in technique of representation with Spielberg's fetal-photographic images of "others" who arrive from another planet in *Close Encounters of the Third Kind*, with the transcendent grace of the figures of love in Marcel Carné's *Les Enfants du Paradis*, with the starry cityscape of Woody Allen's *Manhattan*. I also think instantly of Deren's work when I watch MTV. My point is not that these films and videos are necessarily and explicitly informed by Deren's urgings and examples, but that her work does provide not only a distinctive vocabulary and syntax for film, but an approach that, in a range of filmic contexts, has great power. That some of Deren's filmic vocabulary is similar both to that which preceded her work and that which has followed is not a matter of claiming or disclaiming credit for her, but of noting the good and unpredictable company her filmic style keeps.

Nonetheless, and perhaps in contradiction to what I have just said, there remains in Deren's work an almost constant tutorial tone. That exem-

---

7. Maya Deren, "Cinematography: The Creative Use of Reality," in *Film Theory and Criticism*, ed. Gerald Mast, Marshall Cohen, and Leo Braudy (Oxford University Press, 1992), 70

plifying quality of Deren's films is a source of my unease with her work. Like certain kinds of teachers, Deren's films rely on my irritation. Deren's films instruct, provide original models, but do not stand easily on their own, and if we are not looking for models, her films leave us unsituated as spectators. This has something to do with the absence of anything we could identify as resolution in several of her films, an absence essential to the authenticity of the work. This resistance to resolution (more than absence of resolution) coheres with the sense Deren's films give of their existence as examples of what she calls "invented events."[8] The latter she defines as filmic gestures that exploit and transform the ordinary in the world—"the natural blowing of the hair," "the welcoming gesture of a hand"—in order to project new worlds on the screen. The combination of the exemplifying quality of Deren's films with the desire to exploit the world in order to reconstruct it may be another element of my irritation with nonfiction film.

In search of more clues, I want to swing the projector to the opposing side of the terrain of nonfiction film, the side I earlier identified with prose and the essay form in literature and that is usually called documentary. If Deren's goal is to create film that always at least transforms, and attempts to abolish, real-world referents, documentary film is oppositionally concerned with what André Bazin thought of as the illumination of the actual world. Here, in a realm closer to that of recording rather than inventing events, the instances of nonfiction films by women are plentiful, especially since the early seventies, and are better known to general audiences. Connie Field's *Rosie the Riveter*, Julia Reichert and Jim Klein's *Union Maids* and their *Seeing Red*, Shirley Clarke's *Portrait of Jason*, Perry Miller Adato's *Gertrude Stein: When This You See, Remember Me*, Amalie Rothschild's *It Happens to Us*, and Michelle Citron's *Daughter-Rite* are among a much longer list of nonfiction films by women that address diverse problems in modern society, especially, but not exclusively, those encountered by women. Several of these films are intended primarily for women; the topics they address define their audience. Childbirthing, women's work, rape, women's roles as unionized or nonunionized workers, women's

8. Ibid., 64.

contributions to war industries, women's relationships to their mothers and to mothering are subjects that particularly engage and trouble contemporary women. A case could be made, without cynicism, that the relative success of some of these films as adjuncts to the women's movement has little to do with the quality or process of film itself.

If all this is, in general, the case about nonfiction "documentary" films, what is it about a film like Barbara Kopple's *Harlan County, U.S.A.* that not only gained it an Academy Award, but draws new viewers and reviewers to the screen long after the event about which the film was made? The opening of *Harlan County* provides one answer: shots of men, the sound and smoke images of an explosion, followed by a cut to a series of men throwing themselves onto a flat conveyer belt in motion, moving into the deep, dark blue of the mine, all yields quickly to a dark blue and black screen lit in disorienting spots such that we glimpse in a montage within the frame, as well as from shot to shot, aspects of men's faces and bodies as well as markers in what we may guess is a mine. These visuals are accompanied by an upbeat country song that doubles and clarifies the information we get from what we see: "It's dark as a dungeon way down in the mine." Underneath this song, there is a constant dull, annoying noise.

There is an unnerving moment of quiet as coal comes out on the belt, followed by the recurrence of the song, a distance shot of two men walking away from the mine, and a cut to an old man, hypnotically gaunt and wrinkled, his face triangular in shape, the source of the song and a commentary that begins, "Coal mining was rough . . . they work you like a mule." As the old man continues his narrative of life as a miner in Harlan County, the film cuts back and forth from his face to men digging inside the mine. Miners, the old man tells us, work twenty-hour days, their bodies wet, their clothes stiff. Once, the old man relates in a parched voice, the boss man approached him. "'Be sure you put that mule in a safe place,'" he commanded. "What about me?" the old man asked. "'We can always hire another man,'" the boss-man had responded. "'We have to buy a mule.'" The words in their vocal frame of the old man's memories, juxtaposed to shots of mine work and its human toll, efficiently establish the tensions of Harlan County, the place and the film.

**Barbara Kopple, *Harlan County, U.S.A.* (1976)
Women on the picket line.**

In the next segment, the one element missing from the beginning, the union, takes its place. Voiceover narrative and a subtitle
announce "a moment in history": "In the summer of 1973, the men at the
Brookside Mine in Harlan, Kentucky, voted to join the United Mine
Workers of America." The film cuts to a young woman who is talking about
a man who died and about her support for the union; the next cut reveals
strikers attempting to stop a van from bringing scab workers to the mine;
in a third cut, a man on the strike line tells an anecdote about a boss who
made him work the day after a three-hundred-pound weight of coal had
fallen on him, splitting open his head. Yet another edit undercuts pity by
historicizing the current events: in black and white, in contrast to the color
photography of the previous shots, we see a photograph of John L. Lewis
with his dates—1920–1960—and a citation: "Organize the unorganized.
Without organization, you suffer." Immediately, as if in response to Lewis,
we hear a female voiceover saying, "We're protesting . . . they're treating
us like dogs, telling us we can't choose our own union . . . " As she speaks
to the camera it moves from her to women wearing "Impeach Nixon" but-

tons; there is a lag edit of several male voices arguing the pros and cons of the union, and we go back to the old man and another story, his "first political lesson," about how strikes get corrupted. Additional shots of a policeman, and of male and female workers with handouts warning of dangers to stock owners who invest in "the enemy," Duke Power Corporation, culminate in a meeting of miners and outside union leaders. Kopple does not attempt to present a historically detailed, causally determined narrative of the struggles of miners and their families against corporate and labor leaders. The fragments of stories, the filmic records of the pain and fury of men in the mines and the women who wait for the men to emerge from the mines, the account of the murder of Carl Yablonski and his family, teach grounds for rage against Duke Power Company and its spokesmen.

Throughout the next segment of *Harlan County*, and again in subsequent sequences, the song, "Which Side Are You On?" calls from the soundtrack as well as from location shots. It is the film's central question, and we already know that, from Kopple's point of view, there is only one side we can choose with honor. It allows us, as spectators, to feel good about the choice Kopple demands that we make, without moving from our seats. It allows an audience of the lingering sixties generation, and perhaps some for whom the thirties was the shaping decade, to feel political juice running in their veins. Among the more potent images that provoke this sensation is a shot taken near the entrance to a coal mine, of a wooden scaffold covered with wreaths of flowers to commemorate the lives of the men who have died in the mines. Images of the grieving faces of women are intercut with the shots of bright flowers. Over and again, images of men—miners and ex-miners, labor leaders, corporate bosses—are edited to encounter images of the women of Harlan County as these women wait and cook and nurse their men and nurture the young and old and sustain the community.

The remaining hour of film follows relentlessly and predictably; yet each time I see *Harlan County*, I am again surprised by the extent of the cynicism and cruelty of the corporation, the failure of the union to conquer the corporate interests in a lasting way, the repetition of similar strikes and disputes, the subtle care with which images and voices of women take a strong place in the county and in the film, and, then, our willingness to stay with the film for its duration. Not everything stays the same; not everything changes. Over time, fewer men die of black-lung disease, because accurate information about the disease and its symptoms is slowly disseminated; but the attempts to confront the diverse dangers of mining remain the task of the miners and their families. "As long as they're greedy and as long as they're rushing the coal mine and wanting production before lives, there'll always be tragedies," one unlikely coal-miner's wife, distinctive in her helmet of dyed white-blonde hair, concludes. Over time, not only gender but race emerge as issues: a voiceover comment, "when you come out of the mine, we're all the same color," contrasts with still shots of people in white gowns and pointed hoods; whispered comments inform us that Harlan County was a key gathering place for the Ku Klux Klan. The ugliness of Klan behavior and the harm repeatedly inflicted on women and children as well as men add another dimension of evil to the lives of these miners.

Repetition in film can be puzzling or pleasing or annoying; in life it is dangerous. Fiction films use symbolic repetition—of colors, actors, music, and so forth—to give us the pleasure of recognition, but they refuse the authenticity of the repetitions of daily life out of fear that they will bore us. Nonfiction films, including *Harlan County*, sometimes take a different strategy: they present similar events that occur over time—strikes, meetings, violence, deaths—to persuade us that repetition is not meaningless. Three deaths are not the same as one death. Three strikes take on a more oppressive ambiance for the viewer than does one strike. In documentary films, time matters, people age, poverty continues and is worse each day. Although, near the end of this film, there is a victory—better wages and greater safety measures—for the union and the miners, the last shots and sounds of the film hint that there is no lasting end to the strife and the cruelty of daily life in Harlan County. The film, therefore, appears to end arbitrarily, ironically leaving the viewer pleased but wanting more.

This absence of resolution is irritating in one way in *Harlan County* and in another in Kopple's 1990 feature-length film about labor struggles, *American Dream*. In *Harlan County*, the lack of resolution is in the events outside the film, in a future that is subordinated to the momentary triumph of the film's present. The filmic experience is structured so that we become engaged in a familiar pattern of conflict and resolution. In both shooting style and the sheer beauty of some of the cinematography by Hart Perry, the visuals of *Harlan County* are not far from the conventions of fiction film: we know who the good and bad guys are and who should win and who should lose. When *Harlan County*, the movie, is over, we, the spectators, may be left with righteous anger; while only a few people may act out of this anger, there is no ambiguity intended about what should happen. In moments, *Harlan County* is dialogic in its resistance to the creation of a few stars through the camera's conventionally loyal attention; by seeking out the women, the old-timers, and the disabled in addition to the men who work the mines, the union leaders, and the corporate bosses, *Harlan County* appears to be polyphonous in its points of view. But Kopple confirms in interviews that this is at most a partial truth.[9] Her montages of daily life in an Appalachian mining town seek and imply a solution to the array of economically based problems for the mineworkers in some form of applied justice that would pay the miners fairly and simultaneously allow them and their families to sustain the dignity, health, and responsibility of a rural community. We feel empathy for the miners and their families through Kopple's guidance, but after *Harlan County* has unveiled their plight and evoked the audience's concern and anger, it may be clearer where we should stand politically but not how we might get there. The sensation is one reminiscent of fiction.

American Dream, in contrast, projects a world where it is not always clear which is the right side to be on, even from the perspective of a political progressive in late capitalist America. Indeed, in *American Dream*, a movie whose Academy Award seems ultimately far more politically significant than *Harlan County's*, conventional good American values do not line up predictably or unambiguously with progressive politics. Within the frame of the film, resistance to the money and power politics of the Hormel meat-packing industry comes from several sites and does not map easily onto conventional alliances within the larger left/right political spectrum. This, in turn, evokes an uneasy state for the viewer, and Kopple recognizes this complexity. In a 1991 interview with Gary Crowdus

9. Gary Crowdus and Richard Porton, "American Dream: An Interview with Barbara Kopple," *Cineaste* 18:4 (1991), 37–38, 41–42, esp. 37; and L. A. Winokur, "Barbara Kopple," interview and biography, *Progressive* 56:11 (Nov. 1992), 30–33, esp. 31.

and Richard Porton of *Cineaste*, she emphasized the difference in the concerns of the two films: "*Harlan County* was much easier," she says, "because it was more black and white."[10] *American Dream*, Kopple explains, was complicated both by the intervention of news media and its context in the Reagan era. For Kopple, *American Dream* was about the economic crisis of the eighties for middle-class people all over the United States, not just in Austin, Minnesota, the primary location of the film.

*American Dream* opens with a photograph of a pale, nondescript building that we later recognize as a slaughterhouse, and cuts quickly, in obvious contrast, to the interior of the slaughterhouse where there is a lot of color, rapid movement, and noise. From the start, *American Dream* is less whimsical and less witty in its montage, less seductive in the matching of audio and visual materials. From its title to its red, white, and blue credits to its audio quotations from speeches of Ronald Reagan and commentaries by national newscasters, this is a film that places the viewer at enough distance from the particular troubles of the meat packers in Austin, Minnesota, to see the struggles before us as indicative of numerous other national conflicts. It is a more serious, grueling and tedious film than *Harlan County*. It is also gripping in an unrelievedly somber way.

Early in the film, Kopple establishes Austin as a small Midwestern town, typical in its mix of mostly modest houses, owned by laborers, with a few distinctively grander dwellings owned and occupied by Hormel Meat Company executives. We witness Jesse Jackson preaching to workers and their families from a podium in an Austin church, and cut backwards in time to an exterior, then an interior, shot of the same church, in which people are singing Christian hymns. Hormel's chief legal counsel, a man named Nyberg, tells the camera that "We rub shoulders and go to church with these workers." A male voiceover lauds Hormel's generous initiatives in relation to its workers, while we see shots of men and women workers in spotless white working clothes, followed by a shot in which workers cut the necks of pigs, which we see as carcasses hanging from an overhead mobile line, slowly moving through stages of slaughter. Here and later, the camera lingers on the slaughtered pig carcasses.

Slaughter is a symbol for what the Hormel workers think is hap-

10. Crowdus and Porton, "American Dream," 37.

pening to them. The issue for the people of Austin is summarized in a sub-title: Hormel has just announced a wage cut, the first of several that would occur during the eighties. Here, as in *Harlan County*, Kopple uses subtitles as well as voiceovers to provide information, but in *American Dream*, even more than in *Harlan County*, in addition to locating the audience in terms of the screen time and place, these printed words within the frame function as a Brechtian device to interrupt our empathy for the strikers and thus distance us from the on-screen men and women.

Temporarily oriented by one of these signs to the date, December, 1984, we and the Hormel workers are introduced to Ray Rogers, a union strategist whom the local union of meat packers hires to help them retain their wages. Slowly and unobtrusively, the camera examines Rogers, much as it might introduce an unknown figure in a fiction film. The film moves quickly from his hiring to the local union leaders' presentation of Rogers, to shots of a notably short, rousing speech by Rogers, to Rogers on television saying that he is going to show workers how to fight back against the bosses at Hormel. If Rogers's role seemed suspect to both the Hormel workers and the film audience when he arrived, it is quickly clarified: his distinction is his knowledge of media, and he will use television, radio, and the press to pressure the Hormel executives and, later, to fight the national union. An unidentified Hormel executive describes Rogers's approach as "nasty." This conclusion is illustrated immediately by a shot from the Hormel executives' point of view of women strikers wearing pig-nose masks. The opening segment ends with overhead shots of half a dozen Hormel bosses; we overhear one of these "suits" saying, "I think it's tragic because the only thing they can do is destroy their own lives." From the dramatic irony of these words, *American Dream* cuts to a shot of hogs hanging on the assembly line, this time with their entrails hanging out. A metaphor is placed in motion.

*American Dream* becomes more complex in its next segment when the camera goes to Washington, D.C., to record a meeting with the United Food and Commercial Workers, the parent union. The dominant figure here is Lewie Anderson, director of the meat-packing division of the national union. Anderson accuses Rogers of "shooting a line of shit" and tells representatives of the Austin local that "they'll lose bigger with

Rogers." The triangle of oppositions is now complete. With media strategist Rogers's encouragement, the local Austin union continues to strike against wage decreases; the national union, in the voice of Anderson, insists that all packing houses have to have the same wages, which means the local should not stand on its position; the corporate bosses are unrelenting in the wage cuts they demand, and start to hire scabs. This is the locus of conflict for the film, complete with male figures of personal power who capture the camera's attention and draw the camera to images of escalating violence of word and deed. At this point, *American Dream* does not seem very different from many fiction films in its basic structure. Rogers is a somewhat ambiguous hero, the obstinate corporate bosses are the bad guys, and Anderson initially seems to be on the side of this corporate evil.

Several differences emerge between *American Dream* and an imaginable fictional version of its events. First, whatever the resemblance of Rogers and Anderson as well as less featured men and women to film characters, these are real people whose lives continue when the camera is not on them. We may imagine the worlds of film characters beyond the margins of the screen in any fiction film, but such imagined worlds cannot be witnessed by others; in *American Dream* the events recorded—as well as, obviously, those unrecorded as life goes on—do occur and can be accounted for by a range of nonfilmic means, including, especially, human memory. History leaves its clues, its markings; film sometimes destroys them.

Second, and perhaps most important, as *American Dream* continues, as time goes on and as we are given more information about each group, its leaders, and their positions, the situation becomes increasingly complex and, paradoxically, simple. Each attempt at resolution of the conflict among Hormel, the national union, and the local union complicates the picture more for the viewer. In contrast to *Harlan County*, in Austin as it appears on the screen, there is no hint of possible change in the position of the corporate heads. Nor is there hope for any kind of negotiations. The workers can either accept a decrease in wages of two dollars an hour as offered by Hormel or be replaced. The intervention of the national union initially seems clearly wrong because Kopple has introduced us first and empathetically to the local workers and their local union, which is at odds with the national union. But Kopple allows us to see and hear the national union's concern for continuity as a substantive issue and this, in turn, allows the audience to recognize the complexities in the conflict.

Kopple pays persistent attention to Rogers and Anderson, but from subtly variant angles. Rogers is initially more attractive in his physical presence and enthusiastic optimism; Lewie (as he is most often called) seems consistently unappealing in visual terms and alienating in his words and gestures to both the local workers and film viewers. Rogers looks buoyant and resilient where Lewie is slow, unforthcoming, and dogmatic. When, in a frame within a frame, Rogers appears on television claiming that Lewie is lying, we want to believe Rogers. But *American Dream* does not allow that to happen or at least to happen easily. Lewie, we are eventually shown, is not a corporation pawn; his fire flames against Hormel and for the national union, and he knows what most of the local workers do not: "When you have to go into a strike it's all out war."

Which side should we be on? The workers who stick with the local union's position, as led by Rogers, at the end of the film have to move and find new jobs. Lewie, enraged by Rogers and the Austin local, screams out, "Don't lay this shit on me." The national union people mock the locals. The corporate executives angrily disallow further protest. The locus of power within the world filmed is clear; it is in the hands of the Hormel corporate bosses from beginning to end. What is not so clear is the right course of action for the local workers. The introduction of Rogers, the supportive outsider, mediates my empathy for the local workers, but not in a consistent direction; uncertain about who Rogers is and what his interests are, I cannot empathize with the striking workers as readily as I could with the striking miners. Alienated by Lewie's rigid rhetoric and arrogance, but caught by his argument for the necessity of national-union consistency and by his opposition to the corporate bosses, I neither see a right resolution within the historical world of the film nor can I easily imagine one.

In *Harlan County*, I think I know who is telling the truth; certainly, I do not trouble about it. I get angry at those whom the film suggests (and I believe) are dishonest. But as Linda Williams suggests, the kind of political truth that is the meat of many nonfiction films is an easy victim for a deconstructive analysis.[11] Any filmmaker can set our sympathies fully in line with the black-lung infested, starving, exploited coal miners of Kopple's *Harlan County*, by shooting some scenes and not others, editing so that we only see and hear the bosses as monsters. (This is not to deny the real awfulness of the behavior of the Duke Power bosses, but to suggest that another filmmaker could reshoot these executives so that they would appear to be rational men choosing what is best for everyone.)

In *American Dream*, I am less certain of where truth lies and, more basically, of how and where it counts. I am drawn to the shots of the striking Hormel workers dancing and making music, and I am touched by the accompanying comment from one of them, "We did what we liked to do [during the strike], worked on each other's cars, helped build houses, cooked together and so on." This memory is one version, perhaps the dominant version for some workers and spectators, of the American Dream. The more irritating, internally oppositional, contingent positions of Kopple's film, are, perhaps, closer to some authentic historical truth. The camera's insistent, unrelieved attention is divided equally among boring union meetings, unattractive leaders, sentimental visions of an idyllic American community, and tough images of workers who accept the national union contract in order to go back to work with some dignity. None of this is easily reducible to a program or position. Nor is any of this easy to dismiss and forget. In terms I borrow from Mikhail Bakhtin, these attributes make *American Dream* a more authentic, truthful film, because any historical moment in any particular place is continually mobile and heterglot, especially in moments of crisis.[12] Without denying the existence of referents, indeed by insisting that any authentic knowledge of the world is replete with contradictions, *American Dream* is genuinely dialogic. It represents the world with several of its alternative voices talking at once, and no voice better or truer than another. In contrast, much as I like what I hear in *Harlan County*, what I hear there is a monologue, and as a form of representation, a monologue cannot provide the whole truth of any world.

11. Linda Williams, "Truth, History and the New Documentary," *Film Quarterly* 46:3 (Spring 1993), 11–20, esp. 11–13.

12. M. M. Bakhtin, *The Dialogic Imagination*, trans. Michael Holquist and Caryl Emerson (University of Texas Press, 1981). Terms such as *heteroglossia* and *dialogic* appear in many places in Bakhtin's writings and are defined and explained in an excellent glossary to this volume, written by its editors.

How much does this matter? Is there anything wrong with a film and its makers taking a position? Can we not argue better, and think more knowingly, when a filmmaker makes her position clear rather than when she blurs or complicates her stance towards her material, deliberately or not? Before I grapple further with these questions, I want to draw on four additional films, all of which fall between the extremes I have thus far described and each of which offers a distinct angle of vision on these problems of the relations of nonfiction films to each other and to annoying questions about how nonfiction film relates to the world before it, complete with its ambiguities.

Since I first started thinking about these films as an arbitrary set (including the films by Deren and Kopple already discussed) I have imagined a chart that depicts these films in relation to categories and in relation to each other. The chart image looks like this:

ABSTRACT/NONREFERENTIAL    CONCRETE/REFERENTIAL
POETRY                                          PROSE
AHISTORICAL                              HISTORICAL

    *Meshes of the Afternoon*         *American Dream*
      *Choreography*           *Harlan County*
*The Very Eye of Night*

                     *Joyce at 34*

        *Clothelines*

*Film About a Woman Who . . . .*

              *Paris Is Burning*

This visual image of the relations of these films in critical terms may suggest why I find it difficult to organize nonfiction film in terms of genre; their positions differ in subtle ways that are too many and varied to comprise one genre, yet too few in my limited sampling to confirm several genres. There may well be a nonfiction genre of social-protest films that would include *Harlan County, U.S.A.* and *American Dream*, and possibly but not necessarily, *Paris Is Burning*. Such a genre would not be gender specific; it would include, for example, most of the films of Peter Davis, one of the people from whom Kopple learned her art. Several critics accept a genre of "Women's Personal Life Films" which includes biographies, autobiographies, interviews with women, diaries, and confessions. All eleven films I discuss here, or perhaps all but Deren's films, might be included in this genre. The elements I note at the top of the chart are not, however, typical genre attributes. Nor are these or other nonfiction films by women made to fill and challenge genre attributes. They cannot be when, as is essential for a nonfiction film, context and event—even invented event—precede style and frame.

Additionally, there is the problem of shift. Dependent on a range of particulars that comprise the context of my seeing at any moment, all of the films shift positions to the right and left. For example, the next film I want to discuss, *Joyce at 34*, by Joyce Chopra and Claudia Weill, seemed to be unhesitatingly realistic, boldly informative, and courageously feminist when I saw it in the mid-seventies; in subsequent screenings at different universities on different coasts, I found it to be lyrical and provocatively ambiguous in its double-voicedness. After several similar films over a decade or more, *Joyce at 34* became for me somewhat of a period piece, but it became new again on a recent viewing. The opening shots—a profile of a pregnant woman, then the seemingly enormous globe of two thirds of her belly in close-up—conjoined with a woman's voiceover, "I'm also a filmmaker" and "I have no belief that the child's going to come," encapsulate several of the tensions of the film. The "I" is Joyce Chopra, a woman filmmaker who is pregnant and delivers her baby on-camera during the first moments of this thirty-five-minute movie. The opening lines are hers; the opening shots are of her. This is not trivial. The woman holding the camera, working the camera, is Claudia Weill, herself a filmmaker and a friend of Chopra's. This film is not, then, exactly what it might seem to be: a typical autobiographical seventies film about women's issues, including woman's body, mothering, and work, that still submits to the conventional male gaze. I can see *Joyce at 34* in this limited, predictable way, as critic E. Ann Kaplan does, and thus use it as an example of "boring realism;" the last two decades have, after all, seen women producing dozens of films that include never-before-seen cinema-verité shots of birthing, nursing, and mothering. Why should I watch this version, again, in 1994?

Because there is at least one alternative way of viewing *Joyce at 34* that transcends the record of pregnancy, labor, and mothering. In this alternative reading, this film does not bore me; it itches at my memory. From the first shots to the last, I am aware of some uncertainty about the film's point of view. This happens because I am aware that it is Claudia Weill, a woman, a filmmaker and Joyce's friend, who is shooting the film. On most screenings I find this to be continually revealing of a dialogue between two women about being a women in the particular Western world in which they live. The familiar profile image of a pregnant woman is the first image of the film, the only image that is conventional, the only image that is consistent with the male gaze. *Joyce at 34* contrasts that familiar first shot with the image of a great global mound of pregnancy, an image of notable intimacy; it is the image to which you awake if you are a woman and nine months pregnant. It is also the image and event that, paradoxically, separates the two women (as with the two women in Weill's feature film *Girlfriends*) and unites them as codirectors of this show.

Men, including Joyce's husband, the father of the baby, exist in the margins of this movie. In *Joyce at 34*, women film and women fill the screen, from the shots of delivery in which the frame appears insufficient to capture the event, to the hovering presence of Joyce's mother, to subsequent images of Joyce's baby as she appears as a little girl. To be sure, the filmic conventions, when watched from the perspective of the nineties, are familiar: fifties music from Joyce's memories of her sixteenth birthday party; still photographs that are Joyce's and the film's archive; unexplained dislocations of time and space—all these are used to capture Joyce's premdeveloping past and the acts of remembering that accompany having a baby, perhaps especially a baby girl. The filmic records of the birth itself and the images of subsequent debates among groups of women about women's obligations to mothering versus working outside the home are also familiar. Made in 1972, *Joyce at 34* now seems almost amusingly like a draft of the climactic episodes of the prime-time series, *Murphy Brown*.

The conventional living-room realism of *Murphy Brown* is not, however, the realism of *Joyce at 34*. Chopra and Weill's "realism" is, ironically, self-conscious and is contested by Joyce's knowledge and ours that her filmmaker friend is filming her. Kaplan dismisses *Joyce at 34* as a typical woman's autobiography shot in mainstream realistic terms. I screen the film with a woman friend and puzzle over Kaplan's claim because what I see and hear is a biography as much or more than it is an autobiography, a dialogue playfully masquerading as a monologue until neither author can resist any longer the admission of the filmic game to the film text.[13]

That *Joyce at 34* is a doubly authored film may not be evident on first viewing for much of the movie, but this knowledge is finally unavoidable and important. Immediately after we see Joyce with her baby in a doctor's office, a scene in which the doctor talks disapprovingly about the detachment of babies from mothers in American culture, the film cuts to shots of Joyce working as a film director with another woman behind the camera. "I feel really good working with Claudia," Joyce says to the camera held by co-director Claudia Weill. The next shot is taken through the glass of a telephone booth in which Joyce is telling someone that for the first time her little girl cried at the presence of a stranger. This has meaning, even if we have not read Freud and Lacan. For the child to cry she must recognize the strangeness, the otherness, of the "stranger." For Joyce to acknowledge her pleasure in working with Claudia is, similarly, to acknowledge her separateness from Claudia and from her child.

We have not escaped to a seamless real world. We watch this film, a mediated representation of a number of experiences that happened in front of a camera, from a significant distance. If in its cheap, grainy texture and thin range of tone, its abrupt cuts and its polyphony, it seems exemplary of cinema-verité, it is cinema-verité telling us of the partialness of its reality, its truths. When Joyce announces to us at the end of the film that she does not want to have another baby because she cannot work and have more than one child, we know that this, too, is only one of several truths. We know this not only because Joyce hedges, but because the camera presses her, brings us so close to her that her face becomes a mask, her words an announcement. Because of the explicitness of the close-up, we are reminded that Joyce's final statement is public, not a confession privately shared. As Roland Barthes claims in "The Face of Garbo," the close-

13. E. Ann Kaplan, *Women and Film* (Methuen, 1983), 128–29. Kaplan is right that the subjects of *Joyce at 34* (and, I might add, of *Murphy Brown*) are middle-class. This does not mean, however, as Kaplan implies, that Joyce, her family, and friends are boring, any more than the film treatment is boring.

up does not reveal, it disguises the self. Chopra and Weill are not having an intimate conversation, nor are they in a consciousness raising group. They are making a film.

I imagine *Clotheslines* as the film Chopra might have made when she returned to filmmaking.[14] In actuality, *Clotheslines* is a film of the eighties made by Roberta Cantow, but this does not change my thought. I see and hear *Clotheslines* as inseparable from the women's movement in a dozen recognizable ways, none of which are pedantic or trivial. Alan Rosenthal, editor of *The Documentary Conscience*, celebrates the appearance in the seventies of new films by women; he stresses particularly what he calls "revelation documentaries," films "shaped as investigations, diaries, portraits, autobiographical confessions in which 'family and roots' provide themes."[15] He would doubtless find *Clotheslines* to epitomize this category, although I cannot imagine that he would love this film as I have.

Painting in motion: my memories of *Clotheslines,* like the film's own memories, are of laundry of diverse shapes and colors, carefully pinned and arranged on lines as evidence of the care and skill of the women who did the wash. For thirty minutes the film itself fills my head with memories of late Cézanne, a bit of Vermeer, some Hopper, the thought of Rothko, all the while distracting me with a soothing female voiceover that recalls the laundry dancing on the line as the wind filled up the legs of the bloomers. The voice remembers more: "Two young blades passing by tipped their hats [to the bloomers on the line]. I always had a lovely picture in my mind of the two young blades showing their respect for the female outline."

This is a film of personal and not-so-personal history. The narrator speaks always in the first person, and is always female, but, with no transitional gesture and without need of chronology, the voices change, returning periodically to what may be the original narrator. Time moves from the black and white of prewar laundry lines to postwar pastels and primary reds on shirts and panties of the fifties and on to a laundromat. Locations shift more emphatically: lines strung between the muted red brick walls of urban courtyards attach one family to another; lines hung

14. Joyce Chopra made *Smooth Talk* in 1985.

15. Alan Rosenthal, "Introduction," *The Documentary Conscience* (University of California Press, 1980), 17.

from house to trees swing in the mid-space of rural farmyards; a clothes-line in an anonymous Indian village displays clothes similar to those we have previously seen washed on a rock in a river that could be in India or China, West Africa or Eastern Europe. These are the clotheslines of the world, and they bind women together across cultures and generations. The faces and bodies of women, washing, hanging, removing laundry are stained by their labor, but the fatigue of these nameless women is van-quished by their pride in the skill with which they hang their laundry and by the satisfaction of their curiosities, a fulfillment available both from the conversations that punctuate each pinched sock and sheet to the abundant social cues in the laundry itself. Judgments were made, too, one narrator recalls: the possible humiliation was beyond endurance if your neighbors witnessed your child's shirt, hung to dry, with a spot in view. The narrator's warning refocuses a particularly brilliant shot of vibrant colors and sexy shapes, returning the image from abstraction to shirts and skirts and bras and pants and sheets and pillowcases. The essentialism implicit in these linkages troubles me, as gender essentialism always does, but on first view-ing I liked these commonalities among women more than I disliked the political position they imply.

Clotheslines is found art and found history and found folklore. A sun-drenched profile shot of a stunning, dark-haired woman hanging her laundry on the roof of a city building, sits gently before us as the narrator proclaims that with each laundry there is "a new beginning and a fresh start." "And when I hang up the clothes," she continues, "I feel connected to all other women." On these clotheslines, in these images of women washing and drying and ironing the things we wear, are the memories and knowledges that awaken women in ways that are rare in conventional film. The camera finds a mother holding her young daughter in her arms; then, sensing sentimentality, Cantow finds a different kind of connection in the water dripping from one tenement clothesline to a line on a floor below. I remember the slogan "the personal is political," and I want to stop the pro-jector and call my mother.

Clotheslines is a memory film, a reminder of competencies that go unacknowledged and losses that will not be replaced in the spinnings of our washers and dryers. My children have no inheritance here. I know just

how to fit a full basket of wet clothes on any decent-length line, how to
double the socks and loop the sheets and let the collars turn to the sun.
*Clotheslines* reminds me of all the "woman's" skills that are slowly being
lost and replaced by activities that are more mechanical and less social.
Living in Madrid a few years ago, I was disconcerted and subsequently
pleased to find a neighbor across the seventh floor who shared my clothes-
line. We had to negotiate the push and pull and wet and dry of our laun-
dries. How proud I was of my skills with a clothespin, how grateful I was
for my neighbor's help with my meager spoken Spanish. How ashamed I
am of the town to which I returned in Southern California, a town where
clothes could dry on a line in minutes almost every day of the year were it
not for a law that forbids outdoor clotheslines. No threats to privacy in my
hometown.

In the map of nonfiction movies I made for this essay, I had a
difficult time placing *Clotheslines*. It is a film about something, about how
some women live portions of their daily lives, about the values of
community and the loss of community, about rituals in families and in
communities that are maintained mainly by women. *Clotheslines* does
ethnography and social protest and personal and public, individual and
community, revelation. At the same time, in its expressionism, in its
photographic representations of clothes freed from their wearers but tied
to a line, and its painterly reminders of bodies in every size and shape, and
thus in its clean affirmations of lust and desire and of line and color, and
of voices sweet and croaking, this film is art. Here, surely, unhesitatingly,
is a nonfiction film that is undoubtedly true but whose truth is not its issue.
This is a film that embraces possibilities of filmmaking as seemingly
different as those of Deren and Kopple and peacefully conjoins art and
social history. And I am not irritated.

Once, this was to be the end of this essay. In that version, I would
have already talked about Yvonne Rainer's *Film about a Woman Who . . .*
and Jennie Livingston's *Paris Is Burning* as examples of full-length, fully
complicated nonfiction films that draw from oppositional traditions of nonfiction film and counter any idea of pure categories or genres. I would then
have turned to *Clotheslines* to demonstrate how a nonfiction film that

relies on reference to a real, historical world can also use images and words of ordinary life to express intangible ideas and feelings. The flaw in this plan is that it would avoid and not comprehend that irritation with nonfiction films from which *Clotheslines* exempts itself.

*Paris Is Burning* and *Film about a Woman Who* . . . not only provoke a sufficient quotient of irritation but reframe the initial questions of this essay. Because it is not without hesitation that I include these films under the heading "nonfiction," they return me to my opening puzzlement about differences between fiction and nonfiction in film and the importance or lack thereof of this distinction. Both these films have an uneasy and provocative relationship to ideas of truth. Both films violate my hypothesis that a distinction of fiction films is to be found in the defining presence of actors, of men and women who play roles that create personas other than their own. In nonfiction films persons present themselves to a camera or allow themselves to be recorded by a camera. This distinction is challenged in *Paris Is Burning*, a film in most ways obviously nonfiction, by the dominant activity recorded, that of gay black men presenting themselves as selected types of women at events in an African-American community that are called "balls." My hypothesis that acting defines fiction film is similarly challenged in *Film about a Woman Who* . . . by the deliberate role-playing by actors and the director, and the multiple re-creations of moments that have shaped Rainer's understandings of love and eros. There is, however, a paradox in considering these films in apposition: the performers in *Paris Is Burning* fervently claim that while their makeup and costumes and walks and postures may all seem to be pretense, they are not masquerading for the sake of spectacle but to become who they "really" are. The players in *Film about a Woman Who* . . . deliberately perform in a flattened and mechanical tonality of voice and gesture, a kind of antirealism that is its own brand of theatricality. Opposite means— intense affect and absence of affect—express a desire to replace the catharsis of classical drama with a gnawing unease about the stability of identity.

Neither of these films is easily summarized, but for somewhat different reasons. *Paris Is Burning* is an interpretive account of a set of spectacles performed by gay black men. Like Kopple's films, *Paris Is Burning* is divided by graphic subtitles into sections. In this case, the titles orient a presumed naïve viewer to a series of recurrent events in the black community. Knowledgeable persons call these events "balls." Balls provide an opportunity for black men, especially gay black men, to recreate themselves in the image of their desires. Elaborate makeup, wigs, and costumes, distinctive gestures (suggestive of a Brechtian "gest"), and highly stylized walks contribute to the creation of characters who perform before audiences. The structure of a ball is much like that of a beauty contest: the contestants promenade before an audience and are judged on several counts relevant to performance qualities, to specialized themes, and to extraordinary names: "Shade," "Luscious Body," "Schoolboy/Schoolgirl Realness," "Venus Xtravaganza," "Movie Stars," "Queens," and "Models." Winners receive prizes. The key ideas and categories of the film are usually spoken aloud but are also emphasized by the film's flashing of the graphic subtitles which are remarkably unparallel and inconsistent in type. The name of one of the narrators, "Dorien Corey," is one of the first signs flashed, but so is a sign labeled "Categories"; signs about aspects of the phenomenon—"Reading," "Voguing"—are crucial to the film. These literary signs fragment the action and remind us that we are watching a film. In *Paris Is Burning*, however, subtitles do not simply provide information as they interrupt our engagement in the film; they also provide a vocabulary specific to the world of this film, a vocabulary that aids us in understanding what we are seeing and hearing and seduces us to continue watching because of the challenge arising from our inability to predict the next title.

*Paris Is Burning* is comprised of fragments of actual balls, footage and commentary on backstage preparations, interviews with club owners, contestants, and producers of balls. A carnivalesque narrator/raisonneur intermittently addresses the camera to explain or reflect on what we see and hear. He functions as a guide through this maze of fabricated society. Where this narrator draws us into the world of the film, numerous subtitles emphasize topics to which the narrator is also drawing our attention. *Paris is Burning* records a theatrical world that combines the cabaret hyperbole of Europe in the late twenties and thirties with the devices of alienation theorized by Brecht in and for that era. In addition to its uses of graphics, Livingston's film is similar in approach to *Harlan County, U.S.A.* in the intensity of human energy captured in sound and image. Like *Harlan County*, *Paris Is Burning* also has a buoyancy, inherent in its context, that makes the difficult lives of its subjects all the more painful to witness.

*Film about a Woman Who* . . . is in its look and sound as different from *Paris Is Burning* as a film could be. Rainer's film instantly seems sufficiently ungrounded and nonnarrative to fit Deren's description of authentic experimental cinema. It takes some time to recognize the continuity of the film's interest in the difficulties of a relationship between a woman and a man, and, contiguously, the relations of these two to a child and to the male lover of the man, and, possibly, of the man to another woman. The nonnarrative "structure of feeling"—to borrow from Raymond Williams—that in most films underlies a series of events shaped by interlocking rational causes and motives, here becomes explicit, while narrative events and characterizations take the hidden site formerly claimed by structures of feeling. What we see in graphic titles and black-and-white images of blank-faced men and women are not causal narrative elements of their relationships but the hidden centers that are requisite to conventional melodramas. The thoughts that typical film characters would only hint at, thoughts that the spectator is expected to project, are in Rainer's film literally and explicitly announced in voiceovers, depicted in images, or spelled out in graphics. This is oddly similar, to my eye and ear, to the runway performances, the objectification of desires, in *Paris Is Burning*.

These two films share a surface frankness about sexuality; both films address the erotic, however, with conventions that deny the spectator a role as voyeur. Both films fulfill Deren's call for presentation of inner consciousness and reaccentuated or created contexts. Neither film is without reference to the ordinary world: the film that looks and sounds most removed from ordinary life, *Film about a Woman Who* . . . begins and ends on a beach and reminds us of the most mundane feelings of love, jealousy, and rejection. *Paris Is Burning* achieves a similar result by an opposite combination of seemingly unexceptional filmic techniques with situations and individuals that are sufficiently disorienting in themselves to undo the notorious passivity of the film spectator.

A key sequence in *Film about a Woman Who* . . . begins with a female voiceover commenting, "With only one other she might have to reveal something about herself. With an audience of two, I become a performer." The screen fills with a tableau of a woman in a fur coat, another, simply dressed, girlish woman, and a young man. All look straight ahead, which as the camera slowly pans before them means each is looking at the camera at some point. Seated on a couch, the only visible object in the frame, the figures hold themselves and move without any individuating gestures; faces are strikingly absent of movement. Accompanied by intermittent overtracking sounds and comments, the young man and young woman help the woman in the fur coat complete a series of actions: they take off her coat, then her wig, her blouse (she wears no bra or slip), her shoes. At this point, all three stand, the man pulls a waist string on the woman's skirt, and removes several of her bracelets. A period of silence and stillness is followed by a cut in which the man now stands behind the couch and caresses the woman who has been stripped and now lies naked on the couch. The hand of the second woman lies still on the couch, a reminder of her presence.

In the next several minutes, the sequence I have just described is recomposed, augmented, and transformed. In one shot, the same woman is lying on the couch but with her skirt on; in a subsequent shot the woman of the fur coat is standing and the man is sitting on the same couch. We see her only from the waist down as he, with his cheek pressed against her hip, very slowly pulls down her long, black-lace underpants. We see her frontally naked except for the continuously changing area covered by her panties as the man pulls them down. An uncomfortably long cut to black interrupts the scene; when the camera finds its light and its personas, the underpants are at just the point where they were before the blackout and the man is finishing lowering them to the woman's ankles. Everything is the same as previously except that the second woman has reappeared and is sitting, motionless, on the couch as the man slowly pulls the first woman's panties back up her legs. This reverse motion appears to be at once a matter of filmic technique and of completion of a ritual without completion as sexual intercourse or as voyeurism. Thinking back to Deren's comments cited earlier, I can read this scene as the imaging of the (personified) camera's desire.

Breaking its previously frustrating stillness, the camera slowly zooms in to the woman's pubic area, which the man re-covers with the woman's underwear as if in competition with the camera, and perhaps with the woman herself, for control over this crucial domain. The next several cuts, which together complete this sequence, include close-ups and extreme close-ups of a woman's face covered with patches on which messages in typescript appear. The woman's desire to reveal herself has been met physically by the man. There is more than the surface of the body to reveal, however. Close-ups of several of the patches indicate that they are the externalizations of the woman's inner thoughts. One message contains a request for permission: "Do you mind if I indulge myself for a few minutes and recall those things which make me laugh all over?" Another patch declares, "I'm totally intoxicated with you." As the camera vertically pans the woman's face, exploring without apparent discovery, it completes its examination with a patch that reads, "It all adds up to one thing. I love you George—." In their apparent directness and emotional clarity, these written messages seem the opposite of the absence of evident feeling in the physical acts of the segment. By separating the words and images of erotic love from each other, emotion appears to be absent. In juxtaposition, however, we can conclude that, were the actions of words and the actions of hands and bodies together, they would match. Perhaps the goal here is intimacy.

Twenty minutes later, at the end of the film, over a visual image of sea and shore that greatly resembles shots early in the film, another graphic message appears on the screen: "She sighs with relief. Now that she knew the truth about her feelings she was free to love him again." The confession, made in the third person, is depersonalized. The private becomes public but remains tantalizing. I am uncertain what "the truth about her feelings" is. I earnestly wish the film would include me and make me laugh all over. And I wonder of what I might have to be stripped in order to laugh at all.

I am not sure that I believe this unnamed woman about whom Rainer's film has been made, whose acts are, by the film's authority, absent. Secretly, I suspect spuriousness, and this leads me to interrogate my own resistances. Is this truth about her feelings a psychoanalytic breakthrough achieved through the disassociation of words and images? If *Film about a Woman Who . . .* is the representation of the subconscious, of the ephemeral "I" implied by the form of the film and by the meanings of words made available by the film, then where am I in relation to the film's discoveries? The process of film as the subject of film that Deren proposed is extended here to include the process of self-analysis as process, but with a goal: truth. I am uncertain what truth means here, other than a fragment of understanding of how a particular person has made sense of her particular history so that she can live with it. Perhaps this is sufficient. But we cannot be, fully, an audience for that history.

I am equally uncertain about my place in relation to *Paris Is Burning*. I know that I am an invited voyeur and I know that what I have watched is the enactment of a wish fulfillment that has a social and political as well as a personal author. Where does this film position me, then, if central to the wish of its personas is the desire to be a white woman? *Paris Is Burning* instructs anyone who is willing to listen and watch, how to read its gay black world; but if we cannot be of this world, as I, a white female, cannot, what do I do with the vocabulary I have learned, except show off in a bit of radical chic?

These uncertainties are elements of my irritation with nonfiction film. My irritation lies in my insecurity about my relation to the world projected. If, as in the case of *Paris Is Burning*, the film teaches me how to read its text, I avoid irritation momentarily, but if my understanding of the text is that the figure I see on the screen is not pretending to be someone or something but is making himself able to be, say, a blonde woman model, where am I in relation to her? The "idea of realness," one person says in *Paris Is Burning*, is to look and act as much as possible like your straight counterpart. In this context, the idea of realness is not a "take-off" or a "satire." We are not in the world of J. L. Austin and the hyena: in Austin's ordinary, commonsensical world, I can pretend to be a hyena but I cannot become one even if I imitate the hyena's imagined actions. In contrast, in the world of *Paris Is Burning* one can become a more "real" person than one was at another time. I think this means that gender defies common assumptions about truth. This, in turn, suggests that film which rests its authority on truth, in which nonfiction means true, rests on very ambiguous ground. As much as Deren and other experimental filmmakers may wish otherwise, every film has its referents, spurious or authentic.

When I say that I understand what I have called my irritation with nonfiction film to be about the insecurity of how and what I am to understand, I am speaking about the instability of point of view. That a goal of some filmmakers is to disturb the passivity of the spectator, and that one way to accomplish this is to disorient point of view, is a central claim of my book on Robert Altman's films. I have spent enough time in the last fifteen years attempting to accustom friends and students to the promiscuous, unstable points of view characteristic of several of Altman's films that I have a sense of what is, and is not, at stake in the acceptance of the irritating text. With Altman's films, while there is always the risk that the complex surface will only alienate the viewer, there is also the chance that the viewer will return. Because I know Cavell is right, that the world of *Nashville* will always be complete without me, I can come closer and closer to knowing where I am in relation to it.[16] Except for those who already inhabit the world filmed before it is recorded, this security of point of view does not occur in nonfiction films. No matter how many times I see *Film about a Woman Who . . .* or *Paris Is Burning*, I stay at the same cautious, unstable distances from the worlds they project. I must stay there, because the world of nonfiction film dares me to enter my own history: the world of these films is not complete without me. Altman, in framing his films as fiction, makes his work vulnerable only to claims of incomprehensibility or inauthenticity. Nonfiction films rest on the irritating instabilities and possibilities of our real and ordinary lives.

*Thanks to Charles Warren for encouraging "The Toil of [My] Thought," and thanks again to Anise and Tracy for patience under my stress, as well as to Tracy for taking me to the mountains to write and for being here on the shore as this goes to print. Also thanks to Gregory Stephens for research well done and to Jill MacDowell for clearing the way.*

16. See Stanley Cavell, *The World Viewed* (1971; expanded edition, Harvard University Press, 1979), 160.

ELIOT WEINBERGER

# The Camera People

T here is a tribe, known as the Ethnographic Filmmakers, who believe they are invisible. They enter a room where a feast is being celebrated, or the sick cured, or the dead mourned, and, though weighted down with odd machines entangled with wires, imagine they are unnoticed—or, at most, merely glanced at, quickly ignored, later forgotten.

Outsiders know little of them, for their homes are hidden in the partially uncharted rain forests of the Documentary. Like other Documentarians, they survive by hunting and gathering information. Unlike others of their filmic group, most prefer to consume it raw.

Their culture is unique in that wisdom, among them, is not passed down from generation to generation: they must discover for themselves what their ancestors knew. They have little communication with the rest of the forest, and are slow to adapt to technical innovations. Their handicrafts are rarely traded, and are used almost exclusively among themselves. Produced in great quantities, the excess must be stored in large archives.

They worship a terrifying deity known as Reality, whose eternal enemy is its evil twin, Art. They believe that to remain vigilant against this evil, one must devote oneself to a set of practices known as Science. Their cosmology, however, is unstable: for decades they have fought bitterly among themselves as to the nature of their god and how best to serve him. They accuse each other of being secret followers of Art; the worst insult in their language is "aesthete."

Ethnos, "a people"; graphe, "a writing, a drawing, a representation." Ethnographic film, then: "a representation on film of a people." A definition without limit, a process with unlimited possibility, an artifact with unlimited variation. But nearly a hundred years of practice have considerably narrowed the range of subjects and the forms of representation. Depending on one's perspective, ethnographic film has become either a subgenre of the documentary or a specialized branch of anthropology, and it teems with contention at the margins of both.

Cinema, like photography sixty years before, begins by making the familiar strange: In 1895 the citizens of La Ciotat observed the arrival of a train with indifference, but those who watched Louis Lumière's version of the event, L'Arrivée d'un Train en Gare, reportedly dove under their seats in terror. In one sense, this was the purest nonfiction film, the least compromised representation of "reality": the passengers walking blankly by Lumière's camera, not knowing that they are being filmed—how could they know?—are the first and, with a few exceptions, the last filmed people who were not actors, self-conscious participants in the filmmaking. In another sense, the film was pure fiction: like Magritte's pipe, the audience in their panic had intuitively grasped that This is not a train.

Recapitulating photography, film's second act was to make the strange familiar. In the same year as Lumière's thrilling train, Félix-Louis Regnault went to the West Africa Exposition in Paris to film a Wolof woman making a ceramic pot. It is Regnault however, not Lumière, who is considered the first ethnographic filmmaker. The reason is obvious: the "people" represented by ethnography are always somebody else. We, the urban white people, held, until recently, the film technology and the "scientific" methodology to record and analyze them: the non-Westerners and a few remote white groups. Moreover, according to our myth of the Golden Age, they lived in societies which had evolved untold ages ago and had remained in suspended animation until their contact with, and contamination by *us*. Ethnographic filmmaking began, and continues as, a salvage operation, as Franz Boas described anthropology. Film, said Regnault, "preserves forever all human behaviors for the needs of our studies." Oblivious to such hyperbole (and formaldehyde), Emilie de Brigard, a historian of the genre, writes that this is the "essential function" of ethnographic film, that it remains "unchanged today."

Where travelers had gone to collect adventures, missionaries to collect souls, anthropologists to collect data, and settlers to collect riches, filmmakers were soon setting out to collect and preserve human behaviors: the only good Indian was a filmed Indian. Within a few years of Regnault's first effort, anthropologists were taking film cameras into the field for their studies, and movie companies were sending crews to strange locales for popular entertainment. It is a curiosity of that era that the two polar allegorical figures in the history of early cinema, the Lumières ("Realism") and Méliès ("Fantasy") were both engaged in shooting such exotica.

By the mid-1920s the representation of other people had evolved into three genres. At one extreme, the anthropological film, largely concerned, as it is today, with recording a single aspect of a culture (a ritual, the preparation of a food, the making of a utilitarian or sacred object) or attempting some sort of inventory. At the other, the fictional romance featuring indigenous people, such as Méliès's *Loved by a Maori Chieftainess* (1913), shot in New Zealand and now lost, or Edward Curtis's *In the Land of the Head-Hunters* (1914), made among the Kwakiutl. Somewhere in-between was a genre inadvertently named by John Grierson in a 1926 review of Robert Flaherty's second film: "Of course, *Moana,* being a visual account of events in the daily life of a Polynesian youth and his family, has documentary value."

*Documentum,* "an example, a proof, a lesson." Grierson's comment was not inaccurate, but there are few cases where it would not be applicable. Fiction, nonfiction, highbrow and low—much of what any of us know of much of the world comes from film: the daily operations of institutions like the police or the army or the prisons or the courts, life on board on a submarine, how pickpockets work the Paris Métro, how Southern California teenagers mate. Filling the frame of every film, no matter how "fictional," is an endless documentation of its contemporary life: a documentation that becomes most apparent with geographical or chronological distance. A Mack Sennett two-reeler is, for us now, much more than a pie in the face: it is long johns and cranked autos, plump women in impossible bathing costumes, and the implicit Middle American xenophobia in the figure of the crazed mustachioed immigrant anarchist. The ditziest Hollywood production bears a subversive documentary message for viewers in China or Chad: this is what ordinary people in the U.S. have in their house, this is what they have in their refrigerator. Even the most fantastical films "document" their cultures: *Nosferatu* and *The Cabinet of Dr. Caligari* are inextricable from Weimar Germany, Steven Spielberg from Reagan America. Above all—and particularly in the United States—many of the greatest works of the imagination begin with the premise that a universe is revealed in the luminous facts of ordinary life. The most extreme case is America's greatest novel: a cosmology derived from the meticulous details, framed in a slight narrative, of an unheroic, low-caste profession that was considered disgusting at the time: the sea-going blubber-renderers of *Moby Dick*.

But in film it is precisely the fuzzy border between "documentary value" and "documentation" (a proof that is independently verifiable) that has led so many filmmakers and critics into acrimonious philosophical debate and methodological civil wars. *Moana* (1926) is a case in point: the work of a revered totemic ancestor in both the documentary and ethnographic lineages. Shot on the Samoan island of Savaii—"the one island where the people still retain the spirit and nobility of their race"—the film is subtitled *A Romance of the Golden Age*. Moana is played by a Samoan named Ta'avale; his "family" was cast from villagers, based on their looks. They are dressed in costumes that had long since been replaced by Western clothes, their hair is done in similarly archaic, "authentic" styles, and the women, almost needless to say, have been returned to their bare-breasted beauty.

There are scenes of "documentary value": gathering taro roots, setting a trap for a wild boar, fishing with spears in the incredibly limpid water, making a dress from mulberry bark. *Moana* also features what is probably the first boy-climbs-coconut-tree scene—though when the boy reaches the top, Flaherty, long before telephoto lenses, is somehow next to him for a close-up. [Superhuman tree-climbing abilities are a trademark of ethnographic filmmakers. Sixty years later, in *Baka: People of the Rain Forest* (1987), Phil Agland has a long shot of a Baka man gathering honey as he spectacularly climbs a 170-foot tree which stands alone and towers over the rest of the forest. In the next shot, he is seen from above, climbing up toward the camera. As he reaches camera-eye level, where the hives are, the narrator intones "80,000 stinging bees pose a serious threat to his life." Evidently the crew brought along their insect repellent.]

To introduce what he called "conflict" into this portrayal of an utterly idyllic life, Flaherty paid Ta'avale to undergo a painful ritual tattooing which had dropped out of practice a few generations before. (The titles read: "There is a rite through which every Polynesian must pass to win the right to call himself a man. Through this pattern of the flesh, to you perhaps no more than cruel, useless ornament, the Samoan wins the dignity, the character and the fiber which keeps his race alive.") It is the conceit of the film that all we have seen so far "has been preparation for the great event": the climactic scene that intercuts the tattooing, frenetic dancing, and an otherwise unexplained "witch woman." (Moana's tattoo, unfortunately, is visible in the first minute of the film.)

In *Nanook of the North: A Story of Life and Love in the Actual Arctic* (1922) the "chief of the Itiumuits, the great hunter Nanook, famous through all Ungara" is played by an Eskimo named Allakariallak. (The character's name seems to be all-purpose: Flaherty planned to make a movie of the Acoma Indians of the Southwest called *Nanook of the Desert*.) The film is also set in the past, without noting the fact. The harpoons with which these "fearless, lovable, happy-go-lucky Eskimos" hunt walruses had long given way to rifles, and, in that crowd-pleasing scene, the gramophone record which Nanook bites was already a familiar item. Other scenes are transparently staged: the seal with which Nanook struggles (and pulls out of the ice-hole twice) in the famous sequence is obviously Dead on Arrival; the unmenacing "wild wolf" is tugging at a leash; and Nanook's family looks pretty chilly pretending to sleep in the half-igloo Flaherty had ordered constructed for sufficient light and his bulky camera. [Another trope of the genre: Agland—to take him again as a recent example—has his family woken by the rain coming through the leaky roof of their hut.] Again, in *Man of Aran* (1934), Flaherty revived customs extinct for as much as a hundred years, including the shark hunts that are the heart of the film. And again, he was sloppy with details: the cottages, lit by shark-oil lamps, clearly have electric wires running from roof to roof.

Flaherty is well-known for the remark, "Sometimes you have to lie. One often has to distort a thing to catch its true spirit." And his editor, Helen Van Dongen, wrote: "To me Flaherty is not a documentarian; he makes it all up." [It would be interesting to compare the "documentary value" of *Nanook* with a film the professionals would surely dismiss as Hollywood trash, Nicholas Ray's *The Savage Innocents* (1960), which is explicitly set in the 19th century, filmed partially on location, tells the story of a great hunter, Inuk (played by Anthony Quinn—a role that would recycle into Bob Dylan's song, "Quinn the Eskimo") and is full of ethnographic information, including culinary preferences and sexual mores, not found in *Nanook*.]

**Robert Flaherty, *Nanook of the North* (1922)**
**Nanook struggles with a seal under the ice.**

But he didn't have to make it up: the struggle against hunger in the Arctic persisted whether the Eskimos carried harpoons or rifles ("Nanook" later died of starvation on a hunt); the Aran Islanders continued to confront a raging sea even if electricity had replaced shark oil as their source of light; and "conflict" in idyllic Samoa was plain enough at the time in the social tensions caused by the missionaries, merchants, and British colonial administrators—which is the theme of an on-location though strictly Hollywood romance only two years later, W. S. Van Dyke's *White Shadows in the South Seas* (1928), where "the last remnants of an earthly paradise . . . from the morning of civilization" is turned into a squalid honkey-tonk.

The essential and largely hidden "conflict," of course, of any ethnographic film—one that, over the decades, was long denied and then debated—is between the filmmaker and the subject matter. It is curious that, a few years later, in a two-part fictional tale of "Paradise" and "Paradise Lost," F. W. Murnau's exquisite *Tabu* (1931)—a project Flaherty dropped out of—the ship that dooms the lovers' fate, a ship so eerily reminiscent of the plague ship of *Nosferatu*, is named "Moana."

Flaherty, unlike many others to come, spent long periods of time living in the communities he was planning to film. (After ten years in the Arctic, exploring for mineral-ore deposits and making home movies, he persuaded the fur company Revillon Frères to finance *Nanook* as a kind of feature-length commercial.) He was the first to screen the daily rushes for the principals for their comments—a participatory filmmaking that would be abandoned until Jean Rouch revived the practice in the 1950s. Many of his scenes remain astonishingly beautiful, particularly the still-unparalleled shots of the sea crashing against the cliffs, bouncing the canoes and kayaks, exploding through blow-holes (perhaps Flaherty was greater as an oceanographic filmmaker than as an ethnographic one). And, above all, his image of humanness, particularly in *Nanook* and *Man of Aran*—the lone individual and the small community valiantly overcoming the brutalities of their environment—has had universal appeal in a century most notable for the victimization of its masses. [An appeal that even extended to the victimizers: Mussolini gave *Man of Aran* a prize, and Goebbels declared that it exemplified the virtue and spirit of fortitude that Hitler wanted the

German people to possess. (Churchill's favorite films were the Marx Brothers', which may have affected the outcome of the war.) It must be recognized, however, that in certain ethnographic films, the emphases on the courageous individual, the "wisdom of the folk," and the eroticization of the pure "savage" human body are equally characteristic of Fascist art. It's a small leap from Leni Riefenstahl's *Olympiad*—particularly in the former's portrayal of Jesse Owens—to her *Last of the Nuba*.] But in the end, Flaherty belongs most exactly to the popular travelogues and "romances" of the silent era, shot on location with native actors—though his films were less stylized, less narrative, and more naturalistic.

With the advent of sound, the expense and the size of the equipment forced most filmmakers to move the exotic to the backlot, and, far more than Flaherty, make it all up. [Richard Leacock was fond of quoting an old Hollywood manual on lighting: "When shooting Westerns, use real Indians if possible; but if Indians are not available, use Hungarians."] The career of Merian Cooper and Ernest Schoedsack is exemplary: They began with *Grass* (1925), a stirring account of the annual migration by 50,000 Bakhtyari shepherds across the Zardeh Kuh mountains of Turkey and Persia. [It is, by the way, probably the only documentary film to end with an actual document: a notarized letter from the British consul in Teheran stating that the filmmakers were indeed the first foreigners to make the journey.] From Persia they went to Siam to film *Chang* (1927), an action-adventure featuring Lao hill people "who have never seen a motion picture" and "wild beasts who have never feared a rifle." By 1933, Cooper and Schoedsack were directing black-faced extras in their ritual worship of King Kong.


The Depression and the Second World War effectively stopped most ethnographic film production. In 1958, the genre revived with the most successful film of its kind since *Nanook*, and one cast strictly in the Flaherty mold: John Marshall's *The Hunters*. Like Flaherty, Marshall had not been trained as an ethnographer, but had spent years living with the people he filmed, the !Kung Bushmen of the Kalahari Desert in southern

Africa. Like *Nanook* and *Man of Aran*, the film portrays courageous men—
it is always men in these films—surviving in a harsh environment: the
!Kung are a "quiet people" engaged in a "ceaseless struggle" for food in a
"bitter land indeed where all the trees have thorns." Rather than one great
hunter, *The Hunters* has four, whom it follows on a hunt that ends with the
killing of a giraffe. One is "a man of many words and a lively mind," the
"perfect man" for the job of headman; another is "the beautiful," "something of a dreamer" and "a natural hunter"; the third is "a simple kindly
man, an optimist"; and the fourth "forthright and humble." These are types
rather than personalities, and we must take the narrator's characterizations
on faith: in the film the four are indistinguishable.

Like Flaherty, Marshall is impossibly sloppy. Though the hunt, for
some reason, is supposed to take place over thirteen consecutive days, it is
clearly a pastiche of footage taken over many years. Not only does the number of giraffes in the herd they are tracking (seen in long shots) keep
changing, the protagonists themselves are not always the same. And, as
anthropologists have pointed out, !Kung subsistence was based more on
gathering than hunting and, at the time, they had plenty of food. (They
began to face starvation when the South African government put them on
reservations.)

The film is sustained by continual narration. At times the narrator
is a crafty insider ("Kaycho water is always brackish this time of year"; the
kudus—a kind of antelope—are "more restless than usual"; and so on). At
other times, Marshall takes the Voice of God, familiar in most documentaries since the invention of sound, to new heights. Not only does he tell us
what the men are thinking—what one critic has wittily called the telepath-
ic fallacy—we even learn the thoughts and feelings of the wounded giraffe.
("She traveled in an open country with a singleness of mind." Later, she is
"troubled," "too dazed to care," and "no longer has her predicament clearly in mind.") Worst of all, God has been reading Hemingway: "He found
the dung of a kudu. A kudu is a big animal. A kudu would be ample meat
to bring home." The machismo of such spoken prose becomes manifest
when the final killing of the female giraffe is described in terms of gang-rape:
The men "exhausted their spears and spent their strength upon her."

The film ends elevating this false narrative into myth: "And old men remembered. And young men listened. And so the story of the hunt was told." But the heroic exploits incessantly emphasized by the narrator are contradicted by what we are actually seeing in the film. They really are lousy hunters. The one kudu they manage to kill (with an utterly unheroic steel trap) is eaten by vultures and hyenas; only the bones are left for the men to rapaciously gnaw. (What, meanwhile, was the film crew eating?) And when the giraffe (also wounded by a trap) is finally cornered and dying, the men keep throwing their spears and missing. No doubt this is what hunting is actually like: Why then should Marshall insist, in his narration, that these "real" people are as unerring as some Hollywood white rajah of the jungle?

Filmmaker David MacDougall, normally quite strict about these matters, has written that *The Hunters* is "one of the few true ethnographic films we have," "a case of synthesis put to the service of truth." Marshall apparently did not agree. In his later films he abandoned the all-seeing eye of traditional fiction film (when the hunters have supposedly lost the track, for example, the film cuts to a shot that lets us know what the giraffe is up to), filmed single events as they occurred, and most important of all, let his subject matter do most of the talking.

The other celebrated ethnographic film of the era, Robert Gardner's *Dead Birds* (1964), employs many of Flaherty's conventions to produce a kind of anti-*Nanook*: a film that, perhaps inadvertently, is far from ennobling. Shot among the Dani, a previously little-documented group in Western New Guinea, the film is a narrative—based, like Flaherty, on a series of archetypal anecdotes rather than the full-blown dramatic structure and developed characterizations of a "plot"—about a warrior, Weyak, and a small boy, Pua. (The boy-figure in *Moana* is named Pe'a.) The characters do not speak; their actions (and, like *The Hunters*, thoughts) are conveyed to us by a continual narration, spoken by Gardner. Perhaps uniquely in ethnographic films, the narration is delivered in a nervous, unnaturally rapid speech, an edginess that considerably adds to the film's dramatic tensions.

Its unforgettable opening clearly announces some sort of allegory: a very long pan of a hawk flying over the treetops, and the spoken words: "There is a fable told by a mountain people living in the ancient highlands of New Guinea . . ." [It is a convention of the genre: the people are remote and as timeless as geography, but will be revealed to be, in some way, just like us. *Grass* opens by promising us the "Forgotten People" who will unlock the "secrets of our own past." *Nanook* opens by taking us to "mysterious barren lands" that, conversely, are "a little kingdom—nearly as large as England."] The fable is the story of the origin of human mortality: a race between a bird and a snake to determine whether people would die like birds or shed their skins and live forever like snakes. Needless to say, the bird won, and *Dead Birds*, in the Flaherty tradition of portraying man against the odds, was apparently intended as a portrayal of one culture's response to the universal destiny. Gardner writes: "I saw the Dani People, feathered and fluttering men and women, as enjoying the fate of all men and women. They dressed their lives with plumage, but faced as certain death as the rest of us drabber souls. The film attempts to say something about how we all, as humans, meet our animal fate."

What the film actually shows is something quite different. With the exception of one quite powerful funeral scene, *Dead Birds* is not concerned with the effects of human destiny—rites, mourning, grief—but rather its provocation. The Dani were among the last people on earth to engage in a rigidly codified ritual war. (One which finally was ended by the local "authorities" shortly after the film was made.) The men of neighboring villages, separated only by their gardens and a strip of no-man's land, would regularly adorn themselves and gather on a battlefield, fighting (theoretically) until there was one fatal casualty. Revenge for that death would provoke the next battle, and so on forever. An endless vendetta war in a land with plenty of food and no particular differences between the villages; where no territory or plunder was captured; with no mass killings and no deviation from the rules.

In fact—or at least according to the film—revenge was rarely achieved on the battlefield. In the battles themselves there is a great deal of back and forth feints and threats, but no hand-to-hand combat; wounds

THE CAMERA PEOPLE

are mainly inflicted haphazardly in the shower of arrows. The two murders in the film, one for each side, occur when a group of men accidentally comes across someone from the other side: a small boy who wandered off, a man trying to steal a pig at night.

A continual, seemingly senseless war; battles where the two sides engage in menacing rhetoric but do relatively little harm; covert killings; a no-man's land lined with tall watchtowers; daily life in a state of permanent dread. The allegorical import of *Dead Birds* must have been obvious to its viewers in 1964, when the Berlin Wall was still new. The film is hardly a meditation on death at all: if it were it would have presented Dani who had died from childbirth, sickness, accidents, age. Rather it is a feathered and fluttering reenactment of the Cold War that was being prolonged and endured by the drab souls of East and West.

The battle sequences in the film are extraordinary. Gardner was especially fortunate to have mountainous terrain where he could get the aerial perspective to lay out what was, quite literally, the theater of war. A brief telephoto shot of the enemy wildly celebrating the death of the small boy becomes particularly unsettling following the moving, rapidly edited sequence of the child's funeral. (The narrator, as throughout the film, fortunately resists the temptation to editorialize.)

The film, in Flaherty style, occasionally concocts an artificial narrative structure: one set of battle scenes, for example, are intercut with shots of women gathering brine who are supposedly waiting for news of casualties, though there was obviously no second unit on the film. (The battles themselves are pastiches, though this is neither apparent nor explained.) And it is the Flaherty "hook"—the focus on the warrior and the boy—that seems misplaced in the film. We learn next to nothing about Weyak, and Pua, who is presented as a pathetic kid, is essentially irrelevant. Once again, women are far in the background. The cruel Dani practice of cutting off the fingers of young girls when there is a death in the village is mentioned only in passing twice. And Gardner, whose films are full of hands— (Flaherty: "Simply in the beautiful movement of a hand the whole story of a race can be revealed")—only gives us a split-second glimpse of the mutilated fingers of Weyak's wife.

After this, his first important film, Gardner would abandon the Flaherty anecdotal narrative of the hunter/warrior, both epitome and paragon of his people, the boy who wishes to emulate him, and the Western bard who sings his praises. In *Dead Birds*, Weyak is introduced by a shot of his hands, Pua by his reflection in a puddle. In later films, Gardner would devolve an ethnographic cinema based entirely on such telling details and oblique images, films that would pose little difficulty to general audiences accustomed to foreign imports, but which the scientists would find incomprehensible.

In the 1950s ethnographic film became an academic discipline with the usual array of specialist practitioners, pedagogues, and critics. It has always seen itself as besieged on two sides. On one flank, the anthropologists, whose conception of a representation of a people has always emphasized the written meaning of *graphe*—and moreover the fixed singularity of the monograph. (As recently as 1988, filmmaker Timothy Asch was complaining that they "have shown little interest in the potential use of ethnographic film.") On the other flank, the aesthetes, or, as Margaret Mead put it: "There's a bunch of filmmakers now that are saying 'It should be art' and wrecking everything we're trying to do."

To prove their mettle to the anthropologists, ethnographic filmmakers have tended to adopt a more-scientific-than-thou attitude. Asch, in a scary comment, writes, "The camera can be to the anthropologist what the telescope is to the astronomer or what the microscope is to the biologist"—which assumes that the matter on the other side of the ethnographic lens is as imperturbable as galaxies or amoebae. Mead, who shot a great deal of footage in Bali in the 1930s with Gregory Bateson, believed that "objective" filming would replace "subjective" field notes, an idea picked up by David MacDougall who, speaking for the reception side, writes that film speaks "directly to the audience, without the coding and decoding inevitable with written language," a notion disproved by the second screening of Lumière's train. And the main textbook in the field, Karl Heider's *Ethnographic Film* (1976), is an attempt to set "standards" and create a "rational, explicit methodology" for the discipline.

Just what some of them have in mind was first articulated by Mead:

> Finally, the oft-repeated argument that all recording and filming is selective, that none of it is objective, has to be dealt with summarily. If tape recorder, camera, or video is set up and left in the same place, large batches of material can be collected without the intervention of the filmmaker or ethnographer and without the continuous self-consciousness of those who are being observed. The camera or tape recorder that stays in one spot, that is not tuned, wound, refocused, or visibly loaded, does become part of the background scene, and what it records did happen.

Such a utopian mechanism—a panopticon with limitless film—has been extrapolated by critic Walter Goldschmidt into a definition of the genre: "Ethnographic film is film which endeavors to interpret the behavior of people of one culture to persons of another culture by using shots of people doing precisely what they would have been doing if the camera were not there."

The ideal, then, is either a dream of invisibility, or worse, the practice of the surveillance camera. Leaving aside the obvious moral and political questions of surveillance—white folks, as usual, playing God, albeit an immobile one with a single fixed stare—the value of such information could be nothing more than slight. The simplest human events unfold in a tangle of attendant activities, emotions, motivations, responses, and thoughts. One can imagine a !Kung anthropologist attempting to interpret the practices and effects of the American cash economy from footage obtained with the cameras in the local bank.

Such films, amazingly, exist. Among them is *Microcultural Incidents at 10 Zoos* (1971) by Ray Birdwhistell, the inventor of *kinesics*, an analysis of body language. Birdwhistell, who might be one of the dotty anthropologists in Barbara Pym's novels, placed hidden cameras in front of the elephant cages in the zoos of ten countries to discover the national traits of behavior revealed by the way families feed the pachyderms. The resulting film is an illustrated lecture with frame numbers running along the top of screen, instant replays and freeze frames (including one of a kid being slobbered on by Jumbo), and phrases like "for those interested in proximics" or "note how the father places the peanut in the child's hand." Birdwhistell maintains that "there is enough information in one 4-second loop for a day's class in anthropology." His film—which is based on the assumption that a nation can be represented by a few members—demonstrates that Italians feed themselves while feeding elephants, the British give a slight formal bow, the Japanese keep a respectful distance, the Americans are easily distracted, and so forth—in other words, the kind of ethnographic information we get from television comedians. Birdwhistell, most tellingly, becomes completely flustered when he gets to India: there are too many people milling around to sort out, and they don't seem terribly interested. Despite his expertise of "organized patterning" and "gambits of caretaking," it apparently doesn't occur to him that in many parts of India an elephant is far less exotic than a cocker spaniel.

Birdwhistell may be an extreme case, but there are thousands of hours of such "scientific" ethnographic film, stored in archives like the Encyclopedia Cinematographica in Göttingen, covering probably every remaining tribe on earth, and devoted, in David MacDougall's words, to "rendering faithfully the natural sounds, structure and duration of events"—a description best applied to Andy Warhol's *Sleep*. [A recent two-hour Dutch film opened with a five-minute fixed shot of a man hacking away with his machete, and these four sentences of narration, with minute-long pauses between them: "Here is Ano. Here is his wife" (nameless, of course). "They are planting manioc. They live in a hut near their garden patch." I confess I never found out what happened next.]

In many other disciplines—including, recently, anthropology itself—a "faithful rendering" is recognized as being entirely subject to the vagaries of current style and individual taste. (As fiction and documentary films forever demonstrate, there is nothing more unreal than yesterday's realism.) But ethnographic film, unlike other filmmaking, thinks of itself as science, and a set of rules has been laid out in a series of charts by Heider. The ethnographic filmic representation of reality is based on:

(1) "Basic technical competence."

(2) "Minimal inadvertent distortion of behavior" (that is, interaction with the camera crew).

(3) "Minimal intentional distortion of behavior" (staging or reconstructing events).

(4) "Ethnographic presence." (Actually, Heider's most radical dictum: an acknowledgment that there's a filmmaker lurking on the premises.)

(5) Minimal "time distortion" and "continuity distortion." Events must be presented in the order they occurred and ideally in the same duration.

(6) "Fully adequate explanation and evaluation of the various distortions" in accompanying printed material.

(7) "Natural synchronous sound" (as opposed to soundtrack music).

(8) "Optimally demystifying" narration, "relevant to the visual materials."

(9) "Cultural and physical contextualization of behavior."

(10) "Whole bodies." ("Long camera shots which include whole bodies of people are preferable . . . to close-ups of faces and other body parts.")

(11) "Whole acts" (beginning, middle, and end).

(12) "Whole people" (emphasis on one or two individuals rather than "faceless masses").

(13) "Ethnographic understanding" (made by/with a professional).

(14) "Full integration with printed materials."

Adhering to most, but not all, of these dicta is Timothy Asch, one of the most respected of the "scientific" filmmakers. Asch, whose writings display unusual candor, has written: "I was ambitious. I wanted to take film that would be valuable for research as well as for instruction and curriculum development." (Clearly not a dream of making *Citizen Kane*, but then ethnographic filmmakers, with the exceptions of Rouch and Gardner, notably rarely or never, in their voluminous writings, mention any films outside of the genre. Apparently they don't go to the movies like the rest

of us.) The kind of film he wants is spelled out elsewhere: a scholarly pill
capable of being semi-sweetened for the masses:

> By focusing on the actions of a few people engaged in activities
> relevant to the research of the anthropologist, and by leaving the
> camera running for long uninterrupted periods, the resulting
> footage is likely to be valuable for research. With the addition of
> a few distant location shots and some cutaways, as well as a few
> rolls of film related to a script, the footage should be equally valu-
> able as a resource for editing film for instruction or for television.

His best-known project, a series of twenty-one films of the
Yanomano people of the Upper Orinoco, made with the anthropologist
Napoleon Chagnon, comes with a "Utilization Chart" which divides cul-
tural research into ten categories and checks off the applicability of each
film. It's a grim taxonomy, and weirdly incomplete: Social Organization,
Kinship, Political Organization, Conflict, Socialization, Women, Field
Work, Ecology & Subsistence, Cosmology & Religion, and Acculturation.
[A world, in other words, without Gastronomy, Music, Stories, Sex,
Leisure, Dreams, Gossip, Body Ornamentation & Dress, Strange
Occurrences, Petty Annoyances . . . or another ten after that.]

The chart's assumption that human life can be contained by such
cubbyholes is identical to the belief that any human activity is most fully
represented by long takes, long shots, and "whole bodies." Worse, it
assumes an existing structure to which all data must be applied; that which
does not is simply excluded:

> Chagnon took a 2 ½ minute sequence of a Yanomano man beat-
> ing his wife over the head with a piece of firewood. We looked at
> it together with James V. Neal and his wife, thinking we might
> include it in our film on genetics [!]. We three men agreed it was
> too disturbing to show. Mrs. Neal saw this as a typically protective
> male view and argued that the beating was no worse than the
> experience of many wives in America. We agree; but we still
> decided not to use the footage.

Asch and Chagnon's *The Ax Fight* (1975) is an example of messy human life reduced to chunks of explainable phenomena. The film is in five parts. Part 1 is the unedited footage of a fight that suddenly erupts in a Yanomano village; the violence of the scene is matched by the frantic quality of the film, as the hand-held camera wobbles, zooms in, and pans rapidly back and forth to keep up with the action. In part 2, the screen is black as the filmmakers discuss what happened; Chagnon speculates that it is the reaction to a case of incest. In part 3, text scrolls up the screen informing us, refreshingly, that the anthropologist was wrong: the fight was the result of a kinship conflict provoked when a woman was ill-treated in a neighboring village; the inevitable kinship charts are then shown. Part 4 replays the original footage with a narrator and pointers identifying the players and their relation to one another. Part 5 presents a polished version of the original, without commentary but edited for narrative continuity. The editing tellingly violates Heider's dictum that events must be presented in the order in which they occurred: as the critic Bill Nichols has pointed out, the original (sequential) footage ends with the wronged woman insulting the men; the narrative version both begins and ends with her, transforming her into a provocateur. (Nichols comments sarcastically, "That's the way women are.")

The opening minutes are an indelible image of community violence, full of unclassifiable data—what filmmaker Jorge Preloran has called the "feel" for a people—a vision of the Yanomano elsewhere unavailable on film. And it is obvious that the sudden outburst and equally sudden resolution of the fight cannot be explained by pointers and kinship charts. One can only imagine the untidy human narrative that would have emerged if the principals and other villagers—who don't speak in the film—were asked to give their versions, if we learned some of their previous history and what happened after the fight. One of the curiosities of ethnographic film, evident to any outsider, is that the strictly scientific films often provide far less information than their reviled "artistic" cousins, which tend to spill over the utilization charts.

Or, more damningly, they provide the same information. There are so many films of the Yanomano that, in Paris in 1978, they could hold a festival of them. These included a number of the Asch-Chagnon films; a

French TV documentary; two films from a Yugoslavian TV series on the rain forest; a Canadian film from the TV series *Full Speed to Adventure*, focusing on two Canadian missionaries living with the community; a Japanese TV film; three videos by New York avant-gardist Juan Downey; and unedited footage shot in the early 1960s by a woman gold prospector. The range of what Heider calls "ethnographic understanding" was obviously great: from experienced scientists to newly arrived television crews (only some of whom were accompanied by anthropologists) to the home movies of a passerby.

There is an account of the festival in *Film Library Quarterly*, written by Jan Sloan. She points out that, despite the diversity of sources, "the actual images were surprisingly similar . . . It is also surprising to note the similarity of information presented in these documentaries. The same limited material is covered in many of the films over and over again . . ."

The recent literary dismantling of written anthropology (by Clifford Geertz, James Clifford, and others) has tried to demonstrate how the sober scientific professionals are no less prone to dubious generalization, manipulation of data, partial explanation, and prevailing ethnocentrism than the enthusiastic amateurs who write accounts of their travels. Similarly, the moment one erases the stylistic differences, the ethnographic differences between a research film and an episode of *Full Speed to Adventure* are less than meets the eye.

The amateurs, in fact, often turn out to be ethnographically richer. Consider the case of an utterly "unscientific" film: *The Nuer* (1970) by Hilary Harris and George Breidenbach, with the assistance of Robert Gardner. Until Gardner's *Forest of Bliss* (1986), this was probably the film most loathed by the professionals. Heider writes: "It is one of the most visually beautiful films ever made . . . But the film is almost without ethnographic integrity. By this I mean that its principles are cinema aesthetic; its framing, cutting, and juxtaposition of images are done without regard for any ethnographic reality." Throughout his book, Heider uses *The Nuer* as the classic example of how not to make an ethnographic film.

The film has no story, little narration, only one brief interview with an individual, no time frame, and no events unfolded in their entirety. Most of it consists of rapidly edited shots of extraordinary beauty, accompanied by a soundtrack of local music and sounds and untranslated speech. There are galleries of close-ups—faces, tobacco pipes, jewelry, houses, corrals—and unforgettable sequences of these astonishingly elongated people simply walking through the dust and mist. Much of the film simply looks at the cows that are central to Nuer life: close-ups of cow legs and cow flanks and cow nostrils and cow horns.

Though this is one of the most "aesthetic" films in the genre, it is full of ethnographic information—far more, ironically, than something like *The Ax Fight*. We see what the Nuer look like, what they make, what they eat, what their music sounds like, their leisure activities, body art, architecture, fishing and cattle-herding, local fauna, diseases, rites of exorcism, spiritual possession, and so on. Most of all, as a study of a community based on cattle, it is a startling revelation of the cow. Even an untrained urban eye finds itself immediately differentiating the cows as individuals— much as the Nuer know the personal history of each; a history which, through bride-prices and ritual exchange, is inextricably tangled with their own histories. Moreover, it becomes evident in the course of the film how an entire aesthetic could be derived from the close observation of cattle— how the shapes and textures of the herds are recapitulated in so much of what the Nuer make.

"The final goal, of which an Ethnographer should never lose sight," wrote Malinowski sixty years ago in a famous dictum, now outdated only in its gender specificity, "is, briefly, to grasp the native's point of view, *his* relation to life, to realize *his* vision of his world." (*his* emphasis.) Of course the ideal is impossible—who can ever see with another's eyes, even within one's own culture? Yet *The Nuer*, rare among ethnographic films, lets us look closely at that which the Nuer look at, but which most of us do not—moreover seeing, as any of us see anything, not the "whole bodies" but the telling details that set each one apart. It is one of the few instances where ethnographic film presents information that is beyond the capabilities of the written monograph. Not observed and analyzed data: it is a physical and intellectual act of seeing. Neither a recapitulation of a foreign vision nor the first-person expression of the filmmakers, it is, most exactly, an act of translation: a reading of their sensibility, recoded into our (film) language. *The Nuer*, like any film, is a metaphor for the Nuer. Its difference is that it does not pretend to be a mirror.

Bill Nichols has written that the central question of ethnographic film is what to do with the people. This is true enough, but it is a center that must be shared by a parallel question: What to do with the filmmaker. Nanook mugged shamelessly for the camera; such footage ever since has tended to be scissored away, to preserve the illusion that the filmed events are being lived as they're always lived, and not being acted out.

David and Judith MacDougall are notable among the ethnographic filmmakers for making their own presence a central feature of their films. Moreover, they have effectively subverted the authority of the all-knowing narrator not only by allowing the subjects to speak—in the late 1960s they introduced subtitled dialogue to the genre—but also by basing their films on conversation. These take three forms: ordinary conversation among the people as observed and recorded by the filmmakers; conversation among the people on topics initiated by the filmmakers; and dialogue between the filmmakers and the people. That the MacDougalls are talking to their subject matter is radical enough in this corner of the film forest; they also allow themselves to be occasionally glimpsed and, in one startling moment, even show us where they're living during the making of the film. (An anthropologist's house is normally more taboo than the interior of a kiva.) They introduce topics with intertitles written in the first person ("We put the following to Lorang . . ."), and their intermittent voiceovers are subjective ("I was sure Lorang's wives were happy together") and sometimes even confessional ("It doesn't feel like we're making progress"). When they don't have certain information or footage, they readily admit it, rather than attempt to patch it over. Most impressively, the films are a visual dialogue between the filmmakers and their subjects: at every moment we know exactly where David MacDougall (the cameraman) is standing. And, thanks no doubt to the presence of Judith MacDougall, their films are full of women talking, and talking freely.

In short, they have found seemingly effortless solutions to most of the political and moral dilemmas of ethnographic film. Contrary to Goldschmidt's definition of the genre, the MacDougalls are shooting people doing precisely what they would have been doing with a camera crew there. The procedure, however, does have its limitations: what they are doing is often not terribly interesting.

Their trilogy—*Lorang's Way, A Wife Among Wives,* and *The Wedding Camels* (1978–81)—shot among the Turkana of northern Kenya is a case in point. The films focus on the family of a wealthy man: the first is a portrait of the patriarch, Lorang; the second talks to his wives; the third concerns the negotiations for the marriage of his daughter. The film rarely leaves the family compound, and for nearly six hours we watch and listen to people largely talking about money and complaining. [Rouch has remarked: "Many recent films of the direct-cinema type are thus spoiled by an incredible regard for the chatting of the people filmed."] Lorang is an Arthur Miller character: the self-made man disgusted by his good-for-nothing sons. But, in the absence of any dramatic catalyst—this being life and not theater—he's a character who goes nowhere: after the first half-hour or so, we only get more of the same. (The wives mainly repeat everything their husbands say.) And the film gives us no way to evaluate whether Lorang is more representative of the Turkana or of the universal *nouveau riche.*

In many ways, the trilogy is like an excruciating evening with one's least favorite relatives. There's no doubt it is a precise representation of this particular family, but can it be considered ethnographic, a representation of a people? We actually learn very little about the Turkana besides work, money, and marriage procedures. No one is born, gets sick, or dies in the films; there are no religious ceremonies; very little singing or eating; conflict with the outside world is alluded to, but not shown; although we come to know the compound well, we are never clear where it is or what its neighbors are up to. The family talks and talks . . . As a record, its style is unusually inventive; but it never solves the perennial questions of the genre: When there are no individuals, who speaks for the people? (Usually the wrong man: the narrator). When there is an individual, to what extent can she or he represent the group?

One answer is a multiplicity of voices—voices that echo, enlarge, and especially contradict one another. Certainly it would be possible in six hours of film, but it would undermine the premises of the genre: *They* have typical members. *We* do not. *They* are unusual, but can be comprehended. *We* are usual, but ultimately incomprehensible. *They* are somewhat like us. *We* are not like us. *They* must be represented in the simplest possible way. *We* must be represented with subtle complexity.

Most ethnographic films document a single event—perhaps, as Rouch has suggested, because such events come with their own ready-made *mise-en-scène*. Such documentation poses a dilemma for scientists. Written ethnography is based on generalization: the ethnographer's description of, say, how a basket is woven is an amalgam based on watching a hundred baskets being made. Filmed ethnography cannot help but be specific: a unique and idiosyncratic instance of basket-weaving. (Often, the differences between what is seen and what is "usual" will be noted by filmmakers in interviews; but never, as far as I know, in the film itself.) Moreover, the filmed event unravels the image of the "traditional" society on which ethnographic film is based, in a way that a written monograph does not: The endlessly repeated becomes the unrepeatable moment; the timeless is suddenly inserted into history; representation of a people becomes representation of a person; ethnography biography, archetype individual. (And a pastiche, like *The Hunters*, is no way out: it cannot help but be subverted by the expectation of a continuity based on matching shots.)

One solution, not so strangely, is surrealism: a superficial discontinuity revelatory of a profound unity. There are films to be imagined that would self-consciously (unlike *The Hunters*) feature different protagonists at different stages of an event, or the same protagonist in different versions, or one where the protagonists perform in a stylized, "unnatural" reenactment. Films that, to represent a people, would attempt to subvert film's natural tendency to specify individuals. (Would a *Discreet Charm of the Bourgeoisie* or a *Heart of Glass* of ethnographic films be any less stylized, or carry less information, than the currently prevailing modes of realism?)

Surrealism moreover introduced an aesthetic based on chance, improvisation, and the found object—an aesthetic which would seem tailored to the actual conditions of a Westerner making an ethnographic film. Yet the genre has had only one surrealist: ironically, the founder of *cinéma vérité*, Jean Rouch. (And there's a parallel to be drawn with another surrealist, the master of photojournalism, Henri Cartier-Bresson.) *Jaguar* (shot in the 1950s and released in 1967), to briefly take one example from a massive amount of work, has the improvisatory exuberance of the 1960s French New Wave—it even includes clips from other Rouch films. One can't anticipate what will happen next, as the film follows its three protagonists traveling from Niger to Ghana to find work; some of the adventures—as when one of the men becomes an official photographer for Kwame Nkrumah—even veer into fantasy. Most important, *Jaguar* is the only inventive exploration of nonsynch sound in the genre. [Baldwin Spencer had taken an Edison cylinder recorder to Australia in 1901, but these possibilities remained unexplored for fifty years.] Shot silently, the soundtrack (recorded ten years later) features the three men commenting on the action: a nonstop patter of jokes, insults, commentary, and light-hearted disagreements that effectively break down the normally unchallenged authority of the single narrator/outsider.

Robert Gardner, in *Deep Hearts* (1978) and *Forest of Bliss* (1987), has adapted another aspect of surrealism to transform the idiosyncratic into the archetypal: he explodes time. By employing the simultaneous time of modern physics, he transforms the linear time of the unrepeatable into the cyclical time of the endlessly repeated. This has been, of course, one of the main projects of the century: through simultaneity—montage, collage, Pound's ideogrammic method—all ages become contemporaneous. It is both a criticism of Western linear time and a bridge to the mythic time which rules most traditional societies. But where the modernists sought to recapture both the formal aspects and the sheer power of so-called "primitive" art and oral epics, Gardner, uniquely, has employed the techniques of modernism to represent the tribal other. A cycle has been completed: with Gardner, James Joyce is our entry into Homer.

*Deep Hearts* is concerned with the annual Garawal ceremony of the Bororo Fulani of Niger. The nomadic groups converge at one spot in the desert, where the young men elaborately make themselves up and, wearing women's dresses, dance for eight days in the sun as the marriageable young women look them over, until one man is selected as the most virtuous and beautiful. According to the few lines of narration in the film, the Bororo consider themselves to be "chosen people" (who doesn't?) but they are threatened by "neighbors, new ideas, disease and drought." Their combination of "excessive self-regard" and "a fear of losing what they have" makes them "easily prey to envy." So they must bury their hearts within them, for "if a heart is deep no one can see what it contains."

If this group-psychological analysis is correct, then the Bororo must remain, particularly to an outsider, unreadable. Everything will remain on the surface, only, at best, inadvertently revealing what is beneath. Gardner's response to this impermeability is to turn it into a dream, a shimmering mirage. Time is scrambled and events keep repeating themselves: men dancing, people arriving, men dancing, preparations for the dance, and so on. Shots of the farewell ceremony, near the end of the film, are followed by a scene we've already seen, near the beginning, of a woman washing her enormous leg bracelets before the dance. Sounds recorded at the dance are played over scenes of preparation for it. There are strange sideways shots of milk being poured from huge bowls that recall the abstract geometries of Moholy-Nagy's films. There are freeze-frames and, in one sequence, slow-motion and distortion of the sound. [Though documentary was born out of slow-motion—Eadward Muybridge's magic-lantern studies of animal locomotion—it remains taboo for ethnographic film, being counter to prevailing notions of realism. Maya Deren's 1947–1951 study of voodoo in Haiti, *Divine Horsemen*, exploits both the hallucinatory quality of slow motion—which rhymes perfectly with the dance and trance possession she is filming—and its ability to let us see details we would otherwise miss in the frenetic action.]

*Deep Hearts* is a dream of the Garawal ceremony, stolen from the sleep of an anthropologist; the woozy memory of events one has witnessed in eight days of desert sun. (Its nearest cousin is the flashbacks to

Guinea-Bissau in Chris Marker's *Sans Soleil*.) As science, it is probably as accurate a description as a more linear recreation. But, unlike science, it leaves its enigmas unsolved. Its last lines of narration are among the most abstract in the genre: "The visitors leave as suddenly as they appeared, and, with the diminishing rains, they will resume their nomadic lives. They go knowing what they would hope to be, an ideal example having been selected from their midst. But this may only serve to remind them of the desires that cannot be met, and which, with the uncertainty of whether choices are really theirs, still lie at the bottom of their deep hearts."

This dream, then, becomes an expression of unfulfilled desire in an unstable society. It is interesting that we barely glimpse, and only from afar, the winner of the contest: this is a study of longing, not achievement. And, uniquely in ethnographic film—which seems to cover everything except what people really think about (other than money)—*Deep Hearts* is a study of erotic longing: the young women posed in tableaux of virginal meekness facing the men (we watch the dancers over the shoulder of one of them); the auto-eroticism of these dancing men dressed as women; the old women who, no longer in the courtship game, must ritually insult them; and the old men who, from the image of their past selves, select the most beautiful.

The film underscores what is obvious elsewhere: there are vast areas of human life to which scientific methodology is inapt; to which ethnographic description must give way to the ethnopoetic: a series of concrete and luminous images, arranged by intuition rather than prescription, and whose shifting configurations—like the points of and between the constellations—map out a piece of a world.

Simultaneous time, the babble of voices overlapping and interrupting each other, the rapid succession of images, the cacophony of programmed and random sounds: all modern art is urban art, and all film—being born with this century—is an image of the city. What then does one do with the subjects of ethnography who, with few exceptions, lead rural lives? The anthropological monograph is, as James Clifford has pointed out, this century's version of the pastoral, and its writing can and does draw on its literary antecedents. Film, however, with its short takes, shifting camera angles and multiple viewpoints is as intrinsically antipastoral as its filmmakers themselves. To take it (and oneself) into the countryside of the tribe, one may either deny its (and one's own) nature—as most ethnographic filmmakers have done—or somehow discover a way into one's subject.

Trinh T. Minh-ha's *Naked Spaces: Living Is Round* (1985) returns ethnography to its origins: the observations of a perceptive and intelligent cosmopolitan traveler. Her ostensible subject is Bachelard's "poetics of space," as exemplified by a dozen ethnic groups in western Africa. The film leisurely shifts from village to village, sound to silence, staring—there is no other word for it—at the people, their dances, and endless architectural details. The soundtrack is local music and the fragmented speech of three women narrators who, at a given moment, may represent different perspectives, but elsewhere in the film exchange roles and even repeat each other's words. Little of what is seen is explained: the voices mention some African beliefs and stories, quote a five-foot shelf of Western literature and philosophy from Heidegger to Novalis to Shakespeare to Eluard, and utter gnomic statements written by the filmmaker herself. (The three narrators, according to Trinh, are an attempt to subvert the patriarchy of the single voice, but it is curious, given her political stance, that no Africans speak in the film.) Contrary to the hardliners—(Walter Goldschmidt: "The ethnographic filmmaker is not engaged in expressing himself")—what holds the film together is precisely its utter subjectivity: these extraordinarily beautiful images of Africa as filtered through the bric-a-brac-cluttered mind of a brilliant academic. And along the way, one sees more than in a hundred "scientific" films.

With *Forest of Bliss*, Robert Gardner has taken his modernist sensibility into an urban setting, however one that is uniquely archaic. The result is a panoramic "city" film in the tradition that begins with Paul Strand and Charles Sheeler's *Mannahatta* (1921) and Walther Ruttmann's *Berlin: Symphony of the City* (1927), and whose latest incarnation is the first half of Wim Wenders's *Wings of Desire* (1987). And yet the nature of his subject, Benares, India, cannot help but insert the film into myth.

Benares is at least three thousand years old, and the oldest continually inhabited city on earth. Moreover, it always has had the same primary function, as the place where each day the countless dead are burned or dropped into the Ganges, and the living purified. To visit the sacred

**Robert Gardner, *Forest of Bliss* (1986)**
**A boat on the Ganges.**

zones of the city, along the river, is like finding priests of Isis still practicing in Luxor. No other living city exists so purely in mythic time.

Similarly, the city itself is an iconographic representation of the
passage from this world to the next: a labyrinth of bazaars, temples, and
houses for the dying opens out onto steps that lead down to the river (at
one section of steps the dead are burned); the wide river itself, cleansing
all, and beyond, distantly visible, the other shore.

These are universally recognizable symbols, from which—with a
host of others: the kite perched between heaven and earth, the scavenging
dogs, the boats that carry the dead to the other side, the purifying fire, the
flowers of veneration—Gardner has constructed a montage of the eternal-
ly repeatable. It is both a study of the mechanics of death (the
organization of Benares's cremation industry) and a map of the Hindu
cosmology of death—almost entirely presented through iconic images. It
is surely the most tightly edited film in the genre, truly a fugue of reiterat-
ed elements, and one whose astonishing use of sound sustains the cyclical

structure by carrying over the natural sounds of one scene into the next—
Godard's technique adapted to a completely different purpose.

Most radically, Gardner has eliminated all verbal explanations.
There is no narration, the dialogue is not subtitled, and there is only one
intertitle, a single line from the Yeats translations of the Upanishads.
*Forest of Bliss*, more than any other film, reinforces the outsider status of
both the filmmaker and the viewer: we must look, listen, remain alert,
accept confusion, draw our own tentative conclusions, find parallels from
within our own experiences. Travelers confronting the exotic, we are also
the living standing before the dead.

I have spent time in Benares on three separate occasions: it is
curious that this, the most artistically crafted of all ethnographic films, has
approached the utopian mimesis of the scientists: for me, at least, it is, as
no other film I know, like being there—though there, of course, in a
two-dimensional space with only two of the senses intact. This is because
the film takes as its center an ultimate incomprehension: of the gods by
man, of the dead by the living, of the blissful by the unenlightened, of the
East by the West, of any culture by another. In Hinduism one attempts to
bridge the gap through the primary form of worship, *darshana*, the act of
seeing—the eyes literally going out to touch the gods. Though I hesitate to
call *Forest of Bliss* a religious experience, it too is dependent on a similar
contemplation of iconic signs: it is an outsider's (refusing to be an insider's)
seeing through Benares into the cycles of life and death.

Needless to say, the film has driven the scientists mad. The
newsletter of the Society of Visual Anthropologists ran a series of polemics
against it, filled with lines like "Technology has left pure imagery behind,
and anthropologists ought to do so too." (The same writer commenting
that, given the sanitary problems of disposing corpses in the river, an interview with a public-health official would have been informative.)

These are the people who prefer a kinship chart to *Anna Karenina*,
but their project is intrinsically doomed: the specificity of their brand of linear film will always subvert their attempts to generalize human behavior.
It is only elaborated metaphor and complex aesthetic structures that are
capable of even beginning to represent human nature and events: configurations of pure imagery will always leave technology behind.

✦

Nearly all ethnographic filmmakers, in interviews, have remarked that the genre is, so many decades later, still in its infancy. It is difficult to disagree. The latest films selected for a recent Margaret Mead Film Festival in New York were generally more of the same: Every film had a narrator, many of them still speaking to a room full of slow children: "This is rice cooking. Rice is grown in their fields." Films still open with lines like, "This is the heart of Africa." There are still moments of incredible chauvinism, as when a narrator explains, "These village children have few toys, yet they are happy," or when, in a British film on the huge Kumbh Mela festival in India, the spiritual leaders of various temples are called bishops, abbots, and deacons, as though this were a tea party in Canterbury.

A few things had changed: thanks to new high-speed films, many featured extraordinary night scenes, lit only by fires or candles. The effects of the West are no longer kept hidden: in one scene, a shaman in a trance stopped chanting to change the cassette in his tape recorder; and it was remarkable how many of the people, from scattered corners of the world, were wearing the same t-shirts with goofy slogans in English. Nearly every film featured synch sound and subtitled dialogue; the films were full of local speech.

The most interesting film I saw at the Festival was *Zulay, Facing the 21st Century* (1989) by Jorge and Mabel Preloran. Feature-length, the entire film is a dialogue between the filmmakers and Zulay, a woman from Otavalo, Ecuador, who comes to Los Angeles to live with them and help in the editing of a film on her community. (The Otavaleños stubbornly retain their traditions and dress, while simultaneously traveling all over the world to sell weavings most charitably described as tourist art.) The film cuts back and forth between the two places: Zulay's family speaking into the camera to give her messages; her reaction as she screens it in L.A.; Zulay in traditional dress posing with Fred Flintstone at Marineland; Otavaleños dressing up as Mexican charros with huge sombreros for a local dance; Zulay operating a movieola with the same precise gestures and impassive face as the weavers in the footage she is editing; her family back home reading her letters out loud; Zulay's return to Otavalo and the local gossip that ultimately drives her back to L.A. (men or married couples may go everywhere, but single women do not leave the village), and so on. Most startlingly for ethnographic film and yet with absolute naturalness, the filmmakers discuss their own lives with Zulay: as expatriate Argentines who still do much of their work in Argentina, they too are adrift between cultures. The film is pure Rouch, and something more: the subject is interacting with the filmmakers not as a recording cultural presence, but as another human. The interview format finally reaches the condition of dialogue. And, in passing, we learn a great deal about Otavalo, all of it presented through the casual conversation.

The film ends with a complex metaphor: Zulay in Los Angeles, wearing traditional dress, screens yet another message from her mother, wearing the same clothes, in Otavalo. Her mother tells her it would be best if she did not come back; Zulay bursts into tears. The filmmakers ask her what she is going to do. Zulay, weeping, says, "I don't know." Film has both erased and created distances: it is Zulay's means of communication with her mother, and yet it is the cause of her expulsion from paradise; going to L.A. to work on the film, she has crossed to the other side of the camera, and though she is the mirror image of what the camera sees, she can't cross back.

It is impossible to separate what may be the next stage of ethnographic film from the fate of its subjects: extinction for some and tremendous cultural change for the rest. But there was an instant in a recent film, Howard Reid's *The Shaman and His Apprentice* (1989), that was, for me, a sudden glimpse into how much has been missing in the genre, and what its future may bring: when film technology is no longer a Western domain; when the observed become the observers; when ethnography becomes a communal self-portraiture, as complex as any representation of *us*; when the erotic can enter in expression, not voyeurism; when *they*, at last, do all the talking.

The film follows a healer named José, of the Yamunawa people of the Peruvian Amazon, as he educates and initiates a young disciple, Caraca. In one scene José takes Caraca for his first visit to the nearest large town. The trip has only one purpose: to go to the local movie house, where there is an important lesson about healing to be learned:

"Cinema," José explains, "is exactly like the visions sick people have when they are dying."

[1990]

ROBERT GARDNER

# The Impulse to Preserve

I do not know at what point I began my life as a filmmaker. Could it have been the day I could at last reach the shelf where my father kept his 16mm. movie projector? It was a Bell and Howell; the kind that had a heavy, round metal base and was made so as to bend in the middle in order to be slid, miraculously, in and out of a velvet-lined box that smelled mysteriously of celluloid and electricity. It was then also that I became the projectionist at our passionate family screenings of Laurel and Hardy, Our Gang, and Charlie Chaplin. I knew that Chaplin was funniest, but Our Gang touched me deeply with its almost true accounts of children trying to outwit a problematic world.

My father also had a 16mm. camera which he used to document the antics of his offspring. I have inherited what has survived of this troubling chronicle. Nowadays I can hardly bear to watch it, so heartbreaking are those conjurings of vanished childhoods. He seems never to have captured in those little yellow boxes of black-and-white film anything except joy, and yet I remember the business of growing up to have had its painful moments. Perhaps my memory is no less faulty than my father's camera, but I think it is a greater certainty that his camera, like all cameras, could be no more telling than the hand that held it.

Philip Larkin wrote that "The impulse to preserve is at the bottom of all art." It must have been some such urge to which my father succumbed when he lifted his camera to capture our somersaults and pony rides. He may not have been thinking of art but only of a way to arrest time and, I would guess, to preserve happiness. As I got older, I would sometimes open the long wooden box that held the tightly wound and silvered screen, slide the projector from its snug little house, thread up a reel getting pungent with neglect, and allow myself a furtive look at the enchantments of a long-forgotten summer.

At a certain point, I came into possession of my own camera and have, ever since, wondered how it should be used. Forty years ago there were no schools in which to learn filmmaking like the ones there are now in London, Paris, Rome, or even in Cambridge, Massachusetts, where I myself sometimes teach. We all learned by doing things and watching others do things who we had reason to think or to hope knew more than we did. We also learned, if lucky enough to be near a good supply, by going to films whenever the opportunity arose.

After college, I moved west to Seattle, where there was not yet a community of filmmaking but where the university had a small art gallery that booked a generous selection of cinema's greatest works. This was the era of Amos Vogel's inspiration, *Cinema 16*, which had already established film as an art in New York City, and the idea had come west to flourish. As I absorbed more and more examples of every available kind of film, I gradually and unexpectedly grew to prefer nonfiction. My first inclinations had been toward narrative, especially as practiced by such innovators as De Sica and Rossellini, who could create so much life from such thin but touching stories. I was also dazzled and sometimes perplexed by what was known then as experimental cinema. Here Maya Deren was my chief delight. Of Deren's films, I am still fondest of *Private Life of a Cat* (1947), which she helped her husband, Alexander Hammid, make, and the arresting visual lyric, *A Study in Choreography for Camera* (1945). I think these two were and still are more engaging of the heart and more commanding visually than her denser, surrealistic work. Also, I have always thought it significant that her final, unfinished venture to document the practice of *voudon* in Haiti was, in the end, her acknowledgment of the power of actuality.

Of all the films that entered my consciousness in those days, Basil Wright's *Song of Ceylon* (1934) appealed in some essential way both to my sensibilities and to any budding ambitions I had as a filmmaker. I was not particularly aware of its importance to me at the time. It is a film whose subtle genius is easily obscured by the obvious charms of Flaherty's *Nanook of the North* (1922) or by the technical mastery of Riefensthal's *Der Triumph des Willens* (*Triumph of the Will*, 1935). I have no idea how many times I have seen Wright's film over the years, but each time I do, it reveals new evidence of an amazing capacity to make images that convey feeling and mood at the same time they are representing, even preserving, the world of reality. When I noticed this in other films like Buñuel's *Land without Bread* (1932), Franju's *Le Sang des Bêtes* (*The Blood of the Beasts*, 1949), and in some of Dziga Vertov's less mannered efforts, I began thinking that perhaps it was possible to give utterance to inner feelings about the world by adroitly seizing it with a camera. For a young man with appropri-

**Luis Buñuel, *Land Without Bread* (1932)**
**A dead child in its coffin is placed in a river, en route to**
**a cemetery.**

ately intense feelings but no demonstrated talent for expressing them, this discovery was an enormously engaging prospect. Besides, I argued easily, I would be able to keep going to films because doing that had already had such good effect. Curiously, I seldom go to films these days unless they are ones that I want to see again or unless they are the most recent work of a few new and old masters, friends or students. It seems there is so much less time than there was when I thought I had no choice but to see everything.

Soon, there was no doubt in my mind that I should set about answering the question of where and how to point my camera at the world. Perhaps this was when my life in filmmaking really began. There was no feeling that if I did not do it the world would be any poorer. It was more that if I did do it I might, just possibly, have a reason for continuing to live in it. My Protestant New England background instructed me to not only work hard but toward some purpose, preferably of the kind that is improving both to one's soul and one's surroundings. Idealism was very much in the air those days. World War II was over and the Cold War had not quite begun. In fact, we were told, there would be no wars if people were fed, housed, and educated. One of the people who was saying this was the great Scottish reformer and producer John Grierson, who went on to establish the National Film Board of Canada with the curious notion that nonfiction film was the only possible teacher for a world just waiting to be taught. This was the idea that lent an air of evangelism to what came to be called the documentary. For me, the possibility of doing something that might lift up humanity and also belong to Art was certainly exciting. However, on looking back I realize that, except for some of the earlier films of Humphrey Jennings, Lindsay Anderson, and especially Wright, I am not particularly attracted to much of what came from the Grierson movement. I now find most of it a trifle bleak and earnest. The movement's goal to instruct was certainly admirable, but the work often seemed to lapse into preaching, and anyhow more Larkin-like impulses to preserve soon began to agitate my mind.

Though they can no doubt be detected in much earlier efforts, these longings to capture human reality in ways that might reveal its essence or significance seem to me to have fully asserted themselves by the time I began making *Dead Birds* (1964). That was in 1961, by which time

I had already absorbed what I most liked in my brief formal study of anthropology and had abandoned any thought of a life in social science. There is no question now that my commitment to filmmaking would be influenced more by one of anthropology's intellectual sources, moral philosophy, than any of its mainstream doctrines. I remember my bewilderment those days with such dismal notions as functionalism and structuralism. For me these systems had in some miraculous way overlooked people entirely. The only appealing concept then current was something called "culture and personality." In this I found the first sensible way of organizing my thoughts about human realities. In fact, its basic premise that there are two fundamental engines of experience whose interaction shapes our lives is related to an underlying theme I detect in many of my films: the tension between individual will and cultural constraint.

I sometimes wonder while thinking about the cinematic inspiration upon which I drew such a long time ago if Grierson may not have had more of an influence than I had supposed. I do not remember in his voluminous and skillful writing that he ever made the observation that film could serve as an agent of moral inspection or even contemplation, but his occasional high-mindedness about our ethical obligations to improve the human lot coincided with some of my own preoccupations. The important difference that I see between his view and my own is that I would prefer any moral to be drawn rather than pointed and I am more concerned with contemplating than improving our ethical natures. This means, I suppose, that I was destined to follow a different esthetic path in my search for imagery and for ways of making it into a film. It has also meant that I belong to a quite different philosophical congregation. I have never had the slightest wish to make instructional films. On the other hand, I would have been happy to follow Wright to the ends of the earth.

In 1961, Western New Guinea, where I went to make *Dead Birds*, was administered by the Netherlands. It was a place largely unknown to even travelers and anthropologists, the two callings specializing in distant and obscure geographies. When I accepted an invitation from the Netherlands New Guinea Office of Native Affairs to make a film in the Central Highlands, I looked without success for a source of reliable background information. There were missionary newsletters carrying fantastic

**Basil Wright, *Song of Ceylon* (1934)**

and self-serving tales of heathen treachery home to the parishioners, but nobody was writing anything sensible about the place to which I was going because nobody had yet gone there to do that. I felt a heavy responsibility to gather as many useful facts as possible. This feeling, which I now think to have been somewhat exaggerated, influenced the way I put together the group that would take part in this undertaking. There would be consideration given to many different interests including humanistic anthropology, botany, natural history and even sociology, an intellectual pursuit that I have yet to embrace with any warmth. What concerns me now is the question of what I wanted of my camera apart from its well-demonstrated faculty for documentation, and also the more practical matter of how I intended to satisfy those wishes. Up to this point, I had made a number of efforts and experiments in cinematography but nothing on the scale of what was to become *Dead Birds*.

I remember hoping, above all else, that whatever I did with a camera should engage the eye. Even in 1961, it was the formal qualities of the image (was I still in thrall to Vertov?) which interested me at least as much as the information toward which I felt responsible. To some extent these two requirements of shape and of content were destined to compete and, although it would be nice not to quarrel with Margaret Mead for having said that in *Dead Birds* "Art neither has been subordinated to, nor has it been allowed to overrule Science," I have come to think she was proposing a most unlikely achievement at least under the circumstances which prevailed in making that film. In any case, even if I was unable at the time to reach an entirely satisfactory solution to this vexing matter, I worked diligently to provide myself with the technical means I thought most suited to the task.

Nineteen-sixty was the precise moment in the history of cinema when workable and lightweight synchronous sound and film equipment was being developed and tested. I had made some trials of my own as early as 1957 when I accompanied John Marshall to the Kalahari and brought a small, soundproofed camera that would run at a constant speed, but it seemed an impossibly awkward and ponderous way to make films. So I chose to use a camera designed for straightforward image making. It was the standard Arriflex, at the time without peer and even today the camera I would choose if noise was not a consideration or if I was looking for an instrument with the greatest reliability and ease of use. I was equipped to expose film using either one-hundred or four-hundred-foot lengths. This would, if I wished, enable me to make a single scene lasting as long as eleven minutes. I never wanted to do this, but I know of occasions (especially in ethnographic filmmaking) when even greater lengths of stock are used to make even longer shots, often on the assumption that doing so will somehow guarantee fidelity or thoroughness. From at least 1960 to the present day, I have thought that the sophistication of the technology employed to make a film, compared to the kind of thinking that instructs its use, is a matter of relatively little consequence. Beautiful films can be made with minimal means, and an abundance of means seems frequently to result in just the opposite. In New Guinea I was adequately but modestly equipped. At least nothing technical was going to submerge the ideas informing the image making.

I wanted to make a film about certain particular individuals through whose lives and situations the film's themes and narrative threads could be developed. This was a decision of the most basic kind. Among other things, it meant that the camera would not be used for passive observation but as an active agent in disclosing the identities and recounting the experiences of some individuals but not others. I wanted to see all I possibly could of the context within which these individuals existed, but I wanted to do this by deliberately, though not exclusively, limiting my gaze to an exploration of the space they occupied. I was interested in entering the lives of some very real and particular people. I was not at all interested in making a film about abstractions like society, culture, and personality, or about items on somebody's ethnographic laundry list. I was once told by a professor of anthropology who had just seen *Dead Birds*: "You sure have some beautiful data." I think he thought I was in the enviable position of being able to put the film through some methodological processor. What he did not realize was that filmmaking is itself a transforming process, and what he was calling "data" had already lost their existential virginity.

My intent here is to try to remember the way my mind dealt with such questions as how pictorial style in filmmaking is formulated and also how once it is, both the shape and content of a film begin to be established. This was not the way I put these questions thirty years ago. In those days I was too preoccupied with problems that confront anyone setting out to make a film largely alone: what camera or cameras to take, how to protect them from heat or humidity, will there be a way to charge batteries, and so on through the endless litany of film's technical worries. I knew only that there was one thing I was sure I wanted and that was for the camera in *Dead Birds* to be active and not passive, to interrogate and not simply observe. To achieve this meant giving some thought to camera technique and then making decisions about how to actually use the camera, where to point it or how to hold it. Among other things and in no particular order of importance, I decided that there would be minimal use of a tripod, a fluid or moving camera, short lenses used in close proximity (as against long lenses used at a distance), and so on through a list of mainly technical considerations. When I turn my thoughts to more recent work, it is interesting for me to note that I have retained many of the prejudices I had when starting *Dead Birds*. Of course, some things do change, such as a recent interest in extremely long lenses as in *Forest of Bliss*, but the underlying intention of telling the story by relying primarily on visual strategies has only grown stronger over time. It is true that *Dead Birds* is in a certain sense extremely literary. I wrote it with as much effort as went into the photography, and its enormous text of words is essential to its comprehension as a tale. However, I can also see that its words were intended as an acknowledgment of a legacy of such glorious commentaries as, say, Robert Knox's in *Song of Ceylon* or Auden's in *Night Mail* (1936). In addition, I feel it was a point not only of arrival but of departure toward more exclusively visual concerns.

There is another bit of visual strategy that should be mentioned, and that is the way the camera is used to follow the action. I am referring to the point of view: the position elected for the camera to "see" events as they unfold. I think a good example of what I mean are the shots of Weyak (the principal adult male in the film) made the morning after the funeral of the little boy killed in ambush by enemy warriors. The camera is traveling, I would like to think it is floating, in a path parallel to the direction in which Weyak is walking. It is at Weyak's side as he moves toward his own watchtower, near which the little boy was killed. What is important in this scene is that the camera never gets in front of Weyak to register an oncoming point of view. This would have meant asking Weyak to wait while I got ahead of him and then telling him to start walking again when I was ready to make the next shot. There is the possibility, of course, that I could have stayed in front of him the whole time he was striding along by somehow walking backwards at the same speed over the uneven terrain he himself was traversing. However, even in 1961, I was neither nimble nor experienced enough to perform such a stunt. The importance of this is that the scene has an inherent integrity that a more contrived, head-on point of view would, on the contrary, have seriously compromised.

Using the camera to follow action has certain consequences apart from simply bolstering a scene's credibility. For one thing, it becomes more than likely that filmmakers who forego directing behavior will find that they are almost always behind whatever they are trying to photograph. They tend to spend a great deal of time and effort trying to catch up with what is going on. Only with considerable effort does one have the opportunity to do any better than stay abreast of things. This kind of camera is not what I would call "privileged." It can be part of the action but it is not permitted to interrupt or intervene in it. Flaherty's camera was frequently put where it could see more than Nanook himself. The audience was thereby privileged in the way they experienced what was represented as reality. Denying the camera these kinds of privileges puts an enormous premium on the ability to anticipate what is going to happen. Nonfiction filmmakers with the interests and scruples that require them to follow rather than lead the action need a sixth sense of what is about to happen just to get onto something visually interesting. Lacking what I suspect is this largely intuitive faculty, it is probably inevitable that what is most important will escape even the best-intentioned filmmaker. The life of a nonfiction filmmaker is really a search for ways to be there *before* something happens.

Two things that determine much of what happens in our lives are circumstance and chance. It is no surprise then that they play equally important roles in the art of telling nonfiction stories about our lives. It is, in a sense, the chance nature of reality that draws our attention to one thing instead of another, that sets in motion the combination of eye and hand movements which point a camera in this direction and not in that and which compels us through some urgency to follow and to preserve what we see.

When I started filming *Forest of Bliss*, I knew that my freedom to move about Benares would be limited by a variety of rules, conventions, and my own hesitation. I would, in short, be limited by circumstances. Owing to my Westernness, there would be places where I would not be immediately welcome. One of those places was of great importance to me, the burning *ghat* called Manikarnika. It was my inadvertent stumbling into that extraordinary space ten years earlier which had filled me with a panic which I kept coming back to Benares to relieve. Another circumstance was that on the shore of the Ganges, very close to Manikarnika, a man was repairing a battered old boat. I saw in this wreck a chance to mentally and pictorially reenter the space from which I felt excluded. Every day I visited the carpenter and filmed the boat's gradual restoration while, at the same time, I got physically and emotionally more ready to enter the larger space that included, a few hundred feet away, Manikarnika. Finally, the boat was finished, and I moved onto the Burning Ground.

As chance plays its decisive part in what finds its way into nonfiction films, it sometimes seems almost to overwhelm all other considerations. By this I mean that occasionally certain coincidences in time and space result in such a powerful rendering of reality that transposing it to the screen runs the risk of its being seen as artifice. This is the phenomenon where actuality outperforms the imagination, outfables the fabulous.

While working on *Forest of Bliss*, I went to nearly absurd lengths to obtain an image of a kite falling from a great height into the Ganges near its far shore. It was the time of year when kites were being flown by hundreds of children every day, but in spite of the innumerable opportunities they provided I was never happy with what I saw in the viewfinder. I was driven by the idea that if I could make this image I would be able to convey a heightened sense of finality or loss: when its string broke, a kite was simply departing forever. One late afternoon coming home up the river, I saw a boat leaving the city shore with what I could see was the shrouded body of a child. I knew from past experience this bundle was being rowed out to be dropped into the middle of the river. As I filmed the scene, I could see a number of kites sailing above the river toward the opposite shore. In what might have been the third or fourth shot, the one in which the child's body was actually slipped into the river, I could see in the background a bright red kite simultaneously entering the water. I do not think this coincidence of burials means to anyone else exactly what it means to me, but I am quite sure that chance, which had brought these two events together, made it possible to make an image of intensified and extended meaning. I learned a short time later that the child who was put into the Ganges had fallen to its death flying a kite from the parapet of a building close to the river's edge. Chance was beginning to weave an improbable web of circumstance. Had there been a voiced commentary in *Forest of Bliss*, and if I had spoken of how this child died, while showing it being put into the river at the very moment a kite was falling into the water a short distance away, audiences might understandably object to an apparent contrivance.

It is easy enough to leave out something that threatens to strain credulity, but much harder to grasp what is in the midst of happening before one's eyes and to point the camera in the right direction at the right time. In any case, it is precisely these kite-falling kinds of stories for which life is the unique source and that, if watched carefully enough, give people like me the opportunity of telling on film. What one must do is maintain the kind of vigilance that will lead to capturing the moments only chance and circumstance provide, and what that seems to require, at the very least, is a state of elevated readiness in which one's eyes are open to all the relationships possible between visible entities. This relatively uncommon state of mind, resembling a sort of trance, seems to me essential in order to see the connectedness of events not only as elements in the physical space they occupy but in their significance as phenomena linked by meaning. There is a way to make films that owe their existence primarily to the act of seeing, and it is quite possible for films to issue forth from a vision as convincingly as from a concept or act of the imagination. Of my own work, I feel this to have happened most recently with *Forest of Bliss*. Both its shape and its content emerged from a personal inspection of the world through a camera. For me, that world remained as mysterious as ever but the camera enabled me to find a way through it.

MAUREEN HOWARD

# You Are There

**M**y father said: "They got it wrong." Or, more likely: "Christ, they got it all wrong." He was speaking of the movie *Boomerang* (1947), a movie that was to gain a modest reputation in the special and suspect category of docudrama. He spoke with authority, for he had been consulted by movie people who came to town, to the courthouse on Golden Hill Street in his city of Bridgeport. *Boomerang* is based on the unsolved murder of Father Hubert Dhame, pastor of St. Joseph's Roman Catholic Church. When the priest was shot once through the head on February 24, 1924, my father, who hacked around as a reporter, had just pinned on a shield to become, in those unprofessional days, the one detective in the State's Attorney's office. With access to court records, what could those movie people have wanted from him twenty-one years later that would make a difference in their story? Perhaps a sense of the city's outrage or an edge of hysteria in the wake of a sensational hometown event; or his take, as a rookie, on the incredible probity of the cool State's Attorney who brought a man to trial and then, by brilliant investigation, famously refuted both his own and the defense's circumstantial evidence and direct testimony, pleading a *nolle prosequi*, dramatically dropping the case.

My father revered that State's Attorney, Homer Cummings. That's not in the plot of *Boomerang*. The detective, played by Lee J. Cobb, is a police-force veteran. Backed by the prosecutor for his integrity, he's not the tough guy who goes for the conviction, but a complicated man finding his way through a subplot of sticky local politics. It's a good script, better than the real detective's 1946 recall, though my father was a man who told grand stories. Interviewed in his office across from Superior Court where the law was the law, he had little use for mere atmosphere surrounding the Dhame case and would have flung himself in the clinker rather than reveal to movie people anything so personal, so irrelevant as his *feelings* about his boss. They got it wrong.

Attempting to get it right, I reconstruct my father's respect for the record, put words in his mouth— the "Christ" was a constant call upon the deity to be a pal, lend divine authority to his every view. He took no offense at the movie version of his experience in which 1924 becomes a vague post–World War II with chubby cars, pageboy hairdos, a simplistic psychiatrist written in—courtesy of an enlightened 1946; or at the predictable fact that the city of Bridgeport, still swollen with wartime prosperity, was turned into a small Connecticut town. I'm not amazed, watching *Boomerang* these many years later, to find Father Dhame resurrected as a genteel Episcopalian minister: his broad Alsatian face and German parish would not have played well in 1947.

As in many a murder mystery, the body of the victim, his goodness documented efficiently, is removed from the scene early on. The drama shifts to the State's Attorney, the old story of the one just man who will succumb neither to self-interest nor to the pressures of the seasoned investigator who is well aware of the moral compromises and political advantages of tying up the case. So we're watching a movie with a thread of legal reality. We know that Arthur Kennedy, who plays the accused drifter, Harold Israel—I need not mention why that name was changed—was apprehended and, unless you are privileged to be my father's child, that we are tracking what really happened. Words appear on the screen, a visible text (which deep down we may read as an imagined construction) says it's a true story. The words, as in many wartime documentaries, are plainly set forth, no fancy graphics. The opening credits of *Boomerang* look as though they were produced on a high-set old Remington. Read quickly, but carefully: the script is taken from an article by one Anthony Abbott in *The Reader's Digest*, 1945.

Abbott wrote "stranger than fiction" pieces by the yard for *Reader's Digest*, or rather by the snippet, for his sensational retellings of murders, cons, and mysterious disappearances were tailored to a few narrow columns. By contrast, his article on the Cummings/Israel case is in-depth reporting, the case fleshed out to story. A disaffected girlfriend, old army buddies come on the scene, and on the page there is a detailed map of downtown Bridgeport. We learn that the Wickersham Commission on Lawlessness commended Cummings for his handling of the case in 1931, that it's in the law books, required reading for all federal prosecutors and, if you believe this one, that Abbott has "heard the yarn as Cummings spins it over coffee cups." A good trick, since the small print at the bottom of the page informs us that his article is condensed from an unsigned piece in *The Rotarian*, December 1945.

At this point I should have given up on the docu in *Boomerang*, gone with the drama, but my response to this lost movie, my making much of it, was more than a testing of documentable hometown reality against the Hollywood version. I wondered at the nature of my project, the claim to investigative work of my own as though the very act of exhaustive research may absolve the liberties that, as a writer of fiction, I take with information. Facts may be fair game, but that notion, which is far from being a fact, does not alleviate the storyteller's anxiety about desired verisimilitude. And for all its empty claims to truth, *Boomerang* was a pretty good movie: it managed to incorporate a convincing reality, no matter that a further discovery undermined the authority of *The Rotarian*. In the archives of the Bridgeport Public Library, I discovered "My Favorite Detective Case," by Admiral Richard E. Byrd, *True Detective*, April 1941: the Israel case, of course, with a few introductory remarks by the honored explorer and aviator who, I surmised, was a Connecticut and D.C. friend of Cummings. Shame on Anthony Abbott and *The Rotarian*. *True Detective* is where they really got the story almost word for word: a decently told account of the case with the bizarre addition of Ethel Barrymore arriving at a legitimate theater across Main Street, thirty feet from and five minutes before the murder, but with the same map of downtown, a meaningless picture of the hospital in which the priest died, and a photo of an impressive man, movie-star handsome. The caption reads: "Admiral Richard E.

Byrd tries to make friends with haughty penguins." At this point, the detective's daughter assembling quaint footnotes and curiosities in a quest for the real case was out of touch with reality, never mind claiming it for *Boomerang*. I was well into folio madness, all for the sake of a late forties movie with a hand-me-down connection to real life, a movie which, if you can idle during the day, may be run off for you on TNT or AMC. It's not in your video emporium.

## II

In my attempt to validate *Boomerang* and other postwar docudramas or near-docudramas that I think succeed—*Call Northside 777* (1948), *Panic in the Streets* (1950), *The Wrong Man* (1957), and *On the Waterfront* (1954)—I'd been after the wrong reality, even the wrong documents. (Documentary film people will note that I'm playing fast with a loose genre.) Reality in these movies depends upon a declaration of reality: in lingo that I am uncomfortable with, reality is a reference. We watch *Boomerang* with a double vision. A folksy voiceover tells us that the bright opening shot of ungritty Stamford (director's location of choice) is *the* street on which . . . but then again we are told that this "might be any main street" in Georgia or Utah. Why bother to locate us? We are obviously in story land. Next: to dim night, a big clock to record exact time. A mix of locals and actors run to the fallen body; stark journalistic camera as we move in on authenticity. Halfway through the first reel, a switch to straight all-knowing voiceover, familiar to the audience at the time from propaganda and army training films, from *Thirty Seconds Over Tokyo* (1944), *Objective Burma* (1945), and even "for real" documentaries.

This confident guide separates legal proceedings from the morass of political corruption and ineptitude in the unnamed city, and from the real-estate scam that may implicate the prosecutor's wife—the murky background of our moral drama. The attempted seduction of Henry Harvey (Cummings) with the lure of the governor's mansion features two greedy clowns, their faces bloated to comic grotesques, their shadows cast expressionistically behind the State's Attorney, Dana Andrews, who offers them not the back of his hand but his boyish rectitude. A grab bag of techniques (newsreel to noir), make-it-up-as-we-move-along, is intentional in *Boomerang.* At times the movie seems as amateurish as a kid's box car made in the garage, wonderfully chancy. Will it kick over at all? Or win? I think it places anyway, because Elia Kazan's firm directorial hand controls the cobbled-together styles. The viewer adjusts to the double deal, the delivery of story with intelligence at a time when information and images of information were felt to be as reliable as paternalistic voiceovers. In speedy newsreel style, we witness apprehension of suspect, line up, third degree, coroner's inquest, and then slip back into the more deliberate story time, culminating in the spectacular reversals and unmaskings of a stunning courtroom scene. "From sea to shining sea" plays behind the resonant voiceover which in a grand finale introduces us to yet another layer of reality: "It may be of interest to you to know that the man we have depicted here as Henry Harvey was in real life Homer Cummings, who was to be appointed Attorney General of the United States."

It may interest you to know that *Boomerang,* for all the plot that accrues to the State vs. Harold Israel, exists in a thirty-five-minute version, cut for the classroom to instruct in procedural and courtroom issues. This version is part bio pic of the young Homer Cummings, and, in greater part, is about the nature of testimony.

In "The Storyteller," Walter Benjamin, who imagined technology he did not live to see, comments on forms of communication already in place: "It is indispensable for information to sound plausible. Because of this it proves incompatible with the spirit of storytelling. If the art of storytelling has become rare, the dissemination of information has had a decisive share in this state of affairs. Actually, it is half the art of storytelling to keep a story free from explanation as one reproduces it." In his argument for the imagination's accuracy, Benjamin does not confuse information with explanation, fact with the gloss on fact. In reading fiction we look for the explanatory or editorial voice to work integrally with the imagined narrative. The epigraphs in George Eliot's *Middlemarch,* the plot foretold before each chapter in Melville's *The Confidence Man,* even the newsreels in Dos Passos's *USA,* do not overinstruct the reader.

But half the art of docudrama is its investment in information, even in the explanatory. In the commercial works that have held my attention for round about forty years, I see a convenient marriage, at times compatible, between information and story as a response to a transitional time: postwar to Cold War; black and white to color; the media's growing awareness of its power; the specter of television; and so forth. I carelessly lump technology with history because technology began to make history. In particular, filmed history—real footage—which had proved effective as propaganda for the war effort, was there for the trumped-up Red Menace and American Legion bombast. The real danger was that the apparatus of documentary—dates, text taken to be fact written on the screen, actual footage—easily persuaded, even coerced, while appearing to dramatize. The danger was to more than storytelling.

Benjamin was fully aware of the inevitable leveling of events, a fear that did not occur to the growing audience in the dark. Might life come to imitate newsreel, that ephemeral compilation of the passing scene in which the signing of treaties, deaths of presidents and movie stars were recorded weekly along with Easter bonnets, baby shows, and Barnumesque curiosities? The public's romance with filmed events recalled the period after the Great War in which technology nourished the Surrealists' aesthetic ambivalence toward reality, freed them to embrace trivia, bottom-of-the-front-page phenomena. It was also not unlike the end of the last century, when architects who had learned to use structural iron and steel gussied up the Chicago World's Fair with Beaux Arts folderol. My postwar docudramas, both the authentic and the phony, looked back to techniques in film that had recently pleased, even awed. *Boomerang, The House on Ninety-Second Street* (1945), *Call Northside 777*, with their nervy verisimilitude and pursuit of information, asked for the ready response of a vast American audience brought together in a common cause. These films are technically reactionary, only as interesting to me as a swatch of William Morris wallpaper or as curious as the current craze for tea ceremony in Japan, but that is interesting enough, an attempt of the decorative and ritualistic to value old visions and by reproduction and reenactment to face off with the contemporary, or at least meet it halfway. There is, however, a great difference between the slow typesetting of

Morris's Kelmscott Press or the spare aesthetics of tea ceremony, which savor time and individual choice as though in a pretechnological world, and my postwar docudramas, which capitalized on what came readily to hand, turned back in time but a few short years.

These black-and-white docudramas were made when Technicolor was blurry but dazzling, when Cinerama played to a packed house on Broadway. It's more to the point to note that the small screen had entered the living room, that these were the few faltering years of live television, when story and information seemingly remained distinct. The box was perceived as an instrument of reality: that fact overshadowed the long history of filmed simulations, reenactments that, from the very beginning of newsreels in 1911, made event into story. Benjamin's judgment—*This new form of communication is information*—was unknown.

The detective work in *Call Northside 777* rests solely on technology. Based on the case of Frank Wiecek, who was imprisoned for the murder of a Chicago cop, the movie demonstrates marvels—linotype and lie detector, the telegraphic transmission of photos. Jimmy Stewart, who had recently learned to play himself in *It's a Wonderful Life*, plays a burnt-out investigative reporter in search of a sensational story. He calls Northside 777 and connects to a heartbreaker. Wiecek's mother has mopped floors for eleven years to save the $5,000 reward that may free him. The use of documents—secreted and disclosed, all displayed on screen—is, I'm tempted to say, lavish. So is the use of location. The Chicago skyline framed through high office windows reflects the power of the city and the view of the people who run it; down to earth, the seedy Northside tenements and bars are foreign, dark, impenetrable, and will not yield the solution. Old gumshoe detection fails. Stewart photographs Wiecek's record of arrest with a mini–spy camera. A photo is found that shows Wanda, the louche, lying witness, entering the precinct with the accused. Inconclusive evidence— and besides, Stewart and his editor (Lee J. Cobb again), caught up in a circulation war, may be exploiting the Wieceks. The reporter stakes his career on untested apparatus that will blow up an indecipherable detail within that discredited photo: the date on a newspaper that proves Frank Wiecek was innocent. So—pictures don't lie: the new technology is our friend, more reliable than human testimony.

**Henry Hathaway, *Call Northside 777* (1948)**
**The photographic blowup that solves the case.**

The show-and-tell of daring devices in *Call Northside 777* might play as a clever schoolroom demonstration of documentation were it not for the forceful old-fashioned plot. Julio Cortazar—an aficionado of American film who wrote the story on which Antonioni based *Blowup* (1966)—may have seen any number of photographic blowups on the screen, including perhaps the ballistics blowup in *Boomerang*, but the date on the paper surfacing in the developing fluid as conclusive evidence in *Call Northside 777* is surely the ur-source of *Blowup*. That's admissible evidence, but only as conclusive as citing a *True Detective* article as the ur-source of *Boomerang*, favorite case of Admiral Bird. Sources—secondary, tertiary—will never reveal why *Blowup* and *Call Northside* approach art and *Boomerang* remains an interesting artifact.

In directing *Call Northside*, Henry Hathaway invested a true story with technological adventure. The demonstration of espionage devices was all he had to pull him through in *The House on Ninety-Second Street*, for the story (counterespionage undermines Nazi attempt to steal A-bomb secrets) is early exposed and overexplanatory, charmless as the summary of Act 4 in an opera program. The documents are under the care of the FBI, and there's J. Edgar Hoover signing papers at his desk, and the agents, except for Lloyd Nolan and supporting actors, are real FBI, and this story could not be told until after we dropped the bomb on Japan, and here is the actual limestone D.C. building of headquarters, and here the poor tired dome of the Capitol called up for service yet again. The house was actually on Ninety-Third Street, but I must not take that tack. The display of technology is worth noting: two-way mirrors, microfilm, short wave, long wave, secret missiles, rockets, new P-38s, cryptology, and the invisible ink out of my first magic set. A great aerodrome holds the files of the FBI where, in one scene, girls (clerks) sit in a Busby Berkeley line up, the New York skyline seen out the window, Sheeler rooftops and gleaming machines: the beauty of industrial design, aesthetics of mechanical power, allocated to our side. At the Nazi spy school in Hamburg the mess they are making is Rube Goldberg. Project 97 or 47, whatever—their attempt at the A-bomb—is kitchen science, maybe the secret action of baking powder in applesauce. We are told by the Daddy of voiceovers that "War is thought and thought is information and he who knows the most. . ." I don't know which end of that sentence that I need not finish unravels me, but I guess it's the middle. Thought is information.

In *The House on Ninety-Second Street* all the terrific gadgets, standard equipment for propaganda movies during the war, don't work. Oh, our people shoot reels of Nazis coming and going from that brownstone not quite in Yorkville. Their every despicable word is recorded, transmitted in code. None of it functions in the plot. At the opening of this drama, a spy (theirs) is accidentally run over by a car. At the end, the Nazis close in on our man, take over his radio station: a short-wave operator, not recognizing the rhythms in the message says, "That's not Bill. I know his fist." As for the crucial scientific information, it's all recorded in the head of a memory artist, a washed-up vaudevillian. Human happenstance and intuition, auditory detection and a filler act left over from the Hippodrome control the central events.

In many docudramas of the period, data functioned merely as decor, as the apparatus of reality. Clocks, addresses, maps were allusions to Time and Place, not *the* time or place of the plot. Maps are posted in precincts and military headquarters; they bleed and swell on the screen, seen in aerial views as though they are landscape. Often maps replace landscape. The shadow of a plane appears over the targeted area. Our maps, their maps, in war docudramas are equally explanatory, equally opaque. In concocted docudramas, *Thirty Seconds Over Tokyo, Confessions of a Nazi Spy* (1939), maps plot where we're going, where we've been, plots we know before we buy our ticket. The black-and-white maps, even those of the more successful postwar docudramas, are almost always throwaways, cartographical gestures that refer to the *idea* of location or event without explanation or story. Unspecial effects, they are hardly the map in Vermeer's *Art of Painting* which, to simplify Svetlana Alpers's interpretation in *The Art of Describing*, hangs on the wall of the artist's studio to inform the foreground of the canvas of scientific knowledge—history—and to inform the artist while in the act of painting of the responsibilities of craft. The maps of docudrama never chart the uncertain relation of land to water, the shallows and ledges of experience which we find in Elizabeth Bishop's "The Map," where "Topography displays no favorites; North's as near as West./More delicate than the historian's are the map-maker's colors."

One exception is *Panic in the Streets*, in which the city of New Orleans is mapped in order to cordon off fear, as fear of a plague spreads to the politicians and the press. The map is kept from the people who do not know (as we do not know) the danger of the moment. *Panic in the Streets*, one of the best docudramas, is a fake docudrama. Routing about in the stacks, I won't come up with a forgettable magazine article about an illegal alien off a boat in the port of New Orleans, about the idealistic Coast Guard doctor as an investigator (a moody Richard Widmark) battling ignorance. The clock figures big, runs against him. Information is crucial, false testimony deadly. Jack Palance (psychotic, evil) and Zero Mostel (cowardly, fawning) are monstrous; their performances, *Grand Guignol*, are too broad to connect to documentary. *Panic in the Streets*, a contamination movie of the fifties with a political agenda concerning foreign infiltration, is drama fed by simulated reportage. The intensity of the story is unhampered by reality. Detection is diagnosis. If the city, indeed the country, is to be saved, information must put an end to the plague, but the carrier—it's harrowing—runs away. The movie succeeds because the acting, directing, and the story overwhelm the coded message. If ever a chase sequence was artistically justified, it's the pursuit of the morally, by this time actually, diseased Palance at the end of *Panic*.

## III

I feel the need of that most magisterial of voiceovers, Lowell Thomas, to narrate the long-standing commerce between image of event and event as image in the shady history of filmed news. We were programmed to trust the authoritative male voice lowering an octave for pathos, underscoring the amusing detail, never alluding to what is excluded from view. Elevating the text by elocutionary means should be declared out of bounds in the nineties, but I can crank the camera fast, not as in wacky chase scenes of the silents, but as the cameramen speeded the action if it seemed appropriate in newsreels right up to World War II. Statesmen and just folks being filmed knew they were being filmed, faced into it, acting a little or a lot. Old news—that Lucky Lindy played his scene of shy triumph next to the Spirit of St. Louis over and over again; that Fiorello La Guardia, who came by gusto naturally, dug into *pasta e fagioli* at his lace-covered table again and again until they got the segment right.

Immensely popular, translated into many languages, newsreels were a reality fix for the audience before giving in to the fantasy of movies. There were newsreel theaters in big cities and every studio had its house brand—Pathé, Fox Movietone, MGM News of the Day. The cameramen were tough, inventive, upon occasion—disasters, war—heroic. Watching Yalta and sneezing contests, the magic of Mexico or Côte d'Azur, the audience never guessed that the studios avoided controversial subjects: 1930 footage of Hitler, too upsetting; Pathé allowed no shots of dead gangsters. Kevin Brownlow's *Behind the Mask of Innocence*, a study of social and political issues in the silents, reveals that the one- and two-reelers, Griffith's especially, looked directly to the news for their often controversial subjects. By the time of the docudramas I'm concerned with, the control of material by the studios, in film and newsreel, was firmly in place.

In 1939, Henry Luce gave Louis de Rochemont, the eventual producer of *Boomerang* and *The House on Ninety-Second Street*, $1,500 to start the newsreel series, *The March of Time*. In an interview on *Camera Three* (1974), de Rochemont comes off a little slick and smug, the man who's made his bit of history and can now show his cards with a flourish. Twenty million people a month watched his movie magazine, in part a Luce promotion, often with grandiose or dramatic *Time-Life* picture-story titles—"The Presidency," "The Lash of Success." Each release was exactly twenty minutes of film that put the news, that "perishable commodity" de Rochemont terms it, "in perspective." Shaped and honed, *The March of Time* rises above the improvisations of newsreel with a good deal of "highlighting." Determined to have it both ways, *The March of Time* made claims to the "excitingly authentic" while happily proclaiming that "If the script didn't fit the pictures we'd make the pictures fit the script until we had a happy marriage." Television delivered a death blow to newsreel, yet this glossy product marched on until 1967. In the *Camera Three* retrospective, Jack Glenn, the chief director of *The March of Time*, lets on how good the early camerawork was, much admired by the arty crowd who, with sophisticated equipment, would later try to imitate the tight stationary shots that inadvertently caught blank walls and windows. He's arrogant, mocking: "Our shows have been called documentary."

Maitland Eddy, in his introduction to *The Great Photo Essays of Life*, whips through the glory days of photo magazines—*Pic, Peek, Click, Look. Life,* the great survivor, is his subject: he is amazingly frank about the editors who dictated policy, their bent for the shocking or "point" photo which commented on an essay, and the decline from straight, unadulterated photography to the interior decoration of layout. Louis de Rochemont's career as producer of docudrama cannot be considered without his Luce connections, for the first *March of Time* preceded by one year the first photo essay. Eddy quotes, with irony and delight, the bloated promo that launched that issue with Margaret Bourke-White's stunning cover shot of the dam at Fort Peck, Montana:

To see life; to see the world; to eyewitness great events; to watch the faces of the poor and the gestures of the proud; to see the strange things—machines, armies, multitudes, shadows in the jungle and on the moon; to see things thousands of miles away, things hidden behind walls and within rooms, things dangerous to come to; the women that men love and many children; to see and take pleasure in seeing; to see and be amazed; to see and be instructed.

The large audience of *Life* seeing the photos in the weekly essays with pleasure and amazement were unaware of the controlling sensibility of the magazine. Would they have been surprised to know that when Bourke-White, Berenice Abbott, Cartier-Bresson, and Eisenstadt threw in their rolls of film, that was the end of their job? I think not. Who was Abbott? Who Cartier-Bresson? In the tough times of the thirties and during the bandwagon effort of the war, the contractual arrangement for professional work took precedent over artistic consideration. (We have only to recall John Huston's wartime career, 1943–1946, to reacquaint ourselves with knocks dealt out and perforce accepted by directors when they worked a government job.) Hollywood docudrama's claim to serious journalistic purpose by way of real footage and real story was familiar to readers of the weekly picture magazines, an easy transfer to accept from page to screen. A *Life* photo essay could be assembled from any one of my docudramas, though a shot of Jimmy Stewart, Lee J. Cobb, or Jack Palance would turn the effort into parody, an empty recycling of movie stills.

Hitchcock's *The Wrong Man* was based on a *Life* photo essay (June 29, 1953), the story of Manny Balestrero, a bass player at the Stork Club who is falsely arrested for murder. It is a dark movie, prefaced by Hitchcock's dour on-screen announcement: "What you see here actually happened." The Hitchcock cameo, his famous trademark, was cut from this film, and it is appropriate that there is no playful shell game of identity, for Manny Balestrero was picked up by the cops in place of an "actual" double. A meticulous use of real location can be window dressing: in *The Wrong Man* it connects the film directly to the photo essay. Here, more than in any other docudrama, I imagine turning the pages for photos of the

**Alfred Hitchcock, *The Wrong Man* (1956)**
**Manny Balestrero (Henry Fonda), the everyman in the typical hat**
**and coat of the period, in the New York subway late at night.**

Stork Club, the F train to Queens, Union City, a prison cell, all so real I
have a fleeting wish to edit out the actor, though Henry Fonda's performance is devastating. The order of a reliable world dissolves on his mild
face as witness after witness testifies against him. In the old issue of *Life*,
the likeness of the right man to the wrong is eerie, unnatural, as though
contrived for a Hitchcock script.

Louis de Rochemont hired the young Elia Kazan to direct
*Boomerang* out of time at the Actor's Studio, where honest internalizing
begot honest simulation. Kazan's direction was a clever patching of documentary technique and story. Seven years later, directing *On the
Waterfront*, documentary has become a remnant. *On the Waterfront* is a
powerful "based on," derived from the actual story of Peter Panto, who
attempted to organize the Brooklyn longshoremen and was seen no more.
Panto did not testify to the Waterfront Commission. Marlon Brando does.
You would never guess that real fighters—Abe Simon, Tony Galento—play
the mob's hoods. The movie is seamless except for the intentionally awkward acting of the two investigators and—isn't it interesting?—a squeaki-

ly staged courtroom scene. In *Boomerang* the direction was so confident that deft arguments were momentarily put aside for an invented melodrama, the courtroom suicide of the real-estate crook who knows his plot is going down. In between the two movies, Kazan was a friendly witness for the House Committee on Un-American Activities. So was Budd Schulberg, who wrote the script of *On the Waterfront*. In *Running Time: Films of the Cold War*, Nora Sayre gives a detailed account of the events, political and professional, leading up to and away from the filming in 1954. "Behind the Waterfront" is upbeat and journalistic, though not all Sayre's passion is reined in. Her cause is to lift the haze that confuses silence, betrayal, and informing with reliable testimony. Sayre's cause would seem to be the insistent theme of each of my valued docudramas. The detective work in the writing of fiction, in which an obsessive verification of sources may be seen as minor or distracting, or as a false claim to the truth, must lead after all to the presentation of the case. The directorial work in the writing of fiction is the impossible one of casting all roles—prosecutor, defender, witness—and playing all three.

## IV

In the fifties at Smith College, where I was an undergraduate much taken with the theater, there was a grand old lady, Mrs. Davis, who was lead to a seat of honor in Davis Hall. She wore evening dress, black velvet and satin, to routine Chekhov and (un)hilarious Restoration comedy, for it was, despite all our shortcomings, opening night. In 1934, Hallie Flanagan Davis had founded the Living Newspaper as part of the WPA Arts Project. She headed the theater division, an enormous administrative task that did not curtail her own artistic endeavors. She had staged docudramas at Vassar, most notably the life of the president of the college, which sounds dreadful, but who knows—Hallie was mistress of the *coup de théâtre*. In the Living Newspaper's "Ethiopia," a touring stage production, actors impersonated Mussolini, Haile Selassie, and Anthony Eden. Problems: "No issue of the Living Newspaper shall contain any representation of the head of foreign states unless such representation shall have been approved by the Department of State." Less than ten years later, Stalin, Churchill, and, as Nora Sayre points out, FDR reduced to an arm pouring tea, would be portrayed in *Mission to Moscow* (1943), a ludicrous docudrama of the Moscow trials, one of our friendship cards to the Russians. Though the Living Newspaper was art out of ideology—one long Left editorial—*The New York Times* and Washington mostly approved. One admiring review called Hallie's work "American as Walt Disney, *March of Time* . . . Congressional Record." A history of American agriculture, "Triple A Plowed Under," was a great success: it made its points by way of skits, radio broadcasts, and pantomimes. An actor played Henry Wallace, who was never a head of state. Props and costumes minimal, spare Meyerhold scenery, Brechtian hi-jinks, circus acts, loudspeaker for voiceover. A giant dime is awarded to Rockefeller; a humongous pickle to Heinz. Audiences heckled, stomped with delight. Davis's sense of play in docudrama, her aesthetic risks and dramatic complexities, never rubbed off on that genre in the movies of the forties and fifties: Hollywood docudramas take themselves very seriously, every one. Hallie Flanagan Davis was called up before the Dies Committee in 1938 and before HUAC as to the theater division of the Arts Project's Communist leanings. Her testimony was dignified and forceful: it is worth reading what she said to those men about her commitment to the theater and her "re-dreaming of America." In the sixties, Julian Beck and Judith Molina founded a theater of radical necessity and poverty. Their Living Theater made reference to the great days of Hallie Flanagan Davis.

The decade of my docudramas falls between the years of protest that brought about both Living Newspaper and Living Theater, and comes after the public certainties of the war. Why, as victors, we were both proud and fearful, smug and unsure, susceptible to the threats of Joe McCarthy, is not my subject, but it is the subtext of these movies, each one searching anxiously for authenticity. But I cannot set McCarthy aside, for it was his show on the box, more than the gentlemanly crime hearings of Estes Kefauver (1951), that threatened the movie industry. As it turned out, Hollywood had nothing to fear from television: in retrospect it seems an arranged marriage, the parties coopting each other. But at the time, the McCarthy hearings (1954) and Milton Berle played along with my docudramas. I see it as a double feature, a triple feature if I introduce one more show, the exemplary television reporting of *See It Now* (1951–1958).

Edward R. Murrow, the most distinguished broadcast journalist of the time, is in the control booth, under the mike, facing the clock, beneath the single small monitor: he swivels to us—"Stand by now. This program is coming to you from Studio 41, New York City." And: "Stand by Dexter, Michigan," "Stand by Chicago," addressing us in his husky smoker's voice, cigarette in hand. To see *See It Now* now is to loathe *Sixty Minutes* and *Nightline*. People are allowed to talk, speak the long yea and nay of it. When Murrow says, "It is our opinion," he includes Fred Friendly, his coproducer. Getting into a dense one—Harold Urey's findings on heavy water—he looks over his shoulders at the controls: "This is our effort to translate that report to television." Opinion, the admission of effort on the part of a talking head, are as inconceivable to us now as the Shroud of Turin. And Murrow gave credit to each cameraman out there in Dexter, Chicago, or Detroit, and he used no Teleprompter. Documents were shown on screen, read to us from the typed or printed page. Murrow dealt with McCarthy by documenting the career of the senator from Wisconsin, and then let the senator have equal time (that program is often cited as the beginning of his end) to document and damn himself.

   *Hear It Now* (radio) and *See It Now* called us to witness as though we were one of the locals hired for the courtroom scene in *Boomerang* or the nurse in *The Wrong Man* who played herself tending to Manny Balestrero's depressed wife. We are to be taken into account. These programs, conscious of the gift and the burden of a wide audience, appealed to us directly, conveyed a need for us. It was a mutual trust, a passing illusion.

   *You Are There* was the zany culmination of the witness craze. You are at the Fall of Rome, the Trial of Thomas More, the Vindication of Savonarola, the Conquest of Cortez. John Daly, Howard K. Smith, foreign correspondents with full credentials, appear as themselves in the TV studio. Let's go to Walter Cronkite: "There is only one story today, Wednesday, May 30, 1431, the Execution of Joan of Arc . . . We have our CBS newspeople standing by in Rouen." The stage sets were thrown up in a week. *You Are There* was a refuge for blacklisted writers, history presumably being safe ground, not subject to manipulation. "This is Harry Marvel inside the chateau at Rouen. We are waiting for the Earl of Warwick." *You Are There* has its enchantments: life in front of the camera, actors hard at work. Sidney Lumet directing Mildred Dunnock, Rod Steiger, Jerome Kilty, babyface Paul Newman, Eartha Kitt. They go up on their lines, recover. You are there. "March 18, the 710th year after the founding of Rome. Let's go to Capitoline Hill . . . Cassius coming this way. I'll try to get him to say something about the main resolution before the Senate today." Sewing machine togas—but enough.

In attempting to frame the few respectable docudramas made at the outset of the Cold War, I cannot dismiss some unamusing propaganda films as camp. *Confessions of a Nazi Spy* is laden with stock documentary gestures out of the bunkum barrel: pompous voiceover and over, animated map seeping poison throughout Europe, real footage of real Nazis, Statue of Liberty for the roundup. There is one great line in this movie, unfortunately often attributed to Hermann Goering: "When I hear the word culture, I reach for my gun." We may dismiss the silly plot: treacherous George Sanders in pursuit of code C, Edward G. Robinson: "As far as I know the FBI has never done any counterespionage"; but the repellent anti-Semitism, set as it is in cheap melodrama, comes off as villainous. A rotten movie, yet no laughing matter: forbidden in Eastern Europe, it is said that seven Polish projectionists were hanged for showing it. Twelve years later, *I Was a Communist Spy for the FBI* (1951) purported to be the real case of Matt Cvetic, union activist in Pittsburgh, a truly insidious piece in which the Reds bait the Pinkos, plot to make use of Negroes "like we did in the race riots of 1943," etc. The actor playing Cvetic does his own voiceover as though, cut loose from this terrible script, he might pass for any number of men who flee the incriminating past in film noir. Will he or won't he get to testify and clear his name? Finally, the scene before the Committee in Washington, D.C., in which his young son proudly sees . . . It's the same story with the same baggage, give or take a twist, as *Dangerous Hours* (1920), in which the Bolshies . . . Indeed, the films were shown together in the fall of 1991 at the Museum of the Moving Image in Long Island City, New York.

*The Commies are Coming, the Commies are Coming* (1951) is "hosted" by *Dragnet's* Jack Webb. I am as bored by this movie as I am by discourse on Disneyland, but I recommend it to devotees of Jean Baudrillard, for there is a simulated American town, peopled and exact in all details, attributed to the evil genius of the Russians: a town that is a perfect Hollywood set, and therefore a simulation of simulation. A court scene, of course, in which the heroic American schlub, who has somehow fallen down this rabbit hole, will not renounce his beliefs. "What you have seen is not entirely fiction," says Webb, before the Warner Brothers movie segues into a training film for G.I.s headed for Korea, instructing them how to behave when captured, how to organize escape patrols.

In Hollywood docudramas, not overtly political, conspiracy is a dominant theme: conspiracy to conceal the truth about disease, corruption, or simply the identity of an innocent man. In *The Haunted Fifties*, I. F. Stone wrote of more than movies: "The cosmic joke of the cold war was the import into America of Russia's traditional spy-mania and constant obsessions about conspiracy." For me, the best of my docudramas come with their thick folder of documentation, with the surround of history. Made at a time when history was not yet nervous about its records, they are anxious movies every one. All except Kazan's self-concealing *On the Waterfront* display the basting threads. There is something crudely appealing and even conspiratorial about *Call Northside 777, Boomerang,* and *The Wrong Man.* They ask us to witness as reality what they have not witnessed. They solve their plots, but only by inspired detection, and we have seen how easily the evidence, seemingly conclusive, can come down the other way. Their duality presents to the writer of fiction the problem of verisimilitude, no matter how fantastic the tale, that must be faced sentence by sentence, day by day.

## V

The wives in each of my "respectable" docudramas—"the women men loved," in Luce-speak—are the gals behind the guys. When the doctor, reporter, or prosecutor falters in his pursuit of truth, the little woman proves to be one notch finer. A comforting sandwich and a glass of milk, administered as nursery food, awaits the tired man. There is home, the private world, and there is out there. Only Manny Balestrero's wife breaks under his arrest, as she did in life, and cannot respond to the reversals at the end of their trials. She, poor woman—it was the fifties—is seen as one more trial for her husband to bear. In *On the Waterfront*, Eva Marie Saint, a convent girl, is drawn into the underworld by the murder of her brother, into the sexual world by Brando. Their story is one of children made to grow up. Unlike the bad girls of the era—Crawford, Stanwyck, Graham— the actresses of my docudramas play archetypal goodies. All—except Eva Marie, who becomes a saintly activist—are lonely and naïve, and live apart from out there.

Out there is the city. These movies exist in an urban enclosure. Politics of the city weigh in each story: the possibility of corruption, of the uncivil within the civil; the probability of mistaken identity, of disappearance in the crowd, of confusion, increases. In these American cities the documents can be lost, faked, withheld as they are in the convoluted plots of Dickens's London. The dissembling or fumbling authorities can be set right only by ingenious detection and full disclosure. Persistence, those of us who live in cities know, becomes a cardinal virtue. In the city we are not known to each other. The accused men in *Call Northside 777*, *Boomerang*, and *The Wrong Man* have paid their dues, but it's of no account when the system cranks up against them. Their credentials are as meaningless as their word. The urban nightmare has similar streets, houses, bars, figures in identical dark coats and slouch hats, misremembered time, and disfiguring shadows.

There was panic in the streets that Robert Moses, the revered urban planner of that time, sensibly but myopically set aside in "The Spreading City": "I dismiss as unworthy of serious consideration the gloomy prophets who label cities as obsolete because of the possibility of atomic bombing." But his prescription for salvage, restoration, and preservation did not reckon with predictable technology, nor with the economic entrapment, hardly a cultivated choice, of the urban masses. Moses's, Mr. City's, lofty recommendation to "approximate the old Roman idea of *rus in urbe*, the country in the city," became yet another footnote to dystopia. Brando, strolling with Eva Marie on the promenade of Brooklyn Heights, the powerful city in their view, asks where she goes when she goes away to the tranquillity of school—"So, that's in the country?" The Balestreros remove to Florida where it is hoped they may reconstruct their lives.

# VI

Boomerang: An Australian missile weapon: a curved piece of hard
wood two to three feet long, with a sharp edge along the convex-
ity of the curve. It is so made as to describe complex curves in its
flight and can be thrown so as to hit an object in a different direction from that of projection, or so as to return to or beyond the
starting point. —*Oxford English Dictionary.*

When my father said they got it wrong in *Boomerang*, he may
have meant that Harold Israel did not go free. He was sent up for six
months on illegal possession of a firearm. Or that, new on the job, he
would not have been the one detective on the case. There was a man
named Garlick, older and wiser, a police officer perhaps, who figures in
several accounts as Cummings's right-hand man. Though he had spent his
life assembling testimony, my father bought Senator McCarthy on television and off. We fell apart, no setting that aside. He liked Joseph Welch,
the prosecutor in the Army-McCarthy trials, too. He liked watching. We
all did, but I could not bear to watch the detective savoring the courthouse
roles, the rhetoric, the senator's spurious documents: instant docudrama.

Searching out old *Reader's Digests* and "true crime," I came up
with sources that might as well be found documents like the simulated
diaries and letters of Samuel Richardson or Daniel Defoe. Such inventions
are not my reality, though I may imitate their fictive premises in writing
fiction. In the introduction to the New York Edition of *The Aspern Papers*,
James is concerned with source as the "visitable past": it is often quoted—
"the poetry of the thing outlived and lost and gone, and yet in which the
precious element of closeness, telling so of connections but tasting so of
differences, remains appreciable." He calls upon a double vision, not
unlike the vision which I attempt re-viewing and writing of these old
movies, hoping to discover the poetry of the thing in the lifeline left in connections, while reaching for the life buoy thrown out in the detection of
differences. For the writer of fiction, the visitable past is never the shallows, but deep, fairly dangerous waters, the pearl diver's place where the
abnormal growth of story must be extracted from the concealing shell of
information.

I came of age in an age of testimony. We were, perhaps, a naïve audience in our response to a naïve genre, too ready to leave unexamined the incorporation of reality into our entertainment. I am aware that I must consider myself a back number tracking where truth may be sacrificed for the sake of story and where it may not. Oliver Stone's *JFK* (1992) appropriates every maneuver of docudrama—the real footage of Ike, Castro, Dulles; the claim to actual events; the decorative maps, authoritative voiceover, technological detection, faked footage—in a fashionable postmodern pastiche. Upon re-viewing, I find it hard to imagine that this movie was taken seriously as a movie. It has some good acting, some good scenes, fancy camerawork throughout with flips from color to black and white (poor old black and white sworn in as the expert witness). *JFK* is laden with exposition, endless and confusing information which slows the action. But Stone is clever; information plays as story conference. "What are we saying here?" Kevin Costner asks. He asks it as Garrison, the District Attorney in New Orleans who staked out his claims in the conspiracy enterprise. But the leading question is rhetorical. What we are hearing is Oliver Stone's answer. It is not necessarily a dismissable answer, but it is surely propaganda in his movie. *JFK* is closer to *The House on Ninety-Second Street* than it is to *Boomerang,* and a great distance from *On the Waterfront* and *Panic in the Streets.* Stone's movie is forty years removed from whatever dubious validity may be claimed for postwar docudramas, and the use of the old techniques becomes, for me, all reference, like the baby carriage from *Potemkin* planted amusingly in De Palma's *The Untouchables* (1988). Frederick Brooks, a great figure in the world of Virtual Reality, might have been speaking of docudrama when he said of a computer model of the Rocky Mountains that "the potentials for misleading are very great in that kind of instance, and the fractal mountains are a good clear visual image of an important distinction between *realism* and *truthfulness.* The danger of more and more realism is that if you don't have corresponding truthfulness, you teach people things that are not so."

The television fundamentalists witness, construct, and reconstruct their testimonies of extraordinary events and revelations, as fundamentalists always have. However subjective, testimony posits the existence of audience, not necessarily of truth. My students speak of their narratives, the multiple narratives available to all which enable us to speak, to create a self. These are texts that connect to the past, tell what happened before the telling began. How can we not welcome this pluralism? Yet I fear an easy visit to the past in which personal testimony, which is not storytelling in Benjamin's sense, loses track of its connection to information and becomes, like much of the nightly news, yet another form of entertainment. And that the witness—like Lucky Lindy, La Guardia, Brando—will begin to act. Remembrance is refracted through desire, and through failure of recollection, and, as in those reenactments that are propaganda, may be supplemented by purpose.

## VII

Teaching in Houston for a month, I took myself to the museums, always alone. In the Museum of Fine Arts, I visited and revisited a favorite work, Braque's *Fishing Boats*, and looked long into a dreamy, welcoming Vuillard, but I came away with one note in my pocket diary: "*Still Life with Musical Instruments*, ca. 1710, Cristofora Monari. A genre painting depicting the perishable and pleasurable in which the weave of an oriental carpet rises 3D out of the canvas, aiming to be real. It's a failure, even as a fake." And in the dazzling Menil collection I noted that Max Ernst, surrealist, when preparing the pieces for his *Histoire Naturelle*, placed paper over raffia, over sand and cherry pits, then, rubbing with a soft pencil, assured the reality of each texture for his imagined reality.

It seems simple in the end—how my intention, which is more than an interest in these old movies, colors memory, is colored and charted by memory. The map on the wall must be precise, exhibit history, and claim knowledge. I see it as a schoolroom map pulled down like a window shade in front of the blackboard. Main Street cuts through neighborhoods, runs right down to the shore. The thick grid of streets is downtown, and there, just there a priest was murdered. It is an old oilcloth map, cracked and faded, that will not do. I must superimpose the latest modeling with fractals revealing the smallest irregularities of coastline and hills. The time, the date recorded as well as all that reliable/unreliable footage from the grave or *True Detective*; the tricks of documentation proving sight is not insight. But the double focus of docudrama reflects my unending anxiety about possession of sources, and that possession is far less than nine-tenths of the law. In this court there is no written law. With the small satisfaction found in the depthless voiceover of proverbs, it is possible to say art witnesses, art invents. So, what the hell, I swivel toward you: "Stand by, Bridgeport. There is only one story tonight." Each task of writing is assembling the evidence, playing it straight like Homer Cummings or at least Dana Andrews, hoping that at the end of my efforts I will not hear it coming at me with its complex curve, that fatherly voice now gently corrective: "Christ, she's got it wrong."

CHARLES WARREN

# Earth and Beyond:

## Dušan Makaveyev's *WR: Mysteries of the Organism*

**D**ušan Makaveyev is one of the world's most remarkable film artists in the period since 1960, working in both fiction and nonfiction film, and notably combining the two. He made two feature-length fiction films in Yugoslavia: *Man Is Not a Bird* (1965) and *Love Affair: or, The Case of the Missing Switchboard Operator* (1967)—the latter a crucial discovery for *Cahiers du Cinéma* at the time; and then *Innocence Unprotected* (1968), about a real man who once appeared in a fiction film, using the old fictional footage as well as Makaveyev's own documentary work to present this man's life. *WR: Mysteries of the Organism* (1971), made partly in Yugoslavia and partly in the United States, has been Makaveyev's most celebrated film. This work about Wilhelm Reich and his ideas and influence, using old and new documentary footage as well as fiction, was seen widely at film festivals and in regular distribution in the early 1970s, and was much discussed; the film script was published in 1972. Makaveyev went on to make *Sweet Movie* (Canada and Holland, 1974), which combines fiction with nonfiction, and then the fiction films *Montenegro* (Sweden, 1981), *The Coca-Cola Kid* (Australia, 1985), *Manifesto* (Yugoslavia again, 1988), and *Gorilla Bathes at Noon* (Germany, 1993). *Hole in the Soul* (1994) is a documentary made in Belgrade.

*WR: Mysteries of the Organism* presents a range of interesting content: documentation of America in 1970, radical politics, Reich's psychological theory and practice, and a fictionalized Yugoslavia. But the heart of it, the basis for it, is how the film alters and refreshes our very sense, our grasp, of film. *WR* reexamines fiction and nonfiction film, and gives us a new ability to respond to film. We are able to see new things in the world, and are perhaps left able to change, because of something new brought about in our relation to film.

*WR* brings to the fore a commitment to the body, a quality of earth, I would like to call it. The film insists on the body and the physical reality of what is before the camera, and it studies the relation of this reality to film imagination and to the imagination in general—the life we come into, the movements of history apprehensible as such, thought and art.

The movement from body to more than body is epitomized in the film's treatment of the issue of male or female—which is one to be identified as? Ordinarily we think of male or female as the most body-determined of issues, but it is not so in this film. Makaveyev identifies himself, as director/presenter, with a woman, the voice that narrates the early documentary part of the film; and it is at least suggested that this woman speaker becomes the lead character, a woman, in the fictional part of the film, who is in turn identified in many ways with Reich, the film's inspiration and first subject. Also, a human being of indeterminate sex, the New York transvestite or transsexual Jackie Curtis, takes over the film at crucial points.

The facing of the body with what is more than the body, yet not apart from it, is also figured in the strange facing of earth with outer space and what may be out there and yet akin to us, maybe a source from which we are drawn. Early in the film Reich's speculation on his possible kinship with extraterrestrials is spoken by the woman narrator (it is *apparently* a woman's voice) as we move down a road through a Maine forest—earth, home, to Reich—and eventually look at Reich's observatory and telescope.

## Humor, Real People, Sex—and Film Fancy

There are three aspects to the earthiness of *WR*: humor; people as real, unidealized people; and sex. These factors all work to ground things in the film, and in a way to comfort us. But they also work to unsettle things, to ready us for transformation. And here humor, people as people, and sex become involved with the techniques and imagination of film showing themselves as such.

Wilhelm Reich, the film's subject, the germ that gives it life, is not notable for humor or for his sense of people as people, despite his abundant presentation of case studies, as in *Character Analysis*. The case studies are very much case studies, conceived in the terms of Reich's theories. He does not have Freud's novelistic quality, sensitive to the unaccountable in people, the narrative of a (Freud) case always taking small unpredictable turns. And the impression one has of Reich in life, as from Myron Sharaf's very sympathetic biography, is of a certain crudeness, a regard for people only in relation to Reich himself and his theories.[1] Even people who loved Reich and are grateful to him for liberating their lives, seem to feel the good done was by virtue of Reich's theoretical passion, something beyond personal consideration.

Reich *is* notable for his preoccupation, like that of Makaveyev's film, with sex. And here Reich works as an emblem for the body as this film conceives of it. Reich, by virtue of his preoccupation with sex, serves as the subject-germ for a film that in significant ways is not Reichian, or is more than Reichian; just as the body in this film's conception allows for, calls for, a going beyond the body. The funny thing is that what in the film is beyond the body takes us right back into the realm of earth and the body. The way up and the way down. . .

Humor begins at the start of the film. White letters—REICH, JOY OF LIFE—on a cheerful blue background ("the color of Orgone energy," the published filmscript informs us[2]) initiate a series of dissolves: REICH, JOY OF LIFE . . . ENJOY . . . FEEL . . . LAUGH. And a bit later: LUIS BUÑUEL AWARD/CANNES FILM FESTIVAL, 1971. The series of dissolves always provokes chuckles in an audience, the quality of the chuckles changing subtly with each phrase as the series goes on, as one may imagine—reread the phrases slowly. Just before this series the film has

1. Myron Sharaf, *Fury on Earth: The Life of Wilhelm Reich* (St. Martin's Press, 1983).

2. Avon Books, 1972. The book contains an interview with Makaveyev conducted by Phillip Lopate and Bill Zavatsky.

given us a paragraph identifying Reich as having discovered "life energy" and having revealed the "deep roots" of various fears, and as believing in a "work-democracy," "an organic society based on liberated work and love." The series of dissolves and the mention of Buñuel tell us that there will be nothing overbearing about the psychoanalysis and the projection of an ideal society in this film. We will not be overwhelmed by any fearful new future. That first paragraph of prose begins, "This film is in part a personal response . . ." The *person* behind this film—and I am not saying it is Makaveyev exactly—will allow for our common humanity. We will be left as we are, to the extent that we must be. We will be all right in the hands of this film. (Of course we may be being seduced.)

In the ensuing sequence we contemplate a couple of dogs—life that is not human, always potentially humorous—and then the film begins to observe, or to collaborate with, a man who comes onto this slum street, puts on a mock-military costume, and begins parading around. (Some will recognize him as Tuli Kupferberg, "poet of the Lower East Side" according to the published script, and sometime lyricist for The Fugs.) This man now provides the humor, as a street-theater satirist of regimes where war is endemic to the state institution. A voiceover (Kupferberg in fact) recites and then sings, "Who will protect us from our protectors? Who shall judge our police?" and eventually, "Very few poems get written. Fewer still get read." The controllers of society, the liberator who is a further controller in a sense—a judge (such as Reich)—then the artist (poet, filmmaker), and ourselves (readers of poems, of films), all are conflated here even as they are named and distinguished. In the written verse and the song the same energy seems to run through everything. Kupferberg's humor is Swiftian—desperate posturing to release energy in the hope of getting a general transformation of things. But the style of the film here is contrastingly calm and observing. The humor *comes into* the film here, from Kupferberg. We are not sure how it will sit with the film itself.

We are not sure, in part because the film's second great quality has come into play, the presentation of people as people. Kupferberg is not a creation of the film just to serve its purposes, but a real man (like those real dogs), gawky, not conventionally attractive. The voice recites, "man cannot clean his sockses and says, 'the world is soiled.'" This man we see is so to speak soiled like anyone—not a movie-person, not a creature of imagination. But then with his mock rifle, tall, lean physique, and upright bearing, he is phallic. This and a certain dirtiness having to do with the black beard and long hair, as well as his humor, make him the perfect embodiment of the imperfect, healthful libido this film wishes to promote. He suits the imagination of the film. And of course he is an imaginative figure in the sense of being theatrical, always in performance—we never see a "real," nonperforming Tuli Kupferberg. Play between the real and the imaginatively perfect will become a major preoccupation of this film. The humor at this point, not being precisely Makaveyev's, and the real-man/art-man question keep us in suspense as to where we are.

The credits sequence, next, with a close shot of an egg yolk being passed from hand to hand, and eventually a fuller view of the people doing this, always elicits chuckles, just as the ENJOY . . . FEEL . . . LAUGH dissolves do. Perhaps the humorous idea is "yes, this was really the sixties," or "yes, this is what all the progressive therapy or ideas about communal living boils down to"—we laugh with the film at its imaging of the silly essence of something; perhaps we laugh at ourselves, or former selves. Of course we do just "enjoy" and "feel"—the yolk slipping around and eventually breaking and smearing engages us without thoughts needing to arise. We laugh as if physically tickled.

There is a disjunction here—perhaps it contributes to the humor, humor always depending on disjunction. We recognize this sequence, interesting for what is "really" going on in it, as fiction. The jaunty and loud, vaguely Eastern piping music, enough in itself to make us smile, seems to belong with a director's created scene; the lighting has the feel of a studio; the intimacy of the moving camera with the subjects looks choreographed; and the people, when we see them fully, behave with a studied air that seems acting (how could we say for sure?). And they are young and beautiful, looking like movie stars, at least little ones, as compared with Tuli Kupferberg. These people are in fact the cast of the Yugoslav fictional part of the film, which begins much later on.

Is the yolk handling itself fiction, the *yolk* and the sheer act of *handling* it, apart from the characters and setting and the way the scene is filmed? What is this very act?—Who can say absolutely what fiction is? The film will press this question again and again. If there is a real distinction between fiction and nonfiction in film, is it something inherent in a film, or a matter of how we see, or use, film? *WR*, with all its mixing of material, will make a great issue of how film is used. Is everything combined in this film to make a great fiction, a feat of imagination, or is it an essay, or a record of our times?

A final note of disorientation in this sequence is that with the appearance of the title, "Directed by Dušan Makaveyev," the darker woman in the group looks right into the camera, and then the others look vaguely toward it, following her lead, then look away before she does. Is this just the cast acknowledging the director? Or is Makaveyev declaring himself, with the title, to "be" this woman whose eyes meet ours? The confusion continues in the next sequence, when the (seeming) woman narrator's voiceover begins. Is this the voice of the film? Of the director? Perhaps the credits sequence as a whole ought to tell us that the voice to come will be one of the group we see, if not the dark woman. The voice we soon hear sounds entirely American, but the published script says it is Milena, who is the blonde woman in the group at the start, and who will be the lead character in the Yugoslavian part of the film.[3] Milena is identified continually with Reich by her speeches and actions; at the end, decapitated—"un-earthed"—but still alive and talking, her image is merged with Reich's photograph by a dissolve. She is identified with the germ—or egg—of the film, Reich, its director in a sense. Milena, the director Makaveyev, the voice or intelligence behind the film, Reich—how far is imaginative identification from being real identification?

The next part of the film, its beginning really, seeks to set out certain facts about Reich, but by indirect, strange, and hurried means. Could the film be plainer here? Is its fancifulness necessary? What is really being conveyed? We see the title *"Filme der Sexpol."* Does this apply to all the rest of *WR* or just to what immediately follows? We see footage of a cou-

---

3. Apparently Makaveyev intended to make a Serbo-Croatian version of the entire film (he never did), where the Milena character (played by Milena Dravic) would in fact read the early narration. I thank Vlada Petric for this information.

ple in a meadow, who are physically well-formed, beautiful, and who eventually undress and make love. One cannot say absolutely whether they are doing it, as one can say with hardcore fictional (?) sex films and some documentaries, though we do see the man's erect penis at one point in the scene. All of this is multiplied into several images by a sort of kaleidoscope—is this a declaration of the camera, just an extension of the camera's inevitable fantasy? Is all this Makaveyev's own footage? Is at least the kaleidoscope effect his? Are we conceivably seeing part of an old film of Reich's sex analysis and education group, Sexpol? The film soon intercuts another title, "*Internationalen Institut für Sexualökonomische Forschung (kopieren verboten),*" which looks archival. *WR* seems to want to identify itself with a production of Reich's—saying that *WR* is in a sense Reich's film.

There is footage of Reich as a young man in a meadow with a young woman, and a bit later, footage of the young Reich in a laboratory. A choir is heard singing the hymn-like "Communist Party my fragrant flower. . ." And through all this the woman narrator gives a fast commentary on Reich's ideas and his career in Europe and America, concluding with his prosecution and death in prison in Pennsylvania. The narration elicits laughs at a few lines: "fuck freely" (audiences must now think of AIDS, but they laugh anyway—of course "freely" does not necessarily mean "promiscuously"); "saliva is good"; Reich in the United States "eventually voted for Eisenhower." "Fuck freely" and "saliva is good" sound incongruous in the sober voice of the narrator. And with Eisenhower, the narrator seems not fully to relish who he is, merely offering his name as straightforward support for the idea of Reich's good citizenship. Does the film wish to tell us about Reich as well as it can? It seems to me that the speed and queerness of what we have seen so far is meant just to give us a subject for the film, almost as a foregone conclusion. The film stirs things up as if they already mattered, without yet coming to what might seem its proper business of showing or telling us something directly. Probably by now we have got the couple making love, whom we could not see well enough, irrevocably into our heads. Sex—the earth—is compelling, despite the tricks of art and mind. But can sex and the earth exist without the tricks of art and the mind?

With the next material the film does seem to come to its proper business. There is a cut from the footage of Reich in his laboratory, with narration about his Orgonon Institute in Maine, to a moving camera shot, approaching a shed or outbuilding, then moving through a room of junk to rest on one of Reich's Orgone boxes in the corner. Seemingly this is Maine (though later information suggests it is not). Makaveyev and his film crew are moving into the orbit of those who knew Reich, to get what information they can. The film now becomes pure documentary, if one likes, touching earth as nearly as it can. Dr. Myron Sharaf emerges from the accumulator, as he calls it, with a little boy in a cat mask. Has this image of birth been staged for the film? Just prior to the emergence we have heard Sharaf reading about Pinocchio—"'Hooray!' he cried, 'I am a real boy.' . . . Old Gepetto smiled . . . Pinocchio had much to learn before he could be a real boy." The reading from "Pinocchio" and the little boy we see in the mask stress the idea of metamorphosis and imagination and the hope for development upward, at the heart of all Reich's and Sharaf's realism about the body.

Sharaf talks with the film crew, casually and good-humoredly explaining the accumulator. He is a stocky, swarthy man, who speaks with something of a city, working-people's accent. He is not an ideal figure. We are speaking with a "real" man about things that have to do with his life. With his vividly patterned cardigan—a link to the child's mask—and his city manner, he seems out of place in this country storeroom, if that is what it is; but he wants to be helpful and to be positive about Reich. He is less than fervid about the accumulator; and intercuts of photos of other accumulators and Orgone devices, with some solemn narration from the woman narrator, make all this seem a quaint historical phenomenon, at least a mystery—perhaps it is too fanciful. We have the feeling that for Sharaf, and for the film, the real story is yet to come.

But the film now moves to an interview with a former woman employee of Reich's that underscores, on its face, the seriousness of Reich's work with orgone energy accumulation. This plump country woman with large bare arms—perhaps a kitchen worker or cleaning woman—tells of once having had the bad bleeding of a cut finger suddenly stopped by Reich's applying a small machine to it. Here an almost disturbingly rough-hewn person attests that Reich's fancy really worked. Or was she fooled? (Was Reich fooled?) Are we seeing a bit of the fanaticism of the devoted? Who is this woman really? What is disturbing about her?

We see the woman in profile from the waist up, tightly framed in the left and center of the shot, with another woman—her colleague, or alter-ego—wiping down a car on the right in the background. The camera is fixed, and a little above the woman as well as to her side, so that she acknowledges it awkwardly. She seems caught for a moment, and compromised with—she is not the subject of the camera's flexible play, like Dr. Sharaf and many others in the film. I think most viewers will wonder about her sexual existence. Could she be reached by Reich's orgasm theory? Does she need to be reached by it? Is she a being of another kind than those whom Reich's theory concerns? The film is about the bridging or mixing of different areas, separate realms. The encounter with this woman makes a puzzle of whether people are really alike in some way. Who is reachable by whom or what? In this scene the issue of Reich's fancy about Orgone devices, with a real person testifying to its seriousness, turns into the issue of who a person is.

An encounter with Eva Reich Moise, Reich's daughter, is used with other material to tell us of Reich's trial and death. Eva is in Maine, outdoors, a middle-aged woman who is casual about her hair, clothes, figure. She looks as if she may have been working in the garden she shows us. She is fervid and bitter about Reich's work, his end, and the state of the world, her thoughts seeming to jar with her setting. She too raises the question of disparate sorts of people, or aliens. One cut to her begins with part of a sentence of hers that is never fully explained: she is addressing the crew, ". . . because you came from behind the Iron Curtain . . ." Does she mean that they cannot understand her, that they are too unlike her? She speaks very much like an American, but at moments shows traces of a foreign upbringing and education (which she in fact had), as when she pronounces "good state beings" (what children behind the Iron Curtain, she says—does she know?—are "manufactured into"), "good" rhyming with "mood," the consonants all forceful and distinct, spaces made between the words—"good. state. beings." This woman does not just serve to provide information about Reich. We are made to ask, is she an alien in some sense? Who—what—is she?

Between two sequences with Eva there is material with the Lewisburg, Pennsylvania, prison where Reich died, and with the garbage incinerator in New York City where his books were burned by court order. Outside the prison the camera moves quickly, presumably in a car, down the long wall of the place, then zooms in quickly on the guard towers and on the entrance area, where some men are passing through the gates. All this is accompanied by a waltz for zither and accordion, reminiscent of the music for the egg-yolk sequence. One thing we feel immediately is that Makaveyev and his crew are world travelers and artists. They can get away from Rangeley, Maine—shoot what they like, go where they like. The way the prison is shot has an antic quality, which the music intensifies. This seems filmmaking asserting itself—Makaveyev's fancy. But of course this may be the only way the prison can be filmed: if Makaveyev and his crew had not moved fast, they might have been accosted or arrested. The film may be as direct here with its real subject as it can be. The music may seem fanciful, but it is, like the music for the egg-yolk scene, down to earth too—popular music, folk music, the way a people reacts to and copes with the realities of life. Maybe the humor of the music and camera antics dissolves for a moment any worry over the distinction between what is artificial and what is down to earth.

The music stops just before the end of the sequence, giving way to what is apparently the grinding sound of the prison gates we see. This sound blends with that of the garbage-moving machine at the New York incinerator, which is what we see next. The giant claws moving garbage about quickly over a long distance are fascinating to watch, seen at a distance from below and then above, and seen close up, the camera moving freely about this dangerous-seeming space, like the garbage machine itself. The woman narrator reads off the titles of Reich's books—*The Function of the Orgasm*; *Ether, God, and Devil*; *The Murder of Christ*, and so on—and there is a sense of outrage at their being destroyed. Still, hearing the names as we see the garbage does make the books seem "garbage" in a way. And the fate of garbage does not look so awful, but intriguing and comic—to be the concern of this busy, hurrying machine, with no human operator visible. At any rate, the titles of the books, and presumably their essences, survive the destruction of all these copies. What is more than body comes through, while the body goes its natural, or fated, or arbitrarily unjust way.

These days it is common to speak of filming in terms of machinery—as automatic, possibly out of human hands, inexorable, artificial—and to note that film often makes metaphors of itself with trains and other machines, from the early silent period on.[4] WR first identifies the prison gates with the garbage machine, by juxtaposition, and then identifies both with WR's own filmmaking, as the camera moves about like the garbage machine. WR does something with—makes film of—Reich and his work, just as the state, the courts, the prison, and the incinerator did something with Reich. WR is hardly at one with the state and the justice system, but the film does show suspicions of its own apparatus and story-telling ability as distorting, even death-dealing. Does WR save itself by working to understand its own fancy, holding that against a standard of being down to earth, true to a subject?

At the start of the prison material the film gives us a black-and-white still photograph of Reich, stout, well-dressed, overcoated, handcuffed, and being escorted to trial or to prison, an expression both sorrowful and a bit alarmed on his face (is the alarm due to the presence of photographers, or to the judicial fate that lies ahead of him?). Makaveyev zooms in—not too fast—on the handcuffs. This moment is very affecting. And the affectingness has to do both with the sorrowful state of Reich and with the zoom gesture itself. It seems that the subject matter of the film becomes fully gripping only when we reach the point of persecution and death, the passion—Eva Reich has just brought up the murder of Christ and Reich's book of that name, and the garbage sequence names it again. The zoom gesture to the detail in the photograph is eerie, because a photograph, which might be taken as a metaphor for film, is operated upon by another photographic (filmic) technique. We are far into the realm of the mechanical, the automatic. This particular gesture represents what Makaveyev is doing constantly with his filming techniques and his use of old film. Reich in his passion is subjected to the state, and as a subject for film he is laid before a great power as well.

Where will it lead? Is the power of film in fact the means for Reich to live, as the real man in a sense, and of course as transcendent of the fate of the real man in his body, in his life on earth? If Reich lives in this tran-

---

4. For different approaches to this see *The Cinematic Apparatus*, ed. Teresa de Lauretis and Stephen Heath (St. Martin's Press, 1980); William Rothman, "Psycho," in *Hitchcock—The Murderous Gaze* (Harvard University Press, 1982); and Jay Cantor on *Shoah*, in the present volume.

**Dušan Makaveyev, *WR: Mysteries of the Organism* (1971)**
**The still photograph of Wilhelm Reich under arrest.**

scendent way, it is so that he can reenter our lives as we live in our bodies, here on earth. How crucial is film for this bringing of the transcendent to the body?

Part of the chill of the moment with the photograph is that it is suddenly black and white after (and before, we soon see) color segments. The film is constantly using and studying this contrast—it is in color except for old material, of which there is a good deal. With the handcuffs photograph black and white suggests death, making a *photograph*—a ghostly fancy—of what was alive and really there. But the black and white also suggests reality, truth, if we take color film as always a bit fantastic or unreal.[5] Film started in black and white, and its deep origin is commonly felt to be the older still photograph, or drawing (paint is too rich, *too* still). The photograph is the root, close to truth. Motion and color come later. The world's oldest art is objects, lyrics, prayers; later come elaborate narration and drama, buildings, complications of fancy. (Or do these take us *back* in their way?)

5. Stanley Cavell explores this mood in "The World as a Whole: Color," in *The World Viewed: Reflections on the Ontology of Film* (1971; expanded edition, Harvard University Press, 1979).

## Dream

When Eva Reich criticizes the life in communist countries, Makaveyev asks her about the American dream, and she says immediately, "the American dream is dead." Whereupon the film cuts to what is seen by a camera moving in a car from the country into town and down the main street of Rangeley, Maine, the soundtrack giving us a well-known New York City radio station, "it's a sunny morning, 79 WABC degrees" (dee-grees), then a chorus singing an advertisement, "Coca Cola—it's the real thing." This part of the film, which will include interviews with Rangeley citizens, might be taken as showing the hollowness and absurdity and backwardness of America, following on Eva Reich's suggestion—but only a cynic would so take it, whose mind is fixed on certain ideas, not attending to the vitality of the filmmaking before us.

The film now becomes like a dream, to pick up Makaveyev's and Eva's word. Some dream is there and alive. Or perhaps the film now becomes more of a film. It loses a certain quality of fooling around or just-before-getting-to-the-subject, and takes hold. The affectingness of the brief zoom-in with the still photograph is borne out—film really doing something. This really doing something is what will bring the film to blossom, or change, into fiction film at a point not far down the road. The new dreaminess in the film has to do with imagination—specifically film imagination—that is beyond the body, the earth, the real. And yet *WR* more and more will press the issue of whether the imagination is not the way to, and the very place of, the body, the earth, and the real.

I call the film dreamlike now to suggest the absorption we feel: the feeling of things being weighted with interest beyond what we could ever explain; the feeling of curiosity as we move forward. All of which does not preclude a certain distance and holding back from what we see. I am not saying that we *identify* with the film—and one thing this film has to teach is that film is not there absolutely to be identified with.[6] We often feel less than fully identified with a dream. The holding back or reflectiveness may come and go, in moments, in spaces, or may hover there con-

---

6. Current film studies, roughly beginning with Christian Metz in *The Imaginary Signifier* (essay, 1975; whole volume, Indiana University Press, 1982), often suggests that film is normally entirely identified with. This is too simple a view.

stantly even as we are engaged—this is the transitional moment or field where, the Upanishads teach, all important knowledge comes in. Perhaps *WR* up to the point we have reached, being interesting but up in the air about its subject, has provided the moment or field of transition, the opening for understanding, that will now stay with us at some level as we more let go and live out the film.

We begin now with a camera in motion, taking in an Esso gas station, a purveyor of fuel for motion, a corporate presence in the wooded outskirts of this town. The camera takes in a view of a little bridge down a side road, then moves across a long bridge over a river. A good deal of time is spent here, looking out the side of the car, the bridge railing going by fast in a blur, while a railroad bridge is seen clearly and seemingly more "slowly" at a little distance up or down the river (we cannot tell which direction). This stress on images of bridges goes to the heart of the film's concern with juxtapositions, transitions, getting from here to there—with different kinds of film, different kinds of people, different places, the body as opposed to the mind or imagination, the self unhealed and the self healed or freed, "our sick society" (the narrator's words when she first begins to speak) and the world of revolution—WR: World Revolution. The blurry near railing might represent our sense deep down, anywhere in the film, or in life, that we are already on a bridge; while the more distant railroad bridge gives us a clear image representing something to aspire to, or representing the act of recognizing consciously or clearly where we already are or what we already are doing. The uncertainty of the direction of the flow of the stream might tell us that in bridging, not every consideration of measurement or having our bearings matters.

The poetic condensation of this moment of direct documentary filmmaking (is it that?) is enriched by the soundtrack from WABC, a New York station oddly heard way up here in Rangeley—considerable bridging there. Is this really what is picked up riding in a car here, or is it imported by Makaveyev? Is Coca-Cola (and Esso) harmless or dangerous? Can we feel free and all right, just a little dizzy, listening to the silly, sensuous commercial song? Or is it maddening, even if we do not recognize that it is? Is WABC itself dangerous? This station plays rock and roll (we hear some of it later in the film on this station), at least some of which in 1971 might be

taken as crucial popular art, revolutionary, or healing. WABC dee-grees—
*gradus ad parnassum*, maybe even the commercials.

We move down the main street of Rangeley, and begin to hear in
(apparently) a man's voiceover an account of a local mass uprising against
Reich. People shouted, "Down with the Or-gies!" (hard "g," from
"Orgonon"), "Down with the Commies!" The narrator is identified by a
title as Reich's son, Peter, and he soon appears, dark, gentle, friendly,
though nervously twisting a strand of his hair—a contrast to his somewhat
self-righteous sister Eva, leading us to think about the different ways the
germ of Reich could go. Is the film, moving down the road, an assault on
Reich like that of the group Peter speaks of? Peter is unsure about what
actually happened, as opposed to what he may have seen "out of fear." A
little later the account we hear in Reich's own voice (the only time we hear
his voice in the film) is painfully excited, as he speaks of stopping people
with his gun and denying he is a communist. We wonder if his view of
these people is distorted, as Peter's may have been. Our sense of being
involved in a story-film now—investigating a mystery, concentrating on
one thing for a time—is borne out by the interviews that follow with two
storekeepers and with the deputy sheriff/barber, a big and frightening
looking man who is in fact peaceable and unassuming, and whose barber's
gestures about his own head—to show how Reich liked his hair—are
almost effeminate, certainly belonging to the world of dressers and cos-
meticians. These townspeople knew Reich, and speak amicably of him,
though they found him "unusual" and "not like ordinary people." Could
these men, or people like them, have been among Reich's attackers? Or do
these men prove that Rangeley has more kinds of people than those who
wanted to attack Reich? Finally we wonder about these men, as about the
woman employee earlier, are they suitable for Reich's mission for sexual
and social liberation? What would it mean to change a town like this? Was
it right for the town to resist Reich violently, if that is what it did?

It is just upon meeting these townspeople that the film shifts to
the drive down the forest road with the woman narrator speaking Reich's
words about possibly being the offspring of an extraterrestrial, and thus
belonging to "a new race of earthlings," "an interplanetary race." This
sequence pushes the question of what a man is. What is he kin to? What

is he suited for? Reich's idea about extraterrestrial kinship seems a figure for being transformed into a new kind of being by the power of ideas. (Reich says, as if describing how a poetic figure works, that his speculation about extraterrestrials may seem "irrationality," but that any irrationality will contain "something of truth.") To be liberated is to become of a new race, yet a new race of earthlings, still of the earth—yet it happens by partaking of what is beyond the earth, yet a teaching *about* the earth, essentially *of* the earth.

This sequence has a ghostly quality. The camera moves down the road as the woman narrator's voice speaks quietly; because there is no road noise and very little sound from the woods, the camera seems to float—we do not compensate for the absent sounds as we might with silent film, because we do hear that voice and just a little sound from the woods. Could the moving camera be like the approach of spacemen in their soundless ships (soundlessness representing a stage of technology that is beyond us)? If the spacemen represent what is beyond earth, which is taken into and transforms the earth, so would filming be an act beyond earth that comes to interact with what is of the earth. Film transforms its subject—and may transform its audience—but film allows its subject (and audience), in transformation, to be what they are, still of a race of earthlings—though now such really, maybe for the first time. The play of film art—"concealment," it may seem—is after all "unconcealment." The "untruth" of film after all brings us to truth, to pick up Heidegger's terms from "The Origin of the Work of Art."

The ghost in the present sequence is the spaceman, or Reich's ideas, or the filming. Reich's teacher Freud tells us that the uncanny is the representation, the return, of our primary body-mind reality, which we do not want to admit. That is, the uncanny is a way of admitting this reality. The ghost—Reich's ideas, filming—seems unearthly, but it is really of the body, or body-mind. We find what is real by means of film, as we do by means of Reich's wild ideas. This is *WR*'s perpetual lesson.

The discrepancy between image and soundtrack in the present sequence makes the camera seem to float. Of course there is such a discrepancy everywhere in sound film, even where we believe we are hearing sound simultaneously recorded with the image. How can we *know* this is the case? And what has the recording left out that we would hear if we were "there"? In the sequence just previous to the forest scene, we might ask if the WABC material, perhaps brought in unrealsitically, should make the camera seem to float there too? I do not suggest that we question every sequence of film—a natural-seeming relation between sound and image is a real thing. But the Maine-woods/spaceman sequence calls attention to film's contrivance and to its not having, ever, a sure co-presence of image and sound. Where do we stand in life itself with regard to sights and sounds? How do we perceive? Is there not contrivance, and a lack of certainty, even where we rightly feel presence and connection?

The eeriness of this sequence is due in part to being in woods, which are proverbially spooky. A forest shuts out the world; we feel distant from it. We are amidst beings—trees—that are alive, but of a different kind of life from our own—nymphs or warriors or something unimaginable may be concealed in them. Being amidst or confronted with a different kind of life makes us think of possibly being changed. Might we become that other kind of being? Might we be assaulted by the other and changed? Might it be glorious?

Ghostliness is there in the ensuing material with Reich's Orgonon estate, set here in the woods. We see Reich's observatory and telescope, and eventually an unidentified telescope-like contraption (a "cloudbuster" in fact, for drawing or projecting Orgone energy between heaven and earth). We see old footage of Reich outdoors and people arriving to confer with him. We see, back in the present apparently, Reich's large stone bust outdoors, presumably erected after his death; and here is where we start to hear Reich's voice, speaking of the local uprising. We think about living presence and disappearance, and the after-effects of old film and voice recording.

The camera enters the Wilhelm Reich Museum and drifts past tables with microscopes and other equipment, all covered with semitransparent plastic—like film, it both covers and reveals. This laboratory, this scene of activity—of creation, perhaps—is now emptied of its workers, but we are here moving about with the camera. Where is Reich? Is he here in *WR*'s film activity and our attentiveness to that?

The film cuts from a mystical picture on the wall of two hands with a field of force of some kind running between them, to a camera movement down a hall and into an empty therapy room with a couch—is this the same building, or even at Orgonon? We hear what we take to be a woman's sighs—is this the breath of life? Reich, or his ideas, coming to life? There is a cut to another therapy room—where is it?—and what follows is a session with a reclining woman in a blue leotard doing Reichian exercises, guided by Dr. Alexander Lowen. Time and space are obliterated in getting from Reich's laboratory, via that picture of the two hands, with a hint of the supernatural, to the living activity of Reichian therapy. We are brought to earth, to the therapy, by fancy. We must realize, the film says, that earth and the body coming to the fore is a matter of ideas coming to life; the fancy of the film works as does the fancy of Reich's ideas.

The woman in this scene does deep breathing, moving her pelvis up and down, all aimed at "letting go," Dr. Lowen tells us. Lowen moves about the woman, giving her instructions, touching her, and making explanations to the filmers. Lowen's name is printed over the image of the woman, confusing identity as earlier in the film; the idea man and his patient are one in a sense. The flexibly moving camera contemplates the woman's body and also follows Lowen closely, getting his face close up in profile at times, his fingers close up another time. The filming takes up the activity, the transactions, of the scene. There is strong sunlight coming in a window at the back—the energy of ideas? of film?—so that Lowen, or parts of him, appear almost in silhouette. The session seems a sort of rite, the elegant and dynamic Dr. Lowen a priest or magician or unearthly being.

Reichian therapy comes into its own now as Myron Sharaf, imaged with a river and bridge in the background, explains the therapy and recounts his own experiences with Reich (the scene looks like Boston and the bank of the Charles, and Sharaf is dressed as in the earlier scene in the shed, suggesting that was not Maine but here in Boston). Sharaf is less strange, more down to earth and comforting, than Lowen, but he starts us on a far journey. There are more filmed therapy sessions. A woman on her back, in underpants and an almost transparent bra, is guided by a voice—we do not see the therapist. The camera—standing in for the therapist?—moves back and forth along the woman's body as the primal spasms of the s-shape take her over. She is reasonably fit and attractive, but she definitely has a middle and hips and thighs and flesh that quivers. This is an unidealized human body. And this is what we see with all the people in these sessions, most notably in the large group session later with people screaming and some walking on others' backs. There we see fat and human oddity in all their familiar appearances.

In the present sequence the woman's head and face make only a vague impression, and this is the case too with people in all the sessions, and even with the present woman in the brief postsession interview, where she is smiling and speaking of her satisfaction. The head, face, soul seem to blur, extensions of the body and its experience. All this bears out Dr. Sharaf's final words in his scene of explanation, about "a feeling of fullness and pleasure and not empty feeling that you're just living in your head." Of course at the end of the film Milena's severed head comes to life, and it may seem delightful or wondrous, or to come as a blessed relief—so that Sharaf's ideal picture of life is challenged, or reinterpreted. If the body and common bodily experience become central, it is still by virtue of ideas, thought to live in the head.

The film now begins to move fast, traversing material of various kinds in the moments leading up to the change to fiction. The film seems to press its boundaries, feeling ready to burst (as Reich says the body will feel like doing), until relief can come in a transformation into fiction.

The interview with the satisfied, bland young woman after therapy gives way to a brief meeting with erotic artist Betty Dodson, perky and articulate, as if to show that living in the head and being an individual can go with being liberated in the body. (Or is Betty Dodson so liberated? Who is she, really? —perhaps an artist or theorist who can promote for others what she may not have attained?) Dodson discusses drawing models who masturbate for her, models who at first feel reluctant, but then find the experience freeing and joyful. And the subject of masturbation seems to focus or make pure Reich's emphasis on the individual's integrity in his/her sexual experience. It is for *you*, he says.

Does masturbation also question Reich: is Reichianism for the sake of a cut-off, lonely pleasure, however intense, missing the dimension of acquaintance with another person? D. H. Lawrence writes,

> Masturbation is the one thoroughly secret act of the human being, more secret even than excrementation . . . In sexual intercourse there is a give and take. A new stimulus enters as the

native stimulus departs . . . But in masturbation there is nothing but loss. There is no reciprocity.

But Lawrence does work what he is saying toward a large plea for liberation, like Reich's and this film's. One must get beyond oneself, but one finds there "the very urge of life" that is within one, which asks finally that one "smash up the vast lie of the world, and make a new world."[7]

The meeting with Betty Dodson points us toward art—and toward the phallus. She speaks to us sitting in front of a large painting or color drawing of a black man on his back masturbating, his hand around his large erect penis. The camera moves in on the penis until at the end of the interview there is little else in the frame. The painting seems to represent the film, as if the issues that gave rise to the film had cried out for iconic realization: a film, like a painting. Let there be something we can fix on, contemplate. But let it be as the penis, penetrating, inseminating. — Is art like masturbation? Is it a purer form of the broad reality it is connected to; or is it self-absorbed and isolated?—Then again, is masturbation in front of another person (or art with a viewer, poems with a reader) really masturbation, isolated?

Why is the man black? No reason. Color (of persons—it has already happened in a more general way with color film versus black and white) here enters the film as a zone of flux, like gender. Color or gender is defined, but not absolutely. In the later *Screw* magazine office scene, a beautiful, shocking naked black man with copious pubic hair appears and moves about, causing no stir, part of the group, as others in the office, all white, discuss transformation.

Dodson appears later in the film, interrupting the Yugoslav fictional material. She and her picture, this time of a woman masturbating, seem notably real in contrast to the now surrounding fiction; and this picture is more muted than the first, seeming less an art object (are a woman's genitals more real, less an art object, than is an erect penis?). Dodson speaks against women's having to depend on a male partner for orgasm— but her remarks are intercut with the image of the lovers in the fictional apartment, locked in embrace and in high pleasure if not orgasm, seeming

---

7. D. H. Lawrence, "Pornography and Obscenity," in *Phoenix* (1936).

very happy. Who—or what—is able to tell us more, the fictional film or the painter and critic of real life?

The first meeting with Dodson, and her painting of the black man, is brief, just enough to give a fresh impression in the film and stir up questions. Now there is a cut to a woman on her back at a crisis point in therapy, screaming "Give it to me! Give it to me! . . . It's mine! . . ." as she clutches a towel held or attached out of our view. She seems to ask for the penis we have just been looking at as her right and her deepest desire. Perhaps she asks for art, for being filmed, which she is certainly now getting.

We cut to a moment with Dr. Robert Ollendorf, who stands near a railing with water and a cityscape behind him—he looks to be on a bridge (the script says it is the deck of a ship—a bridge in motion, we might say). He makes a very strange statement, and that is all there is to him: "If any sane man or woman would be produced by a doctor suddenly . . . he very likely would commit suicide."

The spoken emphasis seems to mean the *doctor* would commit suicide, but it might be the sane man or woman produced. Does Ollendorf mean to stress the slow progress of therapy (speedy results would shock one into suicide), or the hopelessness, even the absurdity, of therapy, something the later Freud emphasized (and Reich fiercely rejected)? Or does he mean that "sanity" is not what we are after?—it is something else.

There is a cut to the streets of New York, and Tuli Kupferberg follows an older woman, respectable-looking, even stuffy. Kupferberg is helmeted and marching, his rifle held erect. The woman and Kupferberg start to walk onto what may be a bridge—there is suddenly a low wall beside the sidewalk, and we cannot see beyond it—and the woman notices Kupferberg and steps back to let him go ahead. She shows alarm as the two of them enter a bridge passage. The woman seems to think Kupferberg is dangerous or crazy. This is theater, making art of the issues of bridging and shock, in this case with an unwilling audience/participant. This is Kupferberg's art, which figures the film's art. Is the film dangerous or crazy? Does a bridge passage necessarily seem dangerous or crazy? Are we, the film's audience, unwilling? Now comes the cut to Milena, who is breaking eggs, with the sound of a sigh and more "eastern" piping music. The fictional material begins.

In the moments leading up to this change to fiction, the juxtapositions come fast and are agitating to watch. The thoughts stirred seem greater than the time given to the images. The film seems to be shaking its subject about, or to be shaken by it, as if the film is a dog, or is shaken by one, such as those we saw at the start of the film, now roused to life. The film is looking, out of necessity, for a new approach to the material, a new way to go, or a way out. The hints about art, with Dodson and Kupferberg, give a clue. The change to fiction then suggests that if film lets go, it becomes fiction. Fiction is the letting-go of film. Fiction, fancy, is letting the dimension of earth, the camera's real subject, come to the fore and fully go its way.

Has the film forced this? Or does the subject, or nature itself, call for what happens? We know the film's subject through the film —where else? Does the subject call for what the film does in its effort to know or make known the subject? (Surely we can know a subject *through* a film and still feel that the film mishandles or misperceives the subject.)

Nonfiction, after some excited editing, turns into fiction. Is nonfiction on the road to this from the start? Would people in nonfiction film say and do what we see and hear, if not for the filming? Would people and places and situations be what they are—what are they?—but for the way we see them on film? Does life dream itself this way so as to make itself understood, to be what it is?

## Fiction—and the Film's Real Subject

The change to Milena and her story is like the change in Joyce's *Ulysses* from several hundred pages of more or less narrative prose to the big "Nighttown" section written as a playscript (or filmscript, since what happens is hardly imaginable staged in a theater). "Nighttown" comes, too, just after the reaching about and mounting intensity of the "Oxen of the Sun" section, pressing the borders of prose with parodies of many styles, looking for a new way, at the maternity hospital.

What happens with Nighttown? Is the action of the book suddenly made clearer, our vision allowed to be more direct? Or has the book shifted to a higher, more intense phase of artifice? *Ulysses,* like *WR,* gives the impression of extraordinary openness to the range of human experience, notably experience of the body. All sorts of things immediately recognizable from life just come in, it seems, as they like. But *Ulysses* also seems the most "written" of books, in its phrase-making, in its weaving of themes. The entire book is a crisis of fancy as against subject matter. The Nighttown section challenges the usual medium of novels, prose narration. Is this medium invalid? Ought it to be cast aside? In *WR* the beginning of Milena's story asks us to think: what are nonfiction film and fiction film for? Ought one to cast the other aside?

The fictional story in *WR* is used to show us a number of things: Milena's dark-haired roommate and her friend from the army, who are a sexually liberated couple enjoying themselves; Milena herself, the independent-thinking Reichian Marxist, anxious to preach and promote her ideas; and Milena's encounter with Vladimir, a Soviet figure skater, proud and stellar, but repressed, very committed to the Soviet tradition of state above individual (he means to be a "good state being"). The locale is Yugoslavia—a title announces Belgrade and 1971, the year the film was made. We see a country that is not a utopia. There is a "bourgeois" bureaucratic class, which makes its appearance in a limousine in the first episode in the street at night; and a working-class element that makes demands only for its immediate sensuous interests, represented by Milena's raucous ex-lover Radmilovic. But this Yugoslavia is not the USSR, and it resists Stalinism. Milena and her roommate tell Vladimir that Yugoslavs care about "personal happiness" and do not blur that with state concerns. Yugoslavia is where Milena lives her Reichian life. It is a marginal or transitional place, in formation—in the 1970s and 1980s, still in relatively quiet formation.[8]

The fiction might be taken as carrying out ideas. The earlier part of the film raises Reich's issues, and now there is the need to see them lived out and to see what opposition to them looks like (Vladimir). The fiction shows us the future in a sense, the world of lived-out ideas that is always a step beyond the world as it is.

8. The explosion in Serbia, Croatia, Bosnia, may seem anticipated in a film such as *WR,* with its harsh juxtapositions, its tearing in so many different directions. But *WR* is a bomb for the mind, for the sake of freeing us from bad historical habits—not a bomb in the body of the world, set off by historic hatreds.

Of course these are real people in these roles, and real places and objects before the camera—even the sets are a reality. The link in fictional film, of real people and objects and places, to story, emblematizes that we do live by or with ideas. We direct our lives by ideas and toward ideas. We live with a world of ideas in our minds, imagined as lived out. The bridge of what is real before the camera takes us to the story, which is something that is there in real life such as we live it, such as comes before the camera in the first place.[9]

Milena's story is also allegory. Here it is not so much ideas lived out, but people simply standing for ideas, and the story being a drama of ideas. Milena's roommate and the roommate's lover are Reichian, but naive. Milena is consciousness. Vladimir is Stalinism, openly associated in the film with Hitlerism. In allegory we see not so much the world beyond or above us, which we might live out, as the world deep within us, the ideas we do live, purified of the chaotic details of life. (In allegory complications of detail are representative, not accidental, though the line here is fine.) Allegory can be very compelling by a power of recognition—the ideas and drama are *right*; we know them. Or allegory can seem thin—so much is pared away. Insofar as Milena's story seems thin, in want of more story—other than allegorical story—it calls attention to the rest of the film, the nonfiction, as *being* story. The fiction reveals the rest of the film, with its realism and also its film-fancy, as perhaps being better story than this part. Certainly the fiction reveals the *whole* of the film, which includes the fiction, as being better story than the fictional part alone. (Similarly the Nighttown section of *Ulysses* can seem to run [brilliantly] thin after a time, to provide only images that represent ideas, and to need the return of rich descriptive prose—which comes.)

Perhaps all fictional film is allegorical in one aspect, to a degree. Perhaps we take an interest in fiction only if things stand for ideas, as Aristotle suggests, distinguishing poetry from history. In life itself things do stand for ideas, or want to stand for ideas, actions for contests of ideas, so that allegory is realism, after all.

*WR* has Milena's story, and it has its nonfiction part. This film

9. Wonderful testimonials to our interest in physical reality and the reality of actual people, in film's world of story and imagination, are André Bazin's *What Is Cinema?* (two vols., University of California Press, 1967, 1971) and Cavell's *The World Viewed*.

splits, for emphasis and recognition, what goes on all at once in other films. *Nanook of the North* has a story like Milena's woven in it—a drama, an allegory. *Rules of the Game* has drama and allegory in plenty, and the story is continued or answered back to, developed, at every turn by the filming—the exploring—of real people and behavior and objects and places.

Milena's story seems at first to add something to the rest of the film, to take part in what the film as a whole is doing; unless one feels that the film is really only beginning now. If we regard Milena as the narrator of the earlier part, this would make that, in retrospect, seem her own thought process or some of her proselytizing. Also, Milena's story might seem the center of the film when we realize that a long stretch of this story makes up the film's ending. At any rate, a short way into Milena's story there is a switch back to nonfictional material, and for the rest of the film we get a mixing of the two. What is contributing to, or illuminating, what? Which is the ground, which is the added commentary or added dimension? What is really the subject of the film?

I have cited Heidegger's "The Origin of the Work of Art" in speaking of concealment and unconcealment, of film's allowing of its subject, or the real world, or the down to earth, to become plain through film's very acts of "concealment," its operation of fancy. I have been calling Milena's story a "world" in various senses (of lived-out ideas, of allegory). Now central to Heidegger's essay is his discussion of "world" and "earth." "World" and "earth" are in conflict in the work of art, in intimacy, in an unsettled, active relation that allows each to be what it is. "World," something "set up", has to do with meaning and values and human understanding. "Earth," something "set forth," is a matter of the "thingly"—bronze, stone, paint, words just as words. "Earth" is of its nature "self-secluding." The work of art has earth come forth to us to be acknowledged, while retaining its self-secluding nature. Earth comes into the art's set-up "world." The work of art must be grounded, though the ground does not want to show itself—and this even though ground is only ground in being "set forth" in the making of a "world." It is all a wonderful circle, where the sides are not to be got free of each other.[10]

---

10. I have used Albert Hofstadter's translation of "The Origin of the Work of Art," in Martin Heidegger, *Poetry, Language, Thought* (Harper & Row, 1971)

In film we might conceive earth to be the real world that comes before the camera, or the real subject of the film, even a body of ideas; or, alternately, the mechanism of film, the camera and film and projector, comparable to bronze, stone, paint . . . And we might conceive "world" as what is done with the real world, or real subject; or with the physical fact of film, the mechanics and the celluloid. There is what is done in shooting the real world, making selections and decisions, framing, moving the camera; and what is done in editing, putting parts of film together, sometimes in sheer exuberance with the medium, as in passages of Vertov, or *WR's* passage leading up to the change to fiction. And there is what is done in fictionalization, with scripting, staging, decor.

Does Milena's story in *WR* act as world—a filmic setting-up—to the earth of the rest of the film? This earth might be the real subject of Reich and his ramifications in people's lives, which is perhaps finally unfathomable (self-secluding), though one can look in its direction. Or earth might be the body, Reich's own subject, what he investigated and talked about. Or earth might be the segments of nonfiction film, the material Milena gathers about herself.

But if Milena, the created character, comes to seem the center of the film, its subject, then the nonfiction would be "world" in regard to Milena's story as earth. The nonfiction carries farther, or helps to bring out, Milena.

The subject of *WR* cannot be said absolutely to be Reich and his effect in the real world—our sense of that slips once Milena's story gets under way. Nor, I think, do we want absolutely to call Milena the subject—there is just too much else going on. Heidegger says that it is "unconcealedness as such" that is finally the point with the work of art— the very way the work works, and our involvement with this. This matters more than any particular subject that is being made manifest—though the particular subject, and particularity as such, are crucial to the process. Heidegger says it is process, motion in a sense, even motion within stillness, that matters most to people.

I suggest that *WR's* elusiveness should bring us to realize that the subject or center or purpose of the film lies in just how it works on us. Here we are very close to the question of the political nature of the film.

Meeting with this film, where are we, or where are we left? What are we sent away to do?

We do not get, exactly, a clarification of Reich and of the way the world works (or does not work) along Marxist-Reichian lines. Whenever we would bear down on something that is clarified, the form of the film, its nonfiction as well as fiction, casts us into a state of meditation about perception: What is reality? What is projection of desire? (The form of any film, carefully attended to, will cause this.)

WR puts us in the situation of making an approach to a clarification we finally cannot have. Just the approach, or the realizing of what an approach is, is a great deal. We are left in motion, or motivated.

Earth is what we are aimed at, but we would lose it if we attained it fully in the form of idea or art. Earth—the body, the new world or society of the body—is what we have in the world, or the motion, of film.

## Film

I want to look at two further sequences and what they bring into the film, and then at the ending. The two sequences come fairly soon after the start of the film's fictional material, where the transvestite or transsexual Jackie Curtis is introduced, and where China footage and Stalin footage are introduced.

Milena meets her ex-lover Radmilovic in the street at night and he raises a fuss, creating a roadblock for a Mercedes evidently carrying an important person, shouting at the car, "Down with the red bourgeoisie! Steak Esterhazi! Mitsuko! Marx Factor!" And here there is a cut to New York's 42nd Street, and on the soundtrack the programming of WABC radio again (no one we see is listening to a radio—it is, as it were, the radio sound in these people's heads). We contemplate a person who looks like a man dressed as a woman (identified by the script as Jackie Curtis), as the camera backs down the street in front of him/her, with a few countermoves forward, curious or affectionate. This goes on and on, as Jackie and a friend in male attire walk toward the backing camera, eating ice-cream cones, looking about, having a certain amount of interaction with each

**Dušan Makaveyev, *WR: Mysteries of the Organism* (1971)**
**Jackie Curtis and friend walking down New York's 42nd Street.**

other, never paying direct attention to the camera. "Marx Factor" is a joke
on the corruption of Marxism into a "red bourgeoisie." And the transition
to 42nd Street compares Yugoslavia with America to an extent, evoking
America's making-up, which may be falsity and self-delusion. We hear ecstatic commercials for Maybelline "Hollywood eyelashes" and for Coppertone
tanning lotion—"Who owns the sun? Coppertone"—and eventually we
watch the crowds in New York moving about under movie marquees for
pornography and shallow romance films—*Playmates*, *Without a Stitch*, *A
Walk in the Spring Rain* (though the last is late Ingrid Bergman, so things
are not so simple). In the midst of this is Jackie, conceivably a pathetic figure—the product of this world but clearly somewhat edgy and ill at ease
with the crowd around.

There is a positive side to the "Marx Factor" transition. The
phrase reminds us that Marx or a true Marxist is supposed to be a factor,
a doer or changer or enactor, and the joke points to the valid creativeness
or making-up of Milena, who would keep the revolution going on. Milena
soon comes into her apartment, where she has an American movie poster

(like the 42nd Street marquees), for *The Mating Urge*—presumably she makes good use of what it represents—and she gets busy changing clothes and fixing herself up, positively costuming herself, in army boots, army jacket, and army hat, with bare legs, before going out to preach Reichian-Marxist ideas.

And Jackie Curtis is far from being a negative figure. There is an enormous weight given to her first appearance (let's rest with the feminine pronoun). We are only a short way into the fictional story when we get this switch to a lengthy meeting with Jackie. Perhaps it is the start of a fiction too, but it is shot in daylight in what looks like the true anarchy of 42nd Street, and Jackie and her friend do not seem to be playing parts, beyond being asked to be filmed as they walk down the street. It is an extended meeting of the filmmaker with an interesting real subject. Jackie is right away a figure of charm, self-possession in spite of being a little ill at ease, and bravery. She is extraordinarily alive in the eyes.

But if we come to earth after a bit of Milena's fiction, it is with contemplation of an utter fantasy figure, with glittery make-up and *outré* manner, standing out against the (other) impermeably real people on the street. Jackie looks like a man dressed as a woman—something about the shoulders, stature, bones of the face. But for all we can tell here, Jackie may have been born a woman. In her monologue later in the film she tells of her first sexual experience as a male and with a male, seeming to make clear who she is. But then she speaks of meeting this lover at a later time— "the next time I saw him I was a girl, and he couldn't get ready . . . he was used to sleeping with boys, which is a very limited view on things . . . I mean, since I was the same person, I mean literally the same person!" Has Jackie undergone surgery and hormone treatment to become a girl? We do not know her status really, only the fancy we see, and the appeal of her seemingly real feelings.

Jackie comes back into the film a number of times. She seems to make uncertainty about sexual identity—or sexual identity as fancy—into a metaphor for the film's whole concern with earth as taking us inevitably into the beyond. Is any real person perhaps as strange as Jackie, living with uncertainty of status, calling upon fantasy, attempting self-creation? If only we would let go?

Later in the *Screw* office Jackie comments on her transformation—"glitter on the eyes, glitter on my lips, glitter on the hair"—and says, "unreal, you just don't see things like that," suggesting the impossibility of the—of course—actual. She picks up a framed photograph of the young Gary Cooper, elegantly suited, looking rather like Cary Grant, and shows it to the camera, saying admiringly, being very firm, "just like you don't see things like *that*, you don't see things like that all the time!" If only we could! the film implies. What is encompassed in figures like Gary Cooper or Cary Grant, and the worthiness of this as a realistic ideal, is argued by Stanley Cavell in *Pursuits of Happiness*.[11] Jackie Curtis, invoking movie stars, suggests that the film figures of *WR* itself (fictional, nonfictional) may be more than a mirror of life, or a field for thought—may be an *inspiration*. People are in fact made of inspiration.

After Jackie's first appearance on 42nd Street, she gives a brief monologue in an indoor space, talking of her "marriage"—what is it exactly? we never know for sure—to Eric, whom she calls "the American hero." As she speaks, we suddenly see Tuli Kupferberg doing his street theater in front of Lincoln Center; then Milena in her apartment, preparing to go out and speak. It is as if Jackie has projected these realms of art—street theater, fiction film—to represent the creativity of her own life.

Milena's speech on the courtyard balcony and her interchanges with her audience there, like her conversations with Vladimir later, are full of pure doctrine, as if the film is moving, within the story, to an element of greater realism. But soon Milena works up the crowd in a tribute to love and happiness, and her listeners lock hands and begin dancing in a long column up the stairs and around the balcony—the background music coming from who knows where—eventually taking up Milena, who dances with them, and they all begin to sing,

> Without love
> Life isn't worth a thing.
> Nobody knows . . . Oh, nobody knows
> What tomorrow may bring.
> Life without fucking isn't worth a thing!

11. Stanley Cavell, *Pursuits of Happiness: The Hollywood Comedy of Remarriage* (Harvard University Press, 1981).

Then as if cued by "what tomorrow may bring," we are launched into one of the most intense and remarkable sequences of the film, and the last to introduce major new material, having to do with Stalin. We go intensely into film, and ultimately to earth. There is a cut from the dancing column on Milena's balcony, to a massive rally in China with Mao and a surging crowd. After this we go to a Soviet fictional (adulatory) film about Stalin, which we see a good bit of, and then to upsetting footage of nasal force-feeding and electroshock therapy, with Stalin material intercut, as well as a brief shot of Reich looking unhappy—a detail of the photo where he is handcuffed. All this issues into the prolonged scene of a large group Reichian therapy session with people of all shapes and sizes screaming, walking on each other, pulsating and thrashing about. This seems to be Apocalypse, but we know it is all right and for the best—or do we quite? At least we know that this is honest nonfictional filming, as far as possible from the idealized Stalin film.

Nowhere in the film are we so aware as in this long passage, of being involved in a film experience, of being in the hands of a film, aban-doned—despite our consciousness of it—to be taken where the film will go. At the same time the film seems to reach more profoundly than ever into the real thing it is all about: the bodily element. This last is strongly set forth in the face of all the showy setting up of the choices and timing of the material. What could be more conscious and idea-determined than such an edited series? And yet a physical force, something of the body, seems to generate it or to be brought alive by it. We feel this as we con-centrate intensely on any one piece of footage, and then find ourselves stimulated anew and cast into another piece. From the dancing on the bal-cony we explode into China, and from there into the cold world of the Stalin film, and on and on—just as sex seems to defy gravity.

The camera backs before Milena and her column of people, and the cut goes to Mao and other officials advancing in a similar column, toward a camera, on a high platform or wall. Another shot, panning and high up, surveys an enormous crowd in Tiananmen Square. The singing of Milena and her people merges into the huge sound of the chanting and crying Chinese. It is as if Milena and her people are transfigured into the Chinese, people of the highest, most world-historical political significance.

The Yugoslav fictional characters in a sense come to earth in nonfiction, but it is an earth more glorious, more imaginatively charged than fiction. We realize what a sense of reality we have invested by now in the fiction we have been watching, because the change to the Chinese seems an escape or blossoming into an imaginative or fantasy world. This impression is given in part by the change from the highly realized filming of the Yugoslavs—which at first looked so much of the studio—to the faded color and ragged print quality of the China footage. The Chinese seem ghosts or spirits or demigods.

After some moments, the cut to the film celebrating Stalin makes the Chinese seem firmly real in retrospect. It is a stark contrast—with of course the suggestion that there is Stalinism in Maoism. The bluish black and white looks ghostlier than anything we have seen. The large formal room is like a tomb, with people standing in opposite rows as Stalin advances at the head of followers, all moving slowly, processionally. The open space seems dead because of the stillness or stiffness of the people, whereas the much greater space of the China footage seemed an opportunity for expansion, for life, even if hypertrophied life. Milena has explained to the crowd (and she will say more later to Vladimir), just as Reich explained, that the craving for orgasm turns into politics, conscious and life-promoting, or warped and death-dealing. Stalin seems to represent the ultimate of the warped and death-dealing—and we sense it through his regime's own fiction film meant to praise and idealize him.[12]

With the asylum footage that ensues, almost unbearable to watch, apparently nonfiction, we are thrust into the realm of the horror film, an imaginative genre invoked at the end of *WR* when Milena's severed head comes alive on the pathologist's tray. We think about the huge fact of Stalin and his prison-asylums, about the brutality that was the result of his elevation to power. But whatever realities we grasp, they seem for the moment, in their surprise, mainly a part of *WR*'s fantasy-like flight into footage of different kinds. Then again, the political content and the fancy film editing as well seem mainly to serve what this film does to our own bodies in the confrontation with force-feeding and shock therapy (and later a man

---

12. Despite seeming intentions, the Soviet fiction films about Stalin give us a hollow myth—André Bazin explains very well how this works, in "The Stalin Myth in Soviet Cinema," in *Movies and Methods*, vol. 2, ed. Bill Nichols (University of California Press, 1985)

beating his head against a wall). Are politics and history, like film, fancies in contrast to pure awareness of the body?

What is this material really? With Stalin we see parts of two films, or very different parts of one, with Stalin dressed and coiffed differently in the two places.[13] In both places we wonder, at least briefly, if this is fiction or real footage of Stalin, perhaps Stalin playing himself for fiction filming. A zither plays "Lili Marlene," so popular with German soldiers during World War II. Is this part of the original film, or added by Makaveyev? Added ironically, to remind us that Stalin fought Hitler, with whom he once made a pact? The song is reprised during the shock-therapy material. Is it to suggest the stoic, cheerful bearing of German soldiers whose work covered horrors? Does the film find stoicism and good cheer the only way to do its own work, which involves horrors? Is the asylum footage real? What country is it from? Is the force-feeding conceivably saving the life of someone whose not eating is not from political protest or from antagonism toward those who are feeding him (he looks unconscious)? Is shock therapy good or bad?

The long scene in the group therapy room, concluding the present montage, seems to show the real underpinnings for political-human advancement, for Milena's kind of politics and what might prevent Stalinist fancy. This scene seems to give the grounding for the new departure into fiction that follows, virtually the rest of the film. In this scene we look and look at actual people—doing what they must, is it?—screaming, emoting without restraint, subject to spasms. We take our time. The camera moves here and there, and there are cuts, numerous shots. We see people in rows, in patterns. There are close-ups of distorted faces, close-ups of dental work. Have we come to the element of the body as far as can be from any fancies? Or is there idea and will (even willfulness) at work in all this? Dr. Lowen is there directing things. Is there even self-delusion? Are American Reichian therapy sessions really connected to World Revolution? We do not know. We are watching film here, as much as in the brilliant montage passage leading up to this. We acknowledge the body— there is no doubt—but there is no assurance what the body *is*, what it means, where it may go.

13. The script identifies only *The Vow*—one of the films Bazin discusses.

Dr. Lowen comes on to explain expression through the body, or rather that "you are—you don't have—a body; you are your body"; and he gives apt imitations of distorted postures and expressions, deriving from mental states. All this may seem plain realism and solid doctrine after the wild therapy session with the ambiguous fantastic filming-without-commentary there. Or Dr. Lowen's instruction may seem further fancy, a step away from looking directly at something real, into words. What is the fancy of words good for?

Now a title announces, "The Moscow Ice Follies Visit Belgrade," and soon Milena meets the skater-actor Vladimir and takes him home— whereupon we see Tuli Kupferberg in Manhattan, discoursing on the phrase "Bring the war home." The story line begins that will lead to the end of the film, with intercutting between Milena and Vladimir's life and the doings of Americans—Reichians and others. A woman in therapy begs for "mama," as Milena and Vladimir first feel attraction. A woman in therapy screams, it seems endlessly, upon mention in Milena's story of the murder of Trotsky and the imprisonment of Reich. Jackie Curtis appears upon discussion of Vladimir's identity—"who are you, really?" he is asked. While Vladimir is imprisoned in a cabinet—from which he will eventually emerge blissful, as if from an Orgone box—there is the major interruption by Jackie's monologue about her life, concluding with the focus on transformation and the picture of Gary Cooper. Is Vladimir, in the cabinet, being transformed? How much so? The concern with creation is carried on in the scene where real person(?) Nancy Godrey makes a mold from Jim Buckley's erect penis to produce a plastic-cast sculpture (Godrey and Buckley are identified by titles; we have seen Buckley in the *Screw* office with Jackie when transformation was discussed). The penis sculpture is shown just at the later moment when the Stalin film comes in again. Stalin = prick, or creation, maybe evil creation (maybe necessary to destroy Hitler). In all this material there is constant play with the notion that common impulses, common realities—craving, horror, transformation— underlie politics and personal relations, the sick or cut off and the healthy and growing, the concentration of the East and the abandon of the West. It is all a question of what we do with what is there.

Soon after Vladimir is freed from the cabinet, the film's final episode in a park begins, introduced by two brief shots of Reich's cloud-busters being adjusted—the tools of his late attempt to link to the universe his work with the energies of sex. The film resolves itself now in a universe of fiction.

The snowy park setting for Milena and Vladimir's final time together is extraordinary for the fictional part, its first outdoor scene, a real public place. Lawrence's *Women in Love* likewise ends in a prolonged snowy episode, pitting the steely Gerald against himself and the book's women. The snow fits the spiritual death that becomes literal in both Lawrence's novel and this film. "The esoteric becomes exoteric," F. R. Leavis writes of the novel's last chapters. But the art works in opposite ways in the film and the novel. *Women in Love*, through many imaginative feats, has established a real England; then the book goes to a snowy world of imagination to play out inner concerns in isolated, exposed clarity. *WR* goes from the world of imagination of the Milena-Vladimir story so far to a natural setting, as if that has called the story out, as if the story must be tested against this setting, as if Milena and Vladimir must live here if they are to live at all.

A kiss from Milena provokes a cut and a dreamier portion of film, with the outdoor background noise now muted. Vladimir, who had been at first fussy about protecting his life for his art, now begins, "I like being here." A second kiss brings on soundtrack music for violins and piano. Vladimir eventually slaps Milena, her advances just too much for him, and there is a cut to what becomes an extended stretch of the Stalin film, with a triumphant imaginative scene in Red Square, ethereal buildings in the distance, and the raising of a great banner in the foreground—it is as if projected by Vladimir, a Stalinist motive for his slap, or his bringing of his mind around to a bright state in his terms.

Vladimir and Milena make up, and there is long passionate kissing, going on and on, seen close up. There has been nothing like this between any two people in the film so far—except for a ghostly foreshadowing, seen briefly, when Jackie and her lover kiss in the back area of a station wagon, virtually in silhouette, close up, their feet and costume-like

**Dušan Makaveyev, *WR: Mysteries of the Organism* (1971)**
**Milena and Vladimir's passionate kiss.**

shoes propped up in the middle distance in the back, the world seen rushing away in the distance. Vladimir and Milena's kiss is the felt and long reality the film has been after—done at last by actors in a story—though a story that has come outdoors.

There is a wild image of pirouetting skaters—a bow to the unimaginable. Then a scream or gasp—after an interval of time, it becomes clear later—indicates the murder of Milena. The film turns to horror as we see Vladimir rising up in the dark with bloody hands; and we go to a morgue where a man removes what is supposed to be Milena's head from a basket. The head is placed on a tray, and, after a cut (a trick to permit what follows and a reminder that film assaults, cutting like a knife), the head comes to life and speaks soberly but not painfully of lovemaking with Vladimir and of his restlessness to go "further," into violence—"he's . . . a genuine Red Fascist." At some point, health is resting where one is. After a pause, Milena concludes firmly, with hope, "even now I'm not ashamed of my Communist past!" It is like one of the steadier encounters in Dante.

Vladimir now wanders outdoors in the daylight and sings a song of asking to be remembered, as if needing help. The scene seems done in a way for the sake of another flirtation with real landscape, a few scroungers gathered about a fire, a loose horse; it goes on for a long time. The setting accents by contrast the quality of art or wish in Vladimir's song. Can reality and art or wish ever come together?

Finally Milena's head appears again, smiling, as Vladimir's song continues on the soundtrack; and there is a dissolve to the photo of the smiling Reich, from Milena's apartment—an element of Milena's imaginative world, and yet the photo of a real man, real as the character Milena is not, though the actress we see is—and the *character* Milena may be just one face of the Milena who is the voice of the film, or the film itself, which is what Reich is now—where he lives. In this dissolve, worlds of persons, or of kinds or states of persons, pour through one another.

Vladimir and Milena have become real by this point. The fiction has penetrated, so that the fanciful concluding scenes are straining against—and cooperating with—a reality now established of people as people. Fictional people.

Sex is a motive here, undeniable when we see the kissing (can this be acting?) and then hear Milena's account of lovemaking, and then the pathologists' talk of the "wild night of love," the "huge amount of semen, four or five times the usual" found in Milena's body. Sex is working with or against a most extreme transformativeness. Does sex induce the head to come alive and talk? Or Vladimir to sing? The film seems about to fly off into space. Has sex induced this, or does it anchor this fantasy?

Humor at last cuts two ways, or takes things in a circle. There is humor in the head coming to life, for all the horror, dissipating a bit the grim realism of the murder. We think of the live actress who must be concealed under the table. The film brings us to earth and lets us know things will be all right.—Yet we settle with the speaker into a certain sobriety. We concentrate on her words, telling of her sad experience and her communist beliefs. And the smile at the end is sober, however uplifting. Milena's smile, dissolving into Reich's in the photo, over Vladimir's "Remember, I'm here too," is like the smile of the universe in *The Divine Comedy*, motion and stillness at once, or the smile of the compassionate Buddha for those who are only what they are, a smile that would encourage them to more. This is not the humor derived from things being put together that are unlike. It is the humor of seeing the array of things and realizing that it all might rise, as if against gravity—the humor of a spontaneous response to having seen this, as if being touched.

PHILLIP LOPATE

# In Search of the Centaur:
## The Essay-Film

**M**y intention here is to define, describe, survey and celebrate a cinematic genre that barely exists. As a cinephile and personal essayist, I have an urge to see these two interests combined through the works of filmmakers who commit essays on celluloid. But, while there are cinematic equivalents to practically every literary genre, filmmakers tend to shy away from the essay, and that in itself is intriguing. What it signals to me is that, in spite of Alexandre Astruc's tempting utopian term "caméra-stylo," the camera is not a pencil, and it is rather difficult to think with it in the way an essayist might.

Ever since I began looking for essay-films, the cinema mavens I consulted were quick to suggest candidates that seemed pretty far-fetched, given my idea of what an essay is. I was told, for instance, that Brakhage's abstract film-poems, Jansco's masterly tracking shots, Tarkovsky's transcendental dramas, even the supposedly genre-subversive remake of *Little Shop of Horrors*, were all "essays" of one sort or another. These examples suggested a confusion between a reflective, self-conscious style and an essayistic one. While an essay must reflect or meditate, not all meditative sensibilities are essayistic. Take Brakhage: for all the mythic sweat of his writings or the lyrical satisfaction of his visuals, I am unable to follow a coherent argument or know what he actually thinks about, say, the play of light on an ashtray for forty minutes. So let me propose that, rather than rushing in anxiously to fill the void, it might be important as a starting-point to face the brute absence—the scarcity—of essay-films.

What exactly do I mean by an essay-film? To answer that I have to step back first and convey my sense of the literary essay. To me, the essay is as much a tradition as a form, and a fairly discrete one: prefigured by classical authors such as Cicero, Plutarch, and Seneca, it crystallized with Montaigne and Bacon, thrived with the English familiar essay of Dr. Johnson, Addison and Steele, Hazlitt, Lamb, Stevenson, Orwell, and Virginia Woolf, propagated an American branch with Emerson, Thoreau, Mencken, and E. B. White, down to our contemporaries Didion, Hoagland, Gass, and Hardwick. There is also a European strand of philosophical essay-writing that extends from Nietzsche to Weil, Benjamin, Barthes, Sartre, Cioran, and others; and a Japanese essay tradition that includes Kenko, Dazai, Tanizaki and so on.

It is easier to list the essay's practitioners than to fix a definition of its protean form. "A short literary composition on a single subject, usually presenting the personal views of the author," says the *American Heritage Dictionary*. While I defy anyone to boil down Montaigne's rambling late essays to a single subject or characterize them as short, I do agree that the essay offers personal views. That's not to say it is always first-person or autobiographical, but it tracks a person's thoughts as he or she tries to work out some mental knot, however various its strands. An essay is a search to find out what one thinks about something.

Often the essay follows a helically descending path, working through preliminary supposition to reach a more difficult core of honesty. The narrative engine that drives its form is "What do I *really* think about X?" not, "What are the conventional views I am expected to have?" For this reason the essayist often plays the nonconformist, going against the grain of prevailing pieties.

Essayists often cast themselves in the role of the superfluous man/woman, the marginal belle lettrist. The obverse of this humility, Montaigne's "What do *I* know?" is a mental freedom and a cheekiness in the face of fashion and authority. The essayist wears proudly the confusion of an independent soul trying to grope in isolation toward the truth.

Adorno, in "The Essay as Form," saw precisely the antisystematic, subjective, nonmethodic method of the essay as its radical promise, and he called for modern philosophy to adopt its form, at a time when authoritative systems of thought had become suspect. Nietzsche asserted famously that all philosophies were disguised psychopathologies. The essayist often begins with a confession of pathology, prejudice, or limitation, and then in the best cases rises to a level of general wisdom that might be generously called philosophy.

Whatever twists and turns occur along its path, and however deep or moral its conclusions, an essay will have little enduring interest unless it also exhibits a certain sparkle or stylistic flourish. It is not enough for the essayist to slay the bull; it must be done with more finesse than butchery. Freshness, honesty, self-exposure, and authority must all be asserted in turn. An essayist who produces magisterial and smoothly ordered arguments but is unable to surprise himself in the process of writing will end up boring us. An essayist who is vulnerable and sincere but unable to project any authority will seem, alas, merely pathetic and forfeit our attention. So it is a difficult game to pull off. Readers must feel included in a true conversation, allowed to follow thorough mental processes of contradiction and digression, yet be aware of a formal shapeliness developing simultaneously underneath.

An essay is a continual asking of questions—not necessarily finding "solutions," but enacting the struggle for truth in full view. Lukács, in his meaty "On the Nature and Form of the Essay," wrote: "The essay is a judgment, but the essential, the value-determining thing about it is not the verdict (as is the case with the system) but the process of judging."

I will now try to define the qualities that to my mind make an essay-film. Starting with the most questionable proposition first:

(1) An essay-film must have words, in the form of a text either spoken, subtitled, or intertitled. Say all you like about visualization being at the core of thinking, I cannot accept an utterly pure, silent flow of images as constituting essayistic discourse. Ditto for a movie composed of images with incidental background noises, like Robert Gardner's exquisite *Forest*

*of Bliss* or Johann van der Keuken's *The Eye above the Well*; whatever their other virtues, these are not, to my thinking, essay-films. To be honest, I've never seen a silent-era movie that I could consider an essay-film. I have been told that Dziga Vertov's *Three Songs of Lenin* transmits its ideational content solely through its visuals. I grant that it delivers a clear ideological point, as does, say, Franju's *Blood of the Beasts*, but conveying a message of politics through images does not alone make an essay—or else we would have to speak of advertisements or political posters as essays. Both the Franju and the Vertov films seem (to use Vertov's label) "songlike," rather than essayistic.

(2) The text must represent a single voice. It may be either that of the director or screenwriter, or if collaborative, then stitched together in such a way as to sound like a single perspective. A mere collage of quoted texts is not an essay. There is nothing wrong with lots of citations or quotes in an essay (think of Montaigne), so long as a unified perspective is asserted around them. I know that Walter Benjamin used to fantasize writing an essay composed wholly of quotes, but he never got around to it, and even if he had, it would not be what draws us to Benjamin, which is his compelling, tender voice and thinking process. When I read an Anthology Film Archives calendar description of an "essay-like" Japanese Super-B in which "some words are taken from Dostoevsky, others from Susan Sontag, Rimbaud, Bob Dylan, creating a string of overlapping images that ultimately build into an innate image," I don't even have to see it to know that it is not my idea of an essay-film.

(3) The text must represent an attempt to work out some reasoned line of discourse on a problem. I am not sure how to test this criterion; but I know when it's not there. For instance, Jonas Mekas's haunting text in *Lost, Lost, Lost* functions like an incantatory poem, not an essay.

By now it should be clear that I am using the term "essay film" as a description, not an honorific; there are great cinematic works that do not qualify as essay-films, and highly flawed ones that do.

(4) The text must impart more than information; it must have a strong, personal point of view. The standard documentary voiceover that tells us, say, about the annual herring yield is fundamentally journalistic, not essayistic. Nor is Luis Buñuel's mischievous *Land Without Bread*,

which parodies the faceless, objective documentary perspective while refraining from giving us Buñuel's own private thoughts about Las Hurdes, an essay-film. The missing element becomes immediately apparent when we contrast the film with Buñuel's lovely, idiosyncratic autobiography, *My Last Sigh*.

(5) Finally, the text's language should be as eloquent, well written and interesting as possible. This may seem less a category than an aesthetic judgment. Still, I include it because you would not expect to find, in a collection of the year's best essays, a piece written in condescendingly simple, primer diction; therefore you should not expect to hear such watered-down language in an essay-film. That such wonderful writers of the thirties as Hemingway and Dudley Nichols should have, in attempting to reach the masses, used so cramped and patronizing a discourse in their narratives for Joris Ivens's *The Spanish Earth* and *The 400 Million*, when they could have written genuine essays, seems a sadly missed opportunity.

Those who regard the cinema primarily as a visual medium may object that my five criteria say nothing about the treatment of images. This is not because I mean to depreciate the visual component of movies; quite the contrary, that is what drew me to the medium in the first place, and will always hold me in thrall. I concentrate here on the value of the text, not in order to elevate words above visuals, or to deny the importance of formal visual analysis, but only because I am unconvinced that the handling of the visuals per se dictates whether a work qualifies as an essay-film. I will say more about the relationship between sound and image in this genre later. For now, permit me to look at a few examples.

My first glimpse of the centaur that is the essay-film was Alain Resnais's *Night and Fog* (1955). While watching it in college I became aware of an elegance in Jean Cayrol's screenplay language that was intriguingly at odds with the usual sledgehammer treatment of the Holocaust:

> Sometimes a message flutters down, is picked up. Death makes its first pick, chooses again in the night and fog. Today, on the same track, the sun shines. Go slowly along with it . . . looking for what? Traces of the bodies that fell to the ground? Or the footmarks of

those first arrivals gun-bullied to the camp, while the dogs barked and searchlights wheeled and the incinerator flamed, in the lurid decor so dear to the Nazis?

The voice on the soundtrack was worldly, tired, weighted down with the need to make fresh those horrors that had so quickly turned stale. It was a self-interrogatory voice, like a true essayist's, dubious, ironical, wheeling and searching for the heart of its subject matter. "How discover what remains of the reality of these camps when it was despised by those who made them and eluded those who suffered there?" Meanwhile Resnais's refined tracking shots formed a visual analogue of this patient searching for historical meaning in sites now emptied of their infamous activity.

It may sound grotesque to say this, but I was more delighted with Cayrol's heady use of language than I was depressed by the subject matter—which in any case I knew all too well from growing up in Jewish Brooklyn. What stuck in my mind for years was that voiceover phrase: "The only sign—but you have to know—is this ceiling scored by fingernails." That "but you have to know" (*mais il faut savoir*) inserted so cannily in mid-sentence, thrilled me like an unexpected, aggressive pinch: its direct address broke the neutral contract of spectatorship and forced me to acknowledge a conversation, along with its responsibilities.

A similar *frisson* occurred when, some years later, I was watching an otherwise conventional documentary, Nemec's *Oratorio for Prague*, about the events in Czechoslovakia in 1968. As the visuals displayed Russian tanks advancing on the crowd, the narrator said something like (I am paraphrasing from memory): "Usually we do not know where to pin the blame for massacres, we invoke large historical forces and so on. This time we do know who gave the order to fire. It was Captain —— ," and the camera zoomed in on a Soviet Army man's head. Again I felt sort of an impudent tweak. Not that I had any idea who this Russian officer was, but I loved the sudden way the civilized elegy for Prague Spring was ruptured, and we were catapulted into that more basic Eastern European mentality of tribal scores to settle, long memories, and bitter humor: that Russian pig may have mowed us down, but we hereby name him and show his face— just in case the millennium of justice ever arrives. I later identified that atypically malicious human voice on the commentary as an essayistic intrusion.

There are essayistic elements that color certain films by Chris Marker, Alexander Kluge, Jon Jost, Ralph Arlyck, Jean-Luc Godard, Jean-Pierre Gorin, Joris Ivens, Pier Paolo Pasolini, Dušan Makaveyev, Jean-Marie Straub, Yvonne Rainer, Woody Allen, Wim Wenders, Hartmut Bitomsky, Orson Welles, Ross McElwee, Robb Moss; Alain Resnais's shorts, Fellini's *Roma,* Michael Moore's *Roger and Me,* Isaac Julian's *Looking for Langston,* Tony Buba's *Lightning Over Braddock,* Morgan Fisher's *Academy Leader,* Cocteau's *Testament of Orpheus,* Louis Malle's *My Dinner with André,* Jonathan Demme's *Swimming to Cambodia,* and I'm sure many others that I've forgotten or overlooked. By no means will I be able to able to discuss all these in the limited space allotted. By zeroing in on a handful, I hope to convey a sense of the potentials and pitfalls of the form, as well as weed out the true essay-films from those that have merely a tincture of essayism.

The one great essayist in the film medium is Chris Marker. *Letter From Siberia* (1958), *The Koumiko Mystery* (1965), and *Sans Soleil* (1982) are his purest essay-films, though it seems that he has an inveterate essayistic tendency that peeps out even in his more interview-oriented documentaries, such as *Le Joli Mai,* or his compilation films, such as *Grin without the Cat.* There is a tension in Marker's films between the politically committed, self-effacing, left-wing documentarist style of the thirties/Ivens tendency, and an irrepressibly Montaignesque personal tone. He has a reputation for being elusive and shy—not the best qualities, on the face of it, for a personal essayist—and yet, perhaps because he evolved so diverse and complicated a self (ex-Resistance fighter, novelist, poet, filmmaker), he can emit enough particles of this self to convey a strong sense of individuality and still keep his secrets. He also has the essayist's aphoristic gift, which enables him to assert a collective historical persona, a first-person plural, even when the first-person singular is held in abeyance. Finally, Marker has the essayist's impulse to tell the truth: not always a comfortable attribute for an engagé artist.

A film such as *Letter From Siberia,* which seems at first the sympathetic testimony of a Western fellow-traveler to the Soviet bloc, ends by coiling us in one contradiction after another. What keeps it on the Left is the good-humored, rather than sinister, tone in which Marker unveils the problematic aspects of Siberian life. In a characteristically witty passage, Marker interprets the same footage three different ways, based on three separate ideological positions, thus demystifying the spurious objectivity of documentaries, albeit with a lighter touch than that with which this operation is usually performed. The sequence also points to one of Marker's key approaches as a film-essayist, which is to meditate on the soundtrack, after the fact, on the footage he has shot. In Marker there is often a pronounced time-lag between the quick eye and the slow, digesting mind, which tracks—months or even years later—the meaning of what it has seen, and this delay accounts for a certain nostalgia for the escaping present and a melancholy over the inherently receding reality of photographed images. It is like that passage in *Tristes Tropiques*, in which Claude Lévi-Strauss laments that the traveler/anthropologist always arrives too early or too late. In Marker's case, his camera arrives in time to record events, but his mind and heart take too long to catch up, not appreciating events sufficiently in the moment.

This time delay also allows Marker to project a historical understanding onto otherwise bland or neutral footage. The most dramatic instance of this occurs in the medal-bestowing ceremony in Cape Verde, Africa, shown in *Sans Soleil*. A year later, Marker tells us on the soundtrack, the President would be deposed by the man he is pinning a medal on. As he explains that the army officer thought he deserved a larger reward than this particular medal, we have the chilling sense that we are watching a bloody tragedy like *Macbeth* unfold at the moment the idea first crossed the upstart's brow. But as Marker tells us elsewhere in the film: "Ah well, history only tastes bitter to those who expect it to taste sugar-coated."

*Sans Soleil* is Marker's masterpiece, and perhaps the one masterpiece of the essay-film genre. How ironic, then, that Marker chooses the fictive strategy of a woman's voice (Alexandra Stewart's) reading passages from the letters of a friend, Sandor Krasna. This Krasna fellow is obviously a lightly fictionalized stand-in for the author, like Lamb's Elia. The film was assembled mostly during the seventies, a period when Marker was part of a political commune and preferred to downplay his auteurial signature (the line "Conception and editing: Chris Marker," buried in the long list of credits, is the only indication that it is his film), which may partly explain the diffident whimsy of hiding behind "Krasna." On the other hand,

**Chris Marker, *Sans Soleil* (1982)**
**"To understand it properly one must move forward in time. In a year Luis Cabral, the President, will be in prison, and the man he has just decorated will have taken power."**

putting his comments in the third person has the distancing effect of giving a respect and weight to them they might not have commanded otherwise. As Stewart reads passages from Krasna's letters, prefacing them with "he once wrote to me" or "he said," the effect is almost like a verbal funeral portrait. Marker appears to be anticipating and celebrating, with mordant relish, his own death, projecting a more mythical figure of himself in the process.

"He wrote: 'I've been around the world several times, and now only banality interests me. On this trip I've tracked it like a bounty hunter.'" Place and homesickness are natural subjects for the essay-film: *Sans Soleil* is a meditation on place in the jet age, where spatial availability confuses the sense of time and memory. Unlike Wim Wenders, who keeps whining (in *Tokyo Ga* and elsewhere) that every place is getting to look like every other place—an airport—Marker has an appetite for geography and local difference; his lament is that, if anything, he feels at home in too many places. Particularly drawn to Japan, he visits his favorite Tokyo haunts, and the narrator reflects: "These simple joys he had never felt on returning to a house, a home, but twelve million anonymous inhabitants could supply him with them." Marker/Krasna is a man of the crowd, who revels in anonymity; a romantic who in San Francisco visits all the locations Hitchcock used in *Vertigo*; a collector of memories ("I have spent my life trying to understand the function of remembering") who explicitly associates recollecting with rewriting.

Marker's earlier Japanese film, *The Koumiko Mystery*, can be read as a sort of poignant power struggle between a lively young woman living in the present and a middle-aged filmmaker determined to turn her into past and memory through the process of infatuation. He sucks on her vitality, he "rewrites" her by meditating on her filmed image, thereby, perhaps, possessing her and her mystery in the only way he can.

*Sans Soleil*, a larger work, is about everything but the proverbial kitchen sink: time, emptiness, Japan, Africa, video games, comic strips, Sei Shonagon's lists, pet burials, relics, political demonstrations, death, images, appearances, suicide, the future, Tarkovsky, Hitchcock, religion, and the absolute. What unites it is Marker's melancholy-whimsical, bacheloric approach to the fragments of the modern world, looking at them moment by moment and trying to make at least a poetic sense of them. "Poetry is born of insecurity," he says, "and the impermanence of a thing," at which point we see a samurai sword fight on television.

Given Marker's sterling example, and the video access "revolution," and with more and more conceptual artists and defrocked academics taking to Portapaks and cheap movie rigs, I half-expected to see a whole school of essay-films develop in the seventies and eighties. Not only did the technical potential exist, but a distribution circuit of underground venues, colleges, and museums was in place, promoting "personal cinema" as an alternative to the commercial product. But the essay-film never really arrived. What took its place, instead, was an explosion of films that incorporated essayistic throat-clearings as but one of many noises in an echo chamber of aesthetic cross-reference that ultimately "subverted," to use current jargon, the very notion of a single personal voice.

It was the bad luck of the essay-film that, just as its technical moment arrived, the intellectual trends of the hour—deconstruction, postmodernism, appropriation art, the new forms of feminism and Marxism retrofitted with semiotic media criticism—questioned the validity of the single authorial voice, preferring instead to demonstrate over and over how much we are conditioned and brainwashed by the images around us. Not that these points are invalid, but they mute the essayistic voice: for if the self is nothing but a social construct, and individuality a bourgeois illusion intended to maintain the status quo, then the hip, "transgressive" thing to do is satiric quotation, appropriation, and collage.

Some of the bright, experimental young filmmakers, such as Abigail Child, Laurie Dunphy, and Anita Thatcher, produced "found footage" films, which mocked the patriarchy by deconstructionist editing. Others such as Trinh T. Minh-ha made what I would call "text films" (*Reassemblage, Surname Viet Given Name Nam*), which surrounded a subject such as colonialism or oppression of women through a reshuffling of voices and doctored footage. Steve Fagin's videos on Lou-Andreas Salomé and Flaubert's *Bouvard and Pécuchet* used Syberberg-like puppet stagings, with results that were intriguing, campy, and elusive. DeDe Halleck and Anthony McCall dismantled and slyly reenacted Freud's Dora case in such a way that the filmmakers' politics were never in doubt, but their own interpretation of the case remained unclear.

These films are frightfully intellectual and effective up to a point in circling their chosen themes; and yet the last thing any of their creators would do is tell us directly, consistently what they actually think about their chosen subject.

A recent "collage film" by Yvonne Rainer, *Privilege* (1990), is a case in point: it mixes dramatic scenes, found footage, fake interviews, written texts, documentary sequences, and so forth, in a stimulating, braided exploration of menopause and racism. Jonathan Rosenbaum, defending this film in the *Chicago Reader*, wrote: "Approached as a narrative, Yvonne Rainer's sixth feature takes forever to get started and an eternity to end. In between its ill-defined borders, the plot itself is repeatedly interrupted, endlessly delayed or protracted, frequently relegated to the back burner and all but forgotten . . . Yet approached as an essay, *Privilege* unfolds like a single multi-faceted argument, uniformly illuminated by white-hot rage and wit—a cacophony of voices and discourses to be sure, but a purposeful and meaningful cacophony in which all the voices are speaking to us as well as one another." Much as I sympathize with Rosenbaum's position, he is almost saying that all you have to do is recategorize some plotless stew as an essay and everything immediately belongs. Even essays have plots! Now it so happens that I admire Rainer's film, but I still cannot bring myself to accept a "cacophony of voices and discourses" as an essay. When I left the theater I was still unsure what exactly Rainer's argument was about menopause, or what she was trying to tell me about the relation between it and racism, other than that both involved feeling like an outsider. She would probably say, "I'm not trying to tell you anything, I'm trying to get you to think." Fine; so does an essay, but an essay also tells us what its author thinks.

Jon Jost is another independent filmmaker who has experimented on and off with essayistic elements. I recently checked out Jost's *Speaking Directly: Some American Notes (1972–1974)*, which the filmmaker himself refers to as an "essay-film," and found it insufferably irritating. In part my reaction is to Jost's solemn, humorless, self-hating, tediously lecturing persona. Granted, all essayists have the option to bring out the obnoxious aspect of their personality, but they usually balance it with *something* charming; in Jost's case I wanted to hide under the seat every time he came on screen. Still, if he had made a true essay-film I could have applauded. But instead he created one more hybrid collage, with Vietnam atrocity stories and nightly-news broadcasts quoted simultaneously for ironic effect; with dictionary definitions suggesting something or other about linguistics; with fulminations against imperialism; cinema-verité interviews of his friends and lover; and large, smugly self-reflexive dollops informing us that this was a movie, as if we didn't know. Jost's autobiographical passages when he addresses the camera suggest the most potential for an essay-film; but he makes such vague, unprobing statements about his life or relationships—dismissing his parents in one sentence apiece as a war criminal and a cipher, respectively—that the self-analysis comes off as evasive and shallow. Perhaps all this is intentional; a self-portrait of an unlikable fellow. It finally seems to me, though, that Jost has not really attempted to understand himself, but simply subsumed his self-portrait in larger and more forgiving sociohistorical categories. (I am told that Jost redeemed himself with a much better essay-film called *Plain Talk and Common Sense*. If so, I suppose I look forward to being proved wrong.)

Clearly, the chief influence on early Jost, and indeed on most independent filmmakers who have selectively used essayistic maneuvers only to abandon or undercut them, is Jean-Luc Godard. Now, Godard may be the greatest film artist of our era, I will not dispute that. But strictly considering the development of the essay-film, his influence has been a mixed blessing. The reason is that Godard is the master of hide and seek, the ultimate tease. Just when you think you've got him, he wriggles away. When he whispers observations in *Two or Three Things I Know about Her*, how can we be sure those are really his opinions? He is too much the modernist, fracturing, dissociating, collaging, to be caught dead expressing his views straightforwardly. (This raises an interesting side issue: to what degree is the modernist aesthetic itself inimical to the essay? Certainly the essay allows for a good deal of fragmentation and disjunction, and yet it keeps weaving itself whole again, resisting alienation, if only through the power of a synthesizing, personal voice with its old-fashioned humanist assumptions.)

Godard has often used the word "researches" in describing his filmic approach, particularly after 1968. "Researches" implies a scientific attitude, enabling Godard to present, say, deadpan ten-minute shots of an assembly line, ostensibly invoking, through "real time," the tedium that will encourage us to empathize with the factory worker. (That it does not, alas, but only makes us impatient with the screen, illustrates what I would call the fallacy of real-time magic thinking.) Generally speaking, "researches" is a good term for Godard's nonfiction efforts, not "essays." The two possible exceptions are *Ici et Ailleurs* (1974) and *Letter to Jane* (1972).

*Ici et Ailleurs* (Here and Elsewhere) is both Godard's surprisingly sincere effort to reflect on the frustration of making a movie about the Palestinian struggle, and a typically modernist attempt "to weave a text and to tear it to pieces, to build a fiction and to ruin its pretensions" (André Bleikasten). Two voices, a "He" and a "She," chase each other on the soundtrack, saying things like: "Too simple and too easy to divide the world in two. Too easy to simply say that the wealthy are wrong and the poor are right. Too easy. Too easy and too simple. Too easy and too simple to divide the world in two." Godard is here using the Gertrude Stein method of incantatory repetition and slight variation to create a cubist experience of language. It is effective in making us contemplate whether a truth is no less valid for being simple. But I would hardly call the text, with its blurted slogans undercut by verbal arabesques, an attempt at reasoned essayistic discourse.

*Letter to Jane*, on the other hand, is a closely reasoned, if nasty, provocation by two male-bonded ingrates, Godard and Jean-Pierre Gorin, against the female movie star who so generously collaborated with them on their otherwise unbudgetable feature, *Tout Va Bien*. There is something so preposterously unfair about their impersonal, didactic language as Godard and Gorin, like thought-police interrogators, critique the supposedly neocolonialist, ethnocentric angle of Jane Fonda's head as she appears to listen sympathetically to a Vietnamese peasant. *Letter to Jane* does open up new possibilities for essay-films, though, by audaciously resisting any pressure to dazzle the eye (the visuals consist mostly of the Fonda newspaper photo, with a few other stills thrown in), and allowing the voiceover to dominate unapologetically. Also, *Letter to Jane* solves one of the key problems of essay-films, what to do for visuals, by making semiotic image-analysis its very subject. The result is, like it or not, an essay-film. And, for all its Robespierrean coldness, I mostly like it, if only because of its unshakable confidence in the power of expository prose.

Godard's ex-partner, Gorin, went on to develop a much more truly personal-essay film style in his own features *Poto and Cabengo* (1982) and *Routine Pleasures* (1985). In *Poto and Cabengo* Gorin takes as his departure point a seemingly sensationalistic true story about two sisters who invent their own way of speaking and turns it into a meditation on language acquisition. Just as Joan Didion and other New Journalism–trained essayists injected themselves into the story, so Gorin's narration inserts his own doubts and confusions about what sort of film he is trying to make, thereby interrogating not only himself but the assumptions of the documentary genre. While it has become a cliché of the New Documentary to make the difficulty of getting the necessary footage the gist of the finished film, Gorin brings to this device a flexible, self-mocking voice (the expatriate filmmaker with the French accent, too smart and lazy for his own good) that is very engaging. In *Routine Pleasures* he dispenses entirely with a news "hook," cheekily alternating between two things he happened to take footage of, toy-train hobbyists and painter–film critic Manny Farber, and trying to weave a connection between these unrelated subjects (something about recreating the world ideally?), if for no other reason than to justify his having spent European television-production money. The result is a perversely willed, unpredictable piece about the thin line between art and hobbyism (the film itself seems a demonstration of this), in which we learn still more about Gorin's inertial, seductively intelligent personality. By drawing closer to himself as a subject, however, he raises the ante of our expectation: for instance, having acknowledged Farber as his mentor, Gorin's discreet refusal to be more candid about Farber's personality and the dynamics of mentorship leaves one disappointed. In both features, Gorin seems hot on the trail of the essay-film, but is still too coy and withholding about sharing the fullness of his thoughts.

One of the natural subjects for personal essay-films is movie making itself, since it is often what the filmmaker knows and cares about most. There is already a whole subgenre of essay-films about the Movie That Could Have Been, Or Was, Or Could Still Be. Pasolini's *Notes Toward an African "Orestes"* (1970) is a sort of celluloid notebook into which the filmmaker put his preliminary ideas about casting, music, or global politics for a project that never came to pass. Maybe by shooting these "notes," he used up the enthusiasm that might have gone into filming the classic itself. Given the murkiness of his *Medea*, I would just as soon watch an essay-film of Pasolini thinking about how he would do an *Orestes* in Africa as actually view the finished product. The opening sequences are promising: he casts by shooting passersby in the street, telling us, "This young man could be Orestes," shows a newsreel of an African military parade, saying "These could be Greek soldiers," and conjectures hypothetical locations: "This could be the camp for the Greeks." He delivers ambiguous touristic impressions, such as, "The terrible aspect of Africa is its solitude, the monstrous form that Nature can assume." He tells himself, "the protagonist of my film . . . must be the People," and keeps circling around the question of a chorus. So far so good. But then the film abandons these thoughts for ten minutes of Gato Barbieri noodling around in rehearsal, and an awkward, staged discussion in which Pasolini asks a group of puzzled African exchange students how they feel about the *Oresteia.*

What makes *Notes Toward an African "Orestes"* so tantalizing and frustrating is that a narrator of the intellectual and moral stature of Pasolini lets only slivers of his mind show through. Were he to have written an essay on the same subject, he would surely have struggled harder to pull his thoughts into focus. (Pasolini could be a very compelling and persuasive essayist). The final collage-form seems dictated clearly by the footage available at editing time, rather than any carefully evolved effort to understand. J. Hoberman sees it otherwise: *"Orestes* is a movie that requires an active viewer, the deconstructive narrative demands that you put Pasolini's film together in your head." I am all for the active viewer, but this seems to me letting Pasolini off the hook. "Deconstructive" should not become an all-purpose excuse for presenting unresolved, thrown-together footage.

A much more satisfying essay-film about the process of movie making and what might have been is Orson Welles's *Filming "Othello"* (1978). This brilliant, if rarely seen, self-exegesis consists, for the most part, of Welles seated with his back to a television monitor, talking to the camera in order to have, as he puts it, a "conversation" about the making of *Othello*. Conversation is, of course the heart of the personal essay tradition; Welles could hardly be naïve on this point, having claimed that he read Montaigne every day. He was certainly steeped in the French master's undulating, pungent discourse.

A famous raconteur and compulsively watchable actor, Welles through his own charisma solves the sticky problem of what to do about visuals in an essay-film, by simply filling the screen with himself talking. Suddenly we are face to face with our essayist, rather than hearing a disembodied voice. Cutaways to sequences of *Othello* (reedited), a relaxed luncheon discussion of the play between Welles and actors Michael MacLiammoir and Hilton Edwards, and footage of Welles addressing a Boston audience, provide sufficient visual variety to his talking torso.

What is so refreshing about his talk is that he is speaking in an honest, maximally intelligent way about things he loves, Shakespeare and filmmaking. This Welles bears little resemblance to the arch poseur of late-night talk shows. Indeed, the audience is privileged to eavesdrop on a genius of the dramatic arts as he shares his thoughts and doubts about one

**Orson Welles, *Filming "Othello"* (1978)**
**Over images from *Othello* Welles comments, "My film tried to depict a whole world in collapse."**

of his most important productions. He is both musing to himself and seeming to dictate an essay aloud (though it was probably written out beforehand). On the other hand, he is also giving a performance, and we cannot help but judge him simultaneously as an actor, the way he whips his head from side to side or raises his eyebrows. Our awareness of the contrivance behind this seemingly artless conversation has been enhanced by Jonathan Rosenbaum's research on the making of *Filming "Othello"*: apparently it was shot over a number of years, with changing television crews operating under Welles's tight direction. (See Rosenbaum's "Orson Welles's Essay-Films and Documentary Fictions," *Cinematograph* 4, 1991.)

Welles tells us about the vicissitudes of filming *Othello:* how he was approached by an Italian producer who said "We must make *Othello*"; how he had originally planned to shoot in a studio with fluid long shots and long takes, but after the Italian producer went bankrupt he was forced into improvised location shooting all over the map and quick editing to cover the shifts; how he had to hammer sardine cans into armor; and other war stories. He tells it exotically, "like a tale from Casanova," careening back and forth in his chronology, getting ahead of himself, digressing from meaty Shakespearian analysis to anecdote to critical response. "There is no way to avoid these—lapses into autobiography," he apologizes, as he begs our pardon later for rambling and failing to cite negative reviews. These apologies help to establish trust and rapport, in the classical manner of the personal essayist.

Vlada Petric notes (*"Filming 'Othello,' " Film Library Quarterly*, 1980) that, after reciting soliloquies of both Othello and Iago, as "a kind of compensation for the fact that the sound in the original print is poor," Welles "admits that his Othello 'does not do full justice to the play'; nevertheless he claims that the film is among his favorite works . . . 'I think that I was too young for this part, and I wish I could have done it over again.'" The present film is, in a sense, the "doing it over."

Welles's other so called essay-film, *F for Fake* (1975), is much less successful as such, largely because Welles seems more intent on mystifying and showing off his magician-Prospero persona than in opening his mind to us. I am never convinced that Welles is working hard to say all he can on the subject of counterfeit art; he is so taken up with a glib defense of artifice that he forgets to convey his own sincerity, something an essayist must do. He would rather have our tepid agreement that all art is a kind of lie than move us. Academic film critics, who overrate cinematic self-reflexivity and attention to the narrative "frame," adore the cheap joke he pulls on us when he promises that everything in the next hour will be true, then makes up some cock-and-bull story towards the end, without having told us the sixty minutes were up. Still, I'm grateful for *F for Fake*, because its florid, windbag Welles makes me appreciate all the more the wonderfully civilized, humane Welles of *Filming "Othello."*

Before he died, Welles was planning to make yet another cinematic self-analysis, *Filming "The Trial."* If you count in earlier Welles projects with essayistic elements, such as *Portrait of Gina* and *It's All True*, it is clear that he had become seriously devoted to the essay-film. Welles said himself in a 1982 interview: "The essay does not date, because it represents the author's contribution, however modest, to the moment at which it was made."

It could be said that all first-person narration tends toward the essay, in the sense that, as soon as an "I" begins to define his or her position in and view of the world, the potential for essayistic discourse comes into play. First-person narration in film is complicated by the disjunction between the subjective voice on the soundtrack and the third-person, material objectivity that the camera tends to bestow on whatever it photographs, like it or not. This tension has been cunningly exploited by the filmmakers who are drawn to the first person, such as Robert Bresson, Joseph Mankiewicz, and Woody Allen. First-person narration in movies often brings with it a bookish quality, partly because it has so often been used in movies adapted from novels, but also because it superimposes a thoughtful perspective, looking backwards on the supposed "now" of the film. Even an *I Walked with a Zombie* begins to seem studied and literary the moment we hear Frances Dee's narrative voice orienting us to events that began in the past.

First-person narrative also awakens the appetite for confession. Think of the strange accents of Meryl Streep's Isak Dinesen in the first *Out of Africa* voiceover: we wait for the shaky self-protectiveness of that voice to break down, become more unguarded, and the remainder of the film plays cat-and-mouse with this confessional promise (largely broken, it turns out).

One good place to start looking for shards of the essay-film might be movies with first-person narrators. Particularly autobiographical films, like Ross McElwee's *Sherman's March* and *Backyard,* Michael Moore's *Roger and Me*, Su Friedrich's *The Ties That Bind* and *Sink or Swim*, Ralph Arlyck's films, Tony Buba's *Lightning Over Braddock*, Wim Wenders's *Lightning Over Water* and *Tokyo Ga*, Cocteau's *Testament of Orpheus*, and Joris Ivens's *Story of the Wind*.

Just as the diary is rightly considered a literary form distinct from the essay, so diary films such as *Sherman's March* and *David Holzman's Diary* obey a different structure than essay-films by following a linear chronology and reacting to daily events, rather than following a mental argument. Still, there are many overlaps between the two, as McElwee's thoughtful, digressive narrator in the wonderful *Sherman's March* (1986) demonstrates. Here McElwee plays with self-irony, ostensibly bidding for our sympathy while asking viewers to judge his bachelor persona as rationalizing and self-absorbed. Indeed, the last quarter of the film turns into a contemporary morality play in which the narrator relinquishes his power of judgment to his friend Charlene, who becomes the voice of wisdom and vitality, telling him what he is doing wrong with women. This pat turnabout does provide a conclusion, but it also reinforces the suspicion that McElwee wants us to read his "Ross" the way we would a fictional, self-deluding character.

Use of the first person invokes the potential for an unreliable narrator, a device we usually think of as reserved strictly for fiction; essayists from Hazlitt to Edward Abbey have toyed with a persona balanced between charm and offensiveness, alternately inviting reader closeness and alienation. The difference is that essayists keep the faith with their narrators, while McElwee finally leaves "Ross" hanging out to dry. It is an effective, even purgatively ego-slaying strategy, but it undermines the work's identity as an essay-film: however deluded he may be, the essayist must have the final word in his own essay.

Michael Moore's *Roger and Me* (1989) promises at first to be a model essay-film. The filmmaker sets up, in the first twenty minutes, a very strong, beguiling autobiographical narrator: we see his parents, the town where he grew up, his misadventures in San Francisco cappuccino bars. Then, disappointingly, Moore phases out the personal side of his narrator, making way for a cast of "colorful" interviewees: the rabbit lady, the evicting sheriff, the mystic ex-feminist, the apologist for General Motors. True, he inserts a recurring motif of himself trying to confront Roger Smith, GM's chairman, but this faux-naïf suspense structure becomes too mechanically farcical, and in any case none of these subsequent appearances deepen our sense of Moore's character or mind.

It is as though the filmmaker hooked us by offering himself as bait in order to draw us into his anticorporate capitalist sermon. The factual distortions of *Roger and Me*, its cavalier manipulations of documentary verisimilitude in the service of political polemic, have been analyzed at great length. I still find the film winning, up to a point, and do not so much mind its "unfairness" to the truth (especially as the national news media regularly distort in the other direction), as I do its abandonment of what had seemed a very promising essay-film. Yet perhaps the two are related: Moore's decision to fade out his subjective, personal, "Michael," seems to coincide with his desire to have his version of the Flint, Michigan, story accepted as objective truth.

It must also be said that, unlike a true personal essayist, Moore resists the burden of self-understanding, electing to ridicule the inanities of the rich while not being hard enough on himself. The issue is not whether *Roger and Me* betrays the essay-film, a form that barely exists and that Moore may have no conception of. The real question is why filmmakers find it so difficult to follow a train of thought, using their own personal voice and experience to guide them? In Moore's case, there seems to be a more pressing political agenda. But another reason could be the huge difference between writing about and filming oneself. Filmmakers usually choose that career with the expectation that they can stay behind the camera, and I suspect that immense reticence or bashfulness may set in once a filmmaker who has taken center screen as the governing consciousness and main performer of an autobiographical film realizes how exposed he or she is. (And this exposure may far exceed what a literary essayist feels. Hence the dance of coyness and retreat, mentioned earlier in regard to Gorin.)

*Roger and Me* also raises the question of to what extent an essay-film can welcome and ingest interviews while still being true to its essayistic nature. At what point will the multiplicity of voices threaten a unified presentation of "the personal views of the author"? Of course, a film can be composed entirely of interviews and still exhibit a personal vision—Erroll Morris's or Marcel Ophuls's documentaries, for example. But a personal vision is not necessarily a personal essay. Erroll Morris's works, eccentric and personal as they are, do not seem to me essay-films. We can only guess what he is thinking as he exhibits the weird human specimens in *Vernon, Florida* or *Gates of Heaven*, and our not knowing how we are supposed to interpret them is precisely the ambiguous point. Similarly, other nonfiction movies with essay flavorings, such as Marker's *Le Joli Mai* or Rouch and Morin's *Chronique d'un Été*, employ a degree of interview material that would seem, at least in my mind, to tip the scales away from the essay-film and toward the documentary.

The relationship between documentary and essay-film is uneasy at best. They are often mistaken for each other; frequently, a work starts off as an essay-film and then runs for cover in the protective grooves of the documentary. At times, however, they behave like two different beasts.

When Michael Moore made a splash with *Roger and Me*, he was at pains to tell reporters, somewhat churlishly, that he hated most documentaries and the standards of ethical documentary procedure. He also left the impression that he had invented a whole new type of movie, instead of acknowledging that there were other autobiographical filmmakers such as McElwee, Buba, and Arlyck who had gotten there first.

To my knowledge Ralph Arlyck is, besides Marker, the one consistent essay-film maker. Arlyck, whose last two movies, *An Acquired Taste* (1981) and *Current Events* (1989), were both shown at the New York Film Festival (and hardly anywhere else), reported he was once on a panel discussion and described himself as a maker of essay-films, at which point some industry producer said with an incredulous sneer, "You mean like— *Thoreau*?" After that, Arlyck has been leery of using the term "essay-film," which may be even more box-office poison than "documentary."

*An Acquired Taste* is, in fact, a hilarious half-hour personal essay about the filmmaker's lack of commercial success, his jealousy and career envy, as seen against the American dream of rising to the top. Arlyck pokes fun at his pathetic go-getter attempts: there is one excruciating scene in which we watch him type out a grant application. "Increasingly I feel like the Ferdinand the Bull of filmmaking," he concludes. He prefers to stay home, play with the kids, and make mild little films, while his wife flies off to France to defend her doctoral thesis. The Arlyck character comes across as a likable schlemiel, cousin to Woody Allen—not necessarily because he is influenced by Allen but because both are drawing from the same well of urban Jewish self-deprecating humor. (Indeed, listening to Woody Allen's digressive, epigrammatic narrators in films such as *Annie Hall*, *Hannah and Her Sisters*, or his third of *New York Stories*, I have often thought that with a little push Woody could have ended up a natural essay-film maker— to the great chagrin of his bankbook. Perhaps his most original trick has been to smuggle contraband essayism into the fiction film.)

Arlyck, meanwhile, unabashedly and essayistically sticks to a single subject and presents his personal views about it. His feature-length *Current Events* tackles the question of how an ordinary individual should respond to the problems of the planet. It is essentially a film about a veteran of sixties' protests—an over-the-hill ex-hippie, his sons call him—twenty years later, reflecting on the meaning of political commitment in the face of overwhelming world need and his own ideological skepticism. Since the subject is so much weightier than career vanity, the tone is more serious, and Arlyck strays farther from home, interviewing people whose persistent commitment to doing good he finds exemplary—if impossible for him to imitate. He always brings it back, like a good personal essayist, to his own daily experiences, the examination of his own conscience. And there is the same intact Arlyck persona: the independent filmmaker and family man, puzzled, ineffectual, sardonic, decent, and good-humored.

Of late, many women filmmakers have been making autobiographical films, using family memoirs as a springboard for personal reflection. Su Friedrich's *Sink or Swim* (1990), even more than her earlier *The Ties That Bind* (1984), is particularly noteworthy, in its complex, harrowing exploration of her relationship to her father. Though the film resembles a structuralist film-poem as much as an essay, Friedrich certainly demonstrates the possibility of making essay-films from a feminist perspective.

Another strong essay-film (or rather, videotape) is Vanalyne Green's *A Spy in the House That Ruth Built* (1989)—exemplary in its personal exploration of a subject (baseball), in the singularity of its first-person text, and in its self-mocking humor and elegant language. Green weaves entertaining connections between the national pastime, erotic fantasies, and the family romance. Here she is plotting her wardrobe for a shoot at the ballpark: "I wanted to go as a tramp, to look as if my head just left the pillow, and the gentle touch of a fingertip on my shoulder would topple me back into bed, where I would lie, framed seductively by the finest cotton and pastel pink sheets, smelling simultaneously of adult sex and a newborn baby's powdered bottom . . . But how not to abandon that other part of myself—the adult woman with the twelve-page vita—while a child inside me was willing to whore her soul for a minute of eye contact with big Dave Winfield?" The visuals show us a witty assemblage composed of baseball paraphernalia, brief interviews, and comically homemade, modest visual tropes. If the text seems wrenched at times into a too-programmatically feminist line, Green recognizes the danger and stops herself, saying: "The more rhetoric, the less I said about me." In the end, she manages to say a lot about herself, in a manner that is broadly generous, forgiving, and very appealing.

I began by pointing to the rarity of essay-films, without explaining why this was. Let me try to do that now.

First, there is the somewhat intractable nature of the camera as a device for recording thoughts: its tendency to provide its own thoughts, in the form of extraneous filmed background information, rather than always clearly expressing what is passing through the filmmaker's mind. True, the filmmaker may also register his thoughts through editing; but this does not remove the problem of the promiscuously saturated image.

Second, there may be, as Stanley Cavell has suggested, a sort of resistance on the part of motion pictures to verbal largesse. Screenplays today employ skeletal dialogue, following the received wisdom that the screen cannot "sop up" much language. Whether this is because of an inherent property in the medium, or because its limits have never been sufficiently tested (think of the novelty of Rohmer's *My Night at Maud's* when it first appeared—a real "talkie!"), the amount of rich, ample language a film can support remains uncertain.

Then there are commercial considerations: just as essay collections rarely sell in bookstores, so essay-films are expected to have little popularity; and films, after all, require a larger initial investment than books. Still, this uncommercial aspect hasn't exactly stopped the legion of experimental filmmakers, whose work often takes a more esoteric, impenetrable form than would an intelligently communicative essay-film.

Another reason has to do with the collaborative nature of the medium: it is easier to get a group of people to throw in with you on a fictional story or social documentary or even a surrealistic vision, than to enlist their support in putting your personal essayistic discourse on screen.

Of course, many independent filmmakers receive grants to make 16mm. or video works that are ostensibly personal, and that they shoot or assemble alone; why don't *they* make more essay-films? I suspect there is a self-selection process attracting certain types of people into filmmaking as an art form: they revere images, want to make magic, and are uncomfortable with the pinning down of thoughts that an essay demands. You would probably stand a better chance of getting a crop of good essay-films if you gave out cameras and budgets to literary essayists and told them to write their next essay for the screen, than if you rounded up the usual independent filmmakers and asked them to make essay-films.

I anticipate a howl of protest: if what you are after is a polished literary text, why not simply write an essay? Why make a film at all? Don't you understand that the film medium has certain properties of its own? Yes, I do understand, but I continue to believe that it is worth exploring this underused form, which may give us something that neither literary essays nor other types of films can.

It seems to me that three procedures suggest themselves for the making of essay-films: (1) To write or borrow a text and go out and find images for it. I do not necessarily mean "illustration," which casts the visual component in a subordinate position. The images and spoken text can have a contrapuntal or even contradictory relation to each other. In Edgardo Cozarinsky's *One Man's War* (1984), the text, based on the late Ernst Jünger's diary as an officer in Hitler's army occupying Paris, is juxtaposed with archival footage from the period. The result is a stimulating clash between the ironic sensibilities of a left-wing emigré filmmaker and a displaced reactionary aesthete. But this is not really an essay-film, because Cozarinsky undercuts Jünger's words without providing a record of his own thoughts. (2) The filmmaker can shoot, or compile previously shot, footage and then write a text that meditates on the assembled images. This is often Marker's approach. (3) The filmmaker can write a little, shoot a little, write a bit more, and so on—the one process interacting with the other throughout.

I do not know whether these processes, chance, or the immaturity of the genre are to blame, but so far, almost none of the examples I would consider essay-films have boasted superlative visuals. Serviceable, yes, but nothing that could compare with the shimmering visual nobility of a dramatic film by Mizoguchi, Antonioni, or Max Ophuls. The one exception I know of is *Night and Fog*, a case in which the separation between visual stylist (Resnais) and screenwriter (Cayrol) may have helped both images and text to reach the same level of artistic ripeness. Even when a great cinematic stylist like Welles tries his hand at an essay-film, the visuals are nowhere near as interesting as those in his narrative features. *F for Fake* suffers from too much François Reichenbach, who shot most of its documentary material, and *Filming "Othello"* is a conventional-looking, talking-heads production made for German television. Marker employs a visual style that is notationally engaging and decentered (and occasionally even mournfully beautiful, as in *Le Joli Mai*, when he had the budget for better cameramen); but for the most part, his visuals lack the syntactical rigor and elegance of his language. Arlyck's texts have considerable complexity and charm, but his visuals remain only one cut above the usual neutral documentary or hand-held cinema-verité. It is almost as though when the part of the brain that commands a sophisticated rational discourse springs into action, the visual imagination becomes sluggish, passive, and less demanding.

Here it might be argued by some that the power of cinematic images springs from the unconscious mind, not from rational thought processes—that you need access to the irrational, the dreamscape, to make visually resonant films. I wonder. So much of film theory is prejudiced in favor of the oneiric that I doubt if I have the courage to take on these biases. All I know is that many of the film images that move me most reflect a detachment, serenity, or philosophical resignation toward the wakened world that I can only think of as rational. I do not want to sound too dualistic by implying that essays are written only with the rational mind; certainly I am aware in my own writing of tapping into unconscious currents for imagery or passion. But I still say that the rational component predominates in the essay, which is a form par excellence for the display of reasoning and reflection. So too should be the essay-film.

I am suddenly aware of many larger questions that my discussion may have failed to confront, and of my inability as a mere scribbler to answer any of them. Questions like: What *is* thinking? What is rationality? Is it possible to think exclusively in visual terms, or exclusively in language, without images? Will there ever be a way to join word and image together on screen so that they accurately reflect their initial participation in the arrival of a thought, instead of merely seeming mechanically linked, with one predominating over or fetched to illustrate the other? Finally, is it possible that the literary essay and the essay-film are inherently different—the essay-film is bound to follow a different historical development, given the strengths and limitations of the cinematic medium? Have I been doing an injustice to the essay-film by even asking it to perform like a literary essay?

Look: it is perfectly all right if, after having read this, you decide to call a collage film like Makaveyev's *WR*, or a duet in which the film-maker disclaims agreement with the spoken text, like Cozarinsky's *One Man's War*, or a symphony of interviewed voices like Marcel Ophuls's *The Sorrow and the Pity*, or a dream vision like Brakhage's mythopoetic *Faust*—essay-films, just so long as you understand that you are using the term "essay" in a way that has very little relation to the traditional, literary meaning of the term.

I think this sudden frequency with which the term "essay-film" is being optimistically and loosely invoked in cinematic circles is not surprising. Right now, there is a hunger in film aesthetics and film practice for the medium to jump free of its genre corral, and to reflect on the world in a more intellectually stimulating and responsible way. When a good film with nonfiction elements comes along that provokes thought, such as Rainer's *Privilege*, it is understandably hailed as an essay-film. And it may turn out in the end that there is no other way to do an essay-film, that the type of essay-film I have been calling for is largely impractical, or overly restrictive, or at odds with the inherent nature of the medium. But I will go on patiently stoking the embers of the form as I envision it, convinced that the truly great essay-films have yet to be made, and that this succulent opportunity awaits the daring cine-essayists of the future.

PHILLIP LOPATE

## Postscript

Since writing this piece, I have seen a number of intriguing, thought-provoking nonfiction films that should be included in the discussion. There is Ross McElwee's skillful, moving, yet reticent continuation of his autobiographical musings, *Time Indefinite*; Alan Berliner's complex, funny documentary portrait of his grandfather, *Intimate Stranger*, about a man well loved by his colleagues but judged more harshly by his family; Patrick Keiller's *London*, an elegiac meditation on that city, using the distancing commentary of a third-person fictive figure, "Robinson," much like the device in *Sans Soleil*, though "Robinson" proves more unreliable; and Godard's amazing, layered, multipart montage, *Histoire(s) du Cinéma*, which broods about the medium in an evocatively "essayistic" manner, insistently subverted by Brechtian distancings. Each of these works flirts with and hesitates to commit to the essay-film, bearing out my thesis that it is an increasingly tempting yet problematic form of our era. Finally, Marker's latest essay-film, *The Last Bolshevik* (1993), about the Russian filmmaker Alexander Medvedkin and the vicissitudes of mixing radicalism and art, triumphantly and confidently manages the form, reaffirming Marker's right to hold onto his title as "the cinema's only true essayist."

*Many people helped me in writing this essay, however much they may disagree with my conclusions. I want to thank Jonathan Rosenbaum for his generous sharing of materials and tapes, and his briefings on Welles; also Terrence Rafferty, for his insights into Marker; Amos Vogel, for his sage skepticism; the staff of Women Make Movies, for giving me access to their library; Charles Silver, for loaning me* Ici et Ailleurs; *Ralph Arlyck, for tapes of his films; Richard Pena, David Sterritt, Ralph McKay, and Carrie Rickey for their helpful advice; and last but not least, Vlada Petric for his invitation and steadfast support.*

VLADA PETRIC

# Vertov's Cinematic Transposition of Reality

*The goal is to make things look on the screen like "life-facts,"*
*and at the same time to mean much more than that.*
—Dziga Vertov

**W**orks of art change on two levels: the aesthetic, which is affected by the ongoing evolution of artistic concepts, and the ideological, which is contingent upon socioeconomic circumstances. Only those nonfictional films that transcend mere documentation can continue to exist and function as important cinematic achievements.

These two levels of change are especially an issue with politically engaged cinema, such as Dziga Vertov's films dedicated to the October Revolution and communist society. His works *Forward March, Soviet* (1926), *One Sixth of the World* (1926), *The Eleventh Year* (1928), and *Three Songs about Lenin* (1934) convey political messages through filmic devices, turning recorded "life-facts" [*zhiznenye fakty*] into what he labeled *kinochestvo.* In his 1922 "We" manifesto, he defines this term (which he coined): "*Kinochestvo* is the art of organizing the respective movements of objects in space, as a rhythmic and artistic whole, in harmony with the nature of the given material and the internal rhythm of the events."[1] It is not merely the content of the shot, but the organization and rhythm of the images projected on the screen that constitute a genuinely

---

1. Dziga Vertov, "We: A Variant Manifesto" (1922), in *Articles, Diaries, Projects* [*Stat'i, dnevniki, zamysli*], ed. Sergei Drobashenko (Moscow: Iskusstvo, 1966), 47. Later cited as *Articles*; the translation of the quotations is mine. Also useful is *Kino-Eye: The Writings of Dziga Vertov*, ed. Annette Michelson, trans. Kevin O'Brien (University of California Press, 1984).

cinematic vision of reality. In other words, the recorded content has to undergo a complex structural and aesthetic transposition—both during and after shooting—in order for the world shown on the screen to be more than a mere photographic document.

Vertov's masterpiece, *The Man with the Movie Camera* (1929), represents an outstanding cinematic transposition of "life-facts" by giving priority to aesthetic expressivity over the observational photographic recording of reality. Yet, with all its structural and formal features, the shots per se are perceived as "Life-As-It-Is" [*zhizn' kakaia ona est'*]. For Vertov, the most important goal of the documentary film was to unify the authentic and the abstract. *Enthusiasm* (1931) illustrates this unity or compromise very well with many shots and sequences that convey reality and a political message in a powerful visual way (including the prologue of archival footage showing the masses demolishing churches, and sequences visualizing the dynamism of factory production). *Three Songs about Lenin* was ideologically the most problematic of his films, and it is the most complex in that it involves the expressive means inherent in both silent and sound cinema, while dealing with a highly political subject.

The personal tone and unconventional structure of Vertov's films was incompatible with the Communist Party's prescription for the treatment of Lenin in art. Vertov's subjective and poetic presentation of the communist leader challenged the basic tenets of Socialist Realism, which insisted on the absolute subordination of form to content, requiring artists to show reality as prescribed by Party ideologists, in a plain style. The political commissars responsible for culture and art in the Soviet Union employed a special tactic to express their condemnation of Vertov's method: they slowly restricted his creative activity, and discouraged young filmmakers from following him. Thus even though, together with Lev Kuleshov, Vertov was the first revolutionary educator of cinema, he eventually had to struggle to complete and distribute his films, including the one dedicated to the leader of the October Revolution.

Idealistic and firmly devoted to communism throughout his life, Vertov proved incapable of seeing the real force behind the suppression of his creativity. Instead, he accused the little bureaucrats [*apparatchiki*] of preventing the completion of his numerous films. Each time he was asked to reedit his films, Vertov expressed great surprise, never realizing that the very system within which he worked was antagonistic toward original, imaginative individuals. Deprived in the 1930s and later of the technical means necessary for filmmaking, Vertov found his life increasingly "unbearable" (his term). But his utopian vision of communist society was deeply ingrained; he always tipped his hat in front of the Lenin monument, even after his documentary dedicated to Lenin was quietly withdrawn from a Moscow theater only a few days after its opening.

The reason for the withdrawal is clear: Vertov's vision of Lenin differed from that promoted by the Party. Instead of a political pamphlet illustrated with motion picture images, Vertov constructed his film as a cinematic anthology of visualized songs based on the myth of Lenin created by ordinary people. Both visions departed from the historical facts, but with different intentions. Vertov's, by turning historical facts into a visual poem, identified with the folk imagination of a better future for all people; the official view of Lenin served the interests of the party governing and controlling the country. Vertov's great film conveys, in pure cinematic terms, ordinary people's admiration for the leader they identify with the quest for social equality; in contrast, Party-sponsored movies about Lenin exploit the medium exclusively for the regime's purposes.

In order to go "beyond document," it is essential to achieve an artistic transposition of strictly observational photographic recording. This is one of the most difficult tasks a filmmaker can face, especially in the documentary, a genre that Vertov called the "unstaged" [*neigrovoi*] film. Since newsreel footage of Lenin was scarce (there existed only a few dozen shots, which had been used repeatedly in Soviet documentaries), Vertov decided to create a "poetic documentary film" [*dokumental'no-poeticheskii neinstsenirovannii fil'm*],[2] based on the folk myth nurtured by peasants and workers living in different parts of the country. His ultimate goal was to "construct a cinematic document of Lenin without—or almost without—Lenin's actual image," presenting him on the screen "indirectly [*otrazhennyi pokaz*], in a more complex way than the newsreel would allow and on a high level of cinematic organization."[3] According to Vertov,

2. Vertov, "Notebooks" (October 4, 1944), *Articles*, 259.

3. Vertov, "Without Words" (1934), ibid., 132.

The film's structure was built along an ascending progression of images, through an interaction among various visual and musical movements, represented sometimes by sound, sometimes by voices, sometimes completely without music or words (only through the people's facial expressions), sometimes by intertitles, sometimes by the movement within the shot, sometimes by the juxtaposition of one group of shots with another, sometimes through slow pace or jolts produced by light and darkness, exchange of slow and fast tempo, progression from torpid to energetic movement, noises, silent songs, songs without words . . . so that the ideas run from the screen to the viewers without forcing them to translate thoughts into words.[4]

The film is built into three rhythmically distinct parts ("songs"), each imbued with a different montage pace: the first, *largo*, depicting various nationalities comprising the Soviet Union; the second, *adagio*, associated with Lenin's death and the people's mourning for him; and the third, *vivace*, intensifying the sense of dynamic power in industrial production in the country after Lenin's death. Each of the three parts is distinguished by its own way of having sights and sounds interact, notably the second part, with its images and music of grief which create a powerful cinematic *marcia funebre*.

To enforce "the complex interaction of sound and image, and to unify numerous channels of expression,"[5] Vertov applied to his film the technique of poetic language known as *Zaum*, practiced by the Suprematist poets, who were very concerned with the rhythmic and melodic aspects of poetry. This attitude was akin to Vertov's own preoccupation with the architectonic arrangement of shots and their rhythmic interaction with sound. Unsurprisingly, Vertov's idea of applying the Constructivist *Zaum* principle to "the most important art" (as Lenin proclaimed cinema) was proscribed as anti-Marxist, i.e., ideologically incorrect.

Conceptually, *Three Songs about Lenin* tells more about ordinary people's hope for a better life than about Lenin, either as a man or a politician. In his diaries, Vertov explains how moved he was while listening to

4. Vertov, "My Last Experiment" (1935), ibid., 144.

5. Vertov, "My Last Experiment," 145.

songs in which Lenin was only a symbol through which the peasants expressed their dreams of the future. In his film, Vertov identified with these dreams in an unconventional cinematic way.

Structurally, the film was built on a musical principle applied to montage, with the intention of achieving a "visual symphony" that would mold the content and the ultimate meaning. To understand the nature of folk (oral) poetry, Vertov visited the eastern region of the Soviet Union, researching and recording popular songs eulogizing Lenin. He immediately realized that "these anonymous, spontaneous poets have created a rich stream of folk art, real poetic song-documents, powerful in their outward simplicity, astonishingly sincere, possessing one of the most aesthetic features—*the unity of form and content*—which we writers, composers, and filmmakers have not been able to accomplish."[6] In his earliest experiments (associated with his "Laboratory of Hearing"), Vertov had interrelated sound and image in a contrapuntal manner; in the Lenin film he decided "to present [edit] the shots in the form of a symphonic structure, starting with simple melodies," so that the "inner truth" of the subject would be conveyed through cinematic means.[7] The decision to build his film on the symphonic principle was in accordance with Vertov's general concept of transcending all visually and aurally recorded "life-facts." As he stated: "the goal was poetic truth, and the means was 'Film-Eye'" [*Tsel' byl poeticheskaia pravda, sredstvom byl kinoglaz*].[8]

It turned out that neither the goal of the film nor its expressive means conformed with what the Party had launched as "Socialist Filmmaking," a variant of Socialist Realism, whose only concern was an ideological message suiting the Party's current needs. The consequence of this divergence in attitudes was predictable: shortly after its opening, the original negative of *Three Songs about Lenin* disappeared (the same fate had befallen the original negative of *The Man with the Movie Camera*). As a result, we are uncertain how surviving prints correspond to the original.

In the existing prints, Lenin's image appears in only a dozen shots taken from the newsreels showing his dead body lying in state, several brief shots of Lenin addressing the masses or talking with people around him,

VERTOV'S TRANSPOSITION OF REALITY

6. Vertov, "Notebooks" (February 29, 1936), ibid., 196.

7. Vertov, "Notebooks" (June 26, 1941), ibid., 239.

8. Vertov, "*Three Songs about Lenin* and 'Film-Eye'" (1934), ibid., 139.

**Dziga Vertov, *Three Songs about Lenin* (1934)**
**The still photograph of Lenin on his bench, used at the beginning**
**of the film.**

**Dziga Vertov, *Three Songs about Lenin* (1934)**
**Lenin's bench after his death.**

and a photograph of him sitting on a bench in a park. Vertov rejected the concept of *typage,* as Eisenstein used it in *October* (1927), casting the worker Nikandrov to play Lenin. Because impersonation of Lenin was incompatible with the "Film-Truth" principle, Vertov turned his camera to the people's faces, capturing their spontaneous expressions as they sang or talked about Lenin. This method is comparable to Leni Riefenstahl's practice of focusing her camera on the faces of German citizens as they greeted Hitler with *die echte Begeisterung* (a genuine enthusiasm) in her film *Triumph of the Will* (1935). Both films document popular enthusiasm, manifested through ritualistic collective behavior and reflected on human faces, be it in grief or admiration. These films show that the suppressive nature of autocratic societies apparently intensified the masses' emotional reactions. In contrast to other propagandist movies produced during Stalin's and Hitler's regimes, Vertov's and Riefenstahl's films penetrate into actual realities in the Soviet Union and Germany, uncovering the psychological base of mass behavior. These two documentaries are unique in their photographic execution and montage structure, whereby the exterior world is transcended cinematically and at the same time made to reveal its deep truth.

In the documentary film about her, *The Wonderful Terrible Life of Leni Riefenstahl* (1993), directed by Ray Müller, Riefenstahl states flatly that her film "faithfully documents" the fervor with which the German masses greeted Hitler and the Nazi regime. It perhaps depends on one's worldview to decide whether (1), as part of the Nazis' propaganda Riefenstahl's film contributed to Hitler's manipulation of the people, and therefore should be condemned; or (2), as an outstanding cinematic achievement, Riefenstahl's film exposes the horrifying power of militaristic hysteria stirred by nationalism, and merits critical appreciation. My teaching experience has consistently supported the latter view: whenever I have shown *Triumph of the Will* to my students, the subsequent discussion has demonstrated that they experienced it as the psychological document of an era that should not be repeated, rather than as a dangerous propagandist movie about the Nazi party, let alone one that might stimulate nationalistic and militaristic feelings today.

Apparently, Vertov and Riefenstahl shared the popular enthusiasm for Lenin and Hitler. In fact, without sharing this common attitude of their countrymen, they would not have been able to enter into their subjects so profoundly and to explore their true nature. In spite of Stalinist oppression, Vertov saw Lenin as the incarnation of communist ideals, a cult figure cleansed of the real politician's characteristics. Similarly, for Riefenstahl, Hitler was the builder of a "New Order," not only in Germany, but in all of Europe. (She now admits that when the German troops invaded Paris, she sent the Führer a congratulatory telegram, thanking him for "securing a lasting peace" in Europe.) But as much as they were part of the collective sentiment, Vertov's and Riefenstahl's talent and cinematic perception succeeded in transforming their political thinking, disclosing a deeper meaning to events through the filmic text, rather than "substituting the appearance of truth for truth itself."[9]

More than anything else, Vertov resented as lies the "artistic truth" commonly shown in film. He rejected the practice of having professional actors portray political figures on the screen, impersonating them according to the government's guidelines. Closely supervised by the commissars of the production companies, many quasi-biographical films extolled historical characters in a simplistic manner. Challenging this practice, Vertov conceived *Three Songs about Lenin* as an "open construction, in the style of Meyerhold," a sacrilegious idea at the time of the great Stalinist purges.[10] As always, Vertov cared more for upholding the artistic integrity of his film than for insuring his personal safety. Using Meyerhold's method of alienating the spectator from the event on the stage, Vertov wanted to prevent the film viewer's full identification with the diegetic world on the screen. This allowed him to keep the narrative content from overriding his expression of insight through cinematic means.

The problem of intertitles was a theoretical issue in both the silent and the early stage of the Soviet sound cinema. The revolutionary filmmakers considered intertitles equal to other aspects of the film, especially in the way titles could have a visual impact or be used rhythmically. Eisenstein used intertitles to enforce the film's ideological discourse

9. Vertov, "Notebooks" (September 7, 1938), ibid., 218.

10. The most innovative of Soviet theater directors, Vsevolod Meyerhold staged all of Mayakovsky's satirical plays in the style known as "Biomechanical Acting," which was attacked by Socialist Realism. In 1938, his theater was closed, and he and his wife, the actress Zinaida Raikh, soon disappeared.

through an associative interaction between statements designed to be read and the representational signification of the shots (particularly in *October*). But Vertov used intertitles more as examples of rhetoric, which justified their exaggerated, intentionally bombastic quality. Accordingly, the printed statements inserted within shots and sequences in *Three Songs about Lenin* contain less valid information than emotional intensity. Many of the intertitles are quotations from the daily press, customary propagandistic proclamations, political slogans, parts of the leader's speeches, parts of popular songs, and aphorisms from oral tradition, all treated as "life-facts" with their own rhetorical and political nature, reflecting the grandiloquence, naïveté, sentimentalism, and idealism of a revolutionary era. Cinematically, they function as visual breaks or pauses in the progression of the images.

One particular intertitle in *Three Songs about Lenin* has drawn my attention through its uncanny association with the recent political turmoil in the Soviet Union, acquiring a meaning of which Vertov could not have dreamed. Preparing for the International Conference on Vertov in Moscow (initially scheduled to take place in the fall of 1991), I spent some time analyzing Vertov's film on the editing table. It was late in the afternoon on Wednesday, August 21, 1991, when, suddenly, loud cheers came from the adjoining room. I stopped the rotating reels of the editing table and rushed to where a group of students were watching the live television transmission of Mikhail Gorbachev's return to Moscow after his brief custody in the Crimea. I arrived just in time to see Gorbachev exiting from the plane and greeting government aides who had joined the putsch. When I returned to the editing room, my excitement was further intensified by the sight of the intertitle that I had left on the screen. It marked the climax of the film, proclaiming: "If Lenin could only see our country now!. . . " [*"Esli by Lenin uvidel nashu storonu seichas!. . . "*] In my imagination, the past and present merged instantly, as I replaced Lenin's name with Vertov's, putting a question mark at the end of the sentence. *If Vertov could only see his country now?* The different punctuation was as important as the change of names: while Vertov's phrasing (including the three dots following the exclamation point) suggests Lenin would be proud of his country after the first decade of Communist rule, my question mark expresses curiosity.

Would Vertov continue to dream of communist society after the collapse of the Soviet empire? How would he react to *perestroika,* i.e., Russia's transformation into a capitalist country? What side would Vertov join, the "camera-gun" (as he called it) in his hands, during the tragic events in and around the Russian White House, when Yeltsin used force against the Parliament? How would Vertov's "Film-Eye" present the demolition of the Lenin monuments all over the former Soviet Union? Would he empathize with the women crying over Lenin's severed head thrown in the mud, turning their faces away from the television camera? Would he succeed in going beyond the exterior appearance of postcommunist events and help viewers understand that the women were mourning their unfulfilled dreams of a better life?

Among the best examples of montage as symbolic device is the "Fall of the Tsar" sequence at the beginning of *October,* where people demolish the Emperor's statue in St. Petersburg. To impart connotations for "dethroning," Eisenstein shows again and again (by overlapping the ends of the shots) the various parts of the body falling in slow motion and striking the ground, thus metaphorically indicating the difficulties and obstacles that accompany revolutionary change. Vertov, clearly, would never reconstruct a historical event in this way; instead, he probably would direct his camera toward Lenin's real fallen effigy, perhaps toward the marble face, crosscutting this with close-ups of real citizens, some crying, some rejoicing, some looking perplexed, some spitting on the communist leader, while a group of children unwittingly jump over Lenin's muddy figure, unaware of what has happened. Would the children silently fly over Lenin's motionless, toppled body or, instead, jump over it with staggered acceleration, while producing joyous noises to enhance the tragicomic aspect of the situation?

Many of the intertitles in Vertov's sound films are intended to distance the viewer from the diegetic world shown on the screen, while involving the viewer all the more in a cinematic construction and the filmmaker's ideas. Such is the case with the intertitle, "If only Lenin could see our country now," positioned among shots of workers and peasants laboring in factories and on farms. Repeated five times, the printed question jabs aggressively against the visual beat of the images. By breaking the linear flow of the images, Vertov follows Mayakovsky's method of altering the auditory rhythm of his poems by inserting the same (exclamatory) line repeatedly into emotionally dense stanzas.[11] After the fifth repetition of the same intertitle in *Three Songs about Lenin*, it becomes obvious what kind of response Vertov wanted to elicit from (perhaps impose on) his audience. The repetition of the written text reflects the filmmaker's own thoughts about his country, thoughts which coincide with the optimism expressed in popular songs.

The longest and most rhetorical intertitle, presented in the form of a "rolling panel" moving diagonally over the screen, gains a fuller connotation when associated with the sincerity of the comments, along similar lines, given by the young heroine-worker [*udarnik* (shock-worker)] seen a bit earlier in the film. Representative of Soviet propagandist slogans, the rolling intertitle predicts the imminent victory of communism, encouraging the people to take part in the fight against capitalism. Imitating proclamations printed regularly in the Soviet newspapers, the intertitle, like the speech of the young heroine-worker, urges the citizens to endure in their historic struggle: "Stand firm! Stand together! Advance boldly to meet the foe! We shall triumph! The landlords and capitalists, destroyed in Russia, will be defeated throughout the world! Centuries will pass, and people will forget the names of the countries in which their ancestors lived, but they will never forget the name Lenin, the name Vladimir Ilich Lenin!" The conventional rhetoric of the written words combines with the sincerity of the woman worker to produce something that goes beyond the written words themselves.

I had the opportunity to see *Three Songs about Lenin* in Berlin, New York, and Moscow at the time of *perestroika*. To my surprise, only a Russian émigré responded with bitter laughter at the intertitle which claims that "landlords and capitalists . . . will be defeated throughout the world," and that "the workers of all countries will be united," while "the people will forget the names of the countries in which their ancestors lived." On the other hand, the young viewers I spoke with after the screening appreciated Vertov's idealism as a real sentiment from a past time. They

11. For more information about Vertov's attempt to apply Mayakovsky's method of composing verses to the structuring of film images, see the chapter "Vertov and Mayakovsky" in my book *Constructivism in Film—"The Man with the Movie Camera"* (Cambridge University Press, 1987), 25–35.

took the rhetorical intertitles as literary documents of political grandiloquence, once used as a propagandist weapon, now looking like a fairy tale. What they found most exciting in the film was the visual power in the montage of Vertov's shots, where they also recognized the author's revolutionary enthusiasm. I was stunned by the remark of one of those young people, who said the film is at the same time aggressive and tender, ostentatious and articulate, extrinsic and subjective. Indeed, it is the interaction and contrast between the verbal and the optical, the rational and the intuitive, that produces the Vertovian auditory/visual "film-thing" [*kino-veshch*], conveying more than what the words alone imply.

Analysis of Vertov's films and scripts testifies to his profound interest in women's mentality. In *Three Songs about Lenin* this is demonstrated by the camera's constant concern with women, searching their faces in close-up. Related in a contrasting, interactive way to the intertitles, the close-ups of different women bring out a conflict between feelings triggered by what the photographic apparatus has captured "unawares" and ideas communicated by written proclamation.

*Three Songs about Lenin* contains nearly three times as many close-ups of women as of men. The climax of the third song is enforced by the lengthy medium close-up in which the young heroine-worker talks about her success in "overfulfilling the factory plan," for which she was decorated with the Order of Lenin. While she talks, her eyes are directed toward the camera and the microphone (partially seen in the upper right corner of the frame), clearly indicating she is aware of the recording technique. Yet she is completely relaxed and natural, and her naturalness of behavior and voice help the audience to "go beyond listening to the woman's words, and read her thoughts."[12]

The full transposition of this shot into the "film-thing" is accomplished through its association with numerous close-ups of another young woman, who wears a dark shawl over her head, appearing in the first song and also as the most expressive among the women who seem (through intercutting) to "surround" the dead Lenin lying in state, in the second song. These shots are conceived in a completely different manner from those of the woman worker.

12. Vertov, "Three Songs about Lenin and 'Film-Eye'" (1934), *Articles*, 138.

The distinction between the two young women with respect to the diegetic world on the screen and the film spectator is quite pronounced. Unlike the heroine-worker, the young woman with a dark shawl makes no contact with the camera. She consistently responds to the presented action with a subjective gaze guiding the viewer's attention to what transpires on the screen, especially when she "looks at" the dead Lenin lying in state (who is seen in the next shot, following her look). In contrast, the lengthy close-up of the heroine-worker functions both as something "caught unawares," and as something self-referential, especially when she turns her gaze toward the camera, which might well remind the viewer of Soviet newsreels about factory workers (which were regularly shown in the theaters before feature films). The close-ups of the young woman with the dark shawl have a stronger dramatic impact, creating the illusion of spatial unity among otherwise unrelated shots (edited on the principal of the "Kuleshov Effect").[13] The psycho-emotional distinction between these two kinds of close-ups is symbolic: while the speech of the young heroine-worker demonstrates indoctrinated behavior, the wordless gaze of the woman with a dark shawl reveals the simple, humane state of mind typical of ordinary people. Yet the most important feature of these shots is that they confirm the honesty of both young women. These shots convey "life-facts," as the two referents express their feelings in a profoundly genuine fashion.

The prominent position of the close-ups of women in *Three Songs about Lenin* endows Vertov's film with a feminine sensitivity allowing for a worldview liberated from the male dominance characteristic of Soviet mainstream films. The quantity of the close-ups and the photographic execution of the individual shots featuring women give the film a feminist stance. It is interesting to compare the presentation of women in this and other Vertov works with other Soviet films, particularly those made during the Stalinist era when the gender issue was de facto considered insignificant and treated hypocritically.

13. The "Kuleshov Effect," is achieved by interrelating shots photographed in different places to create an illusion that different actions are occurring simultaneously or to convey a particular mood from one shot to the other. Kuleshov explains: "I alternated the same shot of [the famous actor] Mozhukhin with various other shots (a plate of soup, a girl, [a teddy bear], a child's coffin), and these shots acquired a different meaning." *Kuleshov on Film—Writings of Lev Kuleshov*, trans. and ed. Ronald Levaco (University of California Press, 1974), 200.

The prominence of women's faces in close-up is very powerful in *The Man with the Movie Camera*, including the film's most emblematic shot, in which the metaphoric unification between worker and machine is achieved through the close-up of a smiling young woman worker super-imposed over a huge, rotating spinning-wheel. And the kinesthetic mon-tage finale brings to the fore the eyes of the editor, Elizaveta Svilova, as she puts together a multitude of shots, fashioning the film's closing, symphon-ic climax.

Vertov's attempt to appease both the ideological and creative aspects of his mind is evident in his 1937 *Lullaby* (the film's alternative title is "A Song of the Liberated Soviet Woman"). Inspired by folk art, the film establishes a link between Soviet women and the revolutionary women in other countries, especially those who fought in the Spanish Civil War. Rhetorically, the film complies with the official view of woman as the symbol of "Communist Motherhood," while poetically it glorifies "not *a* mother but *the* Mother, not *a* girl, but *the* Girl," owing to Vertov's unique directorial style, at once personal and general, realistic and abstract.[14] The written and spoken texts in the film support the official communist policy, while the visual execution of the shots expresses the filmmaker's personal attitude toward woman as a "Living Person" (the title of one of Vertov's seminal essays). As a whole, the film works on two rather contradictory lev-els—the ideological, which produces agitprop reverberations, and the artistic, which reveals a strong empathy for working women. To Vertov's astonishment, the Party censors denounced his presentation of women in *Lullaby* as ideologically unacceptable and requested additional shooting and montage changes in the "questionable" sequences. Vertov's refusal to make such compromises did not prevent the release of a mutilated and unauthorized version of the film. With his naïve grasp of political reality, Vertov wrote a letter of protest to Boris Shumyatsky, the head of the Soviet film industry, "but without receiving any answer."[15]

Some of Vertov's scripts, which portray women in a poetic man-ner (he refers to this writing as "cinematic poems"), were rejected by the

14. Vertov, "Notebooks" (February 12, 1937), *Articles*, 229.

15. Vertov, "Notebooks" (December 20, 1937), ibid., 214.

state film companies, who found them "inappropriate" in their depiction of the "typical Soviet woman." One can imagine how painful it was for Vertov to carry on in the face of such sanctimonious accusations.

The conditions under which Vertov worked on *Three Songs about Lenin* in central Asia were "abnormal" [*abnormal'nye usloviia*], and the distribution of the film was handled ignominiously by the authorities.[16] In his diaries, Vertov describes difficulties that he and his crew had to endure throughout the shooting, lacking necessary equipment and even food and water. The hardship associated with the Lenin project continued after Vertov returned from location. When the film opened in one of Moscow's major theaters, it was quickly removed. Surprised and enraged, Vertov wrote, "A group of foreigners complained to me (through an interpreter) that they had searched for *Three Songs about Lenin* all day, and—when they finally reached the theater and tried to purchase tickets—were told that they had all been sold. I found it terrifying to think that a petty, tyrannical bureaucrat could take the film off the central screen because of personal taste or perhaps some other reason, and by doing so, spit with impunity in the face of Soviet public opinion."[17] At least for an instant, Vertov pointed to "some other reason" for the discrimination against his film, but still without giving further consideration to the actual source of such a "terrifying" action. In fact, it was naïve of him to have believed that a "petty, tyrannical bureaucrat" was responsible, when it was well known that such a decision could be made only by Party officials, especially if the film was dedicated to Lenin.

The withdrawal of the film was to have a devastating impact on Vertov, as he explained in his diaries:

> A feeling of anxiety—by day and by night. My organism is like a drawn bow. It seems impossible to ease the tension. It would be easier to endure the ordinary means of torture—needles under the feet, burning at the stake. I thought I would always be tireless.

16. Vertov, "Three Songs about Lenin and 'Film-Eye'" (1934), ibid., 139.
17. Vertov, "Notebooks" (November 9, 1934), ibid., 181-82.

But not so. They have exhausted me—completely. My brain is worn down, and my body would collapse from a light breeze. I walk like that limping eastern woman in the first Song about Lenin.[18]

The situation did not improve even after Jean-Richard Block and André Malraux declared, *"Three Songs about Lenin* is a great film of our times." When Soviet citizens went to the Central Theater at Pushkin Square to see "this 'great film', they were told that the film had been withdrawn from the repertory." "Why," Vertov asks hopelessly.[19] The word *why* reverberates like a fatal leitmotif throughout his diaries. After all, Vertov's attempt had been—like that of the Party—to glorify Lenin as the founder of the first communist state on earth. But the expressive means and emotional goals of Vertov's and the Party's undertakings were different, indeed conflicting—a fact that has often been misrepresented by film historians.

Annette Michelson asserts that *Three Songs about Lenin* "enjoyed a greatly privileged status, indeed, as the only film of Vertov's to which immediate, unanimous and enduring approval was extended within the Soviet Union," and that the film sustained a "wide distribution and prompt incorporation within the canon of officially endorsed films."[20] Such a claim is mistaken and unfair to Vertov. Judging from the filmmaker's memoirs and according to the existing documents, Vertov's Lenin project was unwanted both during its shooting and after its release. Even the workers' repeated demands to see the film could not change the official attitude. It was the price Vertov had to pay for staying away from the road to communism prescribed by the Party and propagated in politically approved films.

Dedicated from the depths of his heart to the revolutionary cause, Vertov carried his camera as a weapon with which the filmmaker could fight for the enlightenment of the masses, including the heightening of their cinematic perception. Vertov's love for cinema obliged him to adhere to the humanistic ideals with which the October Revolution was inaugurated, without closing his "Film-Eye" to the negative side of the

18. Vertov, "Notebooks," (May 17, 1934), ibid., 178.

19. Vertov, "Notebooks" (November 9, 1934) ibid., 181.

20. Annette Michelson, "The Kinetic Icon and the Work of Mourning: Prolegomena to the Analysis of a Textual System," in *The Red Screen: Politics, Society, and Art in Soviet Cinema*, ed. Anna Lawton (Routledge, 1992), 114.

new society. It is not surprising that some of the most authentic and revealing Vertovian newsreels were shelved for exposing "Life-As-It-Is" (especially during the great famines that occurred in 1922–23 and 1932–33, in
the Ukraine, Kazakhstan, and the Volga region) instead of depicting "Life-
As-It-Should-Be-Seen," which the Party insisted that artists do.

     Vertov's individuality and openness dated from the start of his film
career. After spending close to five months at the Moscow Film
Committee as a cameraman, Vertov had to answer an official questionnaire
sent to all employees on December 21, 1918. Under the heading "What
party do you belong to, or, are you affiliated with any party", he stated: "I
am not committed to any party, but I sympathize with the anarchists-indi-
vidualists [*anarkhisti-individualisti*]."[21] By expressing his sympathy with
anarchism and individualism, Vertov disclosed his innate antagonism to
the Bolshevik practice of imposing a social order by brute force. Clearly,
Bolshevism did not suit Vertov's humane concept of a classless society, let
alone his strong commitment to the freedom of the creative spirit, as he
searched for a communism "with a human face," as it was later called by
the communists who opposed Stalinism. In his quest he often acted irra-
tionally, appearing ridiculous, even crazy, in the eyes of colleagues who
were willing to make compromises. Above all, Vertov could not lie or pretend he was following the Party's orders when it was against his innermost
feelings. This generated an irresolvable psycho-emotional tension within
Vertov, which proved detrimental to his well-being. Another deeply committed Soviet revolutionary filmmaker, Alexander Medvedkin, had a similar experience with the authorities. Chris Marker in his video-essay *The
Last Bolshevik* (1993) relates this story in the form of five "visual letters"
to Medvedkin, his recently deceased friend.[22] Documentary maker Esther
Shub, who held perhaps the most uncompromising—yet deeply
humane—vision of communist society, also vigorously defended individu-

21. This information was provided by Vladimir Magidov in his paper, "Dziga Vertov: Archives, Research, and
Findings," at the International Symposium, "The Vertov Jump: Up or Down," Moscow, June 7-13, 1992.

22. Alexander Ivanovich Medvedkin headed the group of filmmakers who organized film-trains [*kinopoezd*] from
1932 to 1934. Equipped with projectors, editing tables, labs, and printers, these trains traveled throughout the
Soviet Union. Among his numerous documentary and feature films, the most original is Medvedkin's "satirical-
philosophical tale," *Happiness* [*Schast'e*, 1935], shelved for decades because of its provocative content and
unconventional style (highly praised by Eisenstein, Pudovkin, and Dovzhenko).

alistic creativity and freedom of expression in art.[23] All three of them, almost certainly, would reject the present capitalistic transformation of Russia, just as they protested the 1920s NEP policy that encouraged commercial film production and promoted the importing of trivial foreign movies, to the detriment of film as an art form.[24]

After repeated complaints to the Ministry of Cinematography for not taking seriously his film proposals (many of his scripts after *Three Songs about Lenin* were rejected), Vertov wrote in 1940: "I am not the one who isolates myself—I *am* isolated."[25] To those of us who have lived under totalitarian regimes, this feeling is quite familiar. Considered ideologically unfit, artists like Vertov were declared out of touch with "the concrete political reality," and therefore unworthy of serious attention. In communist countries this pronouncement was communicated in the form of a sealed letter called *kharakteristika,* containing a political evaluation of a citizen, kept secret from the person to whom it referred. These secret files played a decisive role (perhaps not so different from what happened in the United States during the McCarthy era) in the lives of Soviet citizens, including Vertov. The artists with negative "characterizations" were restricted in their public activities and left to vegetate on the margin of Soviet cultural life. They lived "like lepers," as Vertov described his life in his diaries.

In the environment of secrecy that dominated public life in autocratic societies, the bureaucrats [*apparatchiki*] acted capriciously. They would commute dissidents' death penalties to life sentences, and then—suddenly—bring them back to public awareness, sometimes even decorating them, as Vertov was in 1935 for his "outstanding contribution" to Soviet culture. In truth, the Order of the Red Star did little for Vertov's position as a filmmaker: his proposal to make a monumental documentary about the Spanish Civil War was immediately dismissed. Such decisions on the part of the authorities deeply affected Vertov's psyche, prompting him

23 Esther (Esfir Il'ichnina) Shub began her career as the editor of fictional films at Goskino. Later she specialized in producing archival or compilation films composed exclusively of authentic newsreel footage. They include *The Fall of the Romanov Dynasty* [*Padenie dinastii Romanovikh,* 1927], *The Great Road* [*Velikii put',* 1927], and *The Russia of Nicholas II and Lev Tolstoi* [*Rossia Nikolaia II i Lev Tolstoi,* 1928].

24. NEP stands for "New Economic Policy" [*Novaia ekonomskaia politika*], promoted by Lenin in 1921, with the intention to improve the devastating economic conditions in the Soviet Union. For several years, this policy stimulated certain capitalist forms of trade, including the production of trivial movies for popular consumption.

25. Vertov, "Notebooks" (February 12, 1940), *Articles,* 229.

to question his existence. Mayakovsky committed suicide after realizing communist ideals had been betrayed by the Stalinist regime. But Vertov opted for life, unproductive as it had become. One may admire Mayakovsky's courage in rejecting life under oppression, but Vertov's acceptance of life "as it is" has provided us with the diaries and other late writings of this uncompromising artist who could not agree with the Stalinist practice of building the "iron road toward communism" (this slogan was repeated in many Soviet newsreels and documentary films of the 1930s).

The emotional tone of Vertov's diaries, manifestos, essays, and scripts suggests that writing was for him a substitute for filmmaking. Spiritually, in his later years, the notebook kept him alive, providing a narrow space within which he was able to express his critical views about life, as well as to convey freely his unrealized cinematic version of reality. Although he enjoyed writing, it could never replace filmmaking, for which he had such an innate love. Like all filmmakers who handle the camera themselves, Vertov felt it to be a part of his body, and this was now taken from him. What was left was a tragic creature, "The Filmmaker without the Film Camera."

By 1940, Vertov's professional activity was reduced to the technical supervision of army newsreels. Never invited to teach at the national film school VGIK (The All-State Institute of Cinematography), he spent most of his time in a gloomy editing room at the film studio of the Red Army. At the outset of World War II, increasingly depressed, Vertov asked himself: "Is it possible to die—not from physical but creative hunger," and immediately gave a prophetic answer: "Indeed, it *is* possible!"[26] This question was posed ten years after Mayakovsky's suicide. Attempting to comprehend that tragic event, Vertov wrote: "Suddenly, he could not take it any longer."[27] Again, Vertov fails to specify what the "it" means, while suggesting that it was a burden that he, like Mayakovsky, could no longer bear.

Discouraged and exhausted, Vertov became a recluse and avoided contact even with his closest friends. Feeling "sick and tired of everything," he wrote in his diary in 1941, "I must either depersonalize myself or else end my film career . . . I feel a painful physical reaction . . . Terrible exhaustion . . . is killing me . . . I can hardly stand on my legs without dif-

26. Vertov, "Notebooks" (February 4, 1940), ibid., 228.

27. Vertov, "Notebooks" (December 15, 1945), ibid., 263.

ficulty . . . Everything is in a fog."[28] Torn by the contradiction between the personal and the public, the authentic and the histrionic, the veristic and the aesthetic, Vertov lost what remained of his self-confidence. At this time, the outside world became threatening, as he describes it in his diary at the end of 1942:

> Hour after hour, day by day, year following year, they have looked upon myself—and also on those who surround me—with suspicion, as if I am sick of leprosy. Accusing me of formalism, they have placed me in a hopeless situation by completely isolating me. Who will extend a hand to the leper? Who would agree to work with him? Who would entrust him with a film project that is reserved only for healthy people?[29]

The writer now replaces "it" with "they."

After World War II, when other Soviet filmmakers were given ample opportunity to work, Vertov was again pushed aside. He complained to himself a bit earlier: "I can't understand, why is it just Vertov who has been denied to make films about important subjects, and constantly denied access to valuable film footage? Why has he been cut off from everything that is creative and interesting?"[30] Clearly, Vertov has lost his self-confidence, referring to himself in the third person. His psychological condition did not improve, even after his living situation changed when the government gave him and his wife a more comfortable apartment. Semiramida Pumpanskaya, Vertov and Svilova's close friend and collaborator on montage, recalls Vertov's initial excitement when this happened. But it was only temporary relief and he again became obsessed with Mayakovsky's suicide, frequently repeating the phrase that he had once used to justify the poet's decision to take his own life. According to Pumpanskaya, he changed the phrase into the first person, saying: "I simply cannot take it any longer."[31]

28. Vertov, "Notebooks" (January 7, 1941), ibid., 228.

29. Vertov, "Notebooks" (Late 1942), ibid., 244-45.

30. Vertov, "Notebooks" (October 11, 1944), ibid., 261.

31. I am grateful to Semiramida Nikolaevna for talking to me about Vertov's last days, during the International Film Symposium in Moscow, June 7–13, 1992.

Vertov was particularly concerned with merging theory and practice. His ultimate goal was to develop some sort of "theory of practice" that would help his "kinoks" [*kinoki*], as he called his collaborators and apprentices, to become first-class filmmakers and knowledgeable cinéasts. This is especially significant since Vertov's audience consisted of peasants and workers, many of whom had never seen motion pictures before the "movie trains"—the chief organizers of which were Vertov in the 1920s and Medvedkin in the 1930s—arrived in the remote parts of the country. Vertov and Medvedkin believed in film as a means of changing the people's consciousness, helping the masses perceive reality in a more profound way, which would improve their lives. Of course, the idea of changing consciousness, which was under the constant control of the Party, was considered by the commissars dangerous and subversive.

The Vertov paradox is his merger of a truthful, observing attitude with his aesthetic view of film structure. This is particularly evident in the essays written at the beginning of his career, which are graphically conceived in the Constructivist fashion. Their layout on the page is designed to capture the reader's eye, and altogether they encourage filmmakers to show "Life-As-It-Is" while at the same time transcending the facade of reality. Vertov constantly reminded his "kinoks" that the camera is a weapon by means of which they could extract from "the chaos of movements, a new vision of reality," as he put it in the 1923 manifesto, "Kinoks: Revolution." In this early text, Vertov explains that "the ultimate goal of the 'Film-Truth' method [is] the production of a fresh perspective on reality, deciphered in an unconventional way, in order to create a world unknown to the naked eye."[32] Such a cinematically deciphered reality is most effectively presented in Vertov's masterpiece, *The Man with the Movie Camera*.

Writing about *The Man with the Movie Camera*, Vertov pointed to two aspects of its cinematic structure, emphasizing the shot's dialectical function in relation to reality. In one statement, entitled "The First Soviet Film without Words" and written prior to the shooting, Vertov described the "Film-Truth" principal of capturing "Life-As-It-Is," i.e., without dis-

32. Vertov, "Kinoks: Revolution" (1923), in *Articles*, 54

turbing the ontological authenticity of the shot.[33] In the second statement, entitled "The Man with the Movie Camera—A Visual Symphony," issued immediately after the film's completion, Vertov specifies the montage strategy, concluding that his film "is not only a practical result, but also a theoretical manifestation [of the author's concept of "unstaged" cinema], presented on the screen in the form of a visual symphony."[34] One can imagine the groups of workers and peasants from remote villages, sitting in front of the improvised screen, watching a film without a story and constructed as "music for the eyes." But Vertov had faith in the ability of cinema to change people's attitude toward life, beginning with their artistic tastes, which, in his view, had been deformed by bourgeois melodramas.

Vertov's theoretical essays should be studied in conjunction with a close analysis of his films, to fully understand the "Film-Eye" method as a means of revealing what is hidden beneath the apparent nature of reality. Inner reality can be reached only through the aesthetic use of film language. The dialectic of Vertov's method is its requirement that the filmmaker refrain from interfering with reality, while presenting it on the screen in a highly aesthetic manner. Vertov taught his kinoks to keep in mind the overall structure of the future film as they took every single shot. This implies that the shooting process is an integral part of the overall construction, and that it is not enough to find an interesting subject, event, or referent and imprint it photographically. To go beyond the photographic recording, the shots of the film must be interrelated on numerous levels, the most important of which is the kinesthetic movement taking place within the frame and between the adjacent images.

Inspired by Constructivism (which considered form in art equal to, or even more significant than, content), Vertov was the first filmmaker to raise the documentary film above mere photographic documentation. In this endeavor he was highly concerned with the formal aspects of film: "meter, tempo, type of movement and its exact location within the shot," and "the organization of the object's movements in space, as an artistically rhythmic whole."[35] Here lies the foundation of his "Theory of Intervals."

33. Vertov, "The Man with the Movie Camera," ibid., 109

34. Vertov, "The Man with the Movie Camera—A Visual Symphony," ibid., 279.

35. Vertov, "We: Manifesto," , ibid., 48

In his 1929 essay entitled "The Alphabet of the 'Kinoks',", Vertov explains how the kinesthetic impact of a sequence depends on the dynamic interaction of all movements occurring on the screen. To function kinesthetically, the juxtaposition of the shots must take into account (1) the frame's scale, (2) the pictorial and graphic composition of the image, (3) the shooting angle, (4) the play of light and darkness, (5) the multidirectional motions within the shot, (6) the physical movement of the camera, and (7) the alternate speeds of the camera and projector (in order to create an illusion of fast or slow motion on the screen).[36] Only when all these elements are successfully integrated can the sequence exert a kinesthetic impact on the viewer. Vertov's best works abound in kinesthesia generated by this kind of shot interaction, where auditory-visual power shatters the viewer's conventional perception of reality.

Vertov's greatest achievement of kinesthesia is in *The Man with the Movie Camera*, a documentary ("unstaged") film in which the form itself comes to function as content, without compromising the ontological authenticity of the individual shots. This sort of cinematic abstraction proved to be a major challenge throughout the editing process. Each time Vertov and Svilova decided to cut shots solely on the principal of intervals, the "life-facts" (as recorded by the camera) were jeopardized; each time they tried to preserve the ontological authenticity of the shot in its entirety, the sequence as a whole lacked kinesthetic power. Sensitive to this dilemma, Vertov strove to observe both the "Film-Truth" (the ontological authenticity of the shot) and the "Film-Eye" (the montage structure of the associated shots). By accomplishing this, he made *The Man with the Movie Camera* able to function on both levels, presenting reality "as it is," and generating, through the kinesthesia, a new vision of the world.

For Vertov, the showing of "untruth in the interest of truth" was a truly "forbidden" approach in film.[37] In trying to substitute "truth itself" for the mere "appearance of truth," he immersed his camera in "the chaos of visual phenomena to extract from it complex optical combinations, freed from the limits of time and space."[38] Through a creative use of the

36. Vertov, "From 'Film-Eye' to 'Radio-Eye—The Alphabet of 'Kinoks'" (1929), ibid., 114.

37. Vertov, "Notebooks" (September 7, 1938), ibid., 218.

38. Vertov, "Kinoks: Revolution," ibid., 54.

camera and montage, Vertov's films show the world in a way that only "Film-Eye" can perceive, a better world whose ideological significance cannot be separated from its aesthetic resolution.

Throughout his life, Vertov searched for a genuine cinematic form of expression that could act as an impetus for revolutionary change. While he failed to make changes in the society in which he lived, he succeeded in developing a cinematic language that has inspired filmmakers ever since. Vertov's life ended in depression and pain caused by the sociopolitical circumstances that limited his creative expression; but the artistic experience generated by his works, and the inspiration of his writings, are there to be rediscovered endlessly.

> • *the FACTORY OF FACTS.*
> • *Filming facts. Sorting facts. Disseminating facts. Agitating with facts. Propaganda with Facts. Fists made of facts.*
> • *Lightning flashes of facts.*
> • *Mountains of facts.*
> • *Hurricanes of facts.*
> • *And individual little factlets.*
> • *Against film-sorcery.*
> • *Against film-mystification.*
> • *For the genuine cinematification of the worker-peasant. USSR.*
>
> —Dziga Vertov, 1926

# Sorting Facts;

## or, Nineteen Ways of Looking at Marker

I was asked to contribute to this collection of essays because of a book I once wrote about Emily Dickinson's poetry. Although this seemed a strange reason to assume I could write about nonfiction film, I was drawn to the project because of the fact of my husband's death and my wish to find a way to document his life and work.

David von Schlegell was a second-generation American with a German name. He was born in St. Louis in 1920. His German name embarrassed him, especially the "von," but he didn't change it, maybe because he was an only child. The family moved east shortly after his birth when his father got a job teaching painting at the Art Students League in New York City. His mother's first name was Alice, but people called her Bae (pronounced Bay). She also drew and painted. The three of them loved the Atlantic Ocean, especially the Maine coast at Ogunquit where they spent each summer. As a boy, David designed sailboats. When he was in his teens he built his own and called it Stormy. He hoped to become a yacht designer or an architect, but he was young and healthy enough to be cannon fodder, so from 1943 to 1945 he served as a bomber pilot and armament-systems officer in the Eighth Air Force. Until he died and was cremated he had a large scar on his left arm from where he was shot while piloting a B-17 in the fiery skies over Emden in Germany. The bullet shattered his wrist, but he managed to bring the bomber back to home base in England. Three other crew members were wounded also. It could be said this wound just above his left hand saved his life, because he was hospitalized for several months and then honorably discharged. But the war wounded him in ways he could never recover. After the war he studied painting with his father at the Art Students League. He painted for many years, then switched suddenly to sculpture. He was a shy person. His art was influenced by Russian Constructivism and various American boat designers. He worked in wood, steel, and aluminum, and usually built his own pieces. His best-known sculptures were designed in the 1960s and early 1970s. I didn't meet him until 1965 when he was forty-five and I already loved his sculpture. We lived together for twenty-seven years, most of them by Long Island Sound. Toward the end of his life he had to stop sailing because of severe arthritis in his knees, but he could still row. I liked to watch how he feathered the oars to glide back. Little whirlpools formed where the oar blades tipped under: their entry clean as their exit. These are only some facts. He had a stroke and died three days later on Monday, October 5, 1992, at 5 a.m. Those last days in the hospital were a horror. He was fully conscious, but words failed. He couldn't speak or write. He tried to communicate by gestures. We couldn't interpret them. He kept making the gesture of pointing. In physical space we couldn't see what he saw. He couldn't guide a pencil or form a coherent signal. François Truffaut says that for a filmmaker the basic problem is how to express oneself by purely visual means. The same could be said for a sculptor, except that for two days and three nights in the hospital I don't think David saw what "visual means" meant. Without words what are facts? His eyes seemed to know. His hand squeezed mine. What did he mean? In my writing, I have often explored ideas of what constitutes an official version of events as opposed to a former version in imminent danger of being lost.

Sorting word-facts I only know an apparition. Scribble grammar has no neighbor. In the name of reason I need to record something because I am a survivor in this ocean.

That's why I agreed to meddle in a foreign discipline.

It's almost next October. In Connecticut we call warm days in October Indian summer. In an interview with Phillipe Sollers, Jean-Luc Godard, referring to *Hail Mary*, cited a passage from Antonin Artaud: "I want soul to be body, so they won't be able to say that the body is soul, because it will be the soul which is body." Godard said this helped him to explain things to his film technicians.[1]

Surely nonfiction filmmakers sometimes work intuitively by factual telepathy. I call poetry *factual telepathy.*

**II**

The French documentary filmmaker, photographer, and traveler, Chris Marker, was a poet first. Marker's twenty-eight-minute *La Jetée*, written and photographed during the early 1960s, imagines a third world war. A man, marked by an image from his childhood, travels through some intertranslational fragmented mirror-memory to the original line of fracture no translation will pacify. Many pilots, men and women, survived, though they didn't survive, collective military service during World War II. *La Jetée* (1962) and *Sans Soleil* (1982) are haunted by indwelling flames of spirit. In the beginning of each Marker film jet planes escape the eye of the camera. One is overhead roaring murder. We see the other being concealed under the flight-deck of an aircraft carrier. *La Jetée* is called a ciné-roman; *Sans Soleil* a documentary.

**III**

*Life, Life*

In 1927 one of Vladimir Mayakovsky's directives for a Constructivist Poetics of Revolution was: "Let's drop all this gibberish about unfurl-

---

1. The interview is printed in *Jean-Luc Godard's "Hail Mary": Women and the Sacred in Film*, ed. Maryel Locke and Charles Warren (Southern Illinois University Press, 1993), 123–24.

ing 'the epic canvas' during a period of war on the barricades—your canvas will be torn to shreds on all sides."² Dziga Vertov certainly agreed. Both were iconoclastic image-makers, though this may be an oxymoron. Oxymorons are incongruous; they mimic and contradict. Iconoclastic image-makers and oxymorons parody habitual thought patterns while marking a site of convergence and conflict: split-repetition, acceleration, reverse motion.

"Revolutionary cinema's path of development has been found," Vertov declared boldly in 1929. "It leads past the heads of film actors and beyond the studio roof, into life, into genuine reality, full of its own drama and detective plots"(KE 32). He considered Mayakovsky's aesthetics of poetry to be closely identified with his own aspirations for radical change in film production: change that would emphasize the primacy of the "factual." The essence of fact was to be found in the poetry of reality; in material objects.

Vertov's debut in cinema prophetically involved a fall. The poet-filmmaker-documentarist ordered his cameraman to shoot him as he jumped off the roof of a one-and-a-half-story summer house. The cameraman was instructed to record Vertov's leap so that all of his real thoughts while falling would be visible on film. Vertov hoped to show that while the ordinary human eye can't ever see what a person is really thinking or feeling during the immediate chaos of violent motion, the camera's technical eye, oscillating between presence and absence, can frame and arrest that person with thoughts in place. Accelerated motion, recalled from a distance of constructed stillness, can recuperate the hiddenness and mystery of this "visible" world.

Is it sense perception or depiction I see "thinking"?

A still photo in *Kino-Eye: The Writings of Dziga Vertov* shows the dapper realist, non-acting, quick-change artist, wearing a white cotton shirt, sleeves folded to the elbows, a wristwatch, casual slacks, white socks, and elegant white shoes, on a day before World War II. Vertov's right hand

2. Quoted in *Kino-Eye: The Writings of Dziga Vertov*, ed. Annette Michelson, trans. Kevin O'Brien (University of California Press, 1984), xxvii. Further citations to this book are given with the abbreviation KE.

touches the crown of his head, as if to measure his position inside the space-time of a film frame. His left arm is reaching forward, probably for balance. He is posing while falling upright and cautiously smiling. From this perspective he appears to be an enlightened materialist.

He could be thinking "I told you so," looking out.


In 1934 an older and more subdued enthusiast of realism noted in his journal: "Several years have now passed since Mayakovsky's death. In every area of our life tremendous changes have taken place. And only the script departments continue as before to defend their hackneyed principles against the incursion of poetic filmmakers. The will to produce poetic film, and particularly poetic documentary, still runs up against a wall of perplexity and indifference. It generates panic. Spreads fear" (KE 184). Recalling Mayakovsky's immense energy, and his own hunger to create, Vertov tersely wrote: "We who work in documentary poetic film are dying for work" (KE 186).


"Document [fr.LL *documentum* official paper, fr. L, lesson, example, fr. *docere* to teach + *-mentum* -ment—more at DOCILE]" "Document verb transitive," *Webster's Third New International Dictionary* (1971):

> **doc-u-ment** 1 obs: TEACH, SCHOOL, INSTRUCT 2: to evidence by documents: furnish documentary evidence of 3: to furnish with documents 4a: to furnish (a ship) with ship's papers as required by law for the manifesting of ownership and cargo b: to annex to (a bill of exchange) the shipment documents—see DOCUMENTARY BILL 5a: to provide with factual or substantial support for statements made or a hypothesis proposed esp: to equip with exact references to authoritative supporting information b: to construct or produce (as a movie or novel) with a high proportion of details closely reproducing authentic situations or events.

Under "documentatary adj." the compilers, assemblers, or typographers have set the words "FACTUAL, OBJECTIVE, REPRESENTATIONAL" in caps.

Editorial use of split sequences, "disruptive-associative montage," emphasis on the mysterious patternment and subliminal structures of images (icons), sensitivity to the sound shape (even in a silent film) of each pictured event, awareness of the time-mystery of simultaneous phenomena (co-occurrence and deployment)—I am an American poet writing in the English language. I have loved watching films all my life. I work in the poetic documentary form, but didn't realize it until I tried to find a way to write an essay about two films by Chris Marker.

On January 17, 1937, Vertov asked himself: "Is it possible that I too am acting out a role? The role of seeker after film truth? Do I truly seek truth? Perhaps this too is a mask, which I myself don't realize?" (KE 209).

## IV

*1941!—a hole in history*
—Emmanuel Levinas

The title of *Sans Soleil* is taken from a song cycle by Mussorgsky. Towards the end of the film the narrator imagines a time traveler from the year 4001, "when the human brain has reached the era of full employment." The traveler is a third-worlder of Time. He tells us Mussorgsky's songs are still sung in the 40th century. I read once that the magic of Mussorgsky rises from a sort of catastrophe. Most of *Sans Soleil's* footage was shot in Japan during the early 1970s, but shades of the dead of Hiroshima and Nagasaki hover at the margins because what is the chaos of fire to Memory? The films of Andrei Tarkovsky are also imprinted by signal recollections of our soils and losses. *Ivan's Childhood* (1962) and *Mirror* (1974), are classified as fictional films in video-rental stores, though they incessantly and insistently document the somber confines of experience during the 1940s. In *Sculpting in Time: Reflections on the Cinema* (1986) Tarkovsky examines his position in an aesthetics of film, always wondering weaving measuring intentionalities of consciousness: problems, paradoxes, time-space, dream-time, unexpected necessity, cinematic possibility. What *is* a film, he keeps asking.

• Fact?

- Forms inside a box?
- Imprinted time?
- Time in the form of fact?
- Recorded life?
- Anonymous truth?
- The print of thought?

## V

*Night trains air raids fall out shelters*
—Sandor Krasna, 1982.

*Sans Soleil* opens with an idyllic pastoral sequence. Three children are walking along a country road in Iceland. The camera's knowing eye plucked them out of place and bygone time shortly before a volcano buried their village under ash. Through the medium of film, we watch them passing through the past again. A woman's voiceover tells us the film's editor surrounded or sheltered this particular sequence with black leader. She speaks from inside the black until the next sequence of shots, when the jet plane sinks into the hold of a destroyer or aircraft carrier.

Bearer of lethal invisible material

only an event or nonevent lowering along the scopic field of light or flight in a world flooded with facts.

*La Jetée*, composed almost completely of photo stills, begins abruptly with a violent out-of-field-movement-sound-image, the roar of revving and hovering jet engines. Sometimes I think I hear sirens, until the whine or scream of aviation doubles and dissolves into cathedral music: voices in a choir sing passages from the *Russian Liturgy of the Good Saturday*. In northern Russia, Iceland, and other northern places, the sun never goes out of sight in summer. *La Jetée's* aborted soundtrack takeoff evokes technicist and eschatological worldviews.

Immediately time could be going either way.

Sabbath. Beginning of the world to this day. The end of darkness, even in the first of *Genesis* all will of God all sum of mortal obedience. How fearfully without transition a moving image becomes a view of things according to machine assemblage. "My films are my children." Genres and methods are means washing over the projector's original phantom photogram. Firstness can only be feeling. Vertovian theory of the interval. What if a film never reaches the screen because viewers walk away?

Return to the intrusive camera for shelter.

Marker's list of credits calls *La Jetée* a "ciné-roman," but the camera's preliminary concentration on real signal towers, real runways, real airport machinery, real modernist utilitarian airport architecture, suggests a nonfiction representation of fact: socialist realism versus documentary invention.

"Ceci est l'histoire d'un homme marqué par une image d'enfance."

Concerning a voice through air

it takes space to fold time in feeling

Often in the moving time of speech some spoken words get lost. A voiceover is omnidirectional, though we read from left to right. White intertitles form lines on the circumscribed skin of a screen. Superimposed subtitles form a third chain of translation: a foreign message from someone to someone foreign. "This is the story of a man, marked by an image from childhood." Words written in English tell me the same thing twice, though through another haunted vista and approach. In 1948, just after World War II, Laurence Olivier produced, directed, and starred in *Hamlet*. Olivier's voiceover introduction to the film was a single sentence spliced to an intertitle-quotation from one of Hamlet's soliloquies: "This is the tragedy of a man who could not make up his mind."

In act 1, scene 1, Horatio sees the ghost of Hamlet's father armed, but with the visor of his helmet up. The protagonist of *La Jetée* has been granted to watch, as a child, his own death. The unknown woman, object of his wish, subject of his gaze, sometimes calls him her "Ghost." "*Hamlet*. Farewell, dear mother. *King*. Thy loving father, Hamlet. *Hamlet*. My mother. Father and mother is man and wife, man and wife is one flesh; so my mother. Come, for England."

He loses her to look for her. Escape into air from living underwater, she could be his mother glimmering into sight

if a bird beats the air must it oh


oh must it not resound


across the moving surface of time, a dark wing the hauntedness all that is in the other stream of consciousness. "So oft it chances in particular men." Now whisper about his eyes being stone. Different visor masks. The uneasy distinction. Turned aside by a look he must go back. Her face is a prisoner of Love.


A boy and his parents have come to the main jetty at Orly, the Paris airport, on a Sunday before World War III, to watch the planes taking off. A little family stands together, facing away from the camera. It's unclear if "the child whose story we are telling" is the child who has his back to us in two still shots. The off-screen narrative voice adopts the royal we when telling the story. Image track and soundtrack don't quite connect. Did the boy at the guardrail inside the film frame become the marked man? His story will survive the madness to come because of his obsession with an image he is *bound* to remember. Who or what binds him? Something he saw on that primal Sunday he looked the other way. We see a young woman standing alone at the right corner of the jetty directly under the early morning or late-afternoon sun. There is always a time when day and night are equal. She must have turned, because in another shot we see her face. Glancing our way her expression is hard to determine. Her pensive gaze is wary tender innocent dangerous. She may be remembering beckoning staring apprehending responding reflecting or deflecting his look.

The uncertainty of appearance in a phrase universe.

The subject of Marker's ciné-roman is unable to forget "the sudden roar" [*overhead long shot*] dark underbelly of a plane in the air after takeoff. "the woman's gesture la geste de la femme" [Oh no!—Look out!—Keep away!—Come here quickly!], her fists thrown up against her face stifling [*out of it*] a laugh. Meeting the actor-Ghost she could be trying to stop *h a* escape. Her fingers spread open [*visage selvedge*] both shield and express. "Les clameurs des gens . . . ." He veers to the left "et que cet instant. . . ." Oh quickly! "Where [is] the soul?" [and beautiful] How is it contrived? "L'homme qui l'avait suivi depuis le camp souterrain—" [*run FLIGHT-LEFT reach out HAWK-WING-ARM*] What are your hands thrown up against? Did he give himself away? [*I do not ask you who you are not.*] Where did the protagonist go? [*there is no crowd, only the faces of that couple who may be his parents*] everyone is looking somewhere else [*turned away from the runway not facing the camera*]. >Guardrail in half-light [*a plane on the ground arriving or departing* ] Sirens. {ellipse [Now] spliced on a land of promise <but now> There are no moorings in conversation. [Where is your soul? [ - ] "a crumpling body."

Fall fall my entire weight <bow>

**Chris Marker, *La Jetée* (1962)**
**"The sudden roar, the woman's gesture."**

# VI

*I showed views of Russia: Moscow, the Kremlin, the coronation—and some*
*scenes of France. The Tsar professed great interest and asked many ques-*
*tions concerning the mechanism. I explained, and offered him a fragment*
*of film. He held it up to the light, looking through it, and passed the strip*
*from hand to hand. He thanked me and wished me success with the*
*Lumière invention in Russia.*
—Felix Mesguich, 1897[3]

    1962. *Ivan's Childhood* opens, before the credits, with the solitary
song of an unseen bird and a child's sunlit peacetime dream-image of a
woman, his mother, smiling. The film, based on "Ivan," a popular wartime
short story by Vladimir Bogomolov, had been poorly produced at the
Mosfilm Studios when Andrei Tarkovsky, only recently graduated from the
Institute of Cinematography, remade it. "I am simply in love with the subject. I was his age when the war began. His situation is that of my generation," he later wrote. He took the visual dream imagery for Ivan's first
dream from one of his own early memories of summer in the Ukraine by
the Dnieper river, before World War II. We see Ivan's face behind a spider-

3. Quoted in Jay Leyda, *Kino: A History of the Russian and Soviet Film* (Macmillan, 1960, new ed. 1973), 22.

web between the branches of a tree. Ivan sees a butterfly and follows it. The camera sweeps and pans over the forest, over the sandy bank of a river. His mother comes into view, carrying a pail of water from the well. He runs to meet her. She sets the pail down. He dips his face in the water to get cool. "Mum, there's a cuckoo!" he tells her. She raises her arm over her forehead as if to wipe away sweat and listens with him. Her loving expression is the essence, the very play, of happiness. No voiceover settles linear sequentiality, though sounds do refer to what we see. In a standard pastoral fusion of music, bird songs, and running water, Ivan's high boyish laughter, repeated and repeated, acts as a pivot. Speech represents logical human contact. In *Ivan's Childhood*, spontaneous acoustic signals of delight are hints of immanent reversal. Laughter uncannily suggests a coming breach.

Ivan's image of happiness has no black leader for shelter.


More than twenty million Russians died between 1941 and 1945. Some of the worst fighting of the war took place in the Ukraine between the Dniester and the Dnieper. Ivan was only dreaming. His mother's happy prewar expression cuts to terror. This look wakes him up. Now it is outside-inside freezing winter cramped shelter. *Now* is brute fact. Now he is dressed in a ragged padded jacket and cap. He is hiding in a shed or ruin then slogging through a swamp through blackened stumps and thickets. He has no mother. Death outstripped her life and will cut his memory out soon. In wartime she is foreign to representation. She only returns in dreams. When her son stops sleeping she will leave no trace. In Bogomolov's story, Lieutenant Galtsev is Ivan's witness. Nikolai Burlyaev, then a schoolboy in Moscow, acts the role of the skinny twelve-year-old orphaned reconnaissance scout. Many actors made screen tests for the part. Tarkovsky later wrote: "I had noticed Kolya, the future Ivan, when I was still a student. It is no exaggeration to say that my acquaintance with him decided my attitude to the filming."[4] The director doesn't explain what he means by this. The young actor who plays Galtsev reminds me of

4. Andrei Tarkovsky, *Sculpting in Time*, trans. Kitty Hunter-Blair (University of Texas Press, 1986), 33. Further citations are given with the abbreviation ST.

David, who was only twenty-three during the time he was a second lieu-tenant. In *La Jetée* the boy who may become the man marked by a mem-ory from childhood may or may not be an actor. The three blonde children in *Sans Soleil* are three blonde children living in Iceland. According to the voiceover, spoken by a woman, the cameraman, who may or may not have been Marker, wasn't shooting a film at the time. He captured their images while on his travels because they represented for him the image of happi-ness. Footage of black volcanic ash covering their village, near the end of the film, was shot later by another documentarist. Still later *Sans Soleil's* semifictional narrator-cinematographer-correspondent tells his semific-tional feminine voiceover: "History advances, plugging its memory as one plugs one's ears . . . A moment stopped would burn like a flame of film blocked before the furnace of the projector."

## VII

*In the middle of this warm prewar Sunday, where he could now stay.*
—Chris Marker, *La Jetée*

Yesterday words could come between the distance. Frame light, for example. All living draw near. Knowing no data no something then something. No never and no opposite occident orient. Film with jumps and quick cuts. Dissolves and slide effects. Real chalk. Burnt-out ruins. Without weariness. Without our working conditions. When our forces hadn't been thrown.

What is valid documentary? In the long struggle who transmits the Diaspora?

Kolya, the future Ivan, David, my future husband, pick up the receiver. Real children on a peacetime morning before ruin. No sequence of dust fire smoldering ash. Just back to morning. The June of Everything.

Where in the flame does a film stop time?

## VIII

*Morning is the time of Midnight. Artificial Day*

Some of my earliest memories are film memories confused with facts.

During the 1940s, the confusion or juxtaposition between living truth or acting life, always a part of the double and paradoxical nature of movie-going, involved a guilty reading-effect for American children whose fathers were away fighting as opposed to traveling in Europe Africa the South Pacific.

Murder with clock striking cat scurrying woman screaming.

Historical or geographical accident isolated us from the cold reality of mud and hunger. We were spectators chewing popcorn in a second darkness out of daylight looking at film-fact on one side of the screen not the other sides of oceans.

Superimposition of time: cinema-time immediate-time.

A film you love when you are young is never what you know you saw. Apparently cinema helps to reduce the distortion between a "dear" father and a "dead" father. It's the scene of horror the camera returns to, never the daughter.

"But we are lucky."

In fact space is imaginary.

During the 1940s, children in Cambridge, Massachusetts, went to the University Movie Theater on Saturday morning at 10 a.m. We saw newsreels, cartoons, previews of coming attractions, and a double feature. We didn't talk. We divided the crime from the scene of it.

# IX

*Acts and Monuments.*

In wartime zoo animals get scarce. Human destiny in the space of money. This world of fatherlands is covered in wounds. Subjects await their colonists. Trying to escape being crushed by a propeller I was searching for someone else. A wing flew open. The image through death.

All the war in the nonacted cinema.

BOMBER SUBMARINE BATTLESHIP NIGHT-ATTACK FIRE-BOMB INFANTRY TORPEDO DOODLE BUG KAMIKAZE: The camera may move along the sidewalk it's still a picture.

GESTAPO HIMMLER HITLER GÖRING BAMBI TARZAN JANE: What Eurydice? Love is illusory.

"Can I piece the falling together?"

"David or Ivan."

"Oh it's you."

Banished from the Land of Children.

# X

*The Negative of Time*

Dear Bae & Bill—

Your nice long letter came today, Bae. You asked about the country here. It is bleak and barren. It is real desert with none of the mountains we had around Oxnard. However, it is good country for flying and the weather is great. There are amazing sunrises. I think New Mexico is famous for them. The sky is full of bright colors. Orange, pink, and green. It is really amazing. We take off in the morning as soon as it is light and it is a very dramatic sight. Last week my instructor and three of us cadets took a cross-country to Dallas, Texas, for navigation practice. Dallas is about five hundred miles away. Cross-country trips like that are a lot like a cruise in a boat. Of course a cruise would be nicer. But when we get into bigger airplanes and they have a range of thousands of miles which they can travel in a relatively short time it will be better.

## XI

*This soil'd world*
—Walt Whitman, "Reconciliation"

"Don't be worried by the sound of 'test pilot,'" David wrote home to his father and mother in 1943. "It is nothing glamorous or exciting like the movies make it sound. There are perfectly routine checks which must be made on all the airplanes at certain intervals. That is all there is to it." What he was really learning to do he learned to leave out. Less than a year later he was flying B-17s or "Flying Fortresses" on bombing missions over Germany in what military strategists, historians, and war buffs refer to as "the European Theater of War." Each letter a soldier wrote home from the "Theater" was inspected first by War Department censors. On the march only a language of remains gets past. All lost material in nonacted news-reels here is the real, the coverless.

On September 7, 1938, Dziga Vertov listed among forbidden bat-tle techniques of a documentarist: "Substituting the appearance of truth for truth itself" (KE 216).

Since David died I can look at photographs of him, though I still haven't able to look at the video copy of a home movie his daughter sent us in 1991. It was filmed by his first wife's uncle during a summer in the 1950s. Bae was still alive. She died October 9, 1965, so I never met her.

Here she sits on a garden chair in Ogunquit in summer. She is reading, knitting, or watching her granddaughter, Lisa. Judging from family photograph albums, her husband was usually surrounded by admiring painting students and fellow artists. In this homemade film Bae is a widow in her sixties. I remember that in our last summer together David couldn't look at the recovered black-and-white-film documentation of her moving image without crying. Sometimes he and Lisa's mother are playing in the sand with their daughter. Sometimes he stands at the door of his studio then goes inside. He designed the building himself. Now it has been torn down. I can only perceive its imprint or trace. Lisa remembers listening to the noise of waves breaking over pebbles in the cove at night, how tides pulled them under, how they swirled and regrouped in the drift and came back.

I imagine the noise as fixity gathering like a heartbeat, steady and sure.

I have pushed the video-cassette box onto the bookshelf near your desk, out of sight. Because the camera operates at sixteen frames per second for old home movies, and speed is silent. Because your moving image would rupture the suture of sound projection. Because there is no acoustic parallel, nor is concord possible. *"The bad old days";* mocking scramble for cover torn labor.

October 5, 1993, October of meeting nowhere.


On January 21, 1924, Vladimir Ilich Lenin suffered a massive stroke. He died that evening at 6:50. We close the mouth and the eyes of the dead and arrange their bodies so they look as if they are sleeping peacefully or resting before we burn, bury, or seal them up.

Lenin's body lay in his sickroom at Gorki on a sheet-draped table surrounded by flowers and fir branches. During the night friends, colleagues, and relatives stood guard over his remains. The following day his body was placed in a coffin lined with red cloth, a small red pillow under his head. Pallbearers and mourners carried the coffin to the train and boarded it. When the train reached Moscow, where the dead leader was to lie in state, the route to the Trade Union House with its Hall of Columns was lined with troops. The temperature was forty degrees below zero, but crowds were gathered on streets, rooftops, balconies, everywhere. The hall was draped with black and red ribbons, black banners hung from the ceilings. The coffin was carried from the train by Kalinin, Bukharin, Tomsky, Kamenev, Stalin, Rudzutak, Zinoviev, and Rykov. Over half a million people filed by his bier between January 23 and 26. Outside the temperatures were freezing, yet they stood for hours night and day waiting for a chance to look. In *Lenin Lives! The Lenin Cult in Soviet Russia*, Nina Tumarkin describes Lenin's bizarre progress from mortal revolutionary hero to embalmed cult-icon under glass. It wasn't easy; there were technical and scientific embalming problems, competitions for best sarcophagus designs, committees. In November 1930 the granite porphyry and labradorite mausoleum holding the transparent coffin opened to the public.

"Modern tombs are a skeptical affair . . . the ancient sculptors have left us nothing to say in regard to the great, final contrast." When Henry James wrote this he was referring to the art of stone, not the art of moving pictures.

Throughout 1933, eagerly or devotedly following Lenin's instruction that "the production of new films inspired by Communist ideas and reflecting Soviet reality should begin with the newsreel," Vertov labored to produce *Three Songs about Lenin*, commissioned for the tenth anniversary of their leader's death. In preparation he and Elizaveta Svilova searched through "archival, cinematheque and unprocessed footage" in various cities including Tiflis, Kiev, and Baku, for moving images of the living Lenin that might have been overlooked by newsreel editors. "In each instance the brunt of the work involved in exploring gigantic amounts of archive footage fell on Svilova's shoulders. For the tenth anniversary of Lenin's death she particularly distinguished herself, when, through a painstaking examination of hundreds of thousands of feet of film in various archives and storehouses, she not only located shots essential for [the project] but reported finding, in addition, ten original negatives that render the living Ilyich on film" (KE 153). With the help of a new sound engineer, P. Shtro, they were able, during one brief climactic section, to transfer Lenin's voice to film. Utilitarian pragmatism, iconoclasm, Constructivism, pomposity, sentimentalism, modernity, archaism, and strident nationalism can all be located in this cinematographic memorial with its vivid musical score by I. Shaporin.

"First Song (hand lettered) 'Under a Black Veil My Face . . . '"[5]

Vertov and Svilova collated their newly collected archival documentary material with other footage already gathered between 1919 and 1924 by the Council of Three, or Kinoki (the third member of the triumvirate was the cameraman, Vertov's brother, Mikhail Kaufman). This was juxtaposed with ethnographic segments photographed by D. Sourenski, M. Magidson, and B. Monastyrsky, of women, almost completely shrouded under layers of clothing, from the eastern areas of the Soviet Union. Sometimes, these walking mummies joyfully fling off the veils covering their faces, for the camera. Other women are shown learning to shoot rifles, entering workers' clubs, learning to read, learning to operate heavy machinery.

*Three Songs about Lenin* was produced in 1933 during the unsettling period of transition between silent film and film with synchronous sound. For the first two Songs it's as if two realities are being unified and falsified by the controlling musical score and instructional titles superimposed. By the third Song the materialist conception of history is no longer a hypothesis but a scientifically demonstrated proposition with an understanding of the potentials of the microphone. On the level of subject matter the internalized danger situation of a lost love-object is being projected, printed, and distributed throughout.

Sound effects seesaw through artifices of montage.

---

5. Annette Michelson, "The Kinetic Icon in the Work of Mourning: Prolegomena to the Analysis of a Textual System," *October* 52 (Spring 1990), 43. Further citations are given with the abbreviation O.

Turkish, Turkmen, and Uzbek folk songs about Lenin are hailing a worldview that the old materialism could not satisfy. Late nineteenth-century Romanticism, Siegfried's funeral music from Wagner's *Götterdammerung*, is hailing a delayed reaction to Hegel's faith in human reason. The practical telecommunication of the mid twentieth century is hailing. "Hey, you there!"

December 1932, an efficient machine interrupted by the assassination of Kirov. Other people against the wall. All this behind-the-scenes in the World Market. "Hey, you there!"

Lenin's insistent communicativeness.

"How many times here in the Red Square—"/ "—did we hear him speak?" (O 43)

In the middle of the second Song there is a sequence where the Founder of the Soviet Union, in the very act of haranguing the masses with his raised arm, interrupts the officious narrative commentary. As if he really could be projecting his aggressive instincts on the restrictions of cinematographic plausibility, Lenin, mouthpiece source and limit of realism, talks.

Stress the importance of triumph. Poignancy of its imagos.

Learning to talk is a complicated process. The child's growing skill between two realist poles, hostile impulses as well as "bad" internal objects; a little demon of melodrama. Helping figures quickly blossom in the creative surge of aesthetic necessity. Yes the triumph of split-off illusion no the ambush and defeat.

Some of the mourners are acting looking back.

"THIRD SONG (hand lettered) 'In Moscow . . .'/ 'Ah, in the great city of stone. . .'/ 'On the square stands a "tent". . .'/ 'The "tent" where Lenin lies. . .'" We see workers inspired by "The Country's First Great Electrificator Lenin," laboring joyfully in huge hydroelectric plants, in factories, on collective farms. "'Machinery is now the weapon. . .'/ 'OUR OIL!'/ 'OUR COAL!'/ 'OUR METAL!'/ 'Our mighty Baltic-White Sea Canal. . .'/

'Lenin, we go FORWARD!'" (O 50–51). While the message may be that Leninist-Communism is liberating, particularly so for women, Annette Michelson demonstrates in "The Kinetic Icon in the Work of Mourning: Prolegomena to the Analysis of a Textual System," ways in which this film she calls "a veritable iconostasis" draws its subliminal visionary force by working in and around the ancient Russian tradition, through music, iconography, and literature, of anonymous female oral lamentation at funerals and burial ceremonies.

If, as Melanie Klein says, following Freud, mourning is the pain experienced in the slow process of testing reality, *Three Songs about Lenin* is a cinematographic embodiment of the fluid and passing states, the inter-action and interjection, between sorrow and distress. This innovative postrevolutionary cinematic memorial to the father of the socialist moth-erland, by use of the camera's eye, may bring into arbitrary relief the patient mitigation of hatred by love. But why do women in moving pictures so often serve as representations of the extension of love united before strife, at the same time they are being "caught unawares" by the camera's point of view?

Writing this essay I have no clear idea what value there can be in a fragment of concrete reality in itself multiple and always at the mercy of a national and personal identity. The real time of emotion isn't musical time or background noise of civilization or continuity of exposed film. You can always tell memory, not the coverings it closes first.

*Three Songs about Lenin* runs forward by half removes into those early blacklist days, wonderfully without defense.

Defense as it appears in fortresses and humans.

*La Jetée* is made up almost entirely of stills. It opens with a low-ering sun, departing planes, and World War III about to begin. Marker's use of photograms and freeze frames in this film that calls itself a fiction is a compelling documentation of the interaction and multiple connections perceived separately and at once between lyric poetry and murderous history. That's the secret meaning. I knew it by telepathy in 1948 when I was eleven and first saw the movie of *Hamlet*. André Bazin says in "Theater and Cinema": "When a character moves off screen, we accept the fact he is out of sight, but he continues to exist in his own capacity at some other place in the decor which is hidden from us. There are no wings to the screen."[6]

Chris Marker's filmography lists a twenty-six-minute video, "Tarkovski '86," as part of a longer work called *Zapping Zone*. I haven't been able to see it, but I noticed his name on the list of credits at the end of the ponderously titled *The Genius, The Man, The Legend: Andrei Tarkovsky*, produced by the Swedish Film Institute in 1988.

Tarkovsky directed a stage production of *Hamlet* in 1982. "To begin with, it's a family, a closely-knit family, they mustn't have the slightest inkling of all that lies ahead of them. They are very protective of each other, very dear to each other, they are all together. And that makes them happy!" he wrote in reference to Ophelia, Laertes, and Polonius in act 1, scene 3.[7]

The Russian director Andrei Tarkovsky often mixed documentary footage with fiction. He scattered professional actors, stagehands, friends, and family members throughout his films just as he arbitrarily blended time periods with international and domestic situations. The project he variously titled, *A White, White Day, Atonement, Redemption, Why Are You Standing So Far Away*, even *Martyrology*, was to include fragments of straight interviews between his mother, Maria Ivanova, who had once been an actress, and himself, until he abandoned this early cinema-vérite approach and replaced the interview format with acted scenes. *Mirror* is partially based on his memories and her memories of life before, during,

6. André Bazin, *What Is Cinema?*, ed. and trans. Hugh Gray (University of California Press, 1967), 105.

7. Andrei Tarkovsky, *Time within Time: The Diaries, 1970–1986*, trans. Kitty Hunter-Blair (Verso, 1993), 381.

and after the war. The actress Margarita Terekhova plays both his wife and his mother, while Maria Ivanova is herself and acts her mother. Ignat Daniltsev plays Tarkovsky's son Ignat (really Andriuska) and Alexi (Andrei himself) as a boy. Oleg Yankovsky is the director's film father, while his real father's poems are read off-screen by Arseniy himself. Real or acting, the characters have the same reflection in whichever mirror serves as camera for the filmmaker for his cinematographer. They can pass back and forth from one to the other but that's what movie acting is because there are no wings to the screen any soul can be the body.

Distant woods beautiful auspicious morning at evening a sudden west wind soughing through white flowering meadow.

Facts are perceptions of surfaces.

In *Sculpting in Time*, Tarkovsky writes about his problems begin-ning *Mirror*. First it was to be a novella about the wartime evacuation, with the plot centering on a military instructor at his school. During the second version of the script the idea of the interview with his mother took prece-dence, "but the incident. . . continued to torment me, and lived on in my memory until it had become a minor episode of the film"(ST 128–29). He abandoned the second version because he continued to feel he was missing an essential vision or fact or memory that would raise the project above the level of lyrical autobiography. The constantly changing quality of this work in progress confirmed his feeling that scenario is fragile and con-stantly changes with the material as well as with qualities individual actors bring to it. This improvisational way of working continued throughout the filming and editing stages. At some point he decided to include newsreel shots, though he seems to have been worried about the combination of acted and documentary sequences. He gathered found footage intending to use it, but the collection represented only isolated fragments lacking the single time-sense he wanted. So, just as Vertov and Svilova had done while preparing *Three Songs about Lenin*, he continued searching, until the day he came across a sequence showing Soviet soldiers crossing Lake Sivash. "Suddenly—quite unheard of for a newsreel—here was a record of one of the most dramatic moments in the history of the Soviet advance of 1943. It was a unique piece; I could hardly believe that such an enormous footage of film should have been spent recording one single event continuously observed. It had clearly been filmed by a gifted camera-man. When, on the screen before me, there appeared, as if coming out of nothing, these people shattered by the fearful, inhuman effort of that tragic moment of history, I knew that this episode had to become the centre, the very essence, heart, nerve of this picture that had started off merely as my intimate lyrical memories" (ST 130). The army cameraman who filmed this extraordinary document was killed the same day he shot the footage. Tarkovsky doesn't give us his name. I haven't been able to find it in any writing about the film. Most of the young soldiers were killed also. The Soviet chief of State Cinema advised him to remove the sequence from the wider selection of documentary intervals or detours because the scene showed too much suffering.

When, almost halfway through the film, the director begins to introduce the various black-and-white newsreel documentary inserts, they telescope together, binding his memory-time of youth to the actual geopolitical chain of violence, seemingly everywhere during the second half of the twentieth century. The archival inserts are sometimes shown at a slower speed, sometimes with "wild recording" faked later.

Sent-back poems from the invisible side of events.


The newsreel filmed by the anonymous cameraman at Lake Sivash acts as an open parenthesis for the tragicomic autobiographical episode in which evacuated boys, at target practice in an icy outdoor rifle-range, play a cruel joke on their shell-shocked military instructor. He has no name either.


In fact authentic documentary material blighted the hearts of children all over the world who came to consciousness enveloped by threatened futurity, during the non-nuclear and then nuclear 1940s. We were alert to the subliminal disjunction between actual and fictional cinematographic realism shown in theaters (never called cinemas) because no one had television at home. When I said that in Cambridge, on Saturdays at 10 a.m., the weekly ritual for children at the University Movie Theater consisted of a newsreel, a cartoon, previews, the main feature, and a serial, I left out the intermission. The curtain came down, as if this were a play, and much to our disgust, perhaps because it demonstrated in fact there were wings to the screen, a real man—comedian or magician, his name didn't matter, we never knew it—walked onstage with a blackboard and other props. We scorned him for interrupting our absorption in ritual. We scorned him for being human. "Let's go on with the show! Lets' go on with the show!" I chanted with the crowd firing tickets, spitballs, and popcorn in his direction, no matter that some of us had been sobbing over the death of noble animals in *My Friend Flicka* or *Bob, Son of Battle* not ten minutes earlier. During wartime, quantities of aggressive impulses nullified our terror of the danger of disruption and released our obsessional defense mechanisms. We needed to show triumph, so we persecuted this mortal parenthesis with hoots and jeers. Saturday after Saturday he recited the number lists and little miracles that made up his repertoire of tricks or jokes, until the lights dimmed, he carried his props offstage to the margins from whence he came, and the curtain rose revealing the screen. The soul had returned to the body, the main feature could resume.

According to the narrator of *Sans Soleil*, the baffling part of the Japanese Shinto ritual of Dondo-yaki is that circle of little boys we see shouting and beating the litter of scraps of burnt ornaments or votive offerings with long sticks after the flames have died down. They tell him it's to chase away the moles. He sees it as a small intimate service.

In English *mole* can mean, aside from a burrowing mammal, a mound or massive work formed of masonry and large stones or earth laid in the sea as a pier or breakwater. Thoreau calls a pier a "noble mole" because the sea is silent but as waves wash against and around it they sound and sound is language.

*Specimen Days*, published in 1882, consists of extracts from note-books Walt Whitman kept between 1862 and 1865 when he was visiting sick and wounded soldiers on the field and in hospitals around Washington, D.C. There are other sequences in *Specimen Days* he calls memoranda, later added in Camden, New Jersey, where the poet moved after suffering his first paralytic stroke. One, "pencill'd . . . one warm October noon," titled "Cedar-Plums Like—Names," is about the problem he had naming the book. In a footnote marked by an asterisk he provides a list of suggested and rejected titles. There are thirty-five. "Then reader dear, in conclusion, as to the point of the name for the present collection, let us be satisfied to *have* a name—something to identify and bind it together, to concrete all its vegetable, mineral, personal memoranda, abrupt raids of criticism, crude gossip of philosophy, varied sands clumps—without bothering ourselves because certain pages do not pre-sent themselves to you or me as coming under their own name with entire fitness or amiability." As if to stifle his own egotism, he adds, in parenthe-sis: "(It is a profound, vexatious, never-explicable matter—this of names. I have been exercised deeply about it my whole life.)"[8]

Children know by precognition how precariously names cling to civilization. In order to qualify for language they must stifle unrelenting internalization. "We have a message for you—our spirits being out of body." Images have countries whose streets they cannot fathom. Immense stretches of ocean up to this frame the screen.

"I just dreamed of you mama. By the way when did father leave us?"

"1935, why?"

Mirror: *The Newsreel Sequences*

---

8. Walt Whitman, *Complete Poetry and Collected Prose*, ed. Justin Kaplan (Library of America, 1982), 886.

history does run backwards through endless generations of mur-
derers. The Spanish Civil War zooms in on us because in cinema people
do talk from the grave

eating away at character because public evaluation is troublesome
and wants autobiographical fiction. No the camera pulls away from corresponding impressions lyric pulls away. No the benign circle shed also.
Time itself running through though shot not smoothly but by jolt by static
energy. Checking the cost. No the collision of one objective nonacted
group shot with another.

No by the very facts.

A woman walks quickly down a city sidewalk carrying a long pane
of broken glass. It's a window not a mirror. Bombs are being dropped from
planes. Do they fly across the screen from left to right because we read in
that direction? Cut to bombs exploding though we only hear singing. Two
women, one carrying a bouquet of flowers, run for cover. Other citizens
are seeking shelter. Theater for whom? Some half glance at the camera as
they hurry in

meanwhile the angry retrospective nostalgia of flamenco music
on the soundtrack reiterates the place of Spain while bridging the transition between acted and nonacted scenes. As if by impasse of idealization
cinema can reestablish security and life itself and song will soothe we will
be soothed to silently watch these incessant relentless negative retrieve-
ments this debris rayed over.

Frantic grown-ups are evacuating groups of children probably
from Madrid. It's a question of security but who will love them don't that's
the substitute part. All the pain of the world is concentrated in this place
crammed with people dear to each other. He tries to comfort his mother
before going. His father kisses and kisses him. What do you see camera?

Shouts and not memorized.

Some children haul heavy suitcases, some wear identification badges, some kiss their relations good-bye, some set off eagerly some are sobbing. A young boy uses a large white pocket handkerchief to wipe away his tears. Cries of love and alarm on the soundtrack fade into an air-raid siren, factory whistle, or is it the whistle of a train approaching.

We are as real and near as cinema.

A little girl, half-turned away holding her doll, smiles shyly. When the ambiguous siren or engine wails its warning she turns directly towards the camera. Medium close-up her expression changing to a mixture of astonishment or terror. This child is not acting. Perhaps she knows what the young actor in *Ivan's Childhood* pretends he knows.

Her look pierces the mask of western culture.

(Almost forty years later, in June, 1972, a terrified Phan Thi Kin Phuc, napalmed in error by a South Vietnamese bomber, will come running naked down a road, having torn off her burning clothing.

She is running towards the camera's single eye.)

A man without wings swings slantingly into view through free space mute sky

1 2 3 4 5 6 seconds of silent soundtrack before liturgical music through fade-in to a certain point then tapering emitting wave notes risen from years of other powers. Balancing and hovering he is swinging in a basket as if re-entrance is easy. Swings in again coming home so it's a picture projected through time subtler than poems or a letter because he is working on it. Found footage shown at slower speed here is power. A tremendous stratosphere spinnaker so weightless after the weighty Spanish evacuation sequence hovers preparing for lift-off well he needs no map to return if fiction angel astronaut returning to home base as if he merely floated out of sight for fun as if reentrance is possible and surely there are to be anchorage mooring helpers waiting. Star boat USSR

resembles a light sail of great speed used on yachts when running before the wind, spinnaker because a yacht called *Sphinx* carried such a sail in 1866. Utilitarian loveliness, a huge bubble of nylon pulling tons of boat through water, but sometimes relentless swinging and thrashing shakes the rig out of her tugging

now the spinnaker is drawing now the long chase ahead. Coming next will be other newsreel footage of young soldiers slogging through mud and shallow water not doing well exhausted though one or two smile wanly at the camera

I wish you could see this film. Sometimes I recognize you inside it so scared and young always among those Soviet soldiers who are crossing Lake Sivash why should there be twice as many sick as wounded

you float back to me everything inexpressible

aerodynamic repair experiment for the freshly washed white star boat USSR getting ashore to let you sleep well. Light sail of great spread used on yachts when running before the wind.
Once you could cover my hand completely with your palm.

A huge bubble of nylon pulling tons of boat through skywater swinging and thrashing relentless threatening to shake the rig out now tugging water now touched by science now drawing silence inside the long chase ahead.
Scenes like this men use

clinging vine method to hang on filling out running before the wind but here there is no yacht and open ocean is air. The effect is the same flying-jib out astride the small boom so spinnaker to get north. Smaller balloons circle and touch the mother one as satellites do then sacred chorus singing sanctus sanctus. All is well. Melody for a while.

Melodies antedate languages they do not grow old. A peaceful weightless wingless furlough one or two other balloons revolve around these smaller powers after peace.

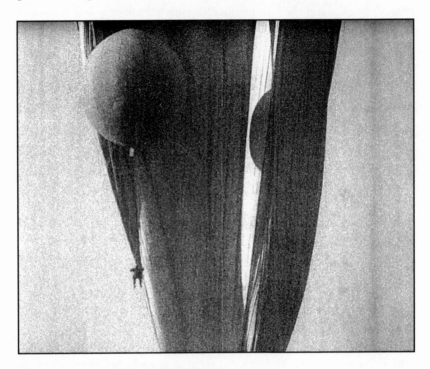

**Andrei Tarkovsky, *Mirror* (1974)**
**Soviet archival footage of military balloons.**

One aerialist sailor attached by a string to a satellite balloon floats in and down across the screen from right to left where are his supports as child attached to a mother? As if he were returning home again a crowd to watch and applaud so from heaven he smiles. Where are you systems of planets around us? Drifting out of sight away out of the frame of the screen behind the wings. Annihilation is the deep chaos answer sheets and white film turmoil. It's a separation wish to be carried out also as if to silence of ether. Irrationality of speech to surrender the beauty of this voyage without baggage to shed earth. Because our fathers have not kept their word. Artificers and builders convey to one another someone was thought to be worthy. Colorlessness prefigures a connection when the unconscious mind mirrors love-partners who are in absolute contrast but by early influence that the child had had time her impressions of her father may have been shaken if there ever was a way to translate the *feeling* of image-juxta-position in these words moving from left to right across this sheet of paper.

Nicely coordinated teamwork between camera crew director actors *Mirror* the private life.

The sea is a theater.

Steerage toward redemptive bourgeois historical resolution what music to windward probably unaware of rocks the motion of waves the swelling fold how quickly the sail becomes a contorted mass of fabric.

Sequences touched off by and surrounding the originary memory of the military instructor without a name. His overanxiousness to keep all his pupils safe. He is a teacher and then about the worry that so perfectly matches these restless boundaries of realism.

Come tell us *young* man.

We can't hear him crying his excessive sorrow because of the world. He has resigned himself in phobia projections and defenses for love. Nothing can remove that split in the film it's too close the masters have been mixed. Double the safe place death. You can see the dramatic force of this central counterpoint ellipse. You know the joke of the boy who tosses the dummy hand-grenade onto the boards. You know the instructor will become the nerve to throw himself down in order to save his young pupils (he is a teacher he thinks he would die for them that sense of omnipotence).

(You hear his heartbeat louder and louder sometimes to the point of martyrdom

Of course the hand-grenade never explodes though his beating heart does change to the beating of drums to a drum-roll marshaling. Poor man this excess of activity no nurse by his side no friend to assist him in his struggles. Some are so young and already representative of current events we are bound to confront

**Andrei Tarkovsky, *Mirror* (1974)**
**Newsreel footage of soldiers crossing Lake Sivash in the Soviet**
**advance of 1943, with Arseniy Tarkovsky's voiceover poem.**

juxtaposed with the newsreel footage, shot by the anonymous cameraman. Soldiers of the Soviet Army slogging through the shallow water and mud flats of Lake Sivash, the "Putrid Sea," in the Russian advance of 1943. During the final shots of this sequence the auteur-director's father, the poet Arseniy Tarkovsky's voiceover recitation of his Whitmanesque poem "Life Life" lends a piercing sadness to these sepia image-traces of patience, fortitude, desperate fatigue, legs stiff from damp and chill, young faces looking blankly at the eye of the camera, the steady, silent, progress forward across seemingly endless shallows. Some of the men are hauling a barge carrying wheels and guns so heavy what could ever be more unlike the floating stratosphere sequence but it's the same war. *No need / To be afraid of death at seventeen / Nor yet at seventy*. Noise of water sloshing synchronized later no extraneous breathing or irrelevant sound-wave energy. *Reality and light/ Exist, but neither death nor dark-*

*ness.* Floating currency. All of us are on the sea-shore now. Drum roll percussion echo reverberation. *And I am one of those who haul the nets/ When a shoal of immortality comes in.* Who are the oldest principal officers? *Live in the house—and the house will stand./ I will call up any century,/ Go into it and build myself a house.* (ST 143) Almost everyone keeps walking, continually proceeding.

The next newsreel footage inserts, juxtaposed with another memory sequence, the young Leningrad blockade orphan and his evacuee companions playing in snow, date from 1945 and after. Antitank guns at night. A banner flapping and snapping. Documentarist shooting dead Nazi. A man with a crutch cowering in a makeshift bomb shelter he could nearly be weeping.

Ardmore Airforce Base
Ardmore, OKLA
Monday, April 12, 1945

Dear Bae & Bill
A little while ago I heard the terrible news about the President's death. What a blow to the world!
This has been an exciting night. There has been a thunderstorm and there were cyclones all around us. But things are quiet now and everything will be OK.

Americans exploded the first atomic bomb at Alamogordo, New Mexico, July 16, 1945 at sunrise. Heat from the blast fused the surrounding desert sand to glass.

Was the next quick newsreel sequence in *Mirror* shot shortly before 8:15 a.m., August 6, 1945? Are those young fliers in the cockpit piloting the *Enola Gay*? Are they on their mission to explode the secret uranium weapon known as Little Boy?

(A little boy who survived Hiroshima remembered the moment the bomb fell, a red dragonfly, the sound of a B-29, his brother reaching out to catch a dragonfly and a flash: "It's strange, those fragmentary scenes remain fixed in my mind like photographs.")

We could be seeing footage from a later test at Bikini Island in the Pacific; in that one some G.I.s were lethally exposed. Maybe the fireball mushroom cloud is from the plutonium one the United States army exploded over Nagasaki on August 9, 1945.

Cut. Gunfire. Flak. Roar. Smoke. Chinese political rally hands waving totalitarian saluting. Sheets of glass framing portraits of Mao. Little icon-busts of Mao. Books leaflets. Mao's little red book. His face on the cover. The Sino-Soviet split. Soviet soldiers forming a human chain to keep oriental peoples back. Some of them shove forward waving photos of Mao. A vast political outdoor ceremony somewhere probably China.

In *La Jetée* and *Mirror*, also in *Sans Soleil*, one finds images associated with, or rising from, Hiroshima. I don't think you can grasp the hauntedness in all of them without understanding this central surrender of soul, in its nuclear plight forgetting and refusing to forget.

The immense indifference of history. The crushing hold of memory's abiding present. Compared to facts words are only nets. We go on hauling in what traces of affirmation we can catch. Action is the movement of memory searching for a lost attachment a make-believe settlement. A screen is a sort of mole or sea wall. It keeps spirit back.

*Thus in silence in dreams' projections,*
—Walt Whitman, "The Wound-Dresser"

# XII

*Because I know that time is always time*
*And place is always and only place*
—T. S. Eliot, *Ash-Wednesday*

This is the epigraph to the English-language version of *Sans Soleil*, released for distribution in the United States in 1982. Documentary and experimental films have a hard time being distributed in North America. Sadly, these films seem to reach only a cosmopolitan coterie of filmmakers, artists, photographers, and film scholars. It's the same situation with experimental poetry. Books and magazines of or about non-mainstream poetry are consigned chiefly to small-press distribution networks or cooperatives, and few bookstores order them. Recently, many independent bookstores are being forced to close when large chains move into their areas. I hear that in Canada things are different.

I thought first about writing something on documentaries about poets because I remembered the recent PBS *Voices and Visions* series, now subtitled for distribution: "A Television Course on Modern American Poetry." The series consists of thirteen one-hour video programs "presenting the life and work of major American poets." I was curious why most of them seemed so flat, though the word "major" was an alert. After watching them all again, this time taking notes, I couldn't think of anything to say. Mike Cartmell, a Canadian filmmaker, suggested I look at *Sans Soleil*. He described it as an autobiographical work about a French filmmaker with an assumed name. *Sans Soleil* wasn't about poetry; it was poetry, he said. I had just finished writing *The Birth-mark: unsettling the wilderness in American literary history*. Marker collided with birth-mark, the assumed name struck home.

# XIII

"So, montage is conflict." Several years ago I plucked this quotation from Eisenstein's "The Cinematographic Principle and the Ideogram" to use as an epigraph to an essay about Charles Olson's *Call Me Ishmael: A Study of Melville*. Franklin D. Roosevelt's sudden death shocked Olson into completing the book he had been unable to pull together for years. Now he started over, cutting, juxtaposing and compressing his material in a radically new way. It was finished "before the 1st A-bomb, 1st week that August." August 6, 1945, marked a point in time after which nothing could be the same. A few months later Olson resigned his government positions (member of the Office of War Information in Washington and Director of the Foreign Nationalities Division of the Democratic National Committee). Olson's critical study of *Moby-Dick* marked his own delayed beginning as a poet.

Short cuts, mixed credits, news items, archival material, nonfictitious science, science fiction, pulp fiction, travel narratives, epigraphs, ballads, and passages from the Bible represent the delayed beginning of Herman Melville's *Moby-Dick*. First the effusive dedication to Hawthorne, next the "Etymology" and "Extracts" sections. Aside from the dedication, and possibly even there, all of these scattered particles of fact and or fable meet in the word-event *whale*.

*Sans Soleil* has a delayed beginning. Marker's film bares the device of its structure first. Credits, quotations, shots filmed by himself and others are spliced and surrounded with black leader. Even the title comes in three languages and colors. For a filmmaker a camera is a screen within a screen; so is a word to a poet. Shots of a Japanese temple consecrated to cats begin and end the main body of Marker's *Sunless* cycle. A couple has come to display an inscribed wooden slat in the cat cemetery in order to protect their missing cat Tora. We see rows of enigmatic porcelain cats, each with one paw raised, as if to deliver some incommunicable communication. Rituals for recovering lost or dead animals occur throughout the movie.

Herman Melville, Emily Dickinson, and Walt Whitman were all using montage before it was a word for a working method. Their writing practice (varied though it was) involved comparing and linking fragments or shots, selecting fragments for scenes, reducing multitudes (chapters or stanzas) and shots (lines and single words) to correlate with one another, constantly interweaving traces of the past to overcome restrictions of temporal framing. The influence Whitman had on Vertov through Mayakovsky is well known. Is the Melville who wrote *Typee, Omoo, Redburn,* "The Encantadas," and "Benito Cereno," a travel writer, a beachcomber, a reporter, or a poet? *Moby-Dick* is a poetic documentary fiction on a grand scale. Often I think of Dickinson's handwritten manuscripts as "Drawings in motion. Blueprints in motion. Plans for the future. The theater of relativity of the screen" (KE 9). With an important difference: if kino-eye signifies, among other things, the conquest of space—"I am kino-eye, I am a mechanical eye. I, a machine, show you the world only as I can see it" (KE 17)—Dickinson's pen-eye aims at the conquest of mechanical reproduction. After reaching the age of consent she refused to be photographed.

Seventeenth- and eighteenth-century American Puritan theologians and historians like Roger Williams, Anne Bradstreet, and Cotton Mather were obsessed with anagrams. Seventeenth-century American Puritans were iconoclasts and animists at once. Ralph Waldo Emerson, Herman Melville, Emily Dickinson, T. S. Eliot, H.D., Marianne Moore, William Carlos Williams, Wallace Stevens, Charles Olson, and John Cage are among many North American writers who inherit this feeling for letters as colliding image-objects and divine messages. "Association, so far as the word stands for an effect, is between THINGS THOUGHT OF—it is THINGS, not ideas, which are associated in the mind. We ought to talk of the association of objects, not the association of ideas"—William James. "If he [the author] make of his volume a mole whereon the waves of Silence may break it is well"—Henry David Thoreau. Needing to translate words into THINGS THOUGHT OF could be the mark of a North American poet

if marks of scattered hues in October sunsets geographically here can ever be translated into English.

Walter Benjamin was also attracted to the idea that single letters in a word or name could be rearranged to cabalistically reveal a hidden purpose. "My thinking relates to theology the way a blotter does to ink. It is soaked through with it. If one were to go by the blotter, though, nothing of what has been written would remain."[9] It's sad to read that one of the reasons given for Benjamin's suicide in 1940 was his reluctance to emigrate to the United States.

Here he didn't expect to go anywhere.


A mark is the face of a fact. A letter is naked matter breaking from form from meaning. An anagram defies linear logic. Any letter of the alphabet may contain its particular indwelling spirit. A mark is a dynamic cut. Dynamic cutting is a highly stylized form of editing. Sequences get magpied together from optical surprises, invisible but omnipresent verbal flashes, flashes of facts. A documentary work is an attempt to recapture someone something somewhere looking back. Looking back, Orpheus was the first known documentarist: Orpheus, or Lot's wife.

> Wavering between the profit and the loss
> In this brief transit where the dreams cross
> —T. S. Eliot, *Ash-Wednesday*


An epigraph is an afterthought. Usually it follows the title of a work. An epigraph is second sight. Severed from its original position, replaced at a foreign margin, the magpied quotation now suggests a theme or acts as talisman. Magpies are pied: mostly black with white patches and white tail stripes. Harbingers of ill omen, they tend to be associated with thresholds and secret ministry. In Ireland, if we saw any, my mother taught us to count quickly: "One is for sorrow, two is for joy, three for a marriage, and four for a boy." The word magpie also refers to the black and white ceremonial dress of an Anglican bishop. In captivity magpies imitate human speech. An early English dictionary describes these members of

---

9. Walter Benjamin, "N [Re the Theory of Knowledge, Theory of Progress]," trans. Leigh Hafrey and Richard Sieburth, in *Benjamin: Philosophy, Aesthetics, History,* ed. Gary Smith (University of Chicago Press, 1989), 61.

the jay family as "the cleverest, the most grotesque, the most musical of crows." In 1852, *Webster's American Dictionary of the English Language* bluntly defines magpie: "a chattering bird of the crow tribe."

> Among twenty snowy mountains,
> The only moving thing
> Was the eye of the blackbird.
> —Wallace Stevens, "Thirteen Ways of Looking at a Blackbird"

People say the magpie has a spot of blood of the devil on its tongue. People who like anagrams are usually attracted to epigraphs.

# XIV

*L'éloignement des pays répare en quelque sorte la trop grande proximité des temps.*
—Racine, *Seconde Préface à Bazajet*

Marker's epigraph to the original French version of *Sans Soleil* is lifted from Racine's second preface to *Bazajet*, one of the seventeenth-century dramatist's least-known works in English. *Bazajet* is a Turkish tragedy set in a seraglio. The magpied lines are the second part of a point Racine was making. "On peut dire que le respect que l'on a pour les héros augmente à mesure qu'ils s'éloignent de nous: *major e longinquo reverentia.*" [We may say the respect that we harbor for heroes increases in proportion to their distance from us.] What Marker didn't let in or cut out contains in itself a quotation without marks lifted by Racine from the *Annals* of the Roman historian Tacitus.

For Roland Barthes the essence of the Racinian eros is sight. In both *La Jetée* and *Sans Soleil* sight is privileged. The image takes the place of the thing. Erotic scenes could be hallucinations. "I see her, she saw me, she knows that I see her, she drops me her glance, just an angle, when it is still possible to act as though it was not addressed to me, and at the end the real glance straightforward that lasted a 24th of a second, the length of a film frame." In *La Jetée* and *Sans Soleil* as in a play by Racine, glances are the equivalents of interviews. A look can be an embrace or a wound. Even the gaze of statues.

## XV

Laertes: *A document in madness: thoughts and remembrance fitted*.

The Capgras syndrome is rare. A patient believes that a person, usually closely related to her, has been replaced by an exact double. When it was first described in 1923 by Capgras and Reboul-Lachaux, they titled it *l'illusion des sosies*. In French, the term *sosie* comes from Plautus's *Amphitryon*. There the god Mercury assumes the appearance of Sosie, Amphitryon's servant, thus becoming his double.

*Sans Soleil* is supposed to be the autobiographical account of a traveling filmmaker named Sandor Krasna. The narrating voiceover is an anonymous woman, perhaps a film editor, a liaison officer, or a sister, remembering letters and camera footage mailed to her from faraway places by a documentarist who is or was a roving reporter. He could be an editor, collaborator, lover, teacher, student, brother, "Sandor Krasna," whatever. There is the suggestion that "he," as she always calls him (the credit list at the end supplies the name Krasna), has gone away some-where, possibly forever. She (the credits say "Florence Delay") says what she says he wrote shows what she says he shot. We aren't sure who is real or imaginary; on the other hand, we understand him to be the cinematog-rapher Chris Marker. Marker's filmography—*Lettre de Sibérie* (1957), *Cuba Si* (1961), *Le Joli Mai* (1962), *La Bataille des Dix Millions* (1970)— beckons his audience in the direction of cinema-verité. Chris Marker: Marxist cinematographer, always on the wing, not to be glimpsed except in flight, doesn't like to be photographed.

Marker's practice of cutting, isolating, grafting, and synthesizing music, languages, machine noises, musical synthesizers, and quotations (Marlon Brando's voice from *Apocalypse Now*) depends on invisible verbal flashes, optical surprises, and split images. Ophelia's mad song evokes Jean Simmons in Olivier's *Hamlet*, although another woman's face is singing. Here Marker introduces what looks like a solarized image. To solarize a shot you reexpose it to light, so solarizing is double exposure. We see what is happening electronically on a machine that separates the darks into lights: we see the process. This sequence recalls the editing sequence from Vertov's *The Man with the Movie Camera* (a classic nonfiction film) at the same time it begins "Krasna's" meditation on, and recollection of, a pilgrimage he made to the sites in San Francisco where Hitchcock's *Vertigo* (a classic mystery film) was shot. The fictional nonfiction filmmaker inserts footage from Hitchcock's earlier fictional movie filmed during the 1950s on location in a city (San Francisco) once almost buried under ash by earthquake and fire. One sequence or mininarrative leads by indirection into another sequence. Meanwhile the unseen narrator repairs or restores psychic reality and its relation to external reality, though we are never really certain who has collected, edited, and marked each shot or short cut.

The American-released version of *Sans Soleil* is narrated in English by Alexandra Stewart. Languages bear particular canny or uncanny acoustical patterns, historical scars. At times her narrative voiceover seems exaggerated in its accentlessness to the point where it impinges on the otherwise wonderfully varied polyphonic soundtrack. Recently I was able to see a showing of Marker's *Le Mystère Kuomiko* (1965), also filmed in Tokyo. I now notice ways in which the memory of this earlier time in Japan crops up in *Sans Soleil*, but I see the resemblance and hear the echoes belatedly. Viewers of *Vertigo*, along with Scotty (James Stewart), don't know, until three quarters of the way through the film, that Judy (Kim Novak) was impersonating Madeleine (Kim Novak). Could it be that the real Kuomiko in the cinema-verité version is a double for Hélène Chatelain (who may or may not be a professional actress), even if she doesn't speak in the ciné-roman *La Jetée*? Where is Kuomiko in the Tokyo of *Sans Soleil*? That's a later mystery. The Ginza owl is here, moving his eyes as usual, the bullet train is here, right- and left-wing radicals are here, but Kuomiko is not. The real Florence Delay is a French novelist, while "Florence Delay" could be here, editing Krasna's movie. Gavin Elster edits Madeleine's story (through Judy) in *Vertigo*. The absent cinematographer could be Delay's double except we know the unseen woman is a figment of Marker's imagination. In 1965 Kuomiko is really a young Japanese woman (perhaps a professional actress now) who speaks fluent French. Her beautiful voiceover is one of the striking elements of the Mystery that bears her name. Kim Novak's two voices as Madeleine and Judy are essential double effects in *Vertigo*. Perhaps the spoken and named voices of Delay and Stewart coappear by chance operation. My favorite sequence in *Sans Soleil* weaves in and around the Hitchcock movie. Here, the person who claims to have seen *Vertigo* nineteen times shows by subterfuge how that film's spiral of time reoccurs in *La Jetée*. So for an English-speaking viewer of *La Jetée*, *The Kuomiko Mystery*, and *Sans Soleil*, the ghostly presence of two women, their trace, is in Stewart's accentless narrative voice.

Often *Sans Soleil* seems to be largely about footage shot somewhere else. This is a film of quotations, outtakes, retakes, tape delays, failed military coups, dead pilots, and ghostly warriors. Everything is acted out on the borderline that divides introjection and incorporation. A double is a facsimile. Is *Sans Soleil's* Sandor Krasna a reflected Gavin Elster?

# XVI

*Film-Truth*

Dziga Vertov and Chris Marker are pseudonyms.

Denis Kaufman was born in 1896 in Bialystock, then a part of the Russian Empire, now a part of Poland. His father was a bookmaker and bibliophile. I can't find information on his mother. In 1915 when he was still a child he moved with his family to Moscow. In 1917 he enrolled in the Psychoneurological Institute (special interest in human perception). The same year he organized "The Laboratory of Hearing" and experimented with sound recording. He also wrote a science-fiction novel since lost. In 1917 Kaufman abandoned his name at the threshold of his working life in film.

Christian François Bouche-Villeneuve was probably born in the Paris suburb of Neuilly-sur-Seine in 1921, possibly to a Russian mother and an American father. Other possibilities for a birthplace are Ulan Bator in Mongolia, or Belville, the Arab quarter of Paris. One bibliographic entry I found says "his early life is shrouded in mystery, much of it perpetrated by the filmmaker himself." During World War II he may have served as a resistance fighter during the occupation of France, some accounts claim he also joined the United States Army as a parachutist—he says he didn't. After the war Marker played music in bars until joining the staff of *Esprit*. He contributed poetry, political commentary, music criticism, short stories, and film essays to the influential Marxist-oriented Catholic journal. He also wrote a wartime aviation novel that has been compared to Saint-Exupéry's *Vol de Nuit* and *Pilote de Guerre*. Marker was founder, editor, and writer of the Planet series of travelogues for Editions de Seuil, which blended impressionistic journalism and still photography. Marker turned to documentary filmmaking in the 1950s.

These are only some facts.

Somewhere else I read his surname may simply be a reference to magic markers, because they highlight or mark a text at the same time you can see through it.

*Sans Soleil* could be a rejection of the documentary form. But what about Japan, Amilcar Cabral, and the historical context? A recent flier for a Marker retrospective at the Museum of Modern Art in New York says he discarded his baptismal name to assume the pseudonym bestowed by his friend and coworker Alain Resnais. In France a filmmaker named Christian François Bouche-Villeneuve would not be foreign, he would be French. In America a person named Chris Marker could be from any place.

The German Anschluss of Austria occurred in 1938. In 1938 Japanese and Soviet forces fought in the Far East, the Munich Conference divided up Czechoslovakia, and the Japanese announced a "New Order in East Asia." In 1938 Dziga Vertov made an entry in his notebook. "You cannot describe a house on fire until the actual event takes place. Perhaps there will be no fire. Either you'll have to deny the description as a fiction,

SORTING FACTS

or burn the house in accordance with the script. Then, however, it will no longer be a newsreel, but the ordinary acted film with sets and actors" (KE 217). In 1938, Bouche-Villeneuve, then seventeen, probably hadn't even thought about changing his name.

Nothing is accidental. Murder is a cipher in the word "Marker."

# XVII

*"The first image he told me about was of three children on a road in Iceland in 1965."* She remembers into the black.

The image we see is of what she says he shot or saw. It doesn't matter who is the author . The image is one of the loveliest I ever remember seeing on film. I can't say why it is so haunting, only that silence has something to do with it. Three children are moving in color but there isn't any soundtrack now. They are blonde and the sun lights their hair from behind. Wind blowing their hair is all. The woman's hair in *La Jetée* is blown by the wind. Two of the children here are definitely girls, the other could be a boy, I'm not sure. The tallest, in the center, gives a shy, quick, furtive look towards the cameraman. All three are moving forward hand in hand, and they seem to be laughing. They could be playing a game, or they could be leading the tall one along to show her something. It's not clear who is leading who following. Just as it's not clear in *La Jetée* if the woman's smile is welcoming or warning. Silence and green fields that resemble ones I remember in Ireland. Salt air of the sea. A lyric fragment cut away. Simply peace and no evidence. They are spirits.

For Vertov, Tarkovsky, and Marker, an image introduced once as a hint or possible symbol may in another context contradict its intended leitmotif. The moment of looking is an arrest.

A minute is a minute a second front. *"One day I'll have to put it alone at the beginning of a film at the end of a long piece of black leader. If they don't see happiness at least they'll see the black leader."*

# XVIII

1929. *The Man with the Movie Camera*. A dynamic tension of citizens moving forward somewhere in a large Soviet city I take to be Moscow, although it's really synthesized from Moscow, Kiev, and Odessa. The material production of life itself in a stranger stasis of silence. These trains and trolleys so flush with smoke and passengers; this young woman waking up, washing herself in her room, pulling up her stockings, fastening her bra. Silence makes it like a dream. Blinking eyes and blinking shutters. The other young woman so poor (in spite of Socialism) she has spent the night on a park bench vagrant and shy. Did physical fitness make that group of women exercising on a concrete platform happy? Did the magician juggling hoops and prestidigitating a mouse ever pass his tricks on to someone else? What are those child spectators in the audience laughing and looking at? Surely not their sure obliteration accelerated second by second. A train moves in from the background it fills the screen. Dark shapes of people then apparitions soon. Silent recesses as if they haven't been leveled already by hard usage by coordinating retrospect.

If a trace is the insertion of words in time, this time what *is* is the wordless acceleration of formal development combined with buoyant enthusiasm.

Disaster is coming; they can't see nor know what we know now.

1982. Dziga Vertov's *The Man with the Movie Camera* is icono-clastic, revolutionary, tectonic, alert. Chris Marker is a man with a movie camera traveling in the wake of World War II. In *Sans Soleil* we sense the failure of revolutionary enthusiasm. "Poetry is born of insecurity," says Marker's voiceover persona, referring to the Japanese habit of living for appearance.

# XIX

The off-screen person speaking and writing through her voice. Three children holding hands. A woman's hand touching the railing of a

ferry. Other fragments of sound without words through thought Mirror the
military instructor's beating heart without having to translate an author's
creative stockpile from past to present. "I'm just back from Hokkaido, the
northern island." Now we know he means Japan. Passengers are sleeping
on the benches of the ferry. Shots of their arms thrown over their faces in
sleep. They could be dead and wounded. Sight of so many sleeping so ran-
domly drifting. He thinks *of a past or future war. Night trains air raids
fallout shelters.*

The title of *Sans Soleil* comes after the first three images. The
next is of a foghorn on the side of a ferry going somewhere. It is almost
sunless. No narration. The sound of the ship's engine resembles the noise
of a heart beating. A heart is an engine. When your heart stops there is
nothing. No color no sun no sound no time. The entrance of the Ghost in
Olivier's *Hamlet* is marked by a heartbeat sound effect suggesting a drum-
beat. Now as then it's dawn. We see a shot of a woman's hand resting on
the rail of the ferry. She has a watch on her wrist, her other hand touches
the railing lightly. She appears to be talking to someone and turns in his
direction. The direction is the same one the ship is moving in, toward the
right-hand frame of the film. The children of the introduction were walking the opposite way.

Something at the margin between thought and sound is somewhere else. The message arrives as a departure. All thoughts are winged.
*La Jetée* forms a sound within sound that is other than jetty. *Sans Soleil*
says one thing, "Sunless" means the same but not exactly.

So many hyphens and parentheses surround him.

That road and that place. Restructuring quickening joy to light
through editing until destiny reverses division. Human beauty and human
clarity carry the force of a reproach. Short cut and black leader. Military

aircraft under the deck of a destroyer. Ethics or aesthetic contrast. Writing is a cutting from inside to paper. Nonfiction footage conveys the world outside. Military background imagery. Too bad for the children.

Another nonfiction attempt at realism.

*Ophelia:* They say the owl was a baker's daughter. Lord, we know what we are, but know not what we may be.

All people captured on film are ghosts. They appear and do not appear. "Be thou, Spirit fierce, / My spirit! Be thou me, impetuous one! / Drive my dead thoughts over the universe" Shelley wrote in "Ode to the West Wind." Emerson, in the essay called "Language," says we are like travelers using the cinders of a volcano to roast their eggs. The woman is reading Marker's written multiple-changeover commentary with practiced utterance. Words are the symbols of spirits. The deer and the dear run away.

After the Third War was there resistance? What happens in current revolutionary institutions when films and tapes rot?

Ivan has gone to reconnoiter in the "dead, flooded forest." Mother of dreams come cover your son's staring photograph.

invisible colliding phenomena.

I entered crazily into the spectacle into the image taking in my arms what is is
to die as Nietzsche did when on January 23, 1889
anagram and each splitting element
I entered crazily into the spectacle into the image taking in my arms what is is
going to die as Nietzsche did when
There may be a number of messages in January 23, 1889
The obscurity of what I felt you felt
There may be a number of messages in
I entered crazily into the spectacle into the image taking in my arms what is is
going to die as Nietzsche did when on January 23, 1889
painting. Nevertheless I love the way
The obscurity of what I felt you felt

The reality of chance. A choice of masks. Political leadership wasn't always an appropriate focus for analysis. Amilcar Cabral approached life dialectically. In his absence he is far from clear. There is a vast literature even during the armed phase.

The poverty of reality in a world market. Viewpoint web-camera equipment.

Editing historical necessity at a periphery.

Blank the crack and mark no language or predator camera can recover.

When a screen seems useless against waves he spreads the sky not by a straightforward movement but in waves

To memory.


1994. *Facsimile*

The village of Pavlovskoe near Moscow. A screening. The small place is filled with peasant men and women and workers from a nearby factory. *Kinopravda* is being shown, without musical accompaniment. The noise of the projector can be heard. On the screen a train speeds past. A young girl appears, walking straight toward the camera. Suddenly a scream is heard in the hall. A woman runs toward the girl on the screen. She's weeping, with her arms stretched out before her. She calls the girl by name. But the girl disappears. On the screen the train rushes by once more. The lights are turned on in the hall. The woman is carried out unconscious. "What's going on?" a worker-correspondent asks. One of the viewers answers: "Its kino-eye. They filmed the girl while she was still alive. Not long ago she fell ill and died. The woman running toward the screen was her mother"
—Dziga Vertov (KE 85).


Refused mourning or melancholia here is the camera the film the projector.

**Chris Marker, *Sans Soleil* (1982)**
**A kamikaze pilot looks solarized on a synthesizer screen.**

# Selected Bibiliography

Listed here are film books mentioned in these essays, plus a selection of additional books on nonfiction film and closely related matters. For further bibliography see Barnouw, Barsam, and Renov.

## General Histories

Barnouw, Erik. *Documentary: A History of the Non-Fiction Film*, rev. ed. Oxford University Press, 1983.

Barsam, Richard Meran. *Non-Fiction Flm: A Critical History*, rev. ed. Indiana University Press, 1992.

Jacobs, Lewis. *The Documentary Tradition*, rev. ed. Norton, 1987.

## Other Books

Acker, Ally. *Reel Women: Pioneers of the Cinema, 1896 to the Present*. Continuum, 1991.

Aitken, Ian. *Film and Reform: John Grierson and the Documentary Film Movement.* Routledge, 1990.

Alexander, William. *Film on the Left: American Documentary Film from 1931 to 1942.* Princeton University Press, 1981.

Barsam, Richard Meran. *The Vision of Robert Flaherty: The Artist as Myth and Filmmaker.* Indiana University Press, 1988.

Barthes, Roland. *Camera Lucida: Reflections on Photography*, trans. Richard Howard. Farrar, Straus & Giroux, 1981.

Bazin, André. *What Is Cinema?* 2 vols., ed. and trans. Hugh Gray. University of California Press, 1967, 1971.

Benson, Thomas W., and Carolyn Anderson. *Reality Fictions: The Films of Frederick Wiseman.* Southern Illinois University Press, 1989.

Berger, John. *About Looking.* Pantheon, 1990.

Berger, John, and Jean Mohr. *Another Way of Telling.* Pantheon, 1982.

Brunsdon, Charlotte, ed. *Films for Women.* British Film Institute, 1986.

Burton, Julianne, ed. *Cinema and Social Change in Latin America: Conversations with Filmmakers.* University of Texas Press, 1986.

————, ed. *The Social Documentary in Latin America.* University of Pittsburgh Press, 1990.

Carson, Diane, Linda Dittmar, and Janice R. Welsch, eds. *Multiple Voices in Feminist Film Criticism.* University of Minnesota Press, 1994.

Cavell, Stanley. *Contesting Tears: The Hollywood Melodrama of the Unknown Woman.* University of Chicago Press, 1995.

————. *Pursuits of Happiness: The Hollywood Comedy of Remarriage.* Harvard University Press, 1981.

————. *Themes Out of School.* North Point Press, 1984.

————. *The World Viewed: Reflections on the Ontology of Film,* 1971; expanded ed., Harvard University Press, 1979.

Chanana, Opender, ed. *Docu-Scene India.* Indian Documentary Producers Association, 1987.

Cholodenko, Alan Robert. *The Films of Frederick Wiseman.* Harvard University Ph.D. thesis, 1987. University Microfilms International.

Clark, Vèvè, Millicent Hodson, and Catrina Neiman. *The Legend of Maya Deren: A Documentary Biography and Collected Works,* 2 vols., Anthology Film Archives/Film Culture, 1984, 1988.

Cooper, Thomas W. *Natural Rhythms: The Indigenous World of Robert Gardner.* Anthology Film Archives, 1995.

DeBrigard, Emilie. *Anthropological Cinema.* Museum of Modern Art, 1974.

de Lauretis, Teresa, and Stephen Heath, eds. *The Cinematic Apparatus.* St. Martin's, 1980.

Eaton, Mick, ed. *Anthropology-Reality-Cinema: The Films of Jean Rouch.* British Film Institute, 1979.

Godard, Jean-Luc. *Godard on Godard,* ed. and trans. Tom Milne, 1972; Da Capo edition, 1986.

Grant, Barry Keith. *Voyages of Discovery: The Cinema of Frederick Wiseman.* University of Illinois Press, 1992.

Grierson, John. *Grierson on Documentary,* ed. Forsyth Hardy. Harcourt Brace, 1947.

Hanhardt, John G., ed. *Video Culture: A Critical Investigation.* Visual Studies Workshop Press, 1986.

Hardy, Forsyth. *John Grierson: A Documentary Biography.* Faber and Faber, 1979.

Haskell, Molly. *From Reverence to Rape: The Treatment of Women in the Movies.* Holt, Rinehart, Winston, 1973, 1989.

Heider, Karl G. *Ethnographic Film.* University of Texas Press, 1978.

Hodgkinson, Anthony W., and Rodney E. Sheratsky. *Humphrey Jennings—More Than a Maker of Films.* Published for Clark University by the University Press of New England, 1982.

Jennings, Mary-Lou, ed. *Humphrey Jennings: Filmmaker-Painter-Poet.* British Film Institute, 1982.

Kaplan, E. Ann. *Women and Film.* Methuen, 1983.

Keyssar, Helene. *Robert Altman's America.* Oxford University Press, 1991.

Kuleshov, Lev. *Kuleshov on Film,* ed. and trans. Ronald Levaco. University of California Press, 1974.

Lawton, Anna, ed. *The Red Screen: Politics, Society, and Art in Soviet Cinema.* Routledge, 1992.

Levin, Roy G. *Documentary Explorations: 15 Interviews with Film Makers.* Doubleday, 1971.

Leyda, Jay. *Kino: A History of the Russian and Soviet Film.* Macmillan, 1960.

Locke, Maryel, and Charles Warren, eds. *Jean-Luc Godard's "Hail Mary": Women and the Sacred in Film.* Southern Illinois University Press, 1993.

Makaveyev, Dusan. *WR: Mysteries of the Organism,* filmscript. Avon Books, 1972.

Mamber, Stephen. *Cinema Verité in America: Studies in Uncontrolled Documentary.* MIT Press, 1974.

Marker, Chris. *La Jetée: Ciné-Roman.* Zone Books, 1992.

Mast, Gerald, Marshall Cohen, and Leo Braudy, eds. *Film Theory and Criticism.* Oxford University Press, 1992.

Metz, Christian. *The Imaginary Signifier,* trans. Celia Britton et al. Indiana University Press, 1982.

Mohan, Jag, ed. *Documentary Films and the National Awakening.* Publications Division, Ministry of Information and Broadcasting, Government of India, 1990.

Mulvey, Laura. *Visual and Other Pleasures.* Indiana University Press, 1989.

Narwehar, Sanjit, ed. *Films Division and the Indian Documentary.* Publications Division, Ministry of Information and Broadcasting, Government of India, 1992.

Nichols, Bill. *Ideology and the Image.* Indiana University Press, 1981.

———. *Representing Reality.* Indiana University Press, 1991.

———, ed. *Movies and Methods,* 2 vols. University of California Press, 1976, 1985.

Ophuls, Marcel. *The Sorrow and the Pity,* filmscript, trans. Mireille Johnston. Outerbridge and Lazard/Dutton, 1972.

Oshima, Nagisa. *Cinema, Censorship, and the State: The Writings of Nagisa Oshima, 1956–1975,* ed. Annette Michelson, trans. Dawn Lawson. MIT Press, 1992.

Petric, Vlada. *Constructivism in Film—"The Man with the Movie Camera."* Cambridge University Press, 1987.

Portuges, Catherine. *Screen Memories: The Hungarian Cinema of Marta Meszaros.* Indiana University Press, 1993.

Quart, Barbara. *Women Directors: The Emergence of a New Cinema.* Praeger, 1988.

Rainer, Yvonne. *Work 1961–73.* The Press of the Nova Scotia College of Art and Design and New York University Press, 1974.

———. *The Films of Yvonne Rainer.* Indiana University Press, 1989.

Renov, Michael, ed. *Theorizing Documentary.* Routledge, 1993.

Rosenthal, Alan. *The Documentary Conscience: A Casebook in Filmmaking.* University of California Press, 1980.

———. *The New Documentary in Action: A Casebook in Filmmaking.* University of California Press, 1971.

Rosenthal, Alan, ed. *New Challenges for Documentary.* University of California Press, 1988.

Rothman, William. *Hitchcock—The Murderous Gaze.* Harvard University Press, 1982.

———. *The "I" of the Camera.* Cambridge University Press, 1988.

Sitney, P. Adams, ed. *Film Culture Reader.* Praeger, 1970.

Sontag, Susan. *On Photography.* Farrar, Straus & Giroux, 1977.

Stoller, Paul. *The Cinematic Griot: The Ethnography of Jean Rouch.* University of Chicago Press, 1992.

Sussex, Elizabeth. *The Rise and Fall of the British Documentary: The Story of the Film Movement Founded by John Grierson.* University of California Press, 1975.

Tarkovsky, Andrei. *Sculpting in Time*, trans. Kitty Hunter-Blair. University of Texas Press, 1986.

———. *Time within Time: The Diaries 1970–1986,* trans. Kitty Hunter-Blair. Verso, 1993.

Vertov, Dziga. *Kino-Eye: The Writings of Dziga Vertov,* ed. Annette Michelson, trans. Kevin O'Brien. University of California Press, 1984.

# About the Contributors

Jay Cantor is the author of two novels, *Krazy Kat* and *The Death of Che Guevarra*, and two books of essays, *The Space Between: Literature and Politics* and *On Giving Birth to One's Own Mother*. He is a MacArthur Fellow, and a professor of English at Tufts University.

Stanley Cavell's books include *Must We Mean What We Say?*, *The Senses of Walden*, *The Claim of Reason*, and three books about film: *The World Viewed: Reflections on the Ontology of Film*, *Pursuits of Happiness: The Hollywood Comedy of Remarriage*, and the forthcoming *Contesting Tears: The Hollywood Melodrama of the Unknown Woman*. He is a MacArthur Fellow, and a professor of philosophy at Harvard University.

Robert Gardner's films include *Dead Birds*, *Deep Hearts*, *Rivers of Sand*, and *Forest of Bliss*, made in New Guinea, Africa, and India. For many years he has taught filmmaking at Harvard University, where he founded the Film Study Center as a graduate student. Presently he is gathering a group of his essays for publication, preparing two narrative features for production, and undertaking several CD-ROM initiatives.

Patricia Hampl is the author of two autobiographical works, *Virgin Time* and *A Romantic Education; Spillville*, a book about Antonin Dvořák's stay in Spillville, Iowa; and two volumes of poetry, *Woman before an Aquarium* and *Resort and Other Poems*. She is currently writing a screenplay based on *Spillville*, to be filmed by Robin Burke Productions. Hampl is a Mac-Arthur Fellow, and a professor of English at the University of Minnesota.

Maureen Howard has published six novels, including *Bridgeport Bus, Grace Abounding, Expensive Habits,* and *Natural History.* Her memoir, *Facts of Life,* won the National Book Critics Circle Award for nonfiction in 1978. Soon to be published is *A Winter's Tale,* the first season of her *Almanac.* She is a professor in the School of the Arts, Columbia University.

Susan Howe's volumes of poetry include *The Europe of Trusts, Singularities,* and *The Nonconformist's Memorial. Selected Early Poems* is forthcoming. Howe is also the author of two books of criticism, *My Emily Dickinson* and *The Birthmark: unsettling the wilderness in American literary history.* She has twice won the Before Columbus Foundation American Book Award. She is a professor of English at the State University of New York, Buffalo.

Helene Keyssar's books include *Robert Altman's America*; *Right in Her Soul: The Life of Anna Louise Strong,* coauthored with Keyssar's husband, Tracy B. Strong; and *Remembering War: A U.S.–Soviet Dialogue,* an oral history compiled with Vladimir Pozner. She has also written books on black and feminist theater and has recently edited *Feminist Theater Theory and Criticism.* She has directed theater and taught theater, film, and television at Amherst College and at the University of California, San Diego, where she is a professor in the Communication Department.

Phillip Lopate has written *Against Joie de Vivre: Personal Essays, Bachelorhood, The Rug Merchant,* and *Being with Children.* He is the editor of *The Art of the Personal Essay: An Anthology from the Classical Era to the Present.* He served for a number of years on the selection committee of the New York Film Festival, and he is currently writing film scripts for Jane Campion and Tilda Swinton, and "The History of New York," to be directed by Ric Burns for public television. Lopate is a professor of English at Hofstra University.

Vlada Petric is the author of *Constructivism in Film—"The Man with the Movie Camera,"* and editor of *Film and Dreams: An Approach to Bergman.*

He has directed several experimental films and television plays. He is curator of the Harvard Film Archive and senior lecturer in Visual and Environmental Studies at Harvard University.

William Rothman has written *Hitchcock—The Murderous Gaze, The "I" of the Camera,* and the forthcoming *Documentary Film Classics*. He coauthored, with his wife, Katherine Morgan, the screenplay for *Unni,* which was directed in India by G. Aravindan. Rothman has taught film at Harvard University and for several years as director of the International Honors Program in Europe and Asia. He now teaches in the School of Commmunication at the University of Miami, where he is director of graduate film studies.

Charles Warren is the coeditor, with Maryel Locke, of *Jean-Luc Godard's "Hail Mary": Women and the Sacred in Film,* and the author of *T.S. Eliot on Shakespeare*. He has taught literature and film at the New School for Social Research and for the International Honors Program in Europe and Asia. He is currently teaching film at Tufts University and Harvard University.

Eliot Weinberger has published two books of essays, *Outside Stories* and *Works on Paper.* He is the editor and translator of over a dozen books by Octavio Paz, including *The Collected Poems: 1957–87*. Among his other translations are *Altazor* by Vicente Huidobro and *Nostalgia for Death* by Xavier Villaurrutia. He is the editor of *American Poetry Since 1950: Innovators and Outsiders*.

# Index

Film titles are followed by the date of release.

UNIVERSITY PRESS OF NEW ENGLAND

publishes books under its own imprint and is the publisher for Brandeis University Press, Dartmouth College, Middlebury College Press, University of New Hampshire, University of Rhode Island, Tufts University, University of Vermont, Wesleyan University Press, and Salzburg Seminar.


Library of Congress Cataloging-in-Publication Data

Beyond document : essays on nonfiction film / edited by Charles Warren
    p.  cm.
  Includes bibliographical references and index.
  ISBN 0–8195–5287–9 (cl : alk. paper). — ISBN 0–8195–6290–4 (pbk.
  : alk. paper)
  1. Documentary films — History and criticism.   I. Warren, Charles,
1948–
PN1995.9.D6B48       1995
070.1'8—dc20                                            95–16674